# GUIDE TO LITERARY AGENTS

## 30TH EDITION

Robert Lee Brewer, Editor

WRITER'S
DIGEST
BOOKS

**WRITER'S DIGEST BOOKS**

An imprint of Penguin Random House LLC
penguinrandomhouse.com

Printed in the United States of America
1st Printing

ISBN 9780593332092
Book design by Alexis Estoye

# CONTENTS

## MARKETS

## RESOURCES

## INDEXES

# FROM THE EDITOR

////////////////////////////////////////////////////////////////////////////////////////

Welcome to the latest edition of *Guide to Literary Agents*. As usual, it's loaded with listings for literary agents and writers conferences. It also has articles on crafting queries, book proposals, and the perfect synopsis.

But this edition of *Guide to Literary Agents* also features an updated "20 Literary Agents Actively Seeking Writers," which includes what each agent is seeking and how to contact them. It's a great place to start in your search for an agent who may be receptive to your project.

Plus, I've collected one piece of advice from 40 different authors, including debut authors, bestselling authors, and in a variety of genres for both fiction and nonfiction. After all, this guide to literary agents and book publishing is meant to help fiction and nonfiction authors alike.

Until next we meet, keep writing and marketing what you write.

Robert Lee Brewer
Senior Content Editor
*Guide to Literary Agents*

# HOW TO USE
## *GUIDE TO*
## *LITERARY AGENTS*

Searching for a literary agent can be overwhelming, whether you've just finished your first book or you have several publishing credits on your résumé. More than likely, you're eager to start pursuing agents and anxious to see your name on the spine of a book. But before you go directly to the listings in this book, take time to familiarize yourself with the way agents work and how you should approach them. By doing so, you will be more prepared for your search and ultimately save yourself effort and unnecessary angst.

## READ THE ARTICLES

This book begins with feature articles organized into three sections: **Getting Started**, **Contacting Agents**, and **The Writer's Toolbox**. These articles explain how to prepare for representation, offer strategies for contacting agents, and arm you with vital tools in your journey. You may want to start by reading through each one and then refer back to relevant articles during each stage of your search.

These personal accounts from just-published authors offer information and inspiration for any writer hoping to find representation.

## DECIDE WHAT YOU'RE LOOKING FOR

A literary agent will present your work directly to editors or producers. It's the agent's job to get her client's work published or sold, and to negotiate a fair contract. In the **Literary Agents** listings section, we list each agent's contact information and explain both what type of work the agency represents and how to submit your work for consideration.

For face-to-face contact, many writers prefer to meet agents at conferences. By doing so, writers can assess an agent's personality, attend workshops, and have the chance to get more feedback on their work than they get by mailing or e-mailing submissions and waiting for a response. The **Writers Conferences** section lists conferences agents and/or editors attend. In many cases, private consultations are available, and agents attend with the hope of finding new clients to represent.

## UTILIZE THE EXTRAS

Aside from the articles and listings, this book offers a section of **Resources**. If you come across a term with which you aren't familiar, check out the Resources section for a quick explanation. Also, note the gray tabs along the edge of each page. The tabs identify each section so they are easier to flip to as you conduct your search.

Finally—and perhaps most importantly—there are the **Indexes** in the back of the book. These can serve as an incredibly helpful way to start your search because they categorize the listings according to different criteria. For example, you can look for literary agents according to their specialties (fiction/nonfiction genres).

---

**LISTING POLICY AND COMPLAINT PROCEDURE**

Listings in *Guide to Literary Agents* were originally compiled from detailed questionnaires and information provided by agents. However, the publishing industry is constantly in flux, and agencies change frequently. We rely on our readers for information about their dealings with agents, as well as changes in policies or fees that differ from what has been reported to the editor of this book. Write to the editor (*Guide to Literary Agents*, F+W, 10151 Carver Road, Suite 300, Cincinnati, OH 45242) or e-mail (robert.brewer@fwmedia .com) if you have new information, questions, or problems dealing with the agencies listed.

---

Listings are published free of charge and are not advertisements. Although the information is as accurate as possible, the listings are not endorsements or guarantees by the editor or publisher of *Guide to Literary Agents*. If you feel you have not been treated fairly by an agent or representative listed in *Guide to Literary Agents*, we advise you to take the following steps:

- First try to contact the agency. Sometimes one letter or e-mail can clear up the matter. Politely relate your concern.
- Document all your correspondence with the agency. When you write to us with a complaint, provide the name of your manuscript, the date of your first contact with the agency, and the nature of your subsequent correspondence.

- We will keep your letter on file and attempt to contact the agency. The number, frequency, and severity of complaints will be considered when we decide whether or not to delete an agency's listing from the next edition.

**NOTE:** *Guide to Literary Agents* reserves the right to exclude any agency for any reason.

## FREQUENTLY ASKED QUESTIONS

1. **Why do you include agents who are not seeking new clients?** Some agents ask that their listings indicate they are currently closed to new clients. We include them so writers know the agents exist and know not to contact them at this time.

2. **Why are some agents not listed?** Some agents may not have responded to our requests for information. We have taken others out of the book after we received complaints about them.

3. **Do I need more than one agent if I write in different genres?** It depends. If you have written in one genre and want to switch to a new style of writing, ask your agent if she is willing to represent you in your new endeavor. Occasionally an agent may feel she has no knowledge of a certain genre and will recommend an appropriate agent to her client. Regardless, you should always talk to your agent about any potential career move.

4. **Why don't you list more foreign agents?** Most American agents have relationships with foreign co-agents in other countries. It is more common for an American agent to work with a co-agent to sell a client's book abroad than for a writer to work directly with a foreign agent. If you decide to query foreign agents, make sure they represent American writers (if you're American). Some may request to receive submissions only from Canadians, for example, or from United Kingdom residents.

5. **Do agents ever contact a self-published writer?** If a self-published author attracts the attention of the media, or if his book sells extremely well, an agent might approach the author in the hope of representing him.

6. **Why won't the agent I queried return my material?** An agent may not answer your query or return your manuscript for several reasons. Perhaps you did not include a self-addressed, stamped envelope (SASE). Many agents will discard a submission without a SASE. Or the agent may have moved. To avoid using expired addresses, use the most current edition of *Guide to Literary Agents* or access the information online at www.writersmarket.com. Another possibility is that the agent is swamped with submissions. An agent can be overwhelmed with queries, especially if the agent recently has spoken at a conference or has been featured in an article or book. Also, some agents specify in their listings that they never return materials of any kind.

# WHAT AN AGENT DOES

A writer's job is to write. A literary agent's job is to find publishers for her clients' books. Because publishing houses receive more and more unsolicited manuscripts each year, or do not accept unsolicited manuscripts, securing an agent is becoming increasingly necessary. But finding an eager and reputable agent can be a difficult task. Even the most patient writer can become frustrated or disappointed. As a writer seeking representation, you should prepare yourself before starting your search. Learn when to approach agents, as well as what to expect from an author/agent relationship. Beyond selling manuscripts, an agent must keep track of the ever-changing industry, writers' royalty statements, fluctuating market trends—the list goes on.

So you face the question: Do I need an agent? The answer, more often than not, is a resounding yes.

## WHAT CAN AN AGENT DO FOR YOU?

For starters, today's competitive marketplace can be difficult to break into, especially for unpublished writers. Many larger publishing houses will only look at manuscripts from agents—and rightfully so, as they would be inundated with unsatisfactory writing if they did not. In fact, approximately 80 percent of books published by the five major houses are acquired through agents.

But an agent's job isn't just getting your book through a publisher's door. The following describes the various jobs agents do for their clients, many of which would be difficult for a writer to do without outside help.

---

**BEFORE YOU SUBMIT YOUR NOVEL**

- Finish your novel manuscript or short story collection. An agent can do nothing for fiction without a finished product. Never query with an incomplete novel.

---

5

- Revise your manuscript. Seek critiques from other writers or an independent editor to ensure your work is as polished as possible.
- Proofread. Don't ruin a potential relationship with an agent by submitting work that contains typos or poor grammar.
- Publish short stories or novel excerpts in literary journals, which will prove to prospective agents that editors see quality in your writing.
- Research to find the agents of writers whose works you admire or are similar to yours.
- Use the Internet and resources like *Guide to Literary Agents* to construct a list of agents who are open to new writers and looking for your category of fiction. (Jump to the listings sections of this book to start now.)
- Rank your list according to the agents most suitable for you and your work.
- Write your novel synopsis.
- Write your query letter. As an agent's first impression of you, this brief letter should be polished and to the point.
- Educate yourself about the business of agents so you will be prepared to act on any offer. This guide is a great place to start.

## Agents Know Editors' Tastes and Needs

An agent possesses information on a complex web of publishing houses and a multitude of editors to ensure her clients' manuscripts are placed in the right hands. This knowledge is gathered through relationships she cultivates with acquisitions editors—the people who decide which books to present to their publisher for possible publication. Through her industry connections, an agent becomes aware of the specializations of publishing houses and their imprints, knowing that one publisher wants only contemporary romances while another is interested solely in nonfiction books about the military. By networking with editors, an agent also learns more specialized information—which editor is looking for a crafty, Agatha Christie–style mystery for his fall catalog, for example.

## Agents Track Changes in Publishing

Being attentive to constant market changes and shifting trends is another major requirement of an agent. An agent understands what it may mean for clients when publisher A merges with publisher B and when an editor from house C moves to house D. Or what it means when readers—and therefore editors—are no longer interested in Westerns while thrillers are flying off the shelves.

## Agents Get Your Work Read Faster

Although it may seem like an extra step to send your work to an agent instead of directly to a publishing house, the truth is that an agent can prevent you from wasting months sending manuscripts that end up in the wrong inbox or buried in an editor's slush pile. Editors rely on agents to save them time as well. With little time to sift through the hundreds of unsolicited submissions arriving weekly in the mail, an editor naturally prefers work that has already been approved by a qualified reader (i.e., the agent) who knows the editor's preferences. For this reason, many of the larger publishers accept agented submissions only.

## Agents Understand Contracts

When publishers write contracts, they are primarily interested in their own bottom line, not the best interests of the author. Writers unfamiliar with contractual language may find themselves bound to a publisher with whom they no longer want to work. Or they may find themselves tied to a publisher who prevents them from getting royalties on their first book until subsequent books are written. Agents use their experiences and knowledge to negotiate a contract that benefits the writer while still respecting the publisher's needs. After all, more money for the author will almost always mean more money for the agent—another reason they're on your side.

## Agents Negotiate—and Exploit—Subsidiary Rights

Beyond publication, a savvy agent keeps other opportunities for your manuscript in mind. If your agent believes your book also will be successful as an audio book, a Book-of-the-Month-Club selection, or even a blockbuster movie, she will take these options into consideration when shopping your manuscript. These additional opportunities for writers are called subsidiary rights. Part of an agent's job is to keep track of the strengths and weaknesses of different publishers' subsidiary rights offices to determine the deposition of these rights regarding your work. After contracts are negotiated, agents will seek additional moneymaking opportunities for the rights they kept for their clients.

## Agents Get Escalators

An escalator is a bonus an agent can negotiate as part of the book contract. It is commonly given when a book appears on a bestseller list or if a client appears on a popular television show. For example, a publisher might give a writer a $30,000 bonus if he is picked for a book club. Both the agent and the editor know such media attention will sell more books, and the agent negotiates an escalator to ensure the writer benefits from this increase in sales.

## Agents Track Payments

Because an agent receives payment only when the publisher pays the writer, it's in the agent's best interest to make sure the writer is paid on schedule. Some publishing houses are notorious for late payments. Having an agent distances you from any conflict regarding payment and allows you to spend time writing instead of making phone calls.

### Agents Are Advocates

Besides standing up for your right to be paid on time, agents can ensure your book gets a better cover design, more attention from the publisher's marketing department, or other benefits you may not know to ask for during the publishing process. An agent can provide advice each step of the way, as well as guide you in your long-term writing career.

## ARE YOU READY FOR AN AGENT?

Now that you know what an agent is capable of, ask yourself if you and your work are at a stage where you need an agent. Look at the "Before You Submit" lists for fiction and nonfiction writers in this article and judge how prepared you are for contacting an agent. Have you spent enough time researching or polishing your manuscript? Does your nonfiction book proposal include everything it should? Is your novel completely finished? Sending an agent an incomplete project not only wastes your time but also may turn off the agent in the process. Is the work thoroughly revised? If you've finished your project, set it aside for a few weeks, then examine it again with fresh eyes. Give your novel or proposal to critique group partners (or beta readers) for feedback.

Moreover, your work may not be appropriate for an agent. Most agents do not represent poetry, magazine articles, short stories, or material suitable for academic or small presses; the agent's commission does not justify spending time submitting these types of works. Those agents who do take on such material generally represent authors on larger projects first and then adopt the smaller items as a favor to the client.

If you believe your work is ready to be placed with an agent, make sure you're personally ready to be represented. In other words, consider the direction in which your writing career is headed. Besides skillful writers, agencies want clients with the ability to produce more than one book. Most agents say they're looking to represent careers, not books.

## WHEN DON'T YOU NEED AN AGENT?

Although there are many reasons to work with an agent, some authors can benefit from submitting their own work directly to book publishers. For example, if your project focuses on a very specific topic, you may want to work with a small or specialized press. These houses usually are open to receiving material directly from writers. Small presses often can give more attention to writers than large houses can, providing editorial help, marketing expertise, and other advice. Academic books or specialized nonfiction books (such as a book about the history of Rhode Island) are good bets for unagented writers.

Beware, though, as you will now be responsible for reviewing and negotiating all parts of your contract and payment. If you choose this path, it's wise to use a lawyer or entertainment attorney to review all contracts. Lawyers who specialize in intellectual property can help writers with contract negotiations. Instead of earning a commission on resulting book sales, lawyers are paid only for their time.

And, of course, some people prefer working independently instead of relying on others. If you're one of these people, it's probably better to submit your own work instead of potentially butting heads with an agent. Let's say you manage to sign with one of the few literary agents who represent short story collections. If the collection gets shopped around to publishers for several months and no one bites, your agent may suggest retooling the work into a novel. Agents suggest changes—some bigger than others—and not all writers think their work is malleable. It's all a matter of what you're writing and how you feel about it.

**BEFORE YOU SUBMIT YOUR NONFICTION BOOK**

- Formulate a concrete idea for your book. Sketch a brief outline, making sure you'll have enough material for a book-length manuscript.
- Research works on similar topics to understand the competition and determine how your book is unique.
- Write sample chapters. This will help you estimate how much time you'll need to complete the work and determine whether or not your writing will need editorial help. You will also need to include a few sample chapters in the proposal itself.
- Publish completed chapters in journals and/or magazines. This validates your work to agents and provides writing samples for later in the process.
- Polish your nonfiction book proposal so you can refer to it while drafting a query letter—and so you'll be prepared when agents contact you.
- Brainstorm three to four subject categories that best describe your material.
- Use the Internet and resources like *Guide to Literary Agents* to construct a list of agents who are open to new writers and looking for your category of nonfiction.
- Rank your list. Research agent websites and narrow your list further, according to your preferences.
- Write your query. Give an agent an excellent first impression by describing your premise and your experience professionally and succinctly.
- Educate yourself about the business of agents so you can act on any offer.

# ASSESSING CREDIBILITY

Many people wouldn't buy a used car without at least checking the odometer, and savvy shoppers would consult the blue books, take a test drive, and even ask for a mechanic's opinion. Much like the shrewd car shopper, you want to obtain the best possible agent for your writing, so you should research the business of agents before sending out query letters. Understanding how agents operate will help you find an agent appropriate for your work, as well as alert you about the types of agents to avoid.

Many writers take for granted that any agent who expresses interest in their work is trustworthy. They'll sign a contract before asking any questions and simply hope everything will turn out all right. We often receive complaints from writers regarding agents *after* they have lost money or have work bound by contract to an ineffective agent. If writers put the same amount of effort into researching agents as they did writing their full manuscripts, they would save themselves unnecessary angst.

The best way to educate yourself is to read all you can about agents and other authors. Organizations such as the Association of Authors' Representatives (AAR, www.aaronline .org), the National Writers Union (NWU, www.nwu.org), American Society of Journalists and Authors (ASJA, www.asja.org), and Poets & Writers, Inc. (www.pw.org) all have informational material on finding and working with an agent.

The magazine *Publishers Weekly* (www.publishersweekly.com) covers publishing news affecting agents and others in the publishing industry. The Publishers Lunch newsletter (www.publishersmarketplace.com) comes free via e-mail every workday and offers news on agents and editors, job postings, recent book sales, and more.

The Internet also has a wide range of sites where you can learn basic information about preparing for your initial contact, as well as specific details on individual agents. You can find online forums and listservs that keep authors connected and allow them to share experiences they've had with different editors and agents. Keep in mind, however, that not everything printed on the Web is fact; you may come across a writer who is bitter because an agent rejected his manuscript. Your best bet is to use the Internet only to *supplement* your other research.

Once you've established what your resources are, it's time to see which agents meet your criteria. Below are some of the key items to pay attention to when researching agents.

## LEVEL OF EXPERIENCE

Through your research, you will discover the need to be wary of some agents. Anybody can go to the neighborhood copy center and order business cards that say "literary agent," but that title doesn't mean she can sell your book. She may lack the proper connections with others in the publishing industry, and an agent's reputation with editors can be a major strength or weakness.

Agents who have been in the business awhile have a large number of contacts and carry the most clout with editors. They know the ins and outs of the industry and are often able to take more calculated risks. However, veteran agents can be too busy to take on new clients or might not have the time to help develop an author. Newer agents, on the other hand, may be hungrier, as well as more open to unpublished writers. They probably have a smaller client list and are able to invest the effort to make your book a success.

If it's a new agent without a track record, be aware that you're taking more of a risk signing with her than with a more established agent. However, even a new agent should not be new to publishing. Many agents were editors before they were agents, or they worked at an agency as an assistant. This experience is crucial for making contacts in the publishing industry, and learning about rights and contracts. The majority of listings in this book explain how long the agent has been in business, as well as what she did before becoming an agent. After an agent has offered representation, you could ask her to name a few editors off the top of her head who she thinks may be interested in your work and why they sprang to mind. Has she sold to them before? Do they publish books in your genre?

If an agent has no contacts in the business, she has no more clout than you do. Without publishing prowess, she's just an expensive mailing service. Anyone can make photocopies, slide them into an envelope, and address them to "Editor." Unfortunately, without a contact name and a familiar return address on the envelope, or a phone call from a trusted colleague letting an editor know a wonderful submission is on its way, your work will land in the slush pile with all the other submissions that don't have representation. You can do your own mailings with higher priority than such an agent could.

## PAST SALES

Agents should be willing to discuss their recent sales with you: how many, what type of books, and to what publishers. Keep in mind, though, that some agents consider this information confidential. If an agent does give you a list of recent sales, you can call the publishers' contracts department to ensure the sale was actually made by that agent. While it's true that even top agents are not able to sell every book they represent, an inexperienced agent who proposes too many inappropriate submissions will quickly lose her standing with editors.

You can also unearth details of recent sales on your own. Nearly all of the listings in this book offer the titles and authors of books with which the agent has worked. Some of them also note to which publishing house the book was sold. Again, you can call the publisher and confirm the sale. If you don't have the publisher's information, simply check to see if it's available on Amazon. You can also check your local library or bookstore to see if they carry the book. You may want to be wary of the agent if her books are nowhere to be found or are only available through the publisher's website. Distribution is a crucial component to getting published, and you want to make sure the agent has worked with competent publishers.

# TYPES OF FEES

Becoming knowledgeable about the different types of fees agents may charge is vital to conducting effective research. Most agents make their living from the commissions they receive after selling their clients' books, and these are the agents we've listed. Be sure to ask about any expenses you don't understand so you have a clear grasp of what you're paying for. Here are some types of fees you may encounter in your research:

## Office Fees

Occasionally, an agent will charge for the cost of photocopies and postage made on your behalf. This is acceptable, so long as she keeps an itemized account of the expenses and you've agreed on a ceiling cost. The agent should ask for office expenses only after agreeing to represent the writer. These expenses should be discussed up front, and the writer should receive a statement accounting for them. This money is sometimes returned to the author upon sale of the manuscript. Be wary if there is an upfront fee amounting to hundreds of dollars, which is excessive.

## Reading Fees

Agencies that charge reading fees often do so to cover the cost of additional readers or the time spent reading that could have been spent selling. Agents also claim that charging reading fees cuts down on the number of submissions they receive. This practice can save the agent time and may allow her to consider each manuscript more extensively. Whether such promises are kept depends upon the honesty of the agency. You may pay a fee and never receive a response from the agent, or you may pay someone who never submits your manuscript to publishers.

Officially, the Association of Authors' Representatives' (AAR) Canon of Ethics prohibits members from directly or indirectly charging a reading fee, and the Writers Guild of America (WGA) does not allow WGA signatory agencies to charge a reading fee to WGA members, as stated in the WGA's Artists' Manager Basic Agreement. A signatory may charge you a fee if you are not a member, but most signatory agencies do not charge a reading fee as an across-the-board policy.

---

### WARNING SIGNS! BEWARE OF:

- Excessive typos or poor grammar in an agent's correspondence.
- A form letter accepting you as a client and praising generic things about your manuscript that could apply to any work. A good agent doesn't take on a new client very often, so when she does, it's a special occasion that warrants a personal note or phone call.
- Unprofessional contracts that ask you for money up front, contain clauses you haven't discussed, or are covered with amateur clip-art or silly borders.
- Rudeness when you inquire about any points you're unsure of. Don't employ any business partner who doesn't treat you with respect.
- Pressure, by way of threats, bullying, or bribes. A good agent is not desperate to represent more clients. She invites worthy authors but leaves the final decision up to them.
- Promises of publication. No agent can guarantee you a sale. Not even the top agents sell everything they choose to represent. They can only send your work to the most appropriate places, have it read with priority, and negotiate you a better contract if a sale does happen.
- A print-on-demand book contract or any contract offering no advance. You can sell your own book to an e-publisher anytime you wish without an agent's help. An agent should pursue traditional publishing routes with respectable advances.
- Reading fees from $25–$500 or more. The fee is usually nonrefundable, but sometimes agents agree to refund the money if they take on a writer as a client or if they sell the writer's manuscript. Keep in mind, however, that a payment for a reading fee does not ensure representation.
- No literary agents who charge reading fees are listed in this book. It's too risky of an option for writers, plus those who don't charge such fees have a stronger incentive to sell your work. After all, they don't make a dime until they make a sale. If you find that a literary agent listed in this book charges a reading fee, please contact the editor at amy.jones@fwmedia.com.

## Critique Fees

Sometimes a manuscript will interest an agent, but the agent will point out areas requiring further development and offer to critique it for an additional fee. Like reading fees, payment of a critique fee does not ensure representation. When deciding if you will benefit from having someone critique your manuscript, keep in mind that the quality and quantity of comments vary from agent to agent. The critique's usefulness will depend on the agent's knowledge of the market. Also be aware that agents who spend a significant portion of their time commenting on manuscripts will have less time to actively market work they already represent.

In other cases, the agent may suggest an editor who understands your subject matter or genre, and has some experience getting manuscripts into shape. Occasionally, if your story is exceptional, or your ideas and credentials are marketable but your writing needs help, you will work with a ghostwriter or co-author who will either share a percentage of your commission or work with you at an agreed-upon cost per hour.

An agent may refer you to editors she knows, or you may choose an editor in your area. Many editors do freelance work and would be happy to help you with your writing project. Of course, before entering into an agreement, make sure you know what you'll be getting for your money. Ask the editor for writing samples, references, or critiques he's done in the past. Make sure you feel comfortable working with him before you give him your business.

An honest agent will not make any money for referring you to an editor. We strongly advise writers not to use critiquing services offered through an agency. Instead, try hiring a freelance editor or joining a writer's group until your work is ready to be submitted to agents who don't charge fees.

# CRAFTING A QUERY

## How to Write a Stand-Out Letter That Gets Agents' Attention

*Kara Gebhart Uhl*

Think of the hours, days, months, years you've spent writing your book. The thought you've put into plot, character development, scene setting, and backstory. The words you've kept. The words you've cut. The joy and frustration you've felt as you channeled Oscar Wilde: "I spent all morning putting in a comma and all afternoon taking it out."

And then you finish. You write "The End." You have a celebratory drink. You sleep.

But as any aspiring author knows, you haven't truly reached "The End." In terms of publishing, you've only just begun. And the next chapter in your publishing journey is your query. It's imperative you treat this chapter with as much attention to detail as you did to all the chapters in your book. Because a good query is your golden ticket. Your charmed demo tape. Your "in."

A query is a short, professional way of introducing yourself to an agent. If you're frustrated by this step, consider: Agents receive hundreds of submissions every month. Often they read these submissions on their own time—evenings, weekends, on their lunch break. Given the number of writers submitting—and the number of agents reading—it would simply be impossible for agents to ask for and read entire book manuscripts from every aspiring author. Instead, a query is a quick way for you to, first and foremost, pitch your book. But it's also a way to pitch yourself. If an agent is intrigued by your query, she may ask for a partial (say, the first three chapters of your manuscript). Or she may ask for the entire thing.

Remember all the time you've invested in your book. Take your time crafting your query. Yes, it's another step in a notoriously slow process. But it's necessary. Have you ever seen pictures of slush piles—those piles of unread queries on many well-known agents' desks? Imagine the size of those slush piles if they held full manuscripts instead of one-page query letters. Thinking of it this way, query letters begin to make more sense. And a well-crafted query just might help land all your well-placed commas into the public's hands.

Here we share with you the basics of a query, including its three parts and a detailed list of dos and don'ts.

## PART I: THE INTRODUCTION

Whether you're submitting a 100-word picture book or a 90,000-word novel, you must be able to sum up the most basic aspects of your book in one sentence. Agents are busy. And they constantly receive submissions for types of work they don't represent. So up front they need to know that, after reading your first paragraph, the rest of your query is going to be worth their time.

An opening sentence designed to "hook" an agent is fine—if it's good and if it works. But this is the time to tune your right brain down and your left brain up—agents desire professionalism and queries that are short and to the point. Err on the side of formality with only a touch of whimsy. Tell the agent, in as few words as possible, what you've written, including title, genre, and length.

In the intro, you must also connect with the agent. Simply sending one hundred identical query letters out to "Dear Agent" won't get you published. Instead, your letter should be addressed not only to a specific agency but to a specific agent within that agency. (And double, triple, quadruple check that the agent's name is spelled correctly.)

When asked for submission tips, agents always mention the importance of making your letter personal. A good author-agent relationship is like a good marriage. It's important that both sides invest the time to find a good fit that meets their needs. So how do you connect with an agent you don't know personally? Research.

### 1. Make a Connection Based on a Book the Agent Already Represents

Most agencies have websites that list who and what they represent. Research those sites. Find a book similar to yours and explain that, because such-and-such book has a similar theme or tone, you think your book would be a great fit. In addition, many agents will list specific genres/categories they're looking for, either on their websites or in interviews. If your book is a match, state that.

### 2. Make a Connection Based on an Interview You Read

Search agents' names online and read any and all interviews they've given. Perhaps they mentioned a love for X and your book is all about X. Mention the specific interview. Prove that you've invested as much time researching them as they're about to spend researching you.

### 3. Make a Connection Based on a Conference You Both Attended

Was the agent you're querying the keynote speaker at a writing conference you were recently at? If so, mention it, and comment on an aspect of his speech you liked. Even better, did you meet the agent in person? Mention it, and if there's something you can say to jog her memory about the meeting, say it. Better yet, did the agent specifically ask you to send your manuscript? Mention it.

Finally, if you're being referred to a particular agent by an author the agent represents—that's your opening sentence. That referral is guaranteed to get your query placed at the top of the stack.

## PART II: THE PITCH

Here's where you really get to sell your manuscript—but in only three to ten sentences. Consider a book's jacket flap and its role in convincing readers to plunk down $24.95 to buy what's in between those flaps. Like a jacket flap, you need to hook an agent in the confines of a very limited space. What makes your story interesting and unique? Is your story about someone's disappearance? Fine, but there are hundreds of stories about missing persons. Is your story about a teenager who has disappeared, and her frantic family and friends who are looking for her? Again, fine, but this story, too, already exists—in many forms. Is your story about a teenager who has disappeared, but her frantic family and friends who are looking for her don't realize that she ran away after finding out she was kidnapped as a baby and her biological parents are waiting for her in a secret place? *Now* you have a hook.

Practice your pitch. Read it out loud, not only to family and friends, but to people willing to give you honest, intelligent criticism. If you belong to a writing group, workshop your pitch. Share it with members of an online writing forum. Know anyone in the publishing industry? Share it with them. We're not talking about querying magazines here; we're talking about querying an agent who could become a lifelong partner. Spend time on your pitch. Write your pitch, put it aside for a week, then look at it again. Perfect it. Turn it into jacket-flap material so detailed, exciting, and clear that it would be near impossible to read your pitch and not want to read more. Use active verbs. Don't send a query simply because you finished a book. Send a query because you finished your pitch and you are ready to begin the next chapter of your publishing journey.

## PART III: THE BIO

If you write fiction for adults or children, unless you're a household name or you've recently been a guest on some very big TV or radio shows, an agent is much more interested in your pitch than in who you are. If you write nonfiction, who you are—more specifically, your platform and publicity—is much more important. Regardless, these are key elements that must be present in every bio:

## 1. Publishing Credits

If you're submitting fiction, focus on your fiction credits—previously published works and short stories. That said, if you're submitting fiction and all your previously published work is nonfiction—articles, essays, etc.—that's still fine and good to mention. Don't be overly long about it. Mention your publications in bigger magazines or well-known literary journals. If you've never had anything published, don't say you lack official credits. Simply skip this altogether.

## 2. Contests and Awards

If you've won many, focus on the most impressive ones and those that most directly relate to your work. Don't mention contests you entered and weren't named in. Also, feel free to leave titles and years out.

## 3. MFAs

If you've earned or are working toward a master of fine arts in writing, say so and state the program. Don't mention English or journalism degrees, or online writing courses.

## 4. Large, Recognized Writing Organizations

Agents don't want to hear about your book club or the small critique group you meet with once a week. And they really don't want to hear about the online writing forum you belong to. But if you're a member of something like the Romance Writers of America (RWA), the Mystery Writers of America (MWA), the Society of Children's Book Writers and Illustrators (SCBWI), the Society of Professional Journalists (SPJ), the American Medical Writers, etc., say so. This shows you're serious about what you do and you're involved in groups that can aid with publicity and networking.

## 5. Platform and Publicity

If you write nonfiction, who you are and how you're going to help sell the book once it's published become very important. Why are you the best person to write it? What do you have now—public speaking engagements, an active website or blog, substantial cred in your industry—that will help you sell this book?

Finally, be cordial. Thank the agent for taking the time to read your query and consider your manuscript. Ask if you may send more, in the format she desires (partial, full, etc.).

Think back to the time you spent writing your book. The first draft wasn't your final. Don't fret too much over rejection slips. A line agents seemingly love to use on rejections is this: "Unfortunately, this isn't a right fit for me at this time, but I'm sure another agent will feel differently." It has merit. Your book—and query—can be good and still garner a rejection, for a myriad of reasons. Be patient. Keep pitching. And in the meantime, start writing that next book.

---

## DOS AND DON'TS FOR QUERIES

**DO:**

- Keep the tone professional.
- Query a specific agent at a specific agency.
- Proofread. Double-check the spelling of the agency and the agent's name.
- Keep the query concise, limiting the overall length to one page (single-spaced, twelve-point type in a commonly used font).
- Focus on the plot, not your bio, when pitching fiction.
- Pitch agents who represent the type of material you write.
- Check an agency's submission guidelines to see how to query—for example, via e-mail or snail mail—and whether or not to include a SASE.
- Keep pitching, despite rejections.

**DON'T:**

- Include personal info not directly related to the book. For example, stating that you're a parent doesn't make you more qualified than someone else to write a children's book.
- Say how long it took you to write your manuscript. Some best-selling books took ten years to write—others, six weeks. An agent doesn't care how long it took—an agent only cares if it's good. Same thing goes with drafts—an agent doesn't care how many drafts it took you to reach the final product.
- Mention that this is your first novel or, worse, the first thing you've ever written. If you have no other publishing credits, don't advertise that fact. Don't mention it at all.
- State that your book has been edited by peers or professionals. Agents expect manuscripts to be edited, no matter how the editing was done.
- Bring up scripts or film adaptations—you're querying an agent about publishing a book, not making a movie.
- Mention any previous rejections.
- State that the story is copyrighted with the U.S. Copyright Office or that you own all rights. You already own all rights. You wrote it.

---

- Rave about how much your family and friends loved it. What matters is that the agent loves it.
- Send flowers or anything else except a self-addressed stamped envelope (and only if the SASE is required), if sending through snail mail.
- Follow up with a phone call. After the appropriate time has passed (many agencies say how long it will take to receive a response), follow up in the manner you queried—via e-mail or snail mail. And know that "no responses" do happen. After one follow-up and no response, cross the agent off your list.

**KARA GEBHART UHL** (karagebhartuhl.com) writes and edits from Fort Thomas, KY.

## ① SAMPLE QUERY 1: LITERARY FICTION
Agent's Comments: Jeff Kleinman (Folio Literary Management)

From: Garth Stein
To: Jeff Kleinman
Subject: Query: "The Art of Racing in the Rain" ①

Dear Mr. Kleinman:

② Saturday night I was participating in a fundraiser for the King County Library System out here in the Pacific Northwest, and I met your client Layne Maheu. He spoke very highly of you and suggested that I contact you.

③ I am a Seattle writer with two published novels. I have recently completed my third novel, *The Art of Racing in the Rain*, and I find myself in a difficult situation: My new book is narrated by a dog, and my current agent ④ told me that he cannot (or will not) sell it for that very reason. Thus, I am seeking new representation.

⑤ *The Art of Racing in the Rain* is the story of Denny Swift, a race car driver who faces profound obstacles in his life, and ultimately overcomes them by applying the same techniques that have made him successful on the track. His story is narrated by his "philosopher dog," Enzo, who, having a nearly human soul (and an obsession with opposable thumbs), believes he will return as a man in his next lifetime.

⑥ My last novel, *How Evan Broke His Head and Other Secrets*, won a 2006 Pacific Northwest Booksellers Association Book Award, and since the award ceremony a year ago, I have given many readings, workshops, and lectures promoting the book. When time has permitted, I've read the first chapter from *The Art of Racing in the Rain*. Audience members have been universally enthusiastic and vocal in their response, and the first question asked is always: "When can I buy the book about the dog?" Also very positive.

⑦ I'm inserting, below, a short synopsis of *The Art of Racing in the Rain*, and my biography. Please let me know if the novel interests you; I would be happy to send you the manuscript.

Sincerely,
Garth Stein

① Putting the word *Query* and the title of the book on the subject line of an e-mail often keeps your e-mail from falling into the spam folder. ② One of the best ways of starting out correspondence is figuring out your connection to the agent. ③ The author has some kind of track record. Who's the publisher, though? Were these both self-published novels, or were there reputable publishers involved? (I'll read on, and hope I find out.) ④ This seems promising, but also know this kind of approach can backfire, because we agents tend to be like sheep—what one doesn't like, the rest of us are wary of, too (or, conversely, what one likes, we all like). But in this case getting in the "two published novels" early is definitely helpful. ⑤ The third paragraph is the key pitch paragraph and Garth gives a great description of the book— he sums it up, gives us a feel for what we're going to get. This is the most important part of your letter. ⑥ Obviously it's nice to see the author's winning awards. Also good: The author's not afraid of promoting the book. ⑦ The end is simple and easy—it doesn't speak of desperation, or doubt, or anything other than polite willingness to help.

## ② SAMPLE QUERY 2: YOUNG ADULT
Agent's Comments: Ted Malawer (Upstart Crow Literary)

Dear Mr. Malawer:

I would like you to represent my 65,000-word contemporary teen novel *My Big Nose & Other Natural Disasters*.

**①** Seventeen-year-old Jory Michaels wakes up on the first day of summer vacation with her same old big nose, no passion in her life (in the creative sense of the word), and all signs still pointing to her dying a virgin. Plus, her mother is busy roasting a chicken for Day #6 of the Dinner For Breakfast Diet.

**②** In spite of her driving record (it was an accident!), Jory gets a job delivering flowers and cakes to Reno's casinos and wedding chapels. She also comes up with a new summer goal: saving for a life-altering nose job. She and her new nose will attract a fabulous boyfriend. Nothing like the shameless flirt Tyler Briggs, or Tom who's always nice but never calls. Maybe she'll find someone kind of like Gideon at the Jewel Café, except better looking and not quite so different. Jory survives various summer disasters like doing yoga after sampling Mom's Cabbage Soup Diet, Enforced Mother Bonding With Crazy Nose-Obsessed Daughter Night, and discovering Tyler's big secret. But will she learn to accept herself and maybe even find her passion in the creative (AND romantic!) sense of the word?

**③** I have written for *APPLESEEDS*, *Confetti*, *Hopscotch*, *Story Friends*, *Wee Ones Magazine*, the *Deseret News*, *Children's Playmate*, and Blooming Tree Press' *Summer Shorts* anthology. I won the Utah Arts Council prize for *Not-A-Dr. Logan's Divorce Book*. My novels *Jungle Crossing* and *Going Native!* each won first prize in the League of Utah Writers contest. I currently serve as an SCBWI Regional Advisor.

**④** I submitted *My Big Nose & Other Natural Disasters* to Krista Marino at Delacorte because she requested it during our critique at the summer SCBWI conference (no response yet).

Thank you for your time and attention. I look forward to hearing from you.

Sincerely,
Sydney Salter Husseman

**①** With hundreds and hundreds of queries each month, it's tough to stand out. Sydney, however, did just that. First, she has a great title that totally made me laugh. Second, she sets up her main character's dilemma in a succinct and interesting way. In one simple paragraph, I have a great idea of who Jory is and what her life is about—the interesting tidbits about her mother help show the novel's sense of humor, too. **②** Sydney's largest paragraph sets up the plot and the conflict, and introduces some exciting potential love interests and misadventures that I was excited to read about. Again, Sydney really shows off her fantastic sense of humor, and she leaves me hanging with a question that I needed an answer to. **③** She has writing experience and has completed other manuscripts that were prizeworthy. Her SCBWI involvement—while not a necessity—shows me that she has an understanding of and an interest in the children's publishing world. **④** The fact that an editor requested the manuscript is always a good sign. That I knew Krista personally and highly valued her opinion was, as Sydney's main character Jory would say, "The icing on the cake."

## ③ SAMPLE QUERY 3: NONFICTION (SELF-HELP)
Agent's Comments: Michelle Wolfson (Wolfson Literary Agency)

Dear Ms. Wolfson:

❶ Have you ever wanted to know the best day of the week to buy groceries or go out to dinner? Have you ever wondered about the best time of day to send an e-mail or ask for a raise? What about the best time of day to schedule a surgery or a haircut? What's the best day of the week to avoid lines at the Louvre? What's the best day of the month to make an offer on a house? What's the best time of day to ask someone out on a date? ❷

My book, *Buy Ketchup in May and Fly at Noon: A Guide to the Best Time to Buy This, Do That, and Go There*, has the answers to these questions and hundreds more.

❸ As a longtime print journalist, I've been privy to readership surveys that show people can't get enough of newspaper and magazine stories about the best time to buy or do things. This book puts several hundreds of questions and answers in one place—a succinct, large-print reference book that readers will feel like they need to own. Why? Because it will save them time and money, and it will give them valuable information about issues related to health, education, travel, the workplace, and more. In short, it will make them smarter, so they can make better decisions. ❹

Best of all, the information in this book is relevant to anyone, whether they live in Virginia or the Virgin Islands; Portland, Oregon, or Portland, Maine. In fact, much of the book will find an audience in Europe and Australia.

❺ I've worked as a journalist since 1984. In 1999, the Virginia Press Association created an award for the best news writing portfolio in the state—the closest thing Virginia had to a reporter-of-the-year award. I won it that year and then again in 2000. During the summer of 2007, I left newspapering to pursue book projects and long-form journalism.

❻ I saw your name on a list of top literary agents for self-help books, and I read on your website that you're interested in books that offer practical advice. *Buy Ketchup in May and Fly at Noon* offers plenty of that. Please let me know if you'd like to read my proposal.

Sincerely,
Mark Di Vincenzo

---

❶ I tend to prefer it when authors jump right into the heart of their book, the exception being if we've met at a conference or have some other personal connection. Mark chose clever questions for the opening of the query. All of those questions are, in fact, relevant to my life—with groceries, dinner, e-mail, and a raise—and yet I don't have a definitive answer to them. ❷ He gets a little more offbeat and unusual with questions regarding surgery, the Louvre, buying a house, and dating. This shows a quirkier side to the book and also the range of topics it is going to cover, so I know right away there is going to be a mix of useful and quirky information on a broad range of topics. ❸ By starting with "As a longtime print journalist," Mark immediately establishes his credibility for writing on this topic. ❹ This helps show that there is a market for this book and establishes the need for such a book. ❺ Mark's bio paragraph offers a lot of good information. ❻ It's nice when I feel like an author has sought me out specifically and thinks we would be a good fit.

## ④ SAMPLE QUERY 4: WOMEN'S FICTION
### Agent's Comments: Elisabeth Weed (Weed Literary)

Dear Ms. Weed:

❶ Natalie Miller had a plan. She had a goddamn plan. Top of her class at Dartmouth. Even better at Yale Law. Youngest aide ever to the powerful Senator Claire Dupris. Higher, faster, stronger. This? Was all part of the plan. True, she was so busy ascending the political ladder that she rarely had time to sniff around her mediocre relationship with Ned, who fit the three Bs to the max: basic, blond, and boring, and she definitely didn't have time to mourn her mangled relationship with Jake, her budding rock star ex-boyfriend.

The lump in her right breast that Ned discovers during brain-numbingly bland morning sex? That? Was most definitely not part of the plan. And Stage IIIA breast cancer? Never once had Natalie jotted this down on her to-do list for conquering the world. When her (tiny-penised) boyfriend has the audacity to dump her on the day after her diagnosis, Natalie's entire world dissolves into a tornado of upheaval, and she's left with nothing but her diary to her ex-boyfriends, her mornings lingering over *The Price Is Right*, her burnt-out stubs of pot that carry her past the chemo pain, and finally, the weight of her life choices—the ones in which she might drown in if she doesn't find a buoy.

❷ *The Department of Lost and Found* is a story of hope, of resolve, of digging deeper than you thought possible until you find the strength not to crumble, and ultimately, of making your own luck, even when you've been dealt an unsteady hand.

❸ I'm a freelance writer and have contributed to, among others, *American Baby, American Way, Arthritis Today, Bride's, Cooking Light, Fitness, Glamour, InStyle Weddings, Men's Edge, Men's Fitness, Men's Health, Parenting, Parents, Prevention, Redbook, Self, Shape, Sly, Stuff, USA Weekend, Weight Watchers, Woman's Day, Women's Health,* and ivillage.com, msn.com, and women.com. I also ghostwrote *The Knot Book of Wedding Flowers*.

If you are interested, I'd love to send you the completed manuscript. Thanks so much! Looking forward to speaking with you soon.

Allison Winn Scotch

❶ The opening sentence reads like great jacket copy, and I immediately know who our protagonist is and what the conflict for her will be. (And it's funny, without being silly.) ❷ The third paragraph tells me where this book will land: upmarket women's fiction. (A great place to be these days!) ❸ This paragraph highlights impressive credentials. While being able to write nonfiction does not necessarily translate over to fiction, it shows me that she is someone worth paying more attention to. And her magazine contacts will help when it comes time to promote the book.

## ⑤ SAMPLE QUERY 5: MAINSTREAM/COMEDIC FICTION
Agent's Comments: Michelle Brower (Folio Literary Management)

Dear Michelle Brower:

❶ "I spent two days in a cage at the SPCA until my parents finally came to pick me up. The stigma of bringing your undead son home to live with you can wreak havoc on your social status, so I can't exactly blame my parents for not rushing out to claim me. But one more day and I would have been donated to a research facility."

Andy Warner is a zombie.

After reanimating from a car accident that killed his wife, Andy is resented by his parents, abandoned by his friends, and vilified by society. Seeking comfort and camaraderie in Undead Anonymous, a support group for zombies, Andy finds kindred souls in Rita, a recent suicide who has a taste for consuming formaldehyde in cosmetic products, and Jerry, a 21-year-old car crash victim with an artistic flair for Renaissance pornography.

❷ With the help of his new friends and a rogue zombie named Ray, Andy embarks on a journey of personal freedom and self-discovery that will take him from his own casket to the SPCA to a media-driven, class-action lawsuit for the civil rights of all zombies. And along the way, he'll even devour a few Breathers.

*Breathers* is a contemporary dark comedy about life, or undeath, through the eyes of an ordinary zombie. In addition to *Breathers*, I've written three other novels and more than four dozen short stories—a dozen of which have appeared in small press publications. Currently, I'm working on my fifth novel, also a dark comedy, about fate.

Enclosed is a two-page synopsis and the first chapter of *Breathers*, with additional sample chapters or the entire manuscript available upon request. I appreciate your time and interest in considering my query and I look forward to your response.

Sincerely,
Scott G. Browne

❶ What really draws me to this query is the fact that it has exactly what I'm looking for in my commercial fiction—story and style. Scott includes a brief quote from the book that manages to capture his sense of humor as an author and his uniquely relatable main character (hard to do with someone who's recently reanimated). I think this is a great example of how query letters can break the rules and still stand out in the slush pile. I normally don't like quotes as the first line, because I don't have a context for them, but this quote both sets up the main concept of the book and gives me a sense of the character's voice. This method won't necessarily work for most fiction, but it absolutely is successful here. ❷ The letter quickly conveys that this is an unusual book about zombies, and being a fan of zombie literature, I'm aware that it seems to be taking things in a new direction. I also appreciate how Scott conveys the main conflict of his plot and his supporting cast of characters—we know there is an issue for Andy beyond coming back to life as a zombie, and that provides momentum for the story.

# CRAFTING THE PERFECT SYNOPSIS

........................................................

*by Kaitlyn Johnson*

///////////////////////////////////////////////////////////////////////////////////

While writing queries and books is no leisurely picnic, the synopsis is often the most complicated submission material a writer can attempt. Everything else can be perfect—pitch, query, voice, and pages—but it's the synopsis that tells where the story goes, if the plot is fully fleshed out, or if the ending is left dangling without reason. If something in this document foreshadows intense editing, problematic theming, or unresolved endings, it could mean a pass. That's where crafting the synopsis correctly comes into play.

## FORMATTING BASICS

The industry standard for synopses is a document that is one to two pages in length. Single-spacing is only acceptable if the entire document fits on one page. However, the rules change upon hitting the second page. If the synopsis exceeds one page, the writer must double space and ensure they don't exceed two pages. If the synopsis is longer than two pages after applying the double-space format, it's too long. It's as simple as that.

Like the manuscript and query letter, stick to regular margins and fonts: Times New Roman, 12 size font, and one-inch margins. Remember, some houses or agencies have their own guidelines, so always check their websites to double check. While one editor asks for two pages, another may ask for six. Do your research.

But don't panic if this feels complicated! No one expects a synopsis to be perfect. Going over a couple lines isn't a big deal, but breaking limits by page lengths is a fast way to rejection. Style guides are set for a reason; don't give the agent a reason to say no before they even get to your manuscript pages.

## TIPS & TRICKS

Something not often discussed is how to deal with introducing a new character in a synopsis. Always place the name in ALL CAPS when a character makes their first appearance. This tactic draws the eye and alerts the reader that they haven't met this person yet.

Make an attempt to include these first introductions somewhere within the first two-to-three fully-formed paragraphs. If someone pops up near the end of the book, it may be seen as a general red flag that the plot hasn't been seamless throughout.

Obviously, there are outliers, but these late additions can usually be fixed by eliminating a name altogether. If a new character only appears in one scene toward the end, thereby barely influencing the plot, forego the name. They can simply be "a soldier," a "nobleman," a "messenger," etc. Remember, the more names a reader is forced to remember, the more plot details might slip from their heads. Focus in on the big players: the protagonist, antagonist, supporting characters, and/or love interest.

## STRUCTURE

Always write the synopsis in chronological order. This isn't the blurb on the back cover of a book, and it's not the same as the query, either. The synopsis can cover a basic three-step structure: Set-up, Confrontation, and Resolution. The best way to grab a reader is by highlighting the facts unique to the story and giving characters a sense of agency.

### STEP 1: Set-up

When crafting your first paragraph, here's what does not work.

1. **A summary of the world rules/history:** Don't begin with the book's own "In the beginning was light…" scenario and don't start off with "My story is about…" Instead, focus on concise details to save space. Explaining a country/city was overrun and colonized so-and-so years ago is fine, but it should be contained in one short sentence and not a sprawling run-on. In addition, give only the worldbuilding/history that is absolutely essential to the main plot. Hold off on subplot explanations.
2. **A character list:** Don't include what characters look like, their purpose in the story, their motivations, etc. The agent doesn't need character descriptions to understand the plot. Save these discoveries for the page.
3. **The query letter itself:** Do not simply repeat the blurb from the query. Usually, the agent reads the synopsis shortly after reading the query, and this sort of repetition may show the writer didn't do their research or doesn't know how to explain their own story in detail.

Here's what does work when beginning a synopsis. Use the first paragraph to describe the opening scene—explain what the reader will be walking into on page one. Establish the main character's name, age, and the gender they identify as. This helps create a picture of "who" they are to the story. Avoid including any secondary characters who appear only for that scene and disappear for the remainder of the novel. Instead, use those who are key to the central plot.

## STEP 2: Confrontation

Step 2 gets more internal with character and external with plot. Meaning, the main characters' development—their reasoning and motivations—plays a more dominant role. Call it the "getting to know you" section, aka the Journey. Here, readers see bonding or flirting, and often a lot of "so tell me about yourself" moments. This will all lead up to the "Inciting Event." For example, something suddenly goes wrong in the trip and provides the characters with an obstacle (i.e., a rockslide on the path, attack from an unknown assailant, or betrayal by one of those close to the protagonist).

This moment is different from the event in your opening scene. The beginning establishes why the characters are compelled into the plot—examples here could be they are forcibly removed from their homeland, they see their family die, or their power/magic is revealed. That's set-up, not the journey.

The middle inciting event drives the book to its final outcome. It defines pacing, controls character growth, and establishes a climax or high point to the center of the story.

## STEP 3: Resolution

Here, the reader faces the story's darkest/deepest moment, a "rock bottom" for the characters. Explain how the moment is overcome and what the protagonist must do to move onward in the journey. Then comes the moment for the final climax and eventual ending. Sometimes, these are one and the same, while at other times they can be two interlocking scenes. For example, a final battle is the climax, but the true ending is when the victor is crowned as king, not the fighting itself.

## FILLER BITS

Tying major plot points together is just as important as describing the events themselves. Writers often want to include every scene of the story in a step-by-step method. Every crawl or trip or laugh is important—it's their "baby" after all. But to an agent, no two moments are equal.

This is where filler bits come into play—the parts connecting the beginning to the middle or the middle to the end. No more than one-to-two short paragraphs should be spent on these.

Here's a visual aid: Beginning > 1-to-2 paragraph connections > Middle/Inciting Event > 1-to-2 paragraph connections > Final Climax/Ending.

For filler bits, use concrete details vital to understanding how the reader moves from one section to another. Overdoing these elements or adding too many world-specific terms can lead to confusion, so use them sparingly. Names often aren't as important as actions.

## VOICE & POVs

In the synopsis, always maintain an active third person. Avoid using passive voice—such as "there was an obstacle" versus "an obstacle lay in the road"; "he had stared out the window" versus "he stared out the window"; "snow was falling slowly" versus "the snow fell slowly"—as it drags pacing and gives the writing a monotone quality.

For writers who use multiple POVs, choose a dominant voice. Most stories have one or two, usually love interests or mortal enemies or hero and sidekick. Determine who drives the plot the most. It's often easier to write the synopsis from the eyes of one character while mentioning the others' role/impact alongside this main figure.

Dueling timelines throw a wrench in this tactic. There are a couple options to tackling those stories: focus on the separation by character—as in, take the main character in the main timeline and present their journey, proving how the other timeline affects it in significant moments; the writer could also split the synopsis in two—describe events of the first timeline on the first page and the second timeline on the second page, using the last paragraph to reveal how they intersect.

Whether through one or multiple POVs, every story has subplots. These are details, hints, or characters that don't play a major role in the current story's main plot. This can include emotional drive/consequences from secondary or tertiary characters, justification for character actions, or locations that appear in the journey but don't impact the bigger picture. Avoid using up space for these moments. The synopsis should focus on main characters influencing the main plot, with backup from secondary characters only when necessary.

## ENDINGS

Endings in a synopsis are mandatory. That doesn't mean an agent will actually read the ending. Some prefer to leave it unspoiled while others believe it's necessary before requesting more pages. Regardless, it must be included.

A query leaves the finale as a wonderful secret, but the synopsis is the exact opposite. Cutting off the document with subtle comments like, "They enter the castle, intent on fighting the beast," won't cut it. That statement says nothing about the true ending: the outcome of the battle! If a character dies, if unrequited love is announced, or if the reader is faced with a cliffhanger, those details must be disclosed.

Endings are necessary for agents to know if they feel connected to the entirety of the work. If they enter the pages with details already in mind, it's all the better when a writer has the power to change their opinion, to surprise them by making them enjoy something they'd previously disliked.

Another reason for endings in the synopsis is to prove the writer knows how to offer closure. Especially with novels that are intended for a series, the first book should be strong enough to satisfy despite the storyline continuing onward. No story should "depend" on a sequel for strength or entertainment, and the synopsis is a way to determine if the writer achieved this goal.

Remember, it's fine if a synopsis comes across stiff or to-the-point. Voice is key within the query and manuscript pages, but the synopsis acts as a quick summary to outline the need-to-know elements of your story. An agent doesn't expect perfection; they simply desire clarity and honesty.

After receiving a BA in Writing, Literature, and Publishing from Emerson College, **KAITLYN JOHNSON** refused to leave the concept of nightly homework behind. As well as being a junior agent for Corvisiero Literary Agency, she is also a freelance editor at her own company, K. Johnson Editorial, and has worked as a copyeditor for academic publisher codeMantra, a YA editor for Accent Press, and a Conference Assistant for GrubStreet, Boston. She has written various articles for *Writer's Digest* and has had a flash fiction story published in the anthology *A Box of Stars Beneath the Bed.*

# THE SECRET TO A STRONGER NONFICTION BOOK PROPOSAL

*By Nina Amir*

Knowing what's already on bookshelves may be the single most effective (and most overlooked) way to convince an agent where your idea fits in. Here's how your Competitive Analysis can be your secret weapon.

It's a rare book that is "the only one" of its kind. If you want to create a successful nonfiction book proposal, you need to go to the trouble of producing a Competitive Analysis. This proposal section demonstrates to an agent and publisher the uniqueness of your book idea as well as why it's a necessary addition to the category.

One of my author coaching clients once had a book idea resulting from a talk she'd been asked to give for an organization. The more she prepared her presentation, the more excited she became about the topic: women and leadership. In researching her talk, she'd already gone through a process similar to outlining a Table of Contents, and she'd even come up with a catchy acronym for her approach. Here's the problem she faced: This writer had no idea how many other books already existed on the topic of women and leadership—my quick search on Amazon yielded more than 20,000 results.

Not only that, she had not considered:

- How her book would be different from the others
- If the category required another book on the topic
- How to make her book stand out.

The more I explained how a successful nonfiction book had to be both unique and necessary—how it had to "fill a hole on the shelf in the bookstore"—the more she felt that her great idea no longer sounded so good. In fact, it still might have been a great idea. But she needed to shape it strategically. She needed to evaluate her book concept against the competition and show how it would rise above it.

## CONDUCT A SOLID COMPETITIVE ANALYSIS

In the "Competing Books" or "Competitive Analysis" section of your proposal, you provide literary agents and acquisitions editors with a detailed look at recent books on your topic and how yours compares. The savviest authors also use this information to improve the book idea they're proposing—until it's one an agent or publisher can't say no to. (I wrote about this extensively in *The Author Training Manual*.)

You may think stiff competition bodes poorly for your book. In truth, many bestsellers on the subject proves a market exists for books like yours. If you can show that your idea offers new benefits to readers, you can make a case that it will sell just as well—if not better.

Conversely, a category with few books and little competition could represent an opportunity to dominate the niche, if you can load your proposal with facts that show how your book is unique and necessary and that a market exists for it.

Here are a few ways to start your competitive analysis:

- Taking into consideration your book's category and topic, compile a list of competing titles (books that cover similar information or tell a similar story) by searching physical bookstore and library shelves as well as sites such as Amazon, Barnes & Noble, LibraryThing, Goodreads, Book Depository, and general search engines.
- Consider the following factors, looking carefully at each of the competing books you've identified: How does it differ from the book you want to write? Is the scope of the book different? How so? Does it have different benefits? What are they? How is it similar to the book you want to write? What are its pros and cons? How would you improve upon it? What promises does the author make to readers? What promises does the author fail to make that he could or should have (or that you can)?
- Study reviews of the competing books you have identified. You can learn a lot from what readers think is good, bad, or missing. Plan to include in your book the things that are weak or absent in the competition.
- Visit competing authors' websites. See what else you can learn about their books' sales, market, readership, etc.
- Look at the competing authors' bios. Consider: What are the authors' credentials (or lack thereof)? How do yours compare? Will it help or hurt you to have different qualifications or similar ones?

# USE THE ANALYSIS TO IMPROVE YOUR IDEA

Once you've done the initial research for your competitive analysis, use the information to evaluate your book idea.

- Ask yourself: Is there a hole on the shelf in your category? What sort of book is missing? Describe the "perfect" book to fill that hole. Now, how does your book idea compare to the book you just described? Are you offering something other authors have not delivered? Make a list of things you need to do to stand out in your niche.
- Based on your evaluation, decide if you need to make changes to your concept. Drawing on the factors you identified in all the steps leading up to this point, strengthen your idea so that it: Tells a fresh story; offers a different perspective or new angle; presents a compelling argument that other authors have not made; provides different data or more current information; and/or takes readers on a singular journey.
- Compare your credentials to that of the competing authors you have identified. Are you equipped to join the ranks of these authors? What do you need to do or be to compete with them? Do you need a larger platform? What steps can you take to broaden your expertise or reach? What else can you do to show that you are the best person to write this book at this time?

Once you've made your book's concept as original and necessary as possible, add your Competitive Analysis to your book proposal. Narrow the competition to five you feel are the closest (and strongest, favoring books that seem to have sold well) in comparison to your own project. For each one, list the title, subtitle, author, publisher, copyright year, number of pages, format (paperback or hardcover) and price of each format. Then summarize how it's similar to your idea (or how it helps readers) as well as how it's different.

Finish this section with a brief paragraph about how your book stands out from the competition as a whole. With this work done, you've not only completed your proposal's Competitive Analysis but also made your book idea more marketable and, therefore, more likely to get picked up by an agent and, subsequently, a publisher.

**NINA AMIR** is known as the Inspiration to Creation Coach. As an author coach, she supports writers on every step of the journey to successful authorship. Additionally, she is one of 800 elite Certified High Performance Coaches working worldwide but the only one specifically supporting writers with personal development. Nina has written three traditionally published books for aspiring authors, *How to Blog a Book*, *The Author Training Manual*, and *Creative Visualization for Writers*, as well as a host of self-published books and ebooks, including the Write Nonfiction NOW! series of guides. She has had 19 books on the Amazon Top 100 List and as many as six books on the Authorship bestseller list at the same time. She also is an award-winning blogger and journalist. To further support writers, Nina founded www.writenonfictionnow.com, the Nonfiction Writers, University, and Author of Change Transformational Programs. She also established the Inspired Creator Community, which provides personal and spiritual growth coaching with the bonus of group author coaching and nonfiction writing and publishing resources. For more information, visit www.ninaamir.com.

# HOW TO KNOW WHEN YOUR MANUSCRIPT IS READY

*By Tiffany Yates Martin*

"The first draft of anything is shit," Hemingway memorably said, and writers who've been writing for any length of time know that much of the real work lies in the editing and revision process. But once you've polished your story, how do you know when it's good enough to publish or submit?

In a craft and business as subjective as writing, there's no clear finish line to let you know when you've arrived. But there are key areas of your manuscript you can evaluate to determine whether your story is as effective as you can make it—and when you're ready to hit "send" or "publish."

## CHECK YOUR FOUNDATION

The general essence or "formula" of story is this: A character the reader feels invested in is driven to attain or avoid something she cares enormously about, and she takes a series of actions in pursuit of that goal, the result of which engenders a shift in her internal and external situation.

So the first thing to assess is whether that foundation is solidly in place, using this basic definition as a template.

A key factor to keep in mind is that the greatest disconnect—and biggest hurdle—writers face in objectively evaluating their work is that they tend to "fill in the blanks" of the story that lives so vividly in their heads. So in answering the questions below, judge solely on what's actually on the page in the finished draft—specifically, clearly, and concretely.

## Have you created character(s) the reader feels invested in?

- **Do readers immediately see who the character is?** Readers don't care what's happening until we care who it's happening to, and for that we have to have a clear, vivid sense of character from page one. You may know them inside and out, but readers need to see who they are on the page. How do you reveal character from the very beginning in their actions, reactions, interactions, behavior, dialogue, inner life, attitude/beliefs, demeanor, etc., to show what makes them interesting, believable, and three-dimensional?

- **Do we have reasons to care what happens to the character(s)?** What about them—as we see them on the page—draws us in, makes us invest in their experience? They don't necessarily have to be likable, just engaging and compelling enough for us to want to get on the train and take this journey with them as our main traveling companions. Give us a reason to care: Is the character funny? Especially good at what he does, or gifted in some way, or have a driving passion we can root for? Can we invest in her admirable goal, even if we don't like the character herself? Is she fascinating or unique in a way that compels us to pay attention? How do you show that on the page?

## Have you shown that the character is driven to attain or avoid something she cares enormously about (stakes), and the series of actions she takes in direct pursuit of that goal (plot)?

- **Do we see clearly the character(s)' situation/attitude at the beginning of the story?** Before we can care about the character's destination, we have to understand their origination point: the character's "point A." What situation are they in when we meet them, and what is their attitude about it? Where do readers glean both their initial external and internal circumstances and the longing or lack (motivation) that compels them to move out of it?

- **Do we know why it matters?** Readers can't care about what a character has to gain or lose—the stakes—unless the character cares profoundly. Where on the page do we see what drives the character (motivation), and why it's so compelling to her (stakes)? Have you shown concretely and vividly what that character wants, or wants to avoid (goal)? Does what is at stake for him drive every action the character takes in pursuit of that goal? Do the stakes stay strong, urgent, and immediate in each scene, and rise higher over the course of the story as the character moves closer to her goal?

- **Do we see that motivation directly propel the character toward a specific goal she embarks on a journey to attain?** Have you clearly shown what knocks her out of her point-A stasis (inciting event) relatively early in the story that sets her on the journey of the story? Does every scene show either movement toward or setbacks from the character(s)' goal as a result of every event that happens in the story? Is each scene's immediate goal concretely related or in service to the character's pursuit of their overarching goal? Is the character the engine of the action in pursuit of that goal, rather than a passive recipient, witness, or bystander?

Does the journey the character takes in the story engender a meaningful shift in her internal and external situation?

- **Do we clearly see the character's arc?** If your character isn't changed by her journey, it's like disembarking in the same town where you boarded the plane—you must take the reader somewhere. Have you shown how every triumph and setback the character experiences over the course of the story moves her along an arc of growth or change—from her point A to a different situation and attitude, her point B? Have you clearly shown his attainment of or failure to attain his goal? Do we see how the character is changed as a direct result—internally as well as externally?

## OTHER ESSENTIAL ELEMENTS

Having the foundational elements of story rock-solid is vital in creating an effective, competitive manuscript. But that doesn't necessarily mean you're ready to hit "send." There are countless moving parts that make up a compelling, polished story, but several areas are especially key to calibrate:

- Is every scene essential—meaning does it show the character moving along her arc, advance the plot, and/or raise stakes (structure)? The most effective stories accomplish most or all of these goals in each scene.
- Are all the characters essential in moving your protagonist(s) along their arcs? If not, could you more effectively combine minor characters to fill a more intrinsic function in the story?
- Have you introduced some question or uncertainty in every single scene (suspense) to propel readers forward (momentum)? Human beings are curious creatures and crave answers; have you consistently created unknowns to pique that desire in us?
- Do you have elements of friction, conflict, or an obstacle on every page, underlying nearly every line (tension)? Smooth sailing is narrative dead space.
- Does the story action rise to a clear climax where the protagonist faces her greatest challenge or obstacle? Do we see how the growth or lessons she has attained in her

journey to this point equip her to triumph (or cause her to fail), and the outcome of the challenge? Are all loose ends tied up in the story's resolution?

- Is your prose concise, concrete, evocative, and polished? Have you said exactly what you mean, without redundancy or wordiness?

As fundamental as they are, these questions are really the tip of the clichéd iceberg of evaluating your story's effectiveness and competitiveness—you can find a much more extensive checklist on my website.

But one question I heard recently from an author might be the best final gut-check—if you can answer with brutal honesty—of whether your story is ready to compete with hundreds of others on agent slush piles and the millions of books already on the market: Is there any area you intuitively know still needs work and are hoping agents, editors, or readers will overlook?

If you can honestly answer no, you can be fairly confident your story is ready for launch.

**TIFFANY YATES MARTIN** spent nearly 30 years as an editor in the publishing industry, working with major publishers and *New York Times*, *Washington Post*, *Wall Street Journal*, and *USA Today* bestselling and award-winning authors as well as indie and newer writers. She is the founder of FoxPrint Editorial and author of the bestseller *Intuitive Editing: A Creative and Practical guide to Revising Your Writing* Under the pen name Phoebe Fox, she's the author of six novels, including *The Way We Weren't* (Berkley). Visit her at www.foxprinteditorial.com or www.phoebefoxauthor.com.

# 20 LITERARY AGENTS

## Actively Seeking Writers and Their Writing

................................................

*by Robert Lee Brewer*

/////////////////////////////////////////////////////////////////////////////////////

Literary agents are the gatekeepers of the publishing industry for most of the larger book publishers, including many medium-sized presses. As such, they're the only vehicle available for writers to get their writing in front of editors at many houses. However, there are hundreds of literary agents—and not all of them are open to new writers.

That's why I've put together this list of 20 literary agents who are actively seeking writers and their writing. Many of these agents are relatively new to agenting and working hard to build their client lists. Others are established, but they're still looking for the right projects.

In this list, there are agents who represent middle grade, young adult, and adult fiction and nonfiction in a variety of genres. If you're working on a book project, there's likely one or more fits in this list.

## TASNEEM MOTALA OF THE RIGHTS FACTORY

If there's literally anything to do as a kid growing up in rural Niagara, it's read, and Tasneem did so much of it that she turned it into her career with a degree in English and Classical Civilizations and a post-grad in Publishing. Her experience includes writing beauty articles for *Elevate Magazine*, promoting Sonia Faruqi's book, *The Oyster Thief*, to the book-blogging sphere as a marketing manager, and building her very own #OwnVoices literary zine, *KROS Magazine*, from scratch when she was in college.

You can follow her on Twitter @seraphecda.

**Seeking:** Tasneem is actively looking for character-driven MG and YA stories written by BIPOC authors.

Retellings of well-known myths and classics, the enemies-to-lovers trope, and anything with mechas or androids are just a few of Tasneem's favorite things when it comes to fiction. She also adores anything with something important to say hidden within all the actio.

**How to Submit:** Writers can submit their work through my QueryManager (https://query manager.com/query/2005).

## MATT BELFORD OF TOBIAS LITERARY AGENCY

Matt joined The Tobias Agency in 2020 after previously working at the David Black Agency and the Aaron M. Priest Agency. Once he received his Master of Fine Arts in Creative Writing from Emerson College, he decided to apply his talents in representing authors, as opposed to writing himself.

A lover of all things science fiction and fantasy, Matt accepts his nerd status readily.

**Seeking:** Some of my favorite reads include *The Summoner,* by Gail Z. Martin; *Kings of the Wyld,* by Nicholas Eames; *Trail of Lightning,* by Rebecca Roanhorse; and *Red Rising,* by Pierce Brown.

I'm interested in receiving submissions for both graphic memoirs and graphic novels, as well as adult science fiction and fantasy, and some popular nonfiction. I'm not interested in YA.

**How to Submit:** If you would like to query me, please complete the form on my QueryManager (https://querymanager.com/query/MWBelford).

## ANALIEZE CERVANTES OF HARVEY KLINGER LITERARY AGENCY

Analieze Cervantes is a graduate from Cal State San Bernardino where she studied English: Creative Writing along with a minor in Screenwriting. She has also worked as an editorial freelancer for independent authors. She started her career as an intern at a New York literary agency and was mentored by Saritza Hernandez. She then joined the Harvey Klinger Literary Agency in 2020.

Analieze is especially open to BIPOC and LGBTQ voices. She currently resides in Southern California with her five dogs.

**Seeking:** As an agent for the Harvey Klinger Literary Agency, I am looking for character-driven books that grip me from the first page until the very end. I want fantastic world-building, a clear plot, and want to know your main character's desire by the time I get to page 10. Time shouldn't exist when I read your manuscript. I want to be hooked and pulled into your world.

Great writing is awesome, but your characters matter most to me. I want books that make me cry, laugh, and to feel connected to your main character. For thrillers, I want to be on the edge of my seat and have no clue on how your book is going to end. I want to vouch for your main character and cheer them on by the end of your story.

For young adult, I'm looking for sci-fi (a Dystopian feel, think Divergent, hacking, neurolinks, AI blend with reality); contemporary romance (think *If He Had Been with Me* and *To All the Boys*, a sweet romance that develops over time, I want to believe in love again); rom-com (a love story that provides comedic elements, meeting in a unique moment/setting); mystery (think *Riverdale*, twists and turns, should not give me any hints); paranormal (vampires, werewolves, blend of reality and fiction with a love story—but no zombies!); crime fiction (thorough investigation for murders and other cases, strong MC with a clear desire); LGBTQ (a love story that progresses over time, no triangles); and thriller/suspense (cliffhangers, want to be on the edge of my seat).

For adult, I'm seeking physiological and domestic thriller/suspense (think Karin Slaughter's *The Good Daughter*); mystery (twists and turns, want a surprise ending, should not give me hints on who "dun" it); contemporary romance (a love story that conquers all, no love at first sight); romantic suspense (a love story with suspense elements webbed in); rom-com (a love story that provides comedic elements, meeting in a unique moment/setting); paranormal (vampires, witches, etc., blend of reality and fiction with a love story—no zombies); sci-fi (soft sci-fi, blending the two worlds); and crime fiction (want to feel connected to the MC and clearly shows MC's desire to solve a case).

I'm not looking for fantasy (though might be interested in magical realism); short story collections; inspirational works including religious overtones; picture/chapter books; erotica; nonfiction; memoir; graphic novels; horror (please nothing with zombies); Westerns; novellas; anything political; poetry; and screenplays.

**How to Submit:** If you would like to query me, please send your query letter, synopsis, and the first five pages of your manuscript at https://querymanager.com/query/Analieze Cervantes.

I am not accepting emailed submissions.

## ZEYNEP SEN OF WORDLINK LITERARY AGENCY

Zeynep Sen graduated from Sarah Lawrence College with a BA in Literature and Creative Writing. Following her graduation, she started working at the Jennifer Lyons Literary Agency, where she honed her skills as an agent. A few years after, Zeynep moved to WordLink Literary Agency, as their new senior and foreign rights agent.

At WordLink, Zeynep represents her own lists of authors and is in charge of the foreign rights of all the authors of the agency. As such, she frequently travels to various international book fairs. Fluent in Spanish and Turkish, Zeynep is drawn to literary and historical works of fiction and narrative nonfiction of international appeal.

**Seeking:** When it comes to nonfiction, I represent works that try to start a social discussion, that prompt the reader to think on social change or books that unveil inspiring life stories or hidden histories few people know about. A book by one of my authors, *Un-American*, by Erik Edstrom, recently published by Bloomsbury, is an excellent example of this.

When it comes to fiction, I'm drawn to family sagas, historical novels and coming-of-age stories that embrace themes such as LGBTQ+ issues, mental health, interculturality, immigration, identity, belonging, and race.

I do not represent thrillers or mystery/crime. Regardless of genre, though, what's most important to me in a work is character development and relationships, as well as unique narrative voices.

**How to Submit:** I'm currently open to submission and actively looking for new works and authors. The best way to share your work with me is to send a query letter to z.sen@word link.us.

I usually respond to queries within 6 weeks of receipt.

## PETE FORD OF CREDO COMMUNICATIONS

Pete Ford has built websites, planned writers conferences, edited manuscripts, and converted books to ebooks. At the end of high school, he read a biography of the famous editor Max Perkins, which immediately clicked with his passions. As Perkins noted, editing is much more than fixing typos—it includes shepherding authors to write their best.

After graduating from Calvin University with a degree in literature, he joined Credo as a literary agent and publishing coordinator. In his agenting role, he enjoys serving and encouraging authors. Based in Grand Rapids, Michigan, Ford focuses on Credo's fiction program, new and diverse voices, and young authors.

**Seeking:** Some of my favorite reads recently include *The Common Rule* and *Scandalous Witness*. I am interested in receiving submissions for both fiction and nonfiction in the Christian publishing arena.

In fiction, I am especially fascinated with parallel storylines that enhance each other. For nonfiction, "lay academic" titles interest me, from spiritual growth and practical living to topics that bring liturgy to an evangelical audience.

I'm not currently interested in representing YA, children's, or memoir.

**How to Submit:** If you would like to query me, please send your proposal and sample chapters as an attachment to Pete@CredoCommunications.net. Read our full submission guidelines on our website: https://www.credocommunications.net/submissions/.

## CRYSTAL ORAZU OF CONTEXT LITERARY AGENCY

Crystal's love for novels first blossomed among the stacks of many Houston public libraries and it has grown stronger ever since. She hopes to represent and uplift authors whose stories allow readers to feel seen and heard in new and exciting ways.

**Seeking:** What moves Crystal above all else is simple, open, and honest writing true to an author's wild imagination or lived experience. Anything that brings equal measures of humor, introspection, or feelings of second-hand embarrassment appeals to her. She loves both sweet meandering stories as well as more fraught and thrilling narratives in both YA and adult fiction. Perspectives that make her question the way that she or others move in the world, as well as her assumptions/opinions of societies and systems (à la *Black Mirror*), are also welcome in her inbox.

Crystal is especially partial to narratives centering Black, Indigenous, and People of Color (BIPOC), LGBTQ+, and neurodivergent persons that include joyful, romantic, or lighthearted elements (#OwnVoices that aren't solely issue driven). Crystal is also looking for middle grade, young adult, and adult fiction that explores interpersonal relationships amongst traditional/chosen family members and friends using either realistic or fantastical elements (especially from a first or second-gen immigrant perspective). Fun sleight of hand/heist/spy narratives like the *Gallagher Girls* series and darker stories along the lines of *Coraline* are also very welcome.

**How to Submit:** Send a short description, short bio, and 5-10 pages of text pasted into the body of the email to querycrystal@contextlit.com. I do not open attachments.

## BARB ROOSE OF BOOKS & SUCH LITERARY MANAGEMENT

Barb Roose loves partnering with aspiring and established authors to achieve their publishing career goals. With experience as an award-winning pharmaceutical sales representative and executive leader in the megachurch environment, Barb embraces the challenges and opportunities that agenting in Christian publishing offers.

As an author, Barb understands the tensions and triumphs embedded in the publishing process. Her heartbeat is helping others achieve their goals as well as increasing representation and publishing opportunities for people of color. Barb represents both Christian adult fiction and Christian nonfiction, with an emphasis on nonfiction.

**Seeking:** In nonfiction, Roose is looking for women's issues, Christian living issues, devotionals, race and culture, memoirs, and narrative nonfiction. In CBA adult fiction, Roose is looking for women's, romantic suspense, suspense/thriller, historical, romance, and legal and family issues.

**How to Submit:** Prospective writers should email one-page equivalent queries with a brief description of your project and vision for marketing your book to representation@books andsuch.com.

## KATHRYN WILLMS OF THE RIGHTS FACTORY

Kathryn Willms has over 12 years of professional writing, editing, and management experience. Since 2017, she has run Kwill Communications, an editorial firm specializing in educational and academic work, as well as providing substantive, stylistic, and copy editing for nonfiction authors. Prior to this, she was vice president and senior editor at Colborne Communications.

As publisher at Iguana Books, she oversaw acquisitions, production, sales, and marketing for over 25 books, a list that included fiction, nonfiction, and children's. Before her foray into publishing, she worked in financial services and as a journalist. She holds an MA in English from the University of Calgary.

Over the course of her career, Kathryn has taken pride in building strong and supportive relationships with authors, and helping them produce powerful, exciting, and creative work. She is excited to be continuing this work with The Rights Factory.

**Seeking:** Nonfiction that informs, inspires, delights, or surprises. As a generalist who simply likes "good books," she's open to a variety of genres, including history; culture and current affairs; sports; biography and memoir; women's issues; health and wellness; food and drink; self-improvement.

Over and above genre, she's looking for fresh takes; strong voices and points of view; uncovered/recovered stories; and the opportunity to learn something new.

**How to Submit:** Writers can submit their work through my QueryManager (https://query manager.com/query/2039).

## MARGARET DANKO OF PAPER OVER BOARD OF THE IRENE GOODMAN LITERARY AGENCY

Originally from the heart of the south, Margaret Danko received her BA from Oberlin College before continuing on to pursue an MFA from Temple University. While there, she climbed the ranks to become an editor of *TINGE Magazine*, publishing fiction, essays, and poetry. She has worked as a freelance editor and media consultant on projects with a variety of authors and publishers, including assisting Kim Perel of Paper Over Board at the Irene Goodman Literary Agency.

She is now building her own list with Paper Over Board. A lover of the dark, the quirky, and the fantastical, Margaret has a keen eye for projects that take unexpected turns or are told from unusual perspectives.

Margaret believes that all books, whether on an emotional level or through a physical call to action, should move their readers, and she is passionate about empowering authors to find the voice and the story that will engage and inspire each and every person who picks up their books.

**Seeking:** Margaret is actively looking for attention-grabbing voices especially #OwnVoices narratives, literary fiction with teeth, historical fiction with a dash of magical realism, fresh literary and commercial suspense, spooky contemporary and fantasy YA, narratives with a deep sense of place and history, quirky and heartwarming family stories, and rom-coms full of charm and whimsy.

She is also interested in nonfiction in the areas of humor, lifestyle, popular science, health/wellness, true crime, politics, and current affairs.

**How to Submit:** Submissions should be emailed and addressed to Margaret Danko at sub missions@paperoverboard.com.

## STEFANIE ROSSITTO OF THE TOBIAS AGENCY

Originally from the German Alps, Steffi used to spend hours in quaint bookstores as a child. She went on to study English language, American literature, and medieval history at Regensburg University and Edinburgh University. Her master's thesis was based on a *New York Times* article on modern day "suburban" novelists and how these authors shaped American suburban culture. After graduation, she moved to New York City where she started out at three different literary agencies before moving on to Random House to explore the corporate side of the business. At Doubleday and Crown, she worked in their subsidiary rights departments for over five years and dealt with foreign and domestic licensing for every genre.

Before coming to Tobias Literary Agency, she spent five years as a freelance reader evaluating German fiction and nonfiction for the US and international market, while raising her two young daughters. Steffi combines experience in agenting with corporate publishing and a keen understanding of foreign fiction and what will translate into the US market.

**Seeking:** Steffi is currently looking for historical fiction and funny, modern romances. She also enjoys anything and everything medieval as well as exciting historical romances and/ or fiction based on real characters.

**How to Submit:** Steffi only accepts queries through QueryManager (https://querymanager .com/query/1927).

## ARIA GMITTER OF THE WHIMSY LITERARY AGENCY

Aria Gmitter joined the Whimsy Literary Agency in 2020. She is a writer, journalist, and editor who graduated from the Denver Publishing Institute in 2016. Before that, she was a literary assistant to Peter Miller of Global Lion Intellectual Property Management.

She has an MFA from Full Sail University and a Masters of Science in Health Law from Nova Southeastern University. She earned her undergraduate Bachelor of Arts degree from the University of Miami majoring in English Literature and Comparative Religious Studies. Her first short story, "Friend of the Fatherless," was published by Bethany House in *Encountering Jesus: Modern-Day Stories of His Supernatural Presence and Power*, in 2015.

**Seeking:** Aria is looking for nonfiction, mind/body/spirit, pop culture, astrology, mystical arts, self-help, romance, crime/mystery novels, psychological thrillers for adult, middle grade, YA, gift books, illustrated, humor and joke, cookbooks, humorous parodies, and children's books.

**How to Submit:** Writers should send their proposals via email to whimsynyc@aol.com. Proposals should include your media platform and table of contents with a full description of each chapter.

## AYLA ZURAW-FRIEDLAND OF THE DAVID BLACK AGENCY

Ayla Zuraw-Friedland joined the David Black Agency in 2019. Previously, she worked as an editorial assistant and assistant editor at Beacon Press in Boston, and as a development editor for encyclopedias at Oxford University Press. She received her BA in English and Creative Writing from Connecticut College in 2015, and her writing can be found in *GAY the Magazine* and *Publishers Weekly*.

**Seeking:** I am interested in acquiring adult literary fiction and nonfiction that inspect queerness, disability, race, class, and community in fresh new ways. I have a soft spot for short story collections with magical elements, and essay collections that look at identity through an interesting and specific cultural lens (motorcycles, rock climbing, pottery, you name it). Some pitches I've read and loved: a memoir of coming out as trans later in life, a case against high school football from a sociological standpoint, a collection of essays about mental health and climate change, a novel about immigrant ghosts.

A few of my favorite contemporary writers are Carmen Maria Machado, Kristen Arnett, Hanif Abdurraqib, Helen Oyeyemi, Daniel M. Lavery, Raven Leilani, Candice Carty-Williams, Kacen Callender, Alexander Chee, Akwaeke Emezi, and Samantha Irby.

**How to Submit:** Writers can submit via QueryManager (https://querymanager.com/query/azurawfr).

## EMILY FORNEY OF BOOKENDS LITERARY AGENCY

As a self-proclaimed decent writer and the ultimate fangirl of genre fiction, Emily Forney started her publishing career as an editorial assistant for literary journals in college, freelanced for feminist and pop culture presses, and worked as a fiction editor for a small popular fiction press.

She earned her MFA in Creative Writing from Northern Arizona University, where she specialized in YA and speculative fiction. After studying as a publishing and editorial fellow for the *Los Angeles Review of Books*, she joined BookEnds Literary agency as an associate agent.

Emily is currently seeking out kid lit, picture books, MG, YA, and adult fiction. She is especially looking for stories by Black authors that celebrate Black joy and love.

**Seeking:** In picture books, seeking whimsical and fun adventure stories that allow for the setting and the world around the characters to play just as important of a role; progressive stories about childhood strength, trauma, and identity; and something spooky, maybe a little dark humor, and child-appropriate fantasy.

In middle grade fiction, seeking historical fiction that turns typical histories on their head and write about "hidden" stories with plenty of humor and whimsy; paranormal and fantasy stories with conventional twists and character-driven narratives; and something spooky, maybe a little dark humor, and child-appropriate fantasy.

In YA fiction, seeking warm romances that capture the magic of teenage summer nights, road trips, and summer camps; paranormal and fantasy stories with solid world-building and romantic twists; contemporary romances and contemporary stories that delve into how digital media affects social activism for young people; and LGBTQI+ stories that don't use identity as a plot twist.

In adult fiction, seeking fantasy stories that flip traditional tropes; historical fiction centered outside of modern and contemporary eras. I like ancient worlds, Renaissance times, and unique story arcs that don't have to do with wars with modern technology; and chick-lit made for reading on the beach to escape hot summer days.

**How to Submit:** Please submit your query letter, synopsis, and optional page samples to my QueryManager account (https://querymanager.com/query/emilyforney).

You can also check out my calls for submissions and my updated wish list on my Twitter @emilykaitlinnn.

## JENNIFER HERRINGTON OF HARVEY KLINGER LITERARY AGENCY

Jennifer Herrington started her career on the editorial side of publishing with Kensington Books Publishing's Lyrical Press imprint and an internship with Entangled Publishing. She's also worked as a freelance editor for independent authors. After an internship at a New York agency, she joined the Harvey Klinger Agency in 2020. Jennifer graduated with a diploma in Radio and Television Broadcasting and recently completed her Publishing Certificate with a designation in children's literature at Ryerson University.

Jennifer is currently building her list and is interested in representing middle grade, YA, and adult fiction. She's especially open to BIPOC and LGBTQ voices in the mentioned categories. Jennifer lives in Ontario, Canada, with her husband, three sons, and two dogs.

**Seeking:** I am looking for character- and voice-driven books that I connect with on an emotional level. I want a book that makes me laugh or cry and extra points for both!

In middle grade fiction, I'd like to see contemporary stories that deal with tough and realistic issues kids are facing today; stories that feature humor and adventure; and paranormal, fantasy (except high fantasy), mystery, horror, and graphic novels are also of special interest.

In YA fiction, I'd like to see feel-good contemporary and contemporary romance; paranormals with strong world building and an interesting twist in vamps, wolves, or witches; romantic comedy; mystery series featuring a YA detective; and sci-fi, fantasy (except high fantasy), horror, and graphic novels are also of special interest.

In adult fiction, I'd like to see romance with a fresh twist on trope-driven plots, including best friend's little sister/brother, enemies to lovers, friends to lover, etc. (I like sweet to spicy); a strong sports romance (would love a heroine athlete!) or a sexy cowboy; dark paranormal romances with gritty vamps, wolves, or witches (think outside the box for world-building); romantic comedy with snarky protagonists and hilarious plotlines; romantic suspense with equal parts steamy as action; mysteries, thrillers, and suspense that keep me up all night; and sci-fi and fantasy with romance threads are also welcome.

**How to Submit:** Please submit your query letter, synopsis, and first five pages of your manuscript to my QueryManager account (https://querymanager.com/query/JenniferHerrington).

## KRISTINA PÉREZ OF ZENO LITERARY AGENCY

Kristina Pérez is a half-Argentine/half-Norwegian native New Yorker who has spent the past two decades living in Europe and Asia. Before joining the Zeno Literary Agency in London at the end of 2019, she worked as a journalist, academic, and author. This breadth of experience enables her to serve her clients in a variety of fields and she is a very editorial agent.

Kristina holds a PhD in Medieval Literature from the University of Cambridge and has taught at the National University of Singapore and the University of Hong Kong. As a journalist, she's written for many international news outlets including the *Wall Street Journal Asia, Condé Nast Traveler*, and CNN.

She is the author of the YA fantasy Sweet Black Waves trilogy (Imprint/Macmillan), the YA sci-fi *The Tesla Legacy* (Tor Teen), and the academic monograph *The Myth of Morgan la Fey* (Palgrave Macmillan).

**Seeking:** With her diverse background, Kristina's tastes in books are equally eclectic. She is actively building her list in both fiction and nonfiction, and particularly encourages submissions from marginalized writers.

On the adult side, she is looking for fantasy, romance, sci-fi, and nonfiction. Kristina loves lush historical fantasy like Tasha Suri's *Empire of Sand* and well-researched historical romance along the lines of Joanna Shupe or Courtney Milan. She is a huge *Battlestar Galactica* fangirl with a soft spot for light space opera, but she's not the right agent for hard/military SF.

For nonfiction, she is primarily looking for current affairs, cultural history, and popular science. Recently, she's enjoyed *Latinx* by Ed Morales and *Invisible Women* by Caroline Criado Perez.

Kristina is open to all kinds of MG and YA but does not represent picture books or chapter books. She adores retellings with a twist, whether it be contemporary or fantasy, especially LGBTQIA+ and those that draw on non-Western folklore and mythology. She also has a penchant for novels-in-verse. Favorite MG reads include *The War that Saved My Life*, by Kimberly Brubaker Bradley; *The Unicorn Quest*, by Kamilla Benko; and *The Storm Runner*, by J. C. Cervantes.

**How to Submit:** Email queries only to perez@zenoagency.com. Please email your query letter with the first chapter of your manuscript pasted into the body of the email. No attachments will be opened.

## PAM GRUBER OF THE IRENE GOODMAN LITERARY AGENCY

Pam Gruber began her career in publishing as an editor, working for over 10 years at Hachette Book Group with a number of acclaimed authors and illustrators. From there, she went on to serve as the editorial director at the children's media startup Rebel Girls, where she saw firsthand how a great book can expand into other entertainment mediums.

Pam joined Irene Goodman as a literary agent after realizing her favorite part of the publishing business was working directly with authors and artists, helping them to shape not only their stories, but also their careers.

She looks for work that is gripping from page one, whether it makes her break out in a smile or gives her goose bumps (from excitement, not fear!). She loves complicated female protagonists, innovative twists on classic tropes, and getting swept away by fully realized worlds—be it the next town over or an imagined universe unlike our own.

Originally from Philadelphia, Pam knew she wanted to work in publishing from a young age. She brings an inscrutable eye for detail to every book she gets her hands on, and her experience at a publishing house gives her insight into how editors think and what they're looking for.

**Seeking:** Pam is looking for adult, young adult, and middle grade fiction with literary voices and commercial hooks. She is particularly interested in layered fantasy, speculative fiction, fantastical realism, rom-coms, and coming-of-age stories with a twist. She is also open to realistic middle grade and YA graphic novels, as well as select narrative nonfiction on lesser-known subjects. Pam would not be the best fit for prescriptive nonfiction, anthologies, potty humor, paranormal, or erotica.

**How to Submit:** Please send your query letter to pam.queries@irenegoodman.com along with the first 10 pages of your manuscript, a brief synopsis, and your bio in the body of the email.

## MARIA ROGERS OF TOBIAS LITERARY AGENCY

Originally hailing from St. Louis, Missouri, Maria graduated from Kenyon College before cutting her teeth in publishing as an intern at Writers House.

She went on to work as an editorial assistant at W. W. Norton & Co. and later as an editor at Scholastic. Over the course of her publishing tenure she has worked on behalf of Pulitzer Prize winners, National Book Award winners, Guggenheim Fellows, PEN/Hemingway Award winners, and *New York Times* bestsellers.

Her work experience has given her insight into many realms of reading, from nonfiction and poetry to literary and commercial fiction, to books for children and young adults.

**Seeking:** I'm currently looking for nonfiction that explores big events from new angles, whip-smart cultural criticism, as well as original and urgent journalism and science writing. I'm also on the lookout for books to engage kids in nonfiction topics, from ancient history to contemporary issues. I am not currently considering poetry, picture books, romance, science fiction, or fantasy at this time.

Some books I recently enjoyed include *The Unwinding*, by George Packer; *Wayward Lives, Beautiful Experiments*, by Saidiya Hartman; *In the Dream House*, by Carmen Maria Machado; *Bottle of Lies*, by Katherine Eban; *River*, by Elisha Cooper; and *Pet*, by Akwaeke Emezi.

**How to Submit:** For fiction and nonfiction, please submit via Maria's QueryManager page (https://querymanager.com/query/MRogers).

# ERIN CLYBURN OF THE JENNIFER DE CHIARA LITERARY AGENCY

Erin Clyburn joined The Jennifer De Chiara Literary Agency as associate agent in 2019 after an internship and apprenticeship with Corvisiero Literary Agency. She has worked as a copy editor and recipe editor in the magazine industry and was general manager and director of collection development for Turtleback Books. She received her BA in English Literature from Mississippi State University and her MA in Children's Literature from Hollins University.

When not working, Erin loves hiking, cooking, traveling, painting, working on a manuscript or two, and trying to keep her three rabbits, Felix, Agnes, and Valentino, from chewing up every baseboard in the house.

Visit her page at www.jdlit.com/erin-clyburn and find her on Twitter @erin_clyburn to learn more.

**Seeking:** In children's, Erin is looking for nonfiction picture books, high-concept chapter book series, middle grade (especially mysteries, stories with big hearts, and all things creepy), dark YA (horror, thriller, and mystery), graphic novels, high-interest nonfiction, and, across the board, magic realism.

In adult fiction, she is looking for character-driven literary fiction; plot-driven suspense, mysteries, and domestic thrillers; humor; all horror from psychological to gothic to slasher; and multigenerational family sagas.

In adult nonfiction, she is looking for pop science; high-interest nonfiction, particularly stories about fascinating people and issues that haven't been told before; true crime; cookbooks; and science- or culture-focused memoirs.

Across the board, Erin would love to see character-driven sci-fi, stories set in the South, #OwnVoices, and neurodiverse representation. Erin is not the right person for fiction picture books, romance, Westerns, epic fantasy, political or military thrillers, hard sci-fi, short stories, or stories with a strong focus on religion.

**How to Submit:** Queries should be submitted through QueryManager: http://QueryMe.Online/ErinClyburn. Emailed queries will be deleted unread.

For fiction, please include your query letter, synopsis, and first 10 pages of your manuscript. For nonfiction, please send your query, proposal, and the first 10 pages. For picture books, please send the whole text.

# AMARYAH ORENSTEIN OF GO LITERARY

Amaryah Orenstein, founder of GO Literary, is thrilled to help writers bring their ideas to life. Aiming to give voice to a broad range of perspectives, Amaryah represents a wide array of literary and commercial fiction and narrative nonfiction. She is actively seeking works that wed beautiful writing with a strong narrative and tackle big issues in engaging, accessible, and even surprising ways.

In addition to negotiating contracts, Amaryah works closely with each of her clients throughout every step of the publishing process, from concept development through publication and beyond. She takes a particular interest in the editorial process, offering skilled advice and guidance to help clients bring out the best in their writing.

Amaryah began her career at the Laura Gross Literary Agency in 2009 and, prior to that, worked as an editorial assistant at various academic research foundations, including The Tauber Institute, where she edited books for Brandeis University Press/University Press of New England. Originally from Montreal, she earned a BA at McGill University before coming to the US to pursue graduate work in American History. She received her MA from the Contemporary History Institute at Ohio University and her PhD from Brandeis University.

**Seeking:** Thematic interests include but are not limited to: contemporary + historical fiction; family relationship + coming-of-age stories; history + current affairs; social + cultural issues; memoir; food.

**How to Submit:** GO Literary aims to give voice to a broad range of perspectives and welcomes electronic submissions from both established and first-time writers. Please send your queries to submissions@go-lit.com. Emails should include a description of your work and a brief biographical sketch. Please do not send your manuscript, whole or partial, unless it has been specifically requested. Please note: GO Literary does not accept submissions via snail mail or social media.

## ISABEL KAUFMAN OF FOX LITERARY

Isabel Kaufman began her publishing career as an intern with Fox Literary in 2012, while studying the history of stories and storytelling at New York University. After completing a master's degree in literature at the University of Edinburgh, she worked for several years as a freelance writer and editor and as a brand consultant in the luxury travel and lifestyle sector.

She is thrilled to return to the business of agenting and her first and lifelong love: developing new voices and building the scaffolding of enduring literary careers. Follow her on Twitter @isabeljka.

**Seeking:** Isabel is actively looking to build her list in fantasy and science fiction, adult literary fiction, upmarket horror, historical fiction, contemporary commercial fiction, and young adult literature. She is looking for smart, inventive, ambitious storytelling and welcomes speculative elements across all genres. She is also interested in creative nonfiction and microhistories, particularly related to the fields of travel, food, and luxury goods.

Her taste is varied, but she is consistently drawn to dynamic prose and vibrant, specific character voice, particularly from historically underrepresented and marginalized authors. She appreciates purposeful conversations with genre staples, new retellings of old myths and fairy tales, and fresh perspectives on "archaic" genres (such as noir, gothic, and classical revenge tragedy). She has a degree in Shakespeare and Jacobean revenge tragedy and is willing to get bloody.

Recent books she has loved include *The Glass Hotel*, by Emily St. John Mandel; *Severance*, by Ling Ma; The Locked Tomb trilogy, by Tamsyn Muir; *The Idiot*, by Elif Batuman; *Luster*, by Raven Leilani; *Sadie*, by Courtney Summers; *The Priory of the Orange Tree*, by Samantha Shannon; *Plain Bad Heroines*, by Emily Danforth; *Raybearer*, by Jordan Ifueko; *If I Had Your Face*, by Frances Cha; *One Last Stop*, by Casey McQuiston; *Freshwater*, by Akwaeke Emezi; and everything by Helen Oyeyemi and Megan Abbott. Her favorite nonfiction includes *Priestdaddy*, by Patricia Lockwood; *Secondhand Time*, by Svetlana Alexievich; and *The Emperor of Scent*, by Luca Turin.

**How to Submit:** Please send submissions to submissions@foxliterary.com.

# THE AGENT QUERY TRACKER

## Submit Smarter and Follow Up Faster with These Simple Spreadsheets to Revolutionize Your Record-Keeping

...................................

*Tyler Moss*

Everyone knows the real magic of writing comes from time spent in the chair, those sessions in which your fingertips flitting across the keyboard can barely keep pace with the electric current sparking through your brain.

Those in-between periods, full of administrative tasks—the querying, the tracking of payments, the day-to-day doldrums that occupy the interstitial moments of a writer's life—become an afterthought. But when such responsibilities are given short shrift, the inevitable result is disorganization—which at best can impede creativity and at worst can have dire consequences. Missed payments, embarrassing gaffes (querying the same agent twice, or realizing you have no record of where your previous agent submitted your last novel), and incomplete records come tax time are entirely avoidable headaches.

Still, organized record-keeping takes work. Which is why we decided to do it for you.

This does not have to mean you're about to start spending more time on these tasks—in fact, quite the opposite. Once you invest in a standard process up front, each future action will require little more than filling out a few cells in a spreadsheet. (Learn to love them as I have for their clean, quadrilateral beauty.)

You can use the simple guides on the following pages to customize forms of your own, whether you're querying an agent, tracking the places your agent is submitting, or working on your freelancing career between projects.

# AGENT QUERY TRACKER

| AGENT | **Example:** Booker M. Sellington | | |
|---|---|---|---|
| AGENCY | The Booker M. Sellington Agency | | |
| E-MAIL | BMS@bmsagency.com | | |
| DATE QUERIED | 8/1/16 | | |
| MATERIALS SENT | Query, Synopsis, first 10 pages | | |
| DATE FOLLOWED UP | 9/1/16 | | |
| RESPONSE | Request for additional materials | | |
| ADDITIONAL MATE-RIALS REQUESTED | Full manuscript | | |
| DATE FOLLOWED UP | 10/15/16 | | |
| RESPONSE | Offer of representation | | |
| NOTES | Specializes in thrillers | | |

Few writers hit the jackpot and manage to land a literary agent on their first query. As this process can take weeks or months, and as agency guidelines vary widely, it can be helpful to keep a detailed record of whom you have contacted, what agency they work for, what materials you've sent in, and the specifics of their responses. Customize your own tracker starting from these column headings:

- **AGENT, AGENCY & E-MAIL:** Where you are sending your query
- **POLICY AGAINST QUERYING MULTIPLE AGENTS AT AGENCY:** [Optional Field] Some agencies have a no-from-one-agent-means-no-from-the-whole-agency policy; noting this saves you time and embarrassment, particularly at larger firms where multiple reps might seem like a potential fit
- **DATE QUERIED & MATERIALS SENT:** When and what you submitted, always following guidelines (query letter, first ten pages, synopsis, proposal, etc.)
- **"NO RESPONSE MEANS NO" POLICY:** [Optional Field] Agents who specify in their guidelines that no response equates to a rejection, meaning you shouldn't follow up
- **DATE FOLLOWED UP:** In the event of no response and excluding those with the policy noted above
- **RESPONSE:** A rejection, a request to see more, or any constructive feedback
- **ADDITIONAL MATERIALS REQUESTED & DATE SENT:** Typically a full or partial manuscript is requested if your query garners interest

- **DATE FOLLOWED UP:** For a full or partial, follow up after at least four weeks if there's no response (unless you have an offer for representation elsewhere, in which case you'll follow up immediately to request a decision or withdraw your manuscript from consideration)
- **RESPONSE:** The agent's final feedback or response
- **NOTES:** Any helpful info on your interaction with the agent or agency, or feedback that could be addressed before additional querying (e.g., "The protagonist often behaves erratically and inconsistently," or "The manuscript could use a proofread")

If you opt to forgo seeking representation and instead are submitting directly to publishers that accept unagented submissions, then I suggest you make a separate spreadsheet to track that information, swapping the headings **AGENT** and **AGENCY** for **ACQUIRING EDITOR** and **IMPRINT/PUBLISHER**, respectively.

---

**ORGANIZE YOUR QUERIES**

Both versions of the tracker are available for download at writersdigest.com/GLA-18.

---

## AGENT SUBMISSIONS TO PUBLISHER TRACKER

| IMPRINT/PUBLISHER | Example: Pendant Publishing | | |
|---|---|---|---|
| ACQUIRING EDITOR | Elaine Benes | | |
| DATE SENT | 8/1/16 | | |
| DATE FOLLOWED UP | 9/1/16 | | |
| RESPONSE | Pass | | |
| EDITOR'S COMMENTS | Says a "book about nothing" is not right for their Spring 2018 lineup | | |
| ADDITIONAL NOTES | Suggests changes to plot in which the judge sentences protagonist to be the antagonist's butler | | |

After signing with an agent, it's critical to stay in close communication as she sends your manuscript to publishers. Such records allow you to stay involved in the direction of your career, gather essential data about the imprints your agent believes you'd be best suited for, and pinpoint commonalities or contradictions in feedback. And if you must someday sever ties with your agent, you'll have what you need to help your new representation pick up right where your old representation left off. Keep record of the following details:

- **IMPRINT/PUBLISHER, ACQUIRING EDITOR & DATE SENT:** The details of exactly where and when your agent submitted your manuscript
- **DATE FOLLOWED UP:** Date on which your agent followed up with the acquiring editor if you did not receive an initial response
- **RESPONSE:** Accepted, rejected, revise-and-resubmit request
- **EDITOR'S COMMENTS:** A one-line description highlighting any relevant feedback received
- **ADDITIONAL NOTES:** Miscellaneous information about the publisher, editor, or the overall interaction between agent and publishing house

## PRO TIP: SAVE SPREADSHEETS TO GOOGLE DRIVE

Recently I read a news story in which a writer in New Orleans ran into his burning home to save the manuscripts of two completed novels stored on his computer—the only place he had them saved. Luckily, he weathered the blaze and escaped with laptop in hand. Though we can admire his dedication to his work, there are any number of digital-age options that could've prevented this horrible scenario—among them, Google Drive.

The system is ideal for uploading a fresh document of your manuscript every time you make changes, storing files online in addition to on your computer (Google Drive has an online storage function similar to services such as Dropbox and Microsoft OneDrive).

Google Drive allows you to create documents, spreadsheets, slide shows, and more, all of which can be accessed from anywhere—laptop, tablet, smartphone—by logging into a free Google account. Such items are easily shared with your co-author, agent, or publicist for more efficient record keeping or file sharing. It's also a great place to create and modify the trackers from this article.

Simply log in to your account at google.com/drive (or create one for free), hit the New button in the top left corner of the interface and click on Google Sheets. This will open a new window with a clean spreadsheet, where you can then begin entering the appropriate column headings. Title the spreadsheet by clicking "Untitled spreadsheet" at the top of the page. Once complete, you'll be able to open up your Freelance Payment Tracker or Agent Query Tracker on any device with an Internet connection—far from flames or flood.

## FREELANCE PAYMENT TRACKER

| ARTICLE HEADLINE | Example: "Tongue Tied" | | |
|---|---|---|---|
| PUBLICATION/URL | *Ball & String* Magazine | | |
| PAYMENT | $500 | | |
| DATE PUBLISHED | July 2016 | | |
| TOTAL WORDS | 1,000 | | |
| $/WORD | $0.40 cents/word | | |
| INVOICE # | #2014-1 | | |
| INVOICE SUBMITTED | 8/12/16 | | |
| PAID | 8/30/16 | | |

When you've been commissioned to write a piece, it's vital to document the status of your payment. Not only will it keep you from missing a check, but it's incredibly useful for noting what a publication has paid you in the past and comparing the rates of different publications for which you freelance—which can help you prioritize your time by targeting the most lucrative outlets. It's also a lifesaver come April 15.

As depicted in the example spreadsheet above, you can use the following column headings to trace the path of your payments:

- **HEADLINE:** Title of the finished, published piece
- **PUBLICATION/URL:** Outlet that published the article and, if applicable, the URL where the article can be found online
- **PAYMENT:** Total payment received for work
- **DATE PUBLISHED:** Date article went live online, or issue month if for a print magazine or journal
- **TOTAL WORDS & $/WORD:** Length of the piece and amount you were paid per word, found by dividing the total payment by the total number of words (a common standardization for freelance payment rates)
- **INVOICE # & SUBMITTED:** Unique number of the invoice you submitted for this particular article (if applicable), and date on which it was submitted
- **PAID:** Date on which you received the payment, most commonly via check or direct deposit

Of course, you can also use this same basic format to develop a spreadsheet that covers advances, royalties, speaking honoraria, etc. Use the basic format outlined here to construct your own customized version.

**TYLER MOSS** is a former editor-in-chief of *Writer's Digest*. Follow him on Twitter @tjmoss11.

# WORKING WITH A PUBLICIST

*by Cris Freese*

So you found an agent, and he landed you the publishing contract of your dreams. Okay, if you've picked up this book, it's more likely that you're dreaming of that day on the near horizon.

Regardless, you're going to find yourself with three champions when that dream comes true. Two of them are oft-discussed—your agent and your editor—and you'll undoubtedly read plenty of articles about developing a strong, working relationship with them. But your third advocate is just as important, and less discussed—your publicist.

As the former editor of *Guide to Literary Agents*, I found myself often working with publicists to secure interviews with authors (particularly debut authors!), asking for guest posts, and combing through advanced reading copies. That is, publicists sought out places where they could get their clients exposure.

And, as you'll see, publicists are tireless workers, doing their best to secure that interview, byline, or mention that piques the interest of readers enough to pick up the book in a bookstore or read description copy on Amazon—and maybe sell some copies!

I sat down with four publicists—two working with traditional, large publishers, and two working for marketing agencies—to talk about their jobs, how authors can help themselves, and more.

## MEET THE PUBLICISTS

- Katie Bassel is a publicity manager at St. Martin's Press.
- Julia Borcherts is a publicist for Kaye Publicity.
- Jordan Rodman is a publicity manager for Alfred A. Knopf & Pantheon.
- Sara Wigal is a senior book publicist at JKS Communications.

## How did you get started as a publicist?

**Sara Wigal:** When I was in my early twenties I hopped around between a few editorial jobs and also thinking I might want to be an agent. I went to the publishing graduate program at Emerson College to sort out what would really be the best career arc for me, and, while studying for my MA, I took a marketing course with Beth Ineson [now the executive director of NEIBA]. What I learned in that class really resonated with me, and I started to feel like I had more direction, and that something more on the PR side of things would probably be a good fit for what I found most interesting, work-wise. When I saw a job opening with Open Book Publicity, I jumped at the chance to start working in literary publicity while still finishing my degree. I was a radio publicist, meaning that I helped put authors on radio shows, and I really loved both the principals at my company, as well as the radio producers and hosts I got to work with (let alone the authors!). I did that for quite a few years before I had another opportunity to become a comprehensive publicist at my current firm, JKS Communications, where I've been able to grow into a larger role and learn so much about our industry and how to best serve authors on a broad scale.

**Katie Bassel:** I started my career in corporate sales and marketing for the St. Louis Cardinals. When I made the move to New York, I sought out a job in publishing. The skill-set was similar, I'm a journalism major, and I've always been a reader and lover of books, so the switch was easy!

**Julia Borcherts:** I met Dana Kaye in the early 2000s when we were both studying fiction writing at Columbia College Chicago. She was working as a book critic; I was writing features for Chicago publications and producing and hosting literary events, so our paths crossed often, especially after she founded Kaye Publicity. In 2014, she needed to replace a publicist and we talked about how my skills (and my interest in books) would translate to that role. I had long admired the way she managed her business and I knew that I could learn so much from her.

**Jordan Rodman:** While in college, I spent a summer interning in NYC for Barbara Jones, the brilliant executive editor at Henry Holt. I didn't know anything at all about publishing (had no idea how to even pronounce Knopf). She recommended I look into jobs in publicity, because as a publicist, you are able to be close to both the books as well as the authors and are able to think creatively and have much more than a traditional desk job.

At her recommendation, I attended the NYU Summer Publishing Institute and went on informational interviews at many publishing houses. I told everyone I knew (and strangers) that I wanted to work with books (a bank teller I spoke with set me up for an interview with her cousin in publishing). Eventually, I got my dream starting job as a publicity assistant at Pantheon and Knopf.

Can you describe what you feel is your primary goal as a publicist for writers?

**KB:** Book media!

**JR:** I want to place media coverage, create partnerships, and execute stellar events, all with the end goal of driving buzz and word of mouth about my books and authors. I want people to go up to their friends and family and say: "I just read *Sweetbitter* by Stephanie Danler and you literally have to stop everything you are doing and read it immediately, like right now." Or something along those lines.

**SW:** I like to tell all my clients that I have my dream job—I help people learn about good books. The mechanism for that, of course, is by helping authors to get media attention … as well as events opportunities, and because I work for a comprehensive firm, we also do a lot of digital marketing. Basically my job is to find and focus on a lot of different ways to get an author's brand out there and growing in the public sphere. Hopefully the authors I work with find a readership that keeps them writing and creating art for many years to come.

**JB:** The bottom line is to help move the needle on book sales, but we also look at the writer's goals. Is the main objective to become established as an expert in a certain field for speaking opportunities or a tenure-track academic position? Is it to improve the odds that a debut novel will attract enough fans for the publisher to invest in a series? To potentially land a more lucrative deal for the next book? To mobilize the fan base from the author's established social media platforms in the cultural conversation arena? Knowing the answers to those questions helps us to customize our strategy.

What goes into finding places for an author to write guest posts, sign books, speak, participate in an interview/Q&A, etc.?

**JB:** The first question we ask ourselves is, "Who is the target audience for this book and where does that audience go to get their news—and entertainment recommendations?" Newspapers and magazines? Pop culture websites? Morning drive-time radio programs? Mom-centric lifestyle publications? YouTube book reviewers and other social media influencers?

The other piece is the author's brand—where does the author as a person intersect with the characters or themes in the books they write? That can provide possibilities to introduce the author to new readers who'd connect to the themes in the author's books due to shared interests. For example, an athlete who's written a memoir about competing in the Olympics could contribute a "conditioning tips" piece to a fitness publication or participate in an interview for a sports-themed radio show or podcast—both audiences could also be interested in reading that memoir. On the other hand, a rom-com novelist could write a humorous guest post about their own nuptials for a wedding magazine—and someone reading that piece might also be drawn to a lighthearted romance novel with a built-in happily-ever-after.

We do attend conferences and festivals and ask our clients for feedback on those they've attended to get a sense of whether the experience offsets the time and expense involved. Are there opportunities to connect with readers, industry professionals and influencers? Are the panels well-attended? Is there good traffic and interaction at the signing tables?

For events at venues without a built-in audience, such as a library or bookstore, we want to make sure that the author can mobilize their own fan base to attend and buy books there, rather than relying on the venue to drum up an audience (which won't happen). Many writers already have a relationship with a favorite bookstore or library branch so if that place is convenient for their friends, family, and fans, we usually start there. If the author has a local connection (hometown, current residence) we can pitch local media and position the event as a news hook.

**KB:** This may seem obvious, but I always consider where the author lives, where the author was born, and where the book is set when I compile my list of outlets to pitch. Those are three key markets to go after for interviews and reviews. And they're usually the most receptive too, for obvious reasons!

If I'm working with a debut author, I seek out all the debut author opportunities available (Goodreads' Debut Author Snapshot, *Writer's Digest*'s Breaking In, etc.).

When it comes to signings, I work in collaboration with our Author Events Department. I let them know which authors I plan to tour and where I plan to send them, and they seek out requests from the indies and chains across the country. Once I know which stores are interested in hosting an event, I give them a call and we get to planning! The goal is to always also book media in each tour city to support the event, but that is becoming harder and harder as regional newspaper staffs grow smaller in size.

**JR:** Step one is thinking about all of the possible audiences who might be interested in the book you are publicizing. There are always more ways into a story than you might initially think. Next, you match those audiences with the media outlets that cater to them and place content. For events, you think about metros that make sense for the publication and in-conversation partners, big-mouths, influencers, and like-minded brands that can help get the word out.

**SW:** Media and event list building is a never-ending job! Most publicists will have a solid base of contacts, but if you work comprehensively and not with a certain niche, as I do, then you will always have more research to do and can't rely on that base only. Finding new media outlets that cover the specific angles I'm working on, especially in any emerging genres, involves a lot of reading news, googling, and watching other author coverage vigilantly. Quite a bit of in-person networking helps this too—I meet media at conferences and often through my personal social life that end up being good places for coverage. How you approach these contacts is key to whether you can create lasting media relationships—a good publicist spends time learning how each journalist wants to communicate and what their beat is before blasting them with a million requests. That takes a lot of time.

## Do you primarily field requests for authors, or are you seeking out places?

**KB:** For fiction, there's hardly any fielding of requests. For nonfiction, I do usually receive a handful of worthwhile requests. To give two examples: I recently worked on the publicity campaigns for *The Wife Between Us* (women's commercial fiction) and *Gold Dust Woman* (a bio of Stevie Nicks). For *The Wife Between Us*, I'd say 95 percent of the reviews and interviews secured were due to my efforts, and 5 percent due either to the co-authors' connections or requests to my inbox. For *Gold Dust Woman*, however, I'd say it was closer to 50-50!

**SW:** As a publicist at a private firm, the majority of coverage comes from my team and myself pitching the media (and not the media coming to me). I have contacts I've known for years and they do come to me when they need certain things, but the majority of the work is to go after it, not to wait for it to roll in! When it does knock on my door, I'm on cloud nine.

**JB:** The primary focus of every campaign is on outreach we generate, although as an author becomes more established, the incoming media requests and speaking opportunities do multiply and we love to facilitate those as well. Since we customize each campaign to what is unique about that author and book, we are always actively researching interesting new opportunities.

**JR:** I am always actively seeking out! As they say, nothing comes to those who wait!

## What should an author expect from their publicist?

**JR:** An author should expect a publicist to be their ally. To spread the word about the author's work to all of their contacts. To think innovatively about their book, and to help the author see new ways into their writing that they might not have known themselves. To be the author's spirit guide through the publishing process.

**SW:** That's a loaded question! There's so much to say here, but I think one of the important things about the author/publicist relationship that I want to express is that truly the best campaigns are run when I am able to work in partnership with the author. Mutual respect for one another's professionalism, expertise, and time is really key—an author should expect that a qualified publicist will work their hardest to satisfy the goals of their individual campaign.

**KB:** I put this question out to a few of my colleagues, and these were the most popular responses!

- That we read your book!
- That we know what's best for your book, and who to pitch.
- That we are taking advantage of all opportunities for your book.

**JB:** The scope of the campaign should be outlined in the proposal and the publicist should provide regular written updates of their activities on the author's behalf and the outcomes of those efforts. The publicist should collaborate with the author's in-house team. They should listen to the author's ideas and be honest in their assessments of those ideas. And they should provide expert guidance for any questions the author has about their campaign and their career.

## What should an author not expect from their publicist?

**SW:** Oprah appearances and coverage from *The New York Times*. Those are the top two requests every publicist rolls their eyes at. Not because no one ever gets them, but because it's such a given that if a book merits the attention of those major players, of course the publicist will go for it. The author truly doesn't even need to ask—publicists are possibly even more excited than authors when we land a big "gain" like that! Authors should work with publicists they can trust to do what's best for them, and not every book is a fit for those types of outlets. That doesn't make them un-newsworthy or inferior—it just means that how audience factors into the news coverage might not lead to those specific places having interest in that book. But other places will, and we can focus on using time effectively to reach those media contacts.

**KB:** Same for this one! I put this question out to a few of my colleagues, and these were the most popular responses.

- That we be actively pitching your book to the media three, four, five months postpublication. (Most all of the pitching magic, and interest, happens in the months or weeks leading up to publication.)
- That we book media that is unrealistic for your book. (Not every book will be reviewed in *The New York Times* or on NPR.)
- That we find a bookseller for your event a week before it's to take place. (Impossible.)

**JB:** Guaranteed results are not possible—publicity is earned coverage; advertising and "advertorials" are paid coverage. A publicist should also not be hired with the expectation of making an author "famous" or to implement a to-do list of directives issued by an author. And, while a publicist should respond to questions in a timely manner and be available if an emergency occurs—say, a touring author's plane is grounded due to weather and they may be late for a signing—an author shouldn't expect the publicist to be on call 24/7 unless it's outlined in the contract.

**JR:** An author should be respectful of a publicist's time. Publicist's manage their time working on many different projects. That doesn't mean they do not have the time and energy to work on your book, but it means that if you send your publicist fifteen emails a day, they will use the time they have allotted to pitching your book to instead craft responses to all of your emails. Also, a publicist is not a therapist, respect boundaries.

### Is your role different depending on if you're working with an experienced, multi-published author versus a debut author? If so, how?

**KB:** Sometimes, sometimes not. Debut authors are often easier to pitch because reviewers want to be the first to sing their praises and lift their careers. If an author has published, say, twenty books, it's exceedingly difficult to get reviewers to pay attention to this latest release. We've gone back to the well too many times, so to speak!

**JB:** The basics are the same but with a debut author, it's more about introducing a fresh new voice into the conversation. There is often more education involved as well—working to maximize their online presence, coaching them for successful media appearances, showing them ways to promote their book that are engaging rather than obnoxious. If the debut author is already established on another platform—perhaps they're a popular blogger or a sought-after public speaker—then we'd want to look at mobilizing that audience to read the book, too.

For an experienced author, a publicist can determine patterns that have been successful in previous campaigns—which types of outlets provide recurring coverage, what works well to mobilize that audience, where the reader base could be expanded. The experienced author is likely to offer insight into that as well. It's also possible to capitalize on their strengths—and to have links to lively broadcast interviews, well-written guest posts, and starred reviews from their previous campaigns.

But there are also certain types of coverage that will already have been used up— the hometown paper won't review every single book in a series; the pop culture magazine won't repeat the same author in their annual holiday gift guide; the alumni magazine won't profile the same graduate twice. So the publicist has to look for ways to expand into new areas for potential coverage and to take note of any exciting new developments in the life of the author or noteworthy angles in their latest book that would appeal to readers and media outlets.

**SW:** A debut author has so many more questions about how the publishing industry works, so for a lot of those campaigns we build in time for those explanations and some of the necessary coaching that helps them understand vital components of the process. A more veteran author often has a more mature understanding of how their campaign will run and what to expect, so things may run a bit differently for that author because they need less preparation.

**JR:** Yes! With debut authors, I make sure to explain the entire publishing process to them so they are aware of all the ways I can help and what exactly it is that I will need from them.

I still do a lot of hand-holding with multi-published authors, but less about process.

## Is there anything a writer can do to make your job easier?

**SW:** Of course! Going back to that partnering concept, when my clients are responsive to email and also willing to think creatively with me, that makes my job so much easier. When I send over media requests and can get a response quickly, it helps snag opportunities faster, which means less back-and-forth and also downsizes the possibility for missed coverage because we missed a deadline or something like that. Authors who are willing to let me use my expertise to guide them tend to have smoother campaigns—essentially they're paying for consultancy, and letting me have a bit of free rein usually results in a more magical set of media results at the day's end. Publicity work is pretty grueling at times (we tend to work some of the longer hours in this industry) but the payoff of what we can accomplish for an author feels incredible, and often the client is a big part in making that happen.

**KB:** Say "yes" to all opportunities, big and small. Reply to emails with some speed. But above all, trust your publicist is doing everything she/he can for your book. There will be periods of "quiet" during the road to publication, but that doesn't mean we've forgotten about you! Quite the opposite. It means we're following up, and trying to get answers, so we can share the good news with you. And we do share good news, right away (!), when we have it. That's the best part of the job.

**JB:** Authors should also advise their publicist of every opportunity that comes their way directly. The publicist can then give them advice on how to maximize that coverage or avoid conflict with coverage already in the works. No publicist wants an author to post a guest column two months before their book's launch—no one will remember the book by the time they can actually buy it—or to find out that the essay they just pitched *The New York Times* has already been given away to an old high school classmate's blog that currently has 12 followers.

Also, writers should begin making inquiries to publicists earlier than they might think—an ideal campaign timeline usually starts about five or six months ahead of the book launch. There isn't much point in hiring a publicist until after the contract is signed with the publishing house but once that happens and the book has gone through its initial round of edits, that's a good time to think about bringing a publicist on board.

**JR:** Pro-tips for authors re: publicists: Merge all your thoughts and ideas into one email a day if possible. Phone calls are great to get a lot done at once, but please make sure there is a reason for it. Be kind to your publicist. Trust their judgment, realize they have experience and are professionals. They are the person in your corner and want to help you. Help them help you. Provide your publicist with all media connections, big mouths, and influencers that you have connections with. Flowers/wine/gifts can never hurt

**What's the most important thing that an about-to-be-published or just-published author can do?**

**SW:** Connect with other writers! No man is an island and the ones that try to be are often stilted in their ability to grow in their craft and in their brand reach. There's this mythology still of the lone writer in an ivory tower, hacking away at a typewriter and then producing the perfect manuscript that goes straight through to publication and becomes a bestseller. That's truly not the case—friends are first "beta readers" for authors and getting a writing community to rally around you is the best way an author can get the best version of their book started… but it's also the first group of people that will buy the book, show up to bookstore readings, and tell their own networks about the book too.

**KB:** Leverage any and all connections, even if they seem small and insignificant. And don't be shy about it (this is the time to call in favors!), or wait until the eleventh hour to do so. Being active on social media is becoming more and more important, too, with the rise of bookstagrammers and book bloggers taking to Twitter and Facebook to share their reviews. Even some news outlets look for authors with large social presences when making decisions about who to invite onto their shows.

**JR:** Gather a list of all of their media connections and big mouths and give it to their publicist. Work on increasing their social media footprint. Tell every person they know (or don't know) about their forthcoming book. Brainstorm related op-ed ideas. Befriend Oprah and Terry Gross.

**JB:** Right now, it's to create and maintain a newsletter program through a professional-looking, easy-to-use service such as Mailchimp and offer incentives for readers to sign up (such as an early excerpt available nowhere else). In the newsletter, the author should offer exclusive content that does not appear on other platforms. This is something we find to be a crucial asset for authors for connecting to readers and one of our prime marketing initiatives is to help them create and grow that reach organically. It used to be that social media followings were important, but nowadays, none of us controls what those followers see—what shows up in our feeds is at the mercy of algorithms, sponsored content placements, people deleting their accounts, and so many other factors outside our control. You don't "own" your Twitter followers or your Facebook friends—if that platform shuts down tomorrow, your audience there is gone. With a newsletter, you own your following and it's guaranteed that your email will appear in everyone's inbox. And by reaching out every month or two and providing worthwhile, newsletter-only content when you do, they'll look forward to opening it up.

## What's the most difficult job about your role?

**JR:** I honestly love my job so much it is hard to say. To be able to promote incredible books and authors is an honor rather than a job. It can be difficult in this current political climate to compete with the news cycle, and I find that to be frustrating. I just want people to know that books are one of the most important ways to learn and cope and move forward and they house powerful ideas that can change the way we see the world and interact with humans, regardless of whether or not their subject directly relates to politics.

**SW:** Setting expectations. For example, sometimes I will get a pretty big piece of coverage, but if the author isn't familiar with that outlet, he or she may not be appreciative, and ask after other dream "gains" that just aren't within reach for whatever reason (we're past deadline, they don't cover that genre, etc., I am talking about really legitimate reasons why an outlet would decline an author). There are radio shows and online magazines with literally millions of listeners/viewers each week that I've had authors sort of shrug off because they personally might not be familiar with the outlet. The thing is, there is such an abundance of media out there now because of the internet that you never really could know every single media outlet … even publicists find new outlets! Helping authors understand that their personal experience of the media is not necessarily universal is a challenge. It's true that not all media outlets are the same, so I provide circulation and/or social media reach to help an author understand what the coverage means in terms of the exposure they are receiving, and it can be hard to set expectations properly if they are focused on specific places for coverage that might not be reasonable, or the best fit for the book.

**JB:** Finding the time to stay on top of what's happening in the publishing industry, measuring patterns in media coverage, exploring what platforms are trending with different people, looking into technologies and innovations that could benefit writers, discovering what new conversations are happening in the world of writing and books—but these topics are so fascinating and so important that I make the time to delve into them.

**KB:** When you put all of your heart and soul into pitching a book and/or an author you adore, and, for whatever reason, it just doesn't resonate with the media or the buying public. It can be very disheartening.

**CRIS FREESE** is a former editor of *Guide to Literary Agents*, a freelance writer, and literary intern with Corvisiero Literary. Follow him on Twitter @crisfreese.

# 30-DAY PLATFORM CHALLENGE

## Build Your Writer Platform in a Month

....................................................

*by Robert Lee Brewer*

Whether writers are looking to find success through traditional publication or the self-publishing route, they'll find a strong writer platform will help them in their efforts. A platform is not marketing; it's the actual and quantifiable reach writers have to their target audience.

Here is a 30-day platform challenge I've developed to help writers get started in their own platform-building activities without getting overwhelmed. By accomplishing one task for one day, writers can feel a sense of accomplishment and still handle their normal daily activities. By the end of the month, writers should have a handle on what they need to do to keep growing their platform into the future.

## DAY 1: DEFINE YOURSELF

For Day 1, define yourself. Don't worry about where you'd like to be in the future. Instead, take a look at who you are today, what you've already accomplished, what you're currently doing, etc.

Here is a chart I'm using (with my own answers). Your worksheet can ask even more questions. The more specific you can be the better for this exercise.

**NAME (AS USED IN BYLINE):** Robert Lee Brewer

**POSITION(S):** Senior Content Editor—Writer's Digest Writing Community; Author; Freelance Writer; Blogger; Event Speaker; Den Leader—Cub Scouts; Curator of Insta-poetry series

**SKILL(S):** Editing, creative writing (poetry and fiction), technical writing, copywriting, database management, SEO, blogging, newsletter writing, problem solving, idea generation, public speaking, willingness to try new things, community building

**SOCIAL MEDIA PLATFORMS:** Facebook, LinkedIn, Twitter, Tumblr, Blogger

**URLs:** www.writersmarket.com; www.writersdigest.com/editor-blogs/poetic-asides;

http://robertleebrewer.blogspot.com/; www
.robertleebrewer.com

**ACCOMPLISHMENTS:** Named 2010 Poet
Laureate of Blogosphere; spoken at several
events, including Writer's Digest Conference,
AWP, Austin International Poetry Festival,
Houston Poetry Fest, and more; author of
*Solving the World's Problems* (Press 53); pub-
lished and sold out of two limited-edition po-
etry chapbooks, **ENTER** and **ESCAPE**; edit-
ed several editions of **Writer's Market** and
**Poet's Market**; former GMVC conference
champion in the 800-meter run and MVP of
WCHS cross country and track teams; under-
graduate award-winner in several writing dis-
ciplines at University of Cincinnati, including
Journalism, Fiction, and Technical Writing;
BA in English Literature from University of
Cincinnati with certificates in writing for Creative Writing-Fiction and Professional and
Technical Writing.

**INTERESTS:** Writing (all genres), family (being
a good husband and father), faith, fitness (especially running and disc golf), fantasy football, reading.

**IN ONE SENTENCE, WHO AM I?** Robert Lee
Brewer is a married Methodist father of five
children (four sons and one daughter) who
works as an editor but plays as a writer, specializing in poetry and blogging.

As long as you're being specific and honest,
there are no wrong answers when it comes
to defining yourself. However, you may realize that you have more to offer than you
think. Or you may see an opportunity that
you didn't realize even existed.

## DAY 2:
## SET YOUR GOALS

For today's platform-building task, set your
goals. Include short-term goals and long-
term goals. In fact, make a list of goals you
can accomplish by the end of this year; then,
make a list of goals you'd like to accomplish
before you die.

### EXAMPLE GOALS

Here are some of examples from my short-
term and long-term goal lists:

*SHORT-TERM GOALS:*

- Promote new book, *Solving the World's
  Problems*.
- In April, complete April PAD Challenge
  on Poetic Asides blog.
- Get Writer's Market to printer ahead of
  schedule.
- Get Poet's Market to printer ahead of
  schedule.
- Lead workshop at Poetry Hickory event
  in April.
- Etc.

*LONG-TERM GOALS:*

- Publish book on platform development
  for small businesses.
- Raise 5 happy and healthy children into 5
  happy, healthy, caring, and self-sufficient
  adults.
- Continue to learn how to be a better hus-
  band and human being.
- Become a bestselling novelist.
- Win Poet Laureate of the Universe honors.
- Etc.

Some writers may ask what defining yourself and creating goals has to do with platform development. I maintain that these are two of the most basic and important steps in the platform-building process, because they define who you are and where you want to be.

A successful platform strategy should communicate who you are and help you get where you'd like to be (or provide you with a completely new opportunity). If you can't communicate who you are to strangers, then they won't realize how you might be able to help them or why you're important to them. If you don't have any goals, then you don't have any direction or purpose for your platform.

By defining who you are and what you want to accomplish, you're taking a huge step in establishing a successful writing and publishing career.

## DAY 3: JOIN FACEBOOK

For today's task, create a profile on Facebook. Simple as that. If you don't have one, it's as easy as going to www.facebook.com and signing up. It takes maybe 5 or 10 minutes. If that.

### 10 FACEBOOK TIPS FOR WRITERS

Many readers probably already have a Facebook profile, and that's fine. If you have already created a profile (or are doing so today), here are some tips for handling your profile:

- Complete your profile. The most checked page on most profiles is the About page. The more you share the better.
- Make everything public. Like it or not, writers are public figures. If you try to hide, it will limit the potential platform.
- Think about your audience in everything you do. When your social media profiles are public, anyone can view what you post. Keep this in mind at all times.
- Include a profile pic of yourself. Avoid setting your avatar as anything but a headshot of yourself. Many people don't like befriending a family pet or cartoon image.
- Update your status regularly. If you can update your status once per day, that's perfect. At the very least, update your status weekly. If your profile is a ghost town, people will treat it like one.
- Communicate with friends on Facebook. Facebook is a social networking site, but networking happens when you communicate. So communicate.
- Be selective about friends. Find people who share your interests. Accept friends who share your interests. Other folks may be fake or inappropriate connections trying to build their "friend" totals.
- Be selective about adding apps. If you're not sure, it's probably best to avoid. Many users have wasted days, weeks, and even months playing silly games on Facebook.
- Join relevant groups. The emphasis should be placed on relevancy. For instance, I'm a poet, so I join poetry groups.

• Follow relevant fan pages. As with groups, the emphasis is placed on relevancy. In my case, I'm a fan of several poetry publications.

In addition to the tips above, be sure to always use your name as it appears in your byline. If you're not consistent in how you list your name in your byline, it's time to pick a name and stick with it. For instance, my byline name is Robert Lee Brewer—not Robbie Brewer, Bob Brewer, or even just Robert Brewer.

There are times when I absolutely can't throw the "Lee" in there, but the rest of the time it is Robert Lee Brewer. And the reasoning behind this is that it makes it easier for people who know me elsewhere to find and follow me on Facebook (or whichever social media site). Name recognition is super important when you're building your writer platform.

## DAY 4: JOIN TWITTER

For today's task, create a Twitter account. That's right. Go to www.twitter.com and sign up—if you're not already. This task will definitely take less than 5 minutes.

As with Facebook, I would not be surprised to learn that most readers already have a Twitter account. Here are three important things to keep in mind:

- **MAKE YOUR PROFILE BIO RELEVANT.** You might want to use a version of the sentence you wrote for Day 1's task. Look at my profile (twitter.com/robertleebrewer) if you need an example.

- **USE AN IMAGE OF YOURSELF.** One thing about social media (and online networking) is that people love to connect with other people. So use an image of yourself—not of your pet, a cute comic strip, a new age image, flowers, robots, etc.

- **MAKE YOUR TWITTER HANDLE YOUR BYLINE—IF POSSIBLE.** For instance, I am known as @RobertLeeBrewer on Twitter, because I use Robert Lee Brewer as my byline on articles, in interviews, at speaking events, on books, etc. Be as consistent with your byline as humanly possible.

Once you're in Twitter, try finding some worthwhile tweeps to follow. Also, be sure to make a tweet or two. As with Facebook, people will only interact with your profile if it looks like you're actually there and using your account.

### SOME BASIC TWITTER TERMINOLOGY

Twitter has a language all its own. Here are some of the basics:

- **TWEET.** This is what folks call the 140-character messages that can be sent on the site. Anyone who follows you can access your tweets.

- **RT.** RT stands for re-tweet. This is what happens when someone shares your tweet, usually character for character. It's usually good form to show attribution for the author of the original tweet.

- **DM.** DM stands for direct message. This is a good way to communicate with someone on Twitter privately. I've actually had a few opportunities come my way through DMs on Twitter.

- **#.** The #-sign stands for hashtag. Hashtags are used to organize group conversations. For instance, Writer's Digest uses the #wdc to coordinate messages for their Writer's Digest Conferences. Anyone can start a hashtag, and they're sometimes used to add humor or emphasis to a tweet.
- **FF.** FF stands for Follow Friday—a day typically set asides to highlight follow-worthy tweeps (or folks who use Twitter). There's also a WW that stands for writer Wednesday.

## DAY 5: START A BLOG

For today's task, create a blog. You can use Blogger (www.blogger.com), WordPress (www.wordpress.com), or Tumblr (www.tumblr.com). In fact, you can use another blogging platform if you wish. To complete today's challenge, do the following:

- **CREATE A BLOG.** That is, sign up (if you don't already have a blog), pick a design (these can usually be altered later if needed), and complete your profile.
- **WRITE A POST FOR TODAY.** If you're not sure what to cover, you can just introduce yourself and share a brief explanation of how your blog got started. Don't make it too complicated.

If you already have a blog, excellent! You don't need to create a new one, but you might want to check out some ways to optimize what you have.

### OPTIMIZE YOUR BLOG

Here are some tips for making your blog rock:

- **USE IMAGES IN YOUR POSTS.** Images are eye candy for readers, help with search engine optimization, and can even improve clicks when shared on social media sites, such as Facebook and Google+.
- **USE HEADERS IN POSTS.** Creating and bolding little headlines in your posts will go a long way toward making your posts easier to read and scan. Plus, they'll just look more professional.
- **WRITE SHORT.** Short sentences (fewer than 10 words). Short paragraphs (fewer than five sentences). Concision is precision in online composition.
- **ALLOW COMMENTS.** Most bloggers receive very few (or absolutely zero) comments in the beginning, but it pays to allow comments, because this gives your audience a way to interact with you. For my personal blog, I allow anyone to comment on new posts, but those that are more than a week old require my approval.

## DAY 6: READ AND COMMENT ON A POST

For today's task, read at least one blog post and comment on it (linking back to your blog). And the comment should not be something along the lines of, "Hey, cool post. Come check out my blog." Instead, you need to find a blog post that really speaks to you and then make a thoughtful comment.

Here are a few possible ways to respond:

- **SHARE YOUR OWN EXPERIENCE.** If you've experienced something simi-

## FREELANCE PITCH TRACKER

| SUBJECT | **Example:** Essay about meeting Stephen King in the waiting room at the dentist | | |
|---|---|---|---|
| PUBLICATION | *Writer's Digest* | | |
| EDITOR | Tyler Moss | | |
| E-MAIL | wdsubmissions@ fwmedia.com | | |
| PITCH SUBMITTED | 8/1/16 | | |
| FOLLOW UP | 8/15/16 | | |
| RESULT | Accepted | | |
| DEADLINE | 10/15/16 | | |
| NOTES | $0.50 cents/word for 600 words | | |

For freelance writers, ideas are currency—but they don't exist in a vacuum. Once you've brainstormed a solid premise and started to pitch potential markets, the resulting interactions can quickly clutter your inbox. Avoid losing track by recording your pitches in a spreadsheet with the following column headings:

- **SUBJECT:** One-line description of your story idea
- **PUBLICATION:** Name of magazine, website, or newspaper you pitched to
- **EDITOR & E-MAIL:** Where you sent your pitch
- **PITCH SUBMITTED:** When the query was sent
- **FOLLOW UP:** The date on which you plan to follow up if you haven't received a response (typically two weeks later, unless the submission guidelines specify otherwise)
- **RESULT:** Accepted, rejected, asked to rework
- **DEADLINE:** If accepted, date story is due
- **NOTES:** Additional info, based on your interactions with the editor (e.g., "Publication pays too little," or "Editor rejected pitch, but encouraged pitching again soon")

In addition to keeping track of irons currently in the fire, this spreadsheet is invaluable for later looking up contact info of editors you haven't e-mailed in a while.

If you want to track submissions to literary journals, simply switch out the column headings **SUBJECT** and **PUBLICATION** with **STORY TITLE** and **JOURNAL**, respectively, ax the **FOLLOW UP** column (journals tend to operate on slower, more sporadic schedules, sometimes without full-time staff), and replace the **DEADLINE** column with **READING FEE** (so you can evaluate and track any submission expenses where applicable).

lar to what's covered in the post, share your own story. You don't have to write a book or anything, but maybe a paragraph or two.

- **ADD ANOTHER PERSPECTIVE.** Maybe the post was great, but there's another angle that should be considered. Don't be afraid to point that angle out.
- **ASK A QUESTION.** A great post usually will prompt new thoughts and ideas—and questions. Ask them.

As far as linking back to your blog, you could include your blog's URL in the comment, but also, most blogs have a field in their comments that allow you to share your URL. Usually, your name will link to that URL, which should either be your blog or your author website (if it offers regularly updated content).

It might seem like a lot of work to check out other blogs and comment on them, but this is an incredible way to make real connections with super users. These connections can lead to guest post and interview opportunities. In fact, they could even lead to speaking opportunities too.

## DAY 7:
## ADD SHARE BUTTONS
## TO YOUR BLOG

For today's challenge, add share buttons to your blog and/or website.

The easiest way to do this is to go to www.addthis.com and click on the Get AddThis button. It's big, bright, and orange. You can't miss it.

Basically, the site will give you button options, and you select the one you like best.

The AddThis site will then provide you with HTML code that you can place into your site and/or blog posts. Plus, it provides analytics for bloggers who like to see how much the buttons are boosting traffic.

If you want customized buttons, you could enlist the help of a programmer friend or try playing with the code yourself. I recently learned that some really cool buttons on one friend's blog were created by her husband (yes, she married a programmer, though I don't think she had her blog in mind when she did so).

Plus, most blogging platforms are constantly adding new tools. By the time you read this article, there are sure to be plenty of fun new buttons, apps, and widgets available.

Here's the thing about social sharing buttons: They make it very easy for people visiting your site to share your content with their social networks via Facebook, Twitter, LinkedIn, Google+, Pinterest, and other sites. The more your content is shared the wider your writer platform.

## DAY 8:
## JOIN LINKEDIN

For today's challenge, create a LinkedIn profile. Go to www.linkedin.com and set it up in a matter of minutes. After creating profiles for Facebook and Twitter, this task should be easy.

### LINKEDIN TIPS FOR WRITERS

In many ways, LinkedIn looks the same as the other social networks, but it does have its own quirks. Here are a few tips for writers:

- **USE YOUR OWN HEAD SHOT.** You've heard this advice before. People want to connect with people, not family pets and/or inanimate objects.
- **COMPLETE YOUR PROFILE.** The more complete your profile the better. It makes you look more human.
- **GIVE THOUGHTFUL RECOMMENDA-TIONS TO RECEIVE THEM.** Find people likely to give you recommendations and recommend them first. This will prompt them to return the favor.
- **SEARCH FOR CONNECTIONS YOU AL-READY HAVE.** This is applicable to all social networks. Find people you know to help you connect with those you don't.
- **MAKE MEANINGFUL CONNECTIONS WITH OTHERS.** Remember: It's not about how many connections you make; it's about how many meaningful connections you make.
- **MAKE YOUR PROFILE EASY TO FIND.** You can do this by using your byline name. (For instance, I use linkedin.com/in/robertleebrewer.)
- **TAILOR YOUR PROFILE TO YOUR VISI-TOR.** Don't fill out your profile thinking only about yourself; instead, think about what your target audience might want to learn about you.

LinkedIn is often considered a more "professional" site than the other social networks like Facebook, Google+, and Twitter. For one thing, users are prompted to share their work experience and request recommendations from past employers and current co-workers.

However, this site still offers plenty of social networking opportunities for people who can hook up with the right people and groups.

## DAY 9:
## RESPOND TO AT LEAST THREE TWEETS

For today's task, respond to at least three tweets from other tweeps on Twitter.

Since Day 4's assignment was to sign up for Twitter, you should have a Twitter account—and you're hopefully following some other Twitter users. Just respond to at least three tweets today.

As far as your responses, it's not rocket science. You can respond with "great article" or "cool quote." A great way to spread the wealth on Twitter is to RT (retweet) the original tweet with a little note. This accomplishes two things:

- One, it lets the tweep know that you appreciated their tweet (and helps build a bond with that person); and
- Two, it brings attention to that person for their cool tweet.

Plus, it helps show that you know how to pick great resources on Twitter, which automatically improves your credibility as a resource on Twitter.

## DAY 10:
## DO A GOOGLE SEARCH ON YOURSELF

For today's task, do a search on your name.

First, see what results appear when you search your name on Google (google.com). Then, try searching on Bing (bing.com). Finally, give Yahoo (yahoo.com) a try.

By searching your name, you'll receive insights into what others will find (and are already finding) when they do a search specifically for you. Of course, you'll want to make sure your blog and/or website is number one in the search results. If it isn't, we'll be covering SEO (or search engine optimization) topics later in this challenge.

For those who want extra credit, here are some other search engines to try searching (for yourself):

- DuckDuckGo.com
- Ask.com
- Dogpile.com
- Yahoo.com
- YouTube.com

(Note: It's worth checking out which images are related to your name as well. You may be surprised to find which images are connected to you.)

## DAY 11:
## FIND A HELPFUL ARTICLE AND LINK TO IT

For today's task, find a helpful article (or blog post) and share it with your social network—and by social network, I mean that you should share it on Facebook, Twitter, and LinkedIn at a minimum. If you participate on message boards or on other social networks, share in those places as well.

Before linking to an article on fantasy baseball or celebrity news, however, make sure your article (or blog post) aligns with your author platform goals. You should

have an idea of who you are and who you want to be as a writer, and your helpful article (or blog post) should line up with those values.

Of course, you may not want to share articles for writers if your platform is based on parenting tips or vampires or whatever. In such cases, you'll want to check out other resources online. Don't be afraid to use a search engine.

For Twitter, you may wish to use a URL shortener to help you keep under the 140-character limit. Here are five popular URL shorteners:

- bit.ly. This is my favorite.
- goo.gl. Google's URL shortener.
- owl.ly. Hootsuite's URL shortener.
- deck.ly. TweetDeck's URL shortener.
- su.pr. StumbleUpon's URL shortener.

By the way, here's an extra Twitter tip. Leave enough room in your tweets to allow space for people to attribute your Twitter handle if they decide to RT you. For instance, I always leave at least 20 characters to allow people space to tweet "RT @robertleebrewer" when retweeting me.

## DAY 12:
## WRITE A BLOG POST AND INCLUDE A CALL TO ACTION

For today's task, write a new blog post for your blog. In the blog post, include a call to action at the end of the post.

### What's a call to action?

I include calls to action at the end of all my posts. Sometimes, they are links to products and services offered by my employer (F+W Media) or some other entity. Often, I include links to other posts and ways to follow me on other sites. Even the share buttons are a call to action of sorts.

### Why include a call to action?

A call to action is good for giving readers direction and a way to engage more with you. Links to previous posts provide readers with more helpful or interesting information. Links to your social media profiles give readers a way to connect with you on those sites. These calls to action are beneficial to you and your readers when they are relevant.

### What if I'm just getting started?

Even if you are completely new to everything, you should have an earlier blog post from last week, a Twitter account, a Facebook account, and a LinkedIn account. Link to these at the end of your blog post today. It's a proper starting place.

And that's all you need to do today. Write a new blog post with a call to action at the end. (By the way, if you're at a loss and need something to blog about, you can always comment on that article you shared yesterday.)

## DAY 13:
## LINK TO POST ON SOCIAL MEDIA PROFILES

For today's challenge, link your blog post from yesterday to your social networks.

At a minimum, these social networks should include Facebook, Twitter, and LinkedIn. However, if you frequent message boards related to your blog post or other social networks (like Google+, Pinterest, etc.), then link your blog post there as well.

I understand many of you may have already completed today's challenge. If so, hooray! It's important to link your blog to your social media accounts and vice versa. When they work together, they grow together.

### Is it appropriate to link to my blog post multiple times?

All writers develop their own strategies for linking to their articles and blog posts, but here's my rule. I will usually link to each blog post on every one of my social networks at least once. Since I have a regular profile and a fan page on Facebook, I link to each of those profiles once—and I only link to posts once each on Google+ and LinkedIn. But Twitter is a special case.

The way Twitter works, tweets usually only have a few minutes of visibility for tweeps with an active stream. Even tweeps with at least 100 follows may only have a 30-minute to hour window of opportunity to see your tweet. So for really popular and timely blog posts, I will tweet them more often than once on Twitter.

That said, I'm always aware of how I'm linking and don't want to become that annoying spammer that I typically avoid following in my own social networking efforts.

### LINKING TIPS

Some tips on linking to your post:

- Use a URL shortener. These are discussed above.

- Apply title + link formula. For instance, I might Tweet this post as: Platform Challenge: Day 13: (link). It's simple and to the point. Plus, it's really effective if you have a great blog post title.
- Frame the link with context. Using this post as an example, I might Tweet: Take advantage of social media by linking to your blog posts: (link). Pretty simple, and it's an easy way to link to the same post without making your Twitter feed look loaded with the same content.
- Quote from post + link formula. Another tactic is to take a funny or thought-provoking quote from the post and combine that with a link. Example Tweet: "I will usually link to each blog post on every one of my social networks at least once." (link). Again, easy stuff.

## DAY 14:
## JOIN INSTAGRAM

For today's task, create an Instagram (instagram.com) profile.

Many of you may already have Instagram profiles, but this social networking site and app is a little different than Facebook and Twitter. While all three offer opportunities for sharing video and photos, Instagram really emphasizes visual elements.

That might not seem like a good fit for writers, who are often more about text than visual cues. But there are opportunities for writers on this platform. And it's one more venue where the people (or your potential audience) are.

Here are a few getting started tips for Instagram:

- **Complete your profile completely.** Use your name, concisely describe who you are and what you're about, and make your profile public.
- **Use an image of yourself.** Not a cartoon. Not an animal. Not a piece of art. Remember that people like to connect with other people.
- **Post new content regularly.** Let people know you are using your account. A new post every day or three is a good way to achieve this.
- **Use unique and relevant hashtags.** These provide a way for people with similar interests who aren't already connected to you to find you.

## DAY 15:
## MAKE THREE NEW CONNECTIONS

For today's task, make an attempt to connect with at least three new people on one of your social networks.

Doesn't matter if it's Facebook, Twitter, LinkedIn, or Google+. The important thing is that you find three new people who appear to share your interests and that you try to friend, follow, or connect to them.

As a person who has limited wiggle room for approving new friends on Facebook, I'd like to share what approach tends to work the best with me for approving new friend requests. Basically, send your request and include a brief message introducing yourself and why you want to connect with me.

That's right. The best way to win me over is to basically introduce yourself. Something along the lines of, "Hello. My name is Robert Lee Brewer, and I write poetry. I read a poem of yours in *XYZ Literary Journal* that I totally loved and have sent you a friend request. I hope you'll accept it." Easy as that.

Notice that I did not mention anything about checking out my blog or reading my poems. How would you like it if someone introduced themselves and then told you to buy their stuff? It sounds a bit telemarketer-ish to me.

While it's important to cultivate the relationships you already have, avoid getting stuck in a rut when it comes to making connections. Always be on the lookout for new connections who can offer new opportunities and spark new ideas. Your writing and your career will benefit.

## DAY 16:
## ADD E-MAIL FEED TO BLOG

For today's challenge, add an e-mail feed to your blog.

There are many ways to increase traffic to your blog, but one that has paid huge dividends for me is adding Feedblitz to my blog. As the subscribers to my e-mail feed have increased, my blog traffic has increased as well. In fact, after great content, I'd say that adding share buttons (mentioned above) and an e-mail feed are the top two ways to build traffic.

Though I have an account on Tumblr, I'm just not sure if it offers some kind of e-mail/RSS feed service.

The reason I think e-mail feeds are so useful is that they pop into my inbox whenever a new post is up, which means I can check it very easily on my phone when I'm waiting somewhere. In fact, this is how I keep up with several of my favorite blogs. It's just one more way to make your blog content accessible to readers in a variety of formats.

If I remember, this task didn't take me long to add, but I've been grateful for finally getting around to adding it ever since.

## DAY 17:
## TAKE PART IN A TWITTER CONVERSATION

For today's task, take part in a Twitter conversation.

Depending upon the time of month or day of week, there are bound to be any number of conversations happening around a hashtag (mentioned above). For instance, various conferences and expos have hashtag conversations that build around their panels and presentations.

Poets will often meet using the #poetparty hashtag. Other writers use #amwriting to communicate about their writing goals. Click on the hashtag to see what others are saying, and then, jump in to join the conversation and make new connection on Twitter.

## DAY 18:
## THINK ABOUT SEO

For today's task, I want you to slow down and think a little about SEO (which is tech-speak for search engine optimization, which is itself an intelligent way of saying "what gets your website to display at or near the top of a search on Google, Bing, Yahoo, etc.").

So this task is actually multi-pronged:

- Make a list of keywords that you want your website or blog to be known for. For instance, I want my blog to be known for terms like "Robert Lee Brewer," "Writing Tips," "Parenting Tips," "Platform Tips," "Living Tips," etc. Think big here and don't limit yourself to what you think you can actually achieve in the short term.
- Compare your website or blog's current content to your keywords. Are you lining up your actual content with how you want your audience to view you and your online presence? If not, it's time to think about how you can start offering content that lines up with your goals. If so, then move on to the next step, which is . . .
- Evaluate your current approach to making your content super SEO-friendly. If you need some guidance, check out my SEO Tips for Writers below. There are very simple things you can do with your titles, subheads, and images to really improve SEO. Heck, I get a certain bit of traffic every single day just from my own SEO approach to content—sometimes on surprising posts.
- Research keywords for your next post. When deciding on a title for your post and subheads within the content, try researching keywords. You can do this using Google's free keyword tool (googlekeywordtool.com). When pos-

sible, you want to use keywords that are searched a lot but that have low competition. These are the low-hanging fruit that can help you build strong SEO for your website or blog.

A note on SEO: It's easy to fall in love with finding keywords and changing your content to be keyword-loaded and blah-blah-blah. But resist making your website or blog a place that is keyword-loaded and blah-blah-blah. Because readers don't stick around for too much keyword-loaded blah-blah-blah. It's kind of blah. And bleck. Instead, use SEO and keyword research as a way to optimize great content and to take advantage of opportunities as they arise.

### SEO TIPS FOR WRITERS

Here are a few SEO tips for writers:

- Use keywords naturally. That is, make sure your keywords match the content of the post. If they don't match up, people will abandon your page fast, which will hurt your search rankings.
- Use keywords appropriately. Include your keywords in the blog post title, opening paragraph, file name for images, headers, etc. Anywhere early and relevant should include your keyword to help place emphasis on that search term, especially if it's relevant to the content.
- Deliver quality content. Of course, search rankings are helped when people click on your content and spend time reading your content. So provide quality content, and people will visit your site frequently

and help search engines list you higher in their rankings.

- Update content regularly. Sites that are updated more with relevant content rank higher in search engines. Simple as that.

- Link often to relevant content. Link to your own posts; link to content on other sites. Just make sure the links are relevant and of high interest to your audience.

- Use images. Images help from a design perspective, but they also help with SEO, especially when you use your main keywords in the image file name.

- Link to your content on social media sites. These outside links will help increase your ranking on search engines.

- Guest post on other sites/blogs. Guest posts on other blogs are a great way to provide traffic from other relevant sites that increase the search engine rankings on your site.

## DAY 19:
## WRITE A BLOG POST

For today's task, write a new blog post.

Include a call to action (for instance, encourage readers to sign up for your e-mail feed and to share the post with others using your share buttons) and link to it on your social networks. Also, don't forget to incorporate SEO.

One of the top rules of finding success with online tools is applying consistency. While it's definitely a great thing if you share a blog post more than once a week, I think it's imperative that you post at least once a week.

The main reason? It builds trust with your readers that you'll have something to share regularly and gives them a reason to visit regularly.

So today's task is not about making things complicated; it's just about keeping it real.

## DAY 20:
## CREATE AN EDITORIAL CALENDAR

For today's task, I want you to create an editorial calendar for your blog (or website). Before you start to panic, read on.

First, here's how I define an editorial calendar: A list of content with dates attached to when the content goes live. For instance, I created an editorial calendar specifically for my Platform Challenge and "Platform Challenge: Day 20" was scheduled to go live on Day 20.

It's really simple. In fact, I keep track of my editorial calendar with a paper notebook, which gives me plenty of space for crossing things out, jotting down ideas, and attaching Post-it notes.

### EDITORIAL CALENDAR IDEAS

Here are tips for different blogging frequencies:

- Post once per week. If you post once a week, pick a day of the week for that post to happen each week. Then, write down the date for each post. Beside each date, write down ideas for that post ahead of time. There will be times when the ideas are humming and you get ahead on your schedule, but there may also be times when the ideas are slow. So don't wait, write down ideas as they come.

• Post more than once per week. Try identifying which days you'll usually post (for some, that may be daily). Then, for each of those days, think of a theme for that day. For instance, my 2012 schedule offered Life Changing Moments on Wednesdays and Poetic Saturdays on Saturdays.

You can always change plans and move posts to different days, but the editorial calendar is an effective way to set very clear goals with deadlines for accomplishing them. Having that kind of structure will improve your content—even if your blog is personal, fictional, poetic, etc. Believe me, I used to be a skeptic before diving in, and the results on my personal blog speak for themselves.

### One more benefit of editorial calendars

There are times when I feel less than inspired. There are times when life throws me several elbows as if trying to prevent me from blogging. That's when I am the most thankful for maintaining an editorial calendar, because I don't have to think of a new idea on the spot; it's already there in my editorial calendar.

Plus, as I said earlier, you can always change plans. I can alter the plan to accommodate changes in my schedule. So I don't want to hear that an editorial calendar limits spontaneity or inspiration; if anything, having an editorial calendar enhances it.

### One last thing on today's assignment

Don't stress yourself out that you have to create a complete editorial calendar for the year or even the month. I just want you to take some time out today to think about it, sketch some ideas, and get the ball rolling. I'm 100% confident that you'll be glad you did.

## DAY 21:
## SIGN UP FOR SOCIAL MEDIA TOOL

For today's task, try joining one of the social media management tools, such as Tweetdeck, Hootsuite, or Seesmic.

Social media management tools are popular among social media users for one reason: They help save time and effort in managing multiple social media platforms. For instance, they make following specific threads in Twitter a snap.

I know many social media super users who swear by these tools, but I actually have tried them and decided to put in the extra effort to log in to my separate social media accounts manually each day.

Here's my reasoning: I like to feel connected to my profile and understand how it looks and feels on a day-to-day basis. Often, the design and feel of social media sites will change without notice, and I like to know what it feels like at ground zero.

## DAY 22:
## PITCH GUEST BLOG POST

For today's task, pitch a guest blog post to another blogger.

Writing guest posts is an incredible way to improve your exposure and expertise on a subject, while also making a deeper connection with the blogger who is hosting your guest post. It's a win for everyone involved.

In a recent interview with super blogger Jeff Goins, he revealed that most of his blog traffic came as a result of his guest posting on other blogs. Some of these blogs were directly related to his content, but he said many were in completely different fields.

## GUEST POST PITCHING TIPS

After you know where you want to guest blog, here are some tips for pitching your guest blog post:

- Let the blogger know you're familiar with the blog. You should do this in one sentence (two sentences max) and be specific. For instance, a MNINB reader could say, "I've been reading your Not Bob blog for months, but I really love this Platform Challenge." Simple as that. It lets me know you're not a spammer, but it doesn't take me a long time to figure out what you're trying to say.
- Propose an idea or two. Each idea should have its own paragraph. This makes it easy for the blogger to know where one idea ends and the next one begins. In a pitch, you don't have to lay out all the details, but you do want to be specific. Try to limit the pitch to 2-4 sentences.
- Share a little about yourself. Emphasis on "a little." If you have previous publications or accomplishments that line up with the blog, share those. If you have ex-

pertise that lines up with the post you're pitching, share those. Plus, include any details about your online platform that might show you can help bring traffic to the post. But include all this information in 1–4 sentences.

- Include your information. When you close the pitch, include your name, e-mail, blog (or website) URL, and other contact information you feel comfortable sharing. There's nothing more awkward for me than to have a great pitch that doesn't include the person's name. Or a way to learn more about the person.

## What do I do after the pitch is accepted?

First off, congratulations! This is a great opportunity to show off your writing skills. Here's how to take advantage of your guest post assignment:

- **WRITE AN EXCEPTIONAL POST.** Don't hold back your best stuff for your blog. Write a post that will make people want to find more of your writing.
- **TURN IN YOUR POST ON DEADLINE.** If there's a deadline, hit it. If there's not a deadline, try to turn around the well-written post in a timely manner.
- **PROMOTE THE GUEST POST.** Once your guest post has gone live, promote it like crazy by linking to your post on your blog, social networks, message boards, and wherever else makes sense for you. By sending your own connections to this guest post, you're establishing your

own expertise—not only through your post but also your connections.

## DAY 23:
## CREATE A TIME MANAGEMENT PLAN

For today's task, create a time management plan.

You may be wondering why I didn't start out the challenge with a time management plan, and here's the reason: I don't think some people would've had any idea how long it takes them to write a blog post, share a link on Twitter and Facebook, respond to social media messages, etc. Now, many of you probably have a basic idea—even if you're still getting the hang of your new-fangled social media tools.

Soooo... the next step is to create a time management plan that enables you to be "active" socially and connect with other writers and potential readers while also spending a majority of your time writing and publishing.

As with any plan, you can make this as simple or complicated as you wish. For instance, my plan is to do 15 minutes or less of social media after completing each decent-sized task on my daily task list. I use social media time as a break, which I consider more productive than watching TV or playing Angry Birds.

I put my writing first and carve out time in the mornings and evenings to work on poetry and fiction. Plus, I consider my blogging efforts part of my writing too. So there you go.

My plan is simple and flexible, but if you want to get hardcore, break down your

time into 15-minute increments. Then, test out your time management plan to see if it works for you. If not, then make minor changes to the plan until it has you feeling somewhat comfortable with the ratio of time you spend writing and time you spend building your platform.

Remember: A platform is a life-long investment in your career. It's not a sprint, so you have to pace yourself. Also, it's not something that happens overnight, so you can't wait until you need a platform to start building one. Begin today and build over time—so that it's there when you need it.

## DAY 24:
## TAKE PART IN A FACEBOOK CONVERSATION

For today's task, take part in a conversation on Facebook.

You should've already participated in a Twitter conversation, so this should be somewhat similar—except you don't have to play with hashtags and 140-character restrictions. In fact, you just need to find a group conversation or status update that speaks to you and chime in with your thoughts.

Don't try to sell or push anything when you join a conversation. If you say interesting things, people will check out your profile, which if filled out will lead them to more information about you (including your website, blog, any books, etc.).

Goal one of social media is making connections. If you have everything else optimized, sales and opportunities will take care of themselves.

## DAY 25:
## CONTACT AN EXPERT FOR AN INTERVIEW POST

For today's task, find an expert in your field and ask if that expert would like to be interviewed.

If you can secure the interview, this will make for a great blog post. Or it may help you secure a freelance assignment with a publication in your field. Or both, and possibly more.

### How to Ask for an Interview

Believe it or not, asking for an interview with an expert is easy. I do it all the time, and these are the steps I take.

- **FIND AN EXPERT ON A TOPIC.** This is sometimes the hardest part: figuring out who I want to interview. But I never kill myself trying to think of the perfect person, and here's why: I can always ask for more interviews. Sometimes, it's just more productive to get the ball rolling than come up with excuses to not get started.
- **LOCATE AN E-MAIL FOR THE EXPERT.** This can often be difficult, but a lot of experts have websites that share either e-mail addresses or have online contact forms. Many experts can also be reached via social media sites, such as Facebook, Twitter, LinkedIn, Google+, etc. Or they can be contacted through company websites. And so on.
- **SEND AN E-MAIL ASKING FOR AN E-MAIL INTERVIEW.** Of course, you can do this via an online contact form too. If the expert says no, that's fine. Respond with a "Thank you for considering and maybe we can make it work sometime in the future." If the expert says yes, then it's time to send along the questions.

### How to Handle an E-mail Interview

Once you've secured your expert, it's time to compose and send the questions. Here are some of my tips.

- **ALWAYS START OFF BY ASKING QUESTIONS ABOUT THE EXPERT.** This might seem obvious to some, but you'd be surprised how many people start off asking "big questions" right out of the gate. Always start off by giving the expert a chance to talk about what he or she is doing, has recently done, etc.
- **LIMIT QUESTIONS TO 10 OR FEWER.** The reason for this is that you don't want to overwhelm your expert. In fact, I usually ask around eight questions in my e-mail interviews. If I need to, I'll send along some follow-up questions, though I try to limit those as well. I want the expert to have an enjoyable experience, not a horrible experience. After all, I want the expert to be a connection going forward.
- **TRY NOT TO GET TOO PERSONAL.** If experts want to get personal in their answers, that's great. But try to avoid getting too personal in the questions you ask, because you may offend your expert or make them feel uncomfortable. Remember: You're interviewing the expert, not leading an interrogation.
- **REQUEST ADDITIONAL INFORMATION.** By additional information, I

mean that you should request a head-shot and a preferred bio—along with any links. To make the interview worth the expert's time, you should afford them an opportunity to promote themselves and their projects in their bios.

### Once the Interview Goes Live . . .

Link to it on your social networks and let your expert know it is up (and include the specific link to the interview). If you're not already searching for your next expert to interview, be sure to get on it.

## DAY 26: WRITE A BLOG POST AND LINK TO SOCIAL PROFILES

For today's task, write a new blog post.

In your blog post, include a call to action and link it on your social networks. Also, don't forget SEO.

Remember: One of the top rules of finding success with online tools is applying consistency. While it's definitely a great thing if you share a blog post more than once a week, I think it's imperative that you post at least once a week.

The main reason? It builds trust with your readers that you'll have something to share regularly and gives them a reason to visit regularly.

If this sounds repetitive, good; it means my message on consistency is starting to take root.

## DAY 27: JOIN ANOTHER SOCIAL MEDIA SITE

For today's task, join one new social media site. I will leave it up to you to decide which new social media site it will be.

Maybe you'll join Pinterest. Maybe you'll choose Goodreads. Heck, you might go with RedRoom or some social media site that's not even on my radar at the time of this article. Everything is constantly evolving, which is why it's good to always try new things.

### To everyone who doesn't want another site to join . . .

I understand your frustration and exhaustion. During a normal month, I'd never suggest someone sign up for so many social media sites in such a short period of time, but this isn't a normal month. We're in the midst of a challenge!

And no, I don't expect you to spend a lot of time on every social media site you join. That's not always the point when you first sign up. No, you sign up to poke around and see if the site interests you at all. See if you have any natural connections. Try mingling a little bit.

If the site doesn't appeal to you, feel free to let it be for a while. Let me share a story with you.

### How I Came to Rock Facebook and Twitter

My Facebook and Twitter accounts both boast more than 5,000 followers (or friends/subscribers) today. But both accounts were originally created and abandoned, because they just weren't right for me at the time that I signed up.

For Facebook, I just didn't understand why I would abandon a perfectly good MySpace account to play around on a site that didn't feature the same level of music and personal blogging that MySpace did. But then, MySpace turned into Spam-opolis, and the rest is history.

For Twitter, I just didn't get the whole tweet concept, because Facebook already had status updates. Why tweet when I could update my status on Facebook?

But I've gained a lot professionally and personally from Facebook and Twitter—even though they weren't the right sites for me initially. In fact, Google+ is sort of in that area for me right now. I don't use it near enough, but I started an account, because it just feels like a place that will explode sooner or later. It's not like Facebook is going to be around forever.

## The Importance of Experimentation

Or as I prefer to think of it: The importance of play. You should constantly try new things, whether in your writing, your social media networks, or the places you eat food. Not only does it make life more exciting and provide you with new experiences and perspective, but it also helps make you a more well-rounded human being.

So don't complain about joining a new social media site. Instead, embrace the excuse to try something new, especially when there are only three more tasks left this month (and I promise no more new sites after today).

## DAY 28:
## READ, POST, AND COMMENT ON IT

For today's task, read and comment on a blog post, making sure that your comment links back to your blog or website.

If you remember, this was the same task required way back on Day 6. How far we've come, though it's still a good idea to stay connected and engaged with other bloggers. I know I find that sometimes I start to insulate myself in my own little blogging communities and worlds—when it's good to get out and read what others are doing. In fact, that's what helped inspire my Monday Advice for Writers posts—it gives me motivation to read what others are writing (on writing, of course).

## DAY 29:
## MAKE A TASK LIST

For today's task, make a task list of things you are going to do on each day next month. That's right, I want you to break down 31 days with 1 task for each day—similar to what we've done this month.

You see, I don't want you to quit challenging yourself once this challenge is over. Of course, you get to decide what the tasks will be. So if you aren't into new social media sites, don't put them on your list. Instead, focus on blog posts, commenting on other sites, linking to articles, contacting experts, or whatever it is that you are going to do next month to keep momentum building toward an incredible author platform.

Somewhere near the end of the month, you should have a day set aside with one task: Make a task list of things to do on each day of the next month. And so on and so forth. Keep it going, keep it rolling, and your efforts will continue to gain momentum and speed. I promise.

## DAY 30:
## ENGAGE THE WORLD

For today's task, engage the world.

By this, I mean that you should comment on status updates, ask questions, share answers, start debates, continue debates, and listen—that's right, don't be that person who dominates a conversation and makes it completely one-sided.

Engage the world by entering the conversation. Engage the world by having the courage to take risks and share things of consequence. Engage the world by having the courage to make mistakes and fail and learn from those mistakes and failures.

The only people who never fail are those who never try, and those people never succeed at anything except avoiding failure and success. Don't be that person. Engage the world and let the world engage you.

# PITCH PARTY

## Everything You Should Know
## About Twitter Pitch Parties

..........................................

*by Cris Freese*

/////////////////////////////////////////////////////////////////////

Everyone is going to tell you that you should be on social media now to promote your book if you're a published author. But if you're a writer who's currently querying, there's a couple of reasons that you should join Twitter.

The first reason is that you get to be a part of a conversation and interact with literary agents, published authors, and other writers. Take a look at writers and agents currently talking on Twitter—it's a true community. People promoting other people's books, offering writing and querying advice, discussing current events, and more.

The second reason? There's a legitimate chance you could find an editor or publisher.

With the creation of Twitter pitch parties, you have an opportunity to pitch your completed and unpublished manuscript without having to write a query letter. Granted, you still have to condense your story into a compelling idea that's fewer than 280 characters. But it's a great opportunity.

If you're going to participate, you'll want to take a step back and get the lay of the land. Here are a couple of helpful guidelines to follow, no matter what the party:

1. **Read the guidelines!** I've tried to summarize the most important bits of several major pitch parties. However, I can't cover everything in this article. You'll want to make sure you know how many times you can pitch and what the timeframe for each competition is.
2. **Check the hashtags.** And I don't mean the competition hashtags. Use suggested hashtags for age categories (if you're pitching a book for an audience younger than the adult audience) and genres. This will be the easiest way for an agent to find your pitch—they're going to be looking for genres they represent, after all.

3. **Study the competitions.** The great thing about Twitter: Everything stays out there! I'd suggest going back to previous competitions by searching for the hashtag and your genre. See what agents Liked and requested. (This is how agents get your attention, letting you know they'd like you to query them!) This will give you a good feel for what agents are looking for and what's hot. But remember: Trends last only so long, and you're looking at things that are now (probably) a year old.

4. **Use all your characters!** And I don't mean in the pitch itself. I mean the hashtag, your author title, and, perhaps most importantly, potential comps. It can help further clarify your tweet if you add comp titles for your manuscript. The best, and most character-efficient, way to do this is [Title] + [Title] in your tweet.

5. **Research the agents and editors.** There's no reason to participate in a pitch party if there are agents you don't match up with—or there's only one agent you're really looking for. Just query that agent, the old-fashioned way.

And while it's not a guideline, it's a friendly reminder that only interested agents or editors should be Liking tweets. Feel free to support fellow writers by retweeting tweets, but keep your finger away from the Like button!

Now, down to the pitch parties themselves. Here are five major pitch parties that you should take a look at and consider adding to your calendar (just be sure to look up the dates on their websites!):

- **#PBPitch (http://www.pbpitch.com/):** In this Twitter pitch party exclusive to picture books, you'll have a 12-hour window to pitch your manuscript on Twitter twice— once in the morning and once in the evening. Having two times where you can pitch gives agents a larger window to find your pitch; it also gives you the opportunity to try a different approach if your first attempt doesn't snag any coveted Likes.

- **#PitMad (http://pitchwars.org/pitmad/):** Founded by Brenda Drake, #PitMad has grown like crazy over the past few years. It's one of the most widely viewed pitch parties on Twitter by agents and editors. Because of that, you'll have the chance to pitch your manuscript up to three times over the course of the allotted time. The official website suggests you break it up every four hours, and tweet a different pitch. Drake and Heather Cashman continually add sub-hashtags to the list of available hashtags, making it easier for industry professionals to find the manuscripts they're interested in. So, when you're tweeting, be sure to include the age category and/or genre of your project (#YA for young adult, #MG for middle-grade, #H for horror, #LF for literary fiction, and so forth). Check out their official website for a list of genres and sub-genres.

- **#RevPit (http://www.reviseresub.com/annual-contest/how-to-submit):** Off of Twitter, this is known as Revise & Resub—a common term that some writers may be familiar with. Known from the query process, "revise and resubmit" is when agents aren't offering representation, but have taken enough interest in your manuscript to offer true, personalized feedback. There's something special about your writing, but it's not quite there yet. By revising and resubmitting, you're getting another chance at potential representation. Originally founded by a group of editors, this pitch party supports authors with editing-focused chats and mini-events throughout the year. While you won't be pitching directly on Twitter, this event is still worth looking into. By entering, you have the chance to win five weeks of editing of your full manuscript. The website recommends that you spend time with at least one beta reader before submitting. You can only submit one time, and you'll pick two choices of editors, with one alternate. When submitting, be sure to also have your query letter polished and ready to go!

- **#SFFPit (http://dankoboldt.com/sffpit/):** Completely dedicated to those writing science fiction and fantasy (but still open to picture book, middle-grade, young adult, new adult and adult authors!), this contest is held twice a year. Founded by Dan Koboldt, the editor of the upcoming WD book, *Putting the Science in Fiction*, you'll have a 10-hour window to pitch your manuscript via Twitter. And you get one tweet per hour, or 10 pitches total! The website includes a list of subgenres for science fiction and fantasy, so you'll want to check out additional hashtags, like #SO for space opera and #PA for post-apocalyptic science fiction.
- **#DVpit (http://dvpit.com):** Hosted and moderated by literary agent Beth Phelan, #DVpit is massive—and important. This event was created to showcase pitches from marginalized voices that have been historically underrepresented in publishing. Since the first #DVpit in April 2016, more than 60 authors have signed with agents and more than 20 book deals have been contracted as a direct result of this event. This event actually hosts two separate contests on back-to-back days: one for children's and teen fiction and nonfiction, and the other for adult fiction and nonfiction. You'll have a 12-hour window to pitch, but you're limited to just six pitches per project.

This list is certainly not the end-all-be-all for Twitter pitch parties. More will likely crop up over time.

And there are also pitch contests, which are an entirely separate entity, but still valuable. Be sure to check out pitch contests, like Pitch Wars, where you'll often find an online community and a hashtag to follow on Twitter. The kinds of conversations writers, agents, and editors are exchanging there are invaluable as you seek to break out.

**CRIS FREESE** is a former editor of *Guide to Literary Agents*, a freelance writer, and literary intern with Corvisiero Literary. Follow him on Twitter @crisfreese.

# 40 AUTHORS SHARE ONE PIECE OF ADVICE FOR WRITERS

*by Robert Lee Brewer*

I love reading interviews with authors. There are few things better than finding out what inspired their books, how they go about revising stories, why they made certain publishing decisions, and more. But one of my favorite questions is: "If you could share one piece of advice with other writers, what would it be?"

So I've collected one piece of advice from 40 different book authors, writing in several different genres of fiction and nonfiction. You might think I'd get 40 answers that say the exact same thing, but you'd be wrong. While there is definitely a little crossover, it's incredible how many different tips are shared one piece of advice at a time.

Enjoy a little insight and inspiration. Then, get back to writing and marketing what you write.

## IGNORE THE NAYSAYERS

"Don't give up, and don't lose your stubborn belief that you have a story worth telling. I've had so many people tell me over so many years that I didn't have the qualities needed to be a writer. All of my writer friends and I have one thing in common: We didn't listen to the naysayers. We kept writing. And eventually we have all been published."

—Devi S. Laskar, author of *The Atlas of Reds and Blues*

## WRITE WHAT MAKES YOU EXCITED

"Run your own race. Don't worry about how fast someone else writes, how much another author makes, how many followers another author has. Write what makes you excited, and the enthusiasm will come through on the page."
  —Christina Lauren, author of *The Honey-Don't List*

## MAKE ART THAT IS MEANINGFUL TO YOU

"I would advise writers to aim to make the kind of art that is meaningful and amusing to them personally. So much about writing is unknowable, but you (probably) know what you personally find impactful, novel, and cool. So let that be your guide!"
  —Scott Kenemore, author of *Lake of Darkness*

## READ IN AND OUT OF YOUR GENRE

"Read! Read in your genre, of course, but also read outside it and try to analyze the voices you find most appealing. This will help you but it will also spur some teeth-gnashing and garment-rending at your own perceived inadequacies. Or maybe that's just me."
  —Kimmery Martin, author of *The Antidote for Everything*

## DEVELOP WRITER FRIENDSHIPS

"Writer friends are everything! We all know that the act of novel writing is solitary, and sometimes lonesome work, but when you crawl out of your cave it's so important to have friends there waiting who get it, who are ready to read and cheer you on, and who will send you right back into the cave when you need it."
  —Afia Atakora, author of *Conjure Women*

## WRITE STORIES THAT MOVE US

"I used to be a documentary filmmaker, and a film director once told me: 'You can't make a good film unless your hands tremble behind the camera.' Let us write stories that move us to the core, because when our pen is trembling, the reader can feel it, too."
  — Nguyễn Phan Quế Mai, author of *The Mountains Sing*

## LEARN TO LET GO

"Write often. I won't go so far as to say you have to write every day, but I do think you need to make this a part of the texture of your life, something that you do on a regular basis, like a workout schedule.

"Then, learn to let go. Let go of old drafts that aren't going anywhere, or scenes that don't work. Don't spend months tweaking a fundamentally flawed project when you can move on to the wonderful new projects that are percolating in your head. The 'you must start what you finish' attitude—although admirable—can actually be a pitfall, because it prevents you from taking a necessary course correction when you need it."

—Leslie Lutz, author of *Fractured Tide*

## FOLLOW YOUR PASSION

"Write something you are passionate about. Your passion will carry you through the ups and downs of the process."

—Bill Higgs, author of *Culture Code Champions: 7 Steps to Scale & Succeed in Your Business*

## WRITE WHAT YOU CAN'T STOP THINKING ABOUT

"Books are hard and they take an obscenely long time (even my seven-year-old knows this by now!). But if you find that you can't stop thinking about a particular book idea, even on your downtime and in your dreams, it's time to write it."

—Bonnie Tsui, author of *Why We Swim*

## BE DELIBERATE ABOUT THE WORDS YOU USE

"Words have extraordinary power—their definitions and colloquial meanings, the way they evolve, and where they come from. Be deliberate and selective about the words you choose. Be voracious about collecting new words for your authorial toolkit. Always look up words you've never met before. And above all, wield your words for good, for creativity, and for the cultivation of knowledge."

—Jess Zafarris, author of *Once Upon a Word: A Word-Origin Dictionary for Kids*

## WRITE WHAT PIQUES YOUR CURIOSITY

"Write what you love, what truly piques your curiosity every day. I've met authors who have told me they were sick of the subject matter in their books by the time they came out. I'm so glad I don't feel this way!

"I never tired of learning about the stories of strong women and finding a compelling way to tell those stories. I love to discuss the themes in the book—cultural standards, resilience, overcoming odds, equality, breaking barriers—so even when I'm tired, I'm always energized by the opportunity to have meaningful conversations around this work.

"You're most likely going to spend a long time writing a book, and then more time promoting it, so make it something you're passionate about so that even when you collapse into bed exhausted at the end of the day (or fall asleep on your couch with your laptop open, as I'm prone to do), you'll feel fulfilled."

—Haley Shapley, author of *Strong Like Her: A Celebration of Rule Breakers, History Makers, and Unstoppable Athletes*

## KEEP GOING

"The writer's life is one filled with creativity, sure, but there are so many other skill sets you need to practice before bringing your books to your readers (or literary agents and publishers). Keep going. Keep writing. Keep learning.

"Persistence and determination can have amazing results!"

—Kris Spisak, author of *The Novel Editing Workbook: 105 Tricks & Tips for Revising Your Fiction Manuscript*

## SET AMBITIOUS GOALS

"Don't be afraid to set ambitious goals—and try not to settle for anything less than those goals on days when motivation is scarce."

—Camilla Bruce, author of *You Let Me In*

## JOIN A WRITING GROUP

"Find a writing buddy or join a writing group. Writing can be very lonely, and it can be hard to stay motivated on a long project. It's great to have people to hold you accountable."

—Maisy Card, author of *These Ghosts Are Family*

## DIVE DEEPLY INTO RESEARCH

"Be guided by carefully developed chronologies. Establish clear causal relationships. Dive deeply into available research sources (National Archives, CIA Library, Air Force Historical Research Agency, Archives of the NSA, and others)."

—Robert L. Richardson, author of *Spying from the Sky: At the Controls of U.S. Cold War Aerial Intelligence*

## DON'T FOLLOW THE TRENDS

"[S]tay focused and write what you enjoy writing. Don't write for money or follow the trends of what might be selling at the time. Write something that you cannot only be proud of, but also enjoy the process of writing.

"A successful career in writing typically takes too long to achieve to be writing something you're not passionate about. Write from your heart, and write what gets you excited to sit at your computer every day.

"Most of all, make sure you have a life while doing it—exercise, teach, build, vote, explore, learn, grow, fellowship, and most of all, love. It will not only inform your writing but you'll also be a healthier person for it, mentally and physically."

—Christopher J. Moore, author of *The Switch Family*

## TRUST YOUR IDEA

"Trust your idea, and just start writing. It can seem like a huge task, especially if you have had your work commissioned and there is a relatively fixed deadline, but once you start putting words on the page it will come together, and there is always someone you can ask for a little bit of support."

—Jaime Breitnauer, author of *The Spanish Flu Epidemic and Its Influence on History*

## DO THE WORK

"All of my advice is stolen from other writers! I heard Lauren Groff once say something along the lines of how the only real difference between someone who has written a book and someone who hasn't, is the willingness to 'do the work.' It's helpful for me to approach writing as work and not some grand creative endeavor."

—Samantha Mabry, author of *Tigers, Not Daughters*

## BE FLEXIBLE

"The best advice I can offer aspiring authors is to be flexible. Be willing to experiment with new genres. You might find your niche somewhere unexpected."

—Tessa Wegert, author of *Death in the Family*

## FOCUS ON YOUR OWN JOURNEY

"[F]ocus on your own journey, and try not to worry about what's going on in the lane next to you. I know it's hard, because it feels natural to compare. And sometimes it's important, to know what barriers exist and how they impact marginalized writers. But from a productivity standpoint, the comparisons tend to do more harm than good. Because everyone's publishing journey is different.

"Everyone has ups and downs at different moments, and paying too much attention to what other people are getting is only going to slow you down. Focus on the page, and the words, and do what you do best—write."

—Akemi Dawn Bowman, author of *Harley in the Sky*

## STUDY THE CRAFT

"We're all students of the craft and every book we read is another chance to learn. Read voraciously. And write exactly the kinds of books you like best."
—Mindy Mejia, author of *Strike Me Down*

## SHOW UP

"This question always causes me to half-close one eye. By asking it, I feel like you're assuming I know what I'm doing. I've written 20+ books, published over two million words, and the truth is—I'm still figuring this out. Every day I show up to a white page. Books to write themselves. I too have much to learn. If I've done anything well in my career, I've shown up. Put my seat in the seat. Week after week. Year after year. Decade after decade. I sweat my books more than I write them and I'm a better rewriter than I am a writer. I also know that I remain grateful that I get to do what I get to do. It's not lost on me. Sometimes I shake my head. This privilege I live. I pray my words are true."
—Charles Martin, author of *The Letter Keeper*

## TAKE BREAKS

"Don't be afraid to take breaks! Nothing is as important as your mental and physical health, and nurturing those things will help you be a much stronger creator."
—Sandhya Menon, author of *Of Princes and Promises*

## WRITE, WRITE, AND WRITE

"Write, write, and write. And when you've written the best manuscript you are able to write, find a good editor, who will find ways for you to make it better."
—Marilyn Peterson Haus, author of *Half of a Whole: My Fight for a Separate Life*

## HAVE COURAGE TO BE HONEST

"I think it's always great to remember that your honest voice is the most powerful thing you have as a writer. Writers always worry about having what it takes, and we can get turned in circles with advice and have-to's. But what you need is right there inside, if you have the courage to use it."
—Deb Caletti, author of *One Great Lie*

## REMEMBER YOUR WHY

"I think the best advice I can give is to really follow your passion and remember your why. I think it can be so hard when you're in the trenches of querying or revising, or even just the stress surrounding a book release, to really feel that fire and that love for this really special and incredible thing we do. We write because we love it. Sometimes we love it so much we hate it! But it's that passion, that magic, that's really at the core. Above all else nurture that and always, always go back to that when things get tough."

—Rachael Lippincott, author of *The Lucky List*

## PATIENCE!

"Patience! I always say patience. Keep your head down, focus on your own progress, and be patient."

—Nekesa Afia, author of *Dead Dead Girls*

## DON'T GIVE UP ON A STORY YOU LOVE

"If I had taken this book at my first draft and accepted it as is, I'm sure it never would have made its way out there into the world. But something about this story kept me coming back and wanting to make it stronger and stronger. Edit after edit, I saw it slowly but surely becoming the novel I always hoped it would be, so if you believe in your story and it continues to call to you, then keep polishing that beauty until it's everything you dreamed of."

—Kate Bromley, author of *Talk Bookish to Me*

## FIND OUT WRITING PROCESSES OF OTHER AUTHORS

"I'll share the advice I always do: find out the writing processes of other authors, their different ways of plotting, of structuring, of crafting, revising, editing, and try them out. You may find a method that makes better sense for you than your current one. And then, even after you fall in love with 'the (new) way,' don't be hesitant to learn additional methods of approaching the craft, as developing fresh perspectives may lead to unlocking further creative potential.

"Personal perspective on this advice: I find I always teach myself 'how to write a book' anew when I'm starting a new project and in doing so, I've added to my repertoire of skills, my tools of the trade, learned new ways of approaching story-making—which all contribute to a sense of confidence in my ability to respond precisely to editorial direction. Which then makes the process of saying YES to new, exciting ideas easier. And, instead of keeping the act of writing as the sadly-solo endeavor it often is, learning from other authors makes our profession feel like an energetic and fresh space of true discovery."

—S. K. Ali, author of *Misfit in Love*

## FAIL HARD AND FAST

"The biggest piece of advice I give is always, always: fail hard and fast. Rejection can be so terrifying that it can knock us down for long stretches of time while we rebuild the confidence to put ourselves and our work out there again. But you're looking for the *right* fit for your work, and it really is like everyone says: It only takes one 'yes.' So as much as you're able to shorten those moments of imposter syndrome and discouragement to get back out there faster, do so. That's my advice."

—Emily Henry, author of *People We Meet on Vacation*

## ALLOW YOURSELF A ROUGH FIRST DRAFT

"Allow yourself the rough first draft. Chisel the hard marble. Get the story out, its shape and form. Release your emotions and find out what it is you want to say in the novel. In your subsequent drafts, you can pull out your tool belt, listen to select critiques, and use your craft to hone the novel into a finished piece of art."

—Mary Alice Monroe, author of *The Summer of Lost and Found*

## SET ASIDE TIME TO WRITE

"I used to hate when authors dispensed this advice, because as a mom of many kids who also has a day job, I always thought—*when?? Please, author person, show me where to find this magical thing called time.*

"But after I had my last child, I started setting aside her weekend nap time as writing time. It was only one or two hours, but it was one or two hours where I closed myself in a room and allowed zero interruptions. I know it doesn't seem like very much time, but having that designated increment made a *huge* difference. It creates a hyper-focus that spurs production, kind of like sprints, and even though that child is now almost 6 years old and no longer naps, I still type most of my words during that tiny little weekend bubble of minutes."

—Lynn Painter, author of *Better Than the Movies*

## BE CONSISTENT

"Be consistent. Consistent with writing and reading. I use a writing tracker, which I keep in a bullet journal, and it's so important. It wasn't until I started treated writing as a daily, non-negotiable practice that I managed to finish a manuscript. And reading is so essential to allow the writing to develop and, more practically, to be able to pitch your novel to agents. You need to understand the area of the market your book will fit into."

—Christina Sweeney-Baird, author of *The End of Men*

## SEND THE INNER CRITIC AWAY

"Believe in your writing and commit to the process again and again. I cannot tell you how many years I spent wrestling with the Inner Critic—that awful internal voice that knows exactly how to deflate your motivation and creativity. The key is to send the Inner Critic out to lunch (or better yet, to go travel the world) while you allow the Inner Writer to finally play fearlessly."

—Alexander Weinstein, author of *Universal Love*

## DON'T ABANDON YOUR STORY

"Trust your story. The temptation to abandon that manuscript mid-draft can be powerful, so belief in what you found compelling about your tale in the first place must keep you going. Unfortunately, you likely won't know how good—or, conversely, how bad—your book is until you've finished, so keep at it and see how it turns out."

—W.A. Winter, author of *The Secret Lives of Dentists*

## PROTECT YOUR CREATIVE TIME

"The business side of being an author—marketing, promotion, answering emails, etc.—takes a fair amount of time, and sometimes, because it feels more tangible, it's easier to prioritize this type of work. You have to protect the creative time. I do that by writing super early in the morning, before the world and all of its tasks have encroached on me. It's also when my brain feels freshest. I do the 'business side' during my lunch break or just after I sign off from my day job. Find what works for you—but make sure you're writing."

—Natalie Lund, author of *The Sky Above Us*

## FINISH IT

"Goodness … I guess my advice is to *finish it*. Do everything you can to get to 'The End,' before going back and editing a single page. I have to make all kinds of rules for myself like not reading more than two hundred words of the previous day's work and not reopening previous chapters, because I know I'm prone to 'moving the furniture around when I'm supposed to be building the house.'"

—Bridget Foley, author of *Just Get Home*

## BE OPEN TO SUGGESTIONS

"Write the story the way you envision it, but once you have turned in the draft, be open to editorial suggestions that could make it stronger."

—Lorraine Heath, author of *Scoundrel of My Heart*

## LET YOUR CHARACTERS LIVE

"Let your characters live in your head rent-free. Watch them come and go. Observe what they do when they think no one is watching. Record their quirks. Interrogate them. When you dance with them, let them lead. This has greased the storytelling wheels for me and made the writing flow more naturally."

—Nadia Hashimi, author of *Sparks Like Stars*

## ALWAYS LEARN, GROW, AND GET BETTER

"Don't give up. The only way you really fail as a writer is to give up and stop writing. It may take a long time to find your voice, and it may be disheartening along the way, but just remember that you're always learning and growing and getting better."

—Kristin Hannah, author of *The Four Winds*

# LITERARY AGENTS

////////////////////////////////////////////////////////////////////

Literary agents listed in this section do not charge for reading or considering your manuscript or book proposal. It's the goal of an agent to find salable manuscripts: Their income depends on finding the best publisher for your manuscript.

Since an agent's time is better spent meeting with editors, they will have little or no time to critique your writing. Agents who don't charge fees must be selective and often prefer to work with established authors, celebrities, or those with professional credentials in a particular field.

## SUBHEADS

Each agency listing is broken down into subheads to make locating specific information easier. In the first section, you'll find contact information for each agency. Additional information in this section includes the size of each agency, its willingness to work with new or unpublished writers, and its general areas of interest.

**MEMBER AGENTS:** Agencies comprised of more than one agent list member agents and their individual specialties. This information will help you determine the appropriate person to whom you should send your query letter.

**REPRESENTS:** This section allows agencies to specify what nonfiction and fiction subjects they represent. Make sure you query only those agents who represent the type of material you write.

Look for the key icon to quickly learn an agent's areas of specialization. In this portion of the listing, agents mention the specific subject areas they're currently seeking as well as those subject areas they do not consider.

**HOW TO CONTACT:** Most agents open to submissions prefer an initial query letter that briefly describes your work. You should send additional material only if the agent requests it. In this section, agents also mention if they accept queries by online submission forms or e-mail, if they consider simultaneous submissions, and how they prefer to obtain new clients.

**TERMS:** Provided here are details of an agent's commission, whether a contract is offered and for how long, and what additional office expenses you might have to pay if the agent agrees to represent you. Standard commissions range from 10–15 percent for domestic sales and 15–25 percent for foreign or dramatic sales (with the difference going to the co-agent who places the work).

**RECENT SALES:** Some agencies have chosen to list recent book sales in their listing. To get to know an agency better, investigate these published titles and learn about writing styles that the agency has bonded with. It is recommended that you always check an agency's website to see what titles have been published by their authors as well.

**WRITERS CONFERENCES:** A great way to meet an agent is at a writers conference. Here agents list the conferences they usually attend. For more information about a specific conference, check the Writers Conferences section.

**TIPS:** In this section, agents offer advice and additional instructions for writers.

## SPECIAL INDEXES

**LITERARY AGENTS SPECIALTIES INDEX:** This index organizes agencies according to the subjects they are interested in receiving. This index should help you compose a list of agents specializing in your areas. Cross-referencing categories and concentrating on agents interested in two or more aspects of your manuscript might increase your chances of success.

**AGENTS INDEX:** This index provides a list of agents' names in alphabetical order, along with the name of the agency for which they work. Find the name of the person you would like to contact, and then check the agency listing.

## A+B WORKS

**E-mail:** query@aplusbworks.com. **Website:** http://aplusbworks.com. **Contact:** Amy Jameson, Brandon Jameson. Estab. 2004.

○ Amy began her publishing career with esteemed literary agency Janklow & Nesbit Associates, where she launched Shannon Hale's career.

**MEMBER AGENTS** Amy Jameson (picture books, middle grade and young adult).

**REPRESENTS** Novels, juvenile books. **Considers these fiction areas:** middle grade, picture books, young adult.

☞ Does not want women's fiction, or any other books for adults.

**HOW TO CONTACT** Query via online submission form. "Due to the high volume of queries we receive, we can't guarantee a response." Accepts simultaneous submissions.

## ⊘ DOMINICK ABEL LITERARY AGENCY, INC.

146 W. 82nd St., #1A, New York NY 10024. (212)877-0710. **Fax:** (212)595-3133. **E-mail:** agency@dalainc.com. **E-mail:** agency@dalainc.com. **Website:** www.dalainc.com. **Contact:** Dominick Abel. Estab. 1975. Member of AAR. Represents 50 clients.

**REPRESENTS** Fiction, novels. **Considers these nonfiction areas:** business, true crime. **Considers these fiction areas:** action, adventure, crime, detective, mystery, police.

**HOW TO CONTACT** Query via e-mail. No attachments. "If you wish to submit fiction, describe what you have written and what market you are targeting (you may find it useful to compare your work to that of an established author). Include a synopsis of the novel and the first two or three chapters. If you wish to submit nonfiction, you should, in addition, detail your qualifications for writing this particular book. Identify the audience for your book and explain how your book will be different from and better than already published works aimed at the same market." Accepts simultaneous submissions. Responds in 2-3 weeks.

## ADAMS LITERARY

7845 Colony Rd., C4 #215, Charlotte NC 28226. (704)542-1440. **Fax:** (704)542-1450. **E-mail:** info@adamsliterary.com. **Website:** www.adamsliterary.com. **Contact:** Tracey Adams, Josh Adams. Estab.

2004. Member of AAR. Other memberships include SCBWI and WNBA.

**MEMBER AGENTS** Tracey Adams, Josh Adams.

**REPRESENTS** **Considers these fiction areas:** middle grade, picture books, young adult.

☞ Represents "the finest children's book and young adult authors and artists."

**HOW TO CONTACT Submit through online form on website only.** Send e-mail if that is not operating correctly. All submissions and queries should first be made through the online form on website. Will not review—and will promptly recycle—any unsolicited submissions or queries received by mail. Before submitting work for consideration, review complete guidelines online, as the agency sometimes shuts off to new submissions. Accepts simultaneous submissions. Responds in 6 weeks if interested. "While we have an established client list, we do seek new talent—and we accept submissions from both published and aspiring authors and artists."

**TERMS** Agent receives 15% commission on domestic sales; 20% on foreign sales. Offers written contract.

**RECENT SALES** *I'm Not Dying With You Tonight*, by Gilly Segal and Kimberly Jones (Sourcebooks); *None Shall Sleep*, by Ellie Marney (Little, Brown); *Aurora's End*, by Amie Kaufman and Jay Kristoff (Knopf Books for Young Readers); *The Blackbird Girls*, by Anne Blankman (Viking); *The Rice in the Pot Goes Round and Round*, by Wendy Shang (Orchard Books); *The Court of Miracles*, by Kester Grant (Knopf Random House); *Dark Rise*, by C. S. Pacat (Quill Tree Books); *Empire of the Vampire*, by Jay Kristoff (St. Martin's Press).

**TIPS** "Guidelines are posted (and frequently updated) on our website."

## BRET ADAMS LTD. AGENCY

Bret Adams, Ltd., 448 W. 44th St., New York NY 10036. (212)765-5630. **Fax:** (212)265-2212. **Website:** bretadamsltd.net. Member of AAR.

**MEMBER AGENTS** Bruce Ostler; Mark Orsini; Alexis Williams.

**REPRESENTS** Theatrical stage play, stage plays. **Considers these script areas:** stage plays, theatrical stage play.

☞ Handles theatre projects. No books or screenplays. Cannot accept unsolicited material.

**HOW TO CONTACT** Use the online submission form. Because of this agency's submission policy and interests, it's best to approach with a professional recommendation from a client. Accepts simultaneous submissions.

## AEVITAS CREATIVE MANAGEMENT

19 W. 21st St., Suite 501, New York NY 10010. (212)765-6900. **Website:** aevitascreative.com. Member of AAR. Signatory of WGA.

**MEMBER AGENTS** Esmond Harmsworth, managing partner; David Kuhn, managing partner; Todd Shuster, managing partner; Jennifer Gates, senior partner; Laura Nolan, senior partner; Janet Silver, senior partner; Bridget Wagner Matzie, partner; Rick Richter, partner; Jane von Mehren, partner; Rob Arnold, agent; Sarah Bowlin, agent; Michelle Brower, agent; Lori Galvin, agent; David Granger, agent; Jim Kelly, agent; Sarah Lazin, agent; Sarah Levitt, agent; Will Lippincott, agent; Jen Marshall, agent; Penny Moore, agent; Lauren Sharp, agent; Becky Sweren, agent; Erica Bauman, associate agent; Justin Brouckaert, associate agent; Nate Muscato, associate agent; Jon Michael Darga; Maggie Cooper; Chelsey Heller; Georgia Francis King; Karen Brailsford; Chris Bucci; Danya Kukafka; Michael Signorelli; Lauren Sharp, senior agent; Daniella Cohen, associate agent; Catharine Strong, associate agent.

**REPRESENTS** Nonfiction, fiction.

**HOW TO CONTACT** Find specific agents on the Aevitas website to see their specific interests and guidelines. Accepts simultaneous submissions.

## THE AHEARN AGENCY, INC.

3436 Magazine St., #615, New Orleans LA 70115. (504)589-4200. **Fax:** (504)589-4200. **E-mail:** pahearn@aol.com. **Website:** www.ahearnagency.com. **Contact:** Pamela G. Ahearn. Estab. 1992. Memberships include MWA, RWA, ITW. Represents 25 clients.

○ Prior to opening her agency, Ms. Ahearn was an agent for 8 years and an editor with Bantam Books.

**REPRESENTS** Novels. **Considers these fiction areas:** crime, detective, romance, suspense, thriller, women's.

☛ Handles general adult fiction, specializing in women's fiction and suspense. Does not deal with any nonfiction, poetry, juvenile material or science fiction.

**HOW TO CONTACT** Query with SASE or via e-mail. Please send a one-page query letter stating the type of book you're writing, word length, where you feel your book fits into the current market, and any writing credentials you may possess. Please do not send ms pages or synopses if they haven't been previously requested. If you're querying via e-mail, send no attachments unless requested. Accepts simultaneous submissions. Responds in 2-3 months on submissions, 3-4 months on queries. Obtains most new clients through recommendations from others, solicitations, conferences.

**TERMS** Agent receives 15% commission on domestic sales; 20% commission on foreign and dramatic sales. Offers written contract, binding for 1 year; renewable by mutual consent.

**RECENT SALES** *The Founding Treason*, by Jeremy Burns; *Undercover Duke*, by Sabrina Jeffries; *The Dead Husband*, by Carter Wilson; *Much Ado About a Scot*, by Gerri Russell; *Portrait of Peril*, by Laura Joh Rowland; *The Christmas Husband Hunt*, by Kate Moore; *Praying for Time*, by Carlene Thompson.

**WRITERS CONFERENCES** Romance Writers of America, Thrillerfest, Bouchercon.

**TIPS** "Be professional! Always send in exactly what an agent/editor asks for—no more, no less. Keep query letters brief and to the point, giving your writing credentials and a very brief summary of your book. If 1 agent rejects you, keep trying—there are a lot of us out there!"

## 🐌 AITKEN ALEXANDER ASSOCIATES

291 Gray's Inn Rd., Kings Cross, London WC1X 8QJ United Kingdom. (020)7373-8672. **Fax:** (020)7373-6002. **E-mail:** reception@aitkenalexander.co.uk; submissions@aitkenalexander.co.uk. **Website:** www.aitkenalexander.co.uk. Estab. 1976.

**MEMBER AGENTS** Clare Alexander (literary, commercial, memoir, narrative nonfiction, history); Lesley Thorne; Lisa Baker; Chris Wellbelove; Emma Patterson; Steph Adams; Amy St. Johnston; Monica MacSwain.

**REPRESENTS** Nonfiction, novels. **Considers these nonfiction areas:** creative nonfiction, memoirs, music, politics, sports. **Considers these fiction areas:** commercial, literary, mainstream, middle grade, suspense, thriller, young adult.

☛ "We specialize in literary fiction and nonfiction." Does not represent illustrated children's books, poetry, or screenplays.

**HOW TO CONTACT** "If you would like to submit your work to us, please e-mail your covering letter with a short synopsis and the first 30 pages (as a Word document) to submissions@aitkenalexander.co.uk indicating if there is a specific agent who you would like to consider your work. Although every effort is made to respond to submissions, if we have not responded within three months please assume that your work is not right for the agency's list. Please note that the Indian Office does not accept unsolicited submissions." Accepts simultaneous submissions. Obtains most new clients through recommendations from others, solicitations.

**RECENT SALES** *A Country Road, A Tree*, by Jo Baker (Knopf); *Noonday*, by Pat Barker (Doubleday); *Beatlebone*, by Kevin Barry (Doubleday); *Spill Simmer Falter Wither*, by Sara Baume (Houghton Mifflin).

## ⊘ ALIVE LITERARY AGENCY

5001 Centennial Blvd., #50742, Colorado Springs CO 80908. **Website:** www.aliveliterary.com. Estab. 1989. Member of AAR. Other memberships include Authors Guild.

**MEMBER AGENTS** Bryan Norman (popular nonfiction, biography/memoir/autobiography, spiritual growth, inspirational, literary); Lisa Jackson (popular nonfiction, biography/memoir/autobiography, spiritual growth, inspirational, literary, women's nonfiction); Rachel Jacobson.

**REPRESENTS** Nonfiction, fiction, novels, short story collections, novellas. **Considers these nonfiction areas:** autobiography, biography, business, child guidance, economics, health, how-to, humor, inspirational, memoirs, parenting, popular culture, politics, religious, self-help, women's issues, young adult. **Considers these fiction areas:** adventure, contemporary issues, family saga, historical, humor, inspirational, literary, mainstream, mystery, religious, romance, satire, sports, suspense, thriller, young adult.

⌐ This agency specializes in inspirational fiction, Christian living, how-to, and commercial nonfiction. Actively seeking inspirational, literary and mainstream fiction, inspirational nonfiction, and work from authors with established track records and platforms. Does not want to receive poetry, scripts, or dark themes.

**HOW TO CONTACT** "Because all our agents have full client loads, they are only considering queries from authors referred by clients and close contacts. Please refer to our guidelines at http://aliveliterary.com/submissions. Authors referred by an Alive client or close contact are invited to send proposals to submissions@aliveliterary.com." Your submission should include a referral (name of referring Alive client or close contact in the e-mail subject line. In the e-mail, please describe your personal or professional connection to the referring individual), a brief author biography (including recent speaking engagements, media appearances, social media platform statistics, and sales histories of your books), a synopsis of the work for which you are seeking agency representation (including the target audience, sales and marketing hooks, and comparable titles on the market), and the first 3 chapters of your manuscript. Alive will respond to queries meeting the above guidelines within 8-10 weeks.

**TERMS** Agent receives 15% commission on domestic sales. Offers written contract; two-month notice must be given to terminate contract.

**TIPS** Rewrite and polish until the words on the page shine. Endorsements, a solid platform, and great connections may help, provided you can write with power and passion. Hone your craft by networking with publishing professionals, joining critique groups, and attending writers' conferences.

## AMBASSADOR LITERARY AGENCY

P.O. Box 50358, Nashville TN 37205. (615)370-4700. **E-mail:** info@ambassadorspeakers.com. **Website:** www.ambassadorspeakers.com/acp/index.aspx. **Contact:** Wes Yoder. Represents 25-30 clients.

◯ Prior to becoming an agent, Mr. Yoder founded a music artist agency in 1973; he established a speakers bureau division of the company in 1984.

**REPRESENTS** Nonfiction, novels. **Considers these nonfiction areas:** business, creative nonfiction, inspirational, religious, spirituality, women's issues. **Considers these fiction areas:** contemporary issues, religious.

⌐ "Ambassador's Literary department represents a select list of best-selling authors and writers who are published by the leading religious and general market publishers in the United States and Europe."

**HOW TO CONTACT** Authors should e-mail a short description of their ms with a request to submit their work for review. Official submission guidelines will be sent if we agree to review a ms. Direct all inquiries and submissions to info@ambassadoragency.com. Accepts simultaneous submissions.

## BETSY AMSTER LITERARY ENTERPRISES

607 Foothill Blvd. #1061, La Cañada Flintridge CA 91012. **E-mail:** b.amster.assistant@gmail.com (for adult titles); b.amster.kidsbooks@gmail.com (for children's and young adult). **Website:** www.amsterlit.com; www.cummingskidlit.com. **Contact:** Betsy Amster (adult); Mary Cummings (children's and young adult). Estab. 1992. Member of AAR; PEN America (Amster); Society of Children's Books Writers and Illustrators (Cummings). Represents more than 75 clients.

- Prior to opening her agency, Ms. Amster was an editor at Pantheon and Vintage for 10 years and served as editorial director for the Globe Pequot Press for 2 years. She frequently speaks at the *Los Angeles Times* Festival of Books and evaluates manuscripts for UCLA Extension's Master Classes in Novel Writing. Prior to joining the agency, Mary Cummings served as education director at the Loft Literary Center in Minneapolis for 14 years, overseeing classes, workshops, and conferences. She curated the annual Festival of Children's Literature and selected judges for the McKnight Award in Children's Literature.

**REPRESENTS** Nonfiction, novels, juvenile books. **Considers these nonfiction areas:** autobiography, biography, business, child guidance, cooking, creative nonfiction, cultural interests, decorating, design, foods, gardening, health, history, horticulture, how-to, interior design, investigative, medicine, memoirs, money, multicultural, parenting, popular culture, psychology, science, self-help, sociology, travel, women's issues, young adult. **Considers these fiction areas:** crime, detective, family saga, juvenile, literary, middle grade, multicultural, mystery, picture books, police, suspense, thriller, women's, young adult.

- "Betsy Amster is actively seeking strong narrative nonfiction, particularly by journalists; outstanding literary fiction; witty, intelligent commercial women's fiction; character-driven mysteries and thrillers that open new worlds to us; high-profile self-help, psychology, and health, preferably research-based; and cookbooks and food narratives by West Coast–based chefs and food writers with an original viewpoint and national exposure. Does not want to receive poetry, romances, western, science fiction, action/adventure, screenplays, fantasy, techno-thrillers, spy capers, apocalyptic scenarios, or political or religious arguments. Mary Cummings is actively seeking great read-aloud picture books and middle-grade novels with strong story arcs, a spunky central character, and warmth, humor, or quirky charm as well as picture-book biographies and lyrically written children's nonfiction on science, nature, mindfulness, and social awareness."

**HOW TO CONTACT** "For adult fiction or memoirs, please embed the first 3 pages in the body of your e-mail. For nonfiction, please embed the overview of your proposal. For children's picture books, please embed the entire text in the body of your e-mail. For longer middle-grade and YA fiction and nonfiction, please embed the first 3 pages." Accepts simultaneous submissions. Responds in 1 month to queries; 2 months to mss. Obtains most new clients through recommendations from others, solicitations, and conferences.

**TERMS** Agent receives 15% commission on domestic sales; 20% commission on foreign sales. Offers written contract, binding for 1 year; three-month notice must be given to terminate contract. Charges for photocopying, postage, messengers, galleys/books used in submissions to foreign and film agents and to magazines for first serial rights. (Please note that it is rare to incur much in the way of expenses now that most submissions are made by e-mail.)

**RECENT SALES** Betsy Amster: *L.A. Weather*, by María Amparo Escandón (Flatiron); *The Taste of Sugar*, by Marisel Vera (Liveright); *How to Write a Novel in 20 Pies: Sweet and Savory Secrets for Surviving the Writing Life*, by Amy Wallen, illustrated by Emil Wilson (Andrews McMeel); *Sugarproof: The Hidden Dangers of Sugar That Are Putting Your Child's Health at Risk and What You Can Do*, by Michael I. Goran, Ph.D. and Emily Ventura, Ph.D., M.P.H. (Avery); *The Highly Sensitive Parent: Be Brilliant in Your Role, Even When the World Overwhelms You*, by Elaine N. Aron, Ph.D. (Citadel); *Nora Ephron: A Life*, by Kristin Marguerite Doidge (Chicago Review Press); *The Lost Gutenberg: The Astounding Story of One Book's Five-Hundred-Year Odyssey*, by Margaret Leslie Davis (TarcherPerigee). Mary Cummings: *Show the World!*, by Angela Dalton (Philomel); *I Was*, by Katherine

Hocker (Candlewick); *Valenslime*, by Joy Keller (Feiwel & Friends); *Be Black Girl Be*, by T.B. Darks (Balzer & Bray); *The Art of Magic*, by Hannah Voskuil (Carolrhoda); *To Boldly Go*, by Angela Dalton (HarperCollins).

**WRITERS CONFERENCES** Writing by Writers Boot Camps (Amster); Minnesota Writing Workshop and regional SCBWI (Cummings).

## THE ANDERSON LITERARY AGENCY

(917)363-6829. **E-mail:** giles@andersonliteraryagency.com. **Website:** www.andersonliteraryagency.com. **Contact:** Giles Anderson. Estab. 2000.

○ Owner and founder Giles Anderson started the agency in 2000 after working several years at The Waxman Literary Agency, Zephyr Press, and The Carnegie Council for Ethics in International Affairs.

**MEMBER AGENTS** Giles Anderson.

☛ "Over time my interests have increasingly turned to books that help us understand people, ideas and the possibility of change. From an examination of the religious beliefs of a Founder to the science of motivation, I'm looking for books that surprise, inform and inspire."

**HOW TO CONTACT** Send query via e-mail. Accepts simultaneous submissions.

**RECENT SALES** *Mindset: The New Psychology of Sucess*, by Carol S. Dweck, Ph.D.; *9 Things Successful People Do Differently*, by Heidi Grant Halvorson; *Reality-Based Leadership*, by Cy Wakeman.

## ⊘ ARCADIA

159 Lake Place South, Danbury CT 06810. **E-mail:** arcadialit@gmail.com. **Contact:** Victoria Gould Pryor. Member of AAR.

☛ We're not seeking new clients.

**HOW TO CONTACT** Not seeking submissions.

## ⊘ THE AUGUST AGENCY, LLC

**Website:** www.augustagency.com. **Contact:** Cricket Freeman. Estab. 2004. Represents 25-40 clients.

○ Before opening The August Agency, Ms. Freeman was a freelance writer, magazine editor and independent literary agent.

**MEMBER AGENTS** Jeffery McGraw, Cricket Freeman.

**REPRESENTS** Novels. **Considers these nonfiction areas:** art, biography, business, current affairs, history, memoirs, popular culture, politics, sociology, true crime, creative nonfiction, narrative nonfiction,

academic works. **Considers these fiction areas:** crime, mainstream.

☛ "At this time, we are not accepting the following types of submissions: self-published works, screenplays, children's books, genre fiction, romance, horror, westerns, fantasy, science fiction, poetry, short story collections."

**HOW TO CONTACT** Currently closed to submissions.

## THE AXELROD AGENCY

55 Main St., P.O. Box 357, Chatham NY 12037. (518)392-2100. **E-mail:** steve@axelrodagency.com. **Website:** www.axelrodagency.com. **Contact:** Steven Axelrod. Member of AAR. Represents 15-20 clients.

○ Prior to becoming an agent, Mr. Axelrod was a book club editor.

**MEMBER AGENTS** Steven Axelrod, representation; Lori Antonson, subsidiary rights.

**REPRESENTS** Novels. **Considers these fiction areas:** crime, mystery, new adult, romance, women's.

☛ This agency specializes in women's fiction and romance.

**HOW TO CONTACT** Query via e-mail. Accepts simultaneous submissions. Obtains most new clients through recommendations from others.

**TERMS** Agent receives 15% commission on domestic sales; 20% commission on foreign sales. No written contract.

**WRITERS CONFERENCES** RWA National Conference.

## AZANTIAN LITERARY AGENCY

**Website:** www.azantianlitagency.com. **Contact:** Jennifer Azantian. Estab. 2014.

○ Prior to establishing ALA, Ms. Azantian was with the Sandra Dijkstra Literary Agency and Ms. Gunic was an assistant editor at Abrams.

**MEMBER AGENTS** Jennifer Azantian; Renae Moore; T.S. Ferguson; Alexandra Weiss; Andrea Walker; Amanda Rutter; Masha Gunic.

**REPRESENTS** Novels. **Considers these fiction areas:** fantasy, horror, middle grade, science fiction, urban fantasy, young adult.

☛ Stories that explore meaningful human interactions against fantastic backdrops, underrepresented voices, obscure retold fairy tales, quirky middle grade, modernized mythologies, psychological horror, literary science fiction, historical fantasy, magical realism, internally consistent epic fantasy, and spooky stories for younger readers.

**HOW TO CONTACT** During open submission windows only: send your query letter, 1-2 page synopsis, and first 10 pages through the form on ALA's website. Accepts simultaneous submissions. Responds within 6 weeks. Please check the submissions page of the agency website before submitting to make sure ALA is currently open to queries.

## BARONE LITERARY AGENCY

385 North St., Batavia OH 45103. (513)293-7864. **Fax:** (513)586-0795. **E-mail:** baronelit@outlook.com. **E-mail:** baronelit@outlook.com. **Website:** www.baroneliteraryagency.com. **Contact:** Denise Barone. Estab. 2010. Member of AAR. Signatory of WGA. Also member of RWA. Represents 16 clients.

**REPRESENTS** Fiction, novels. **Considers these nonfiction areas:** memoirs, theater, young adult. **Considers these fiction areas:** action, adventure, cartoon, comic books, commercial, confession, contemporary issues, crime, detective, erotica, ethnic, experimental, family saga, fantasy, feminist, frontier, gay, glitz, hi-lo, historical, horror, humor, inspirational, juvenile, lesbian, literary, mainstream, metaphysical, military, multicultural, multimedia, mystery, new adult, New Age, occult, paranormal, plays, police, psychic, regional, religious, romance, satire, science fiction, spiritual, sports, supernatural, suspense, thriller, translation, urban fantasy, war, westerns, women's, young adult. **Considers these script areas:** action, adventure, comedy, contemporary issues.

☛ Actively seeking adult contemporary romance. Does not want textbooks.

**HOW TO CONTACT** Due to the massive number of submissions that I receive, I can no longer respond to queries. You will not hear back from me unless I am interested in your work. Please do not send anything through the mail. I accept only email queries. If I like your query letter, I will ask for the first 3 chapters and a synopsis as attachments. Accepts simultaneous submissions. I no longer provide a response. Obtains new clients by queries/submissions via e-mail only.

**TERMS** Agency receives 15% commission on domestic sales; 20% on foreign sales. Offers written contract.

**RECENT SALES** *The List*, by Yvette Geer (Cayelle Publishing), *Her Hot Alaskan Doc*, by Denise Gwen (Cayelle Publishing), *Hunted, Allied*, and *Fated*, by Molly Zenk and Sarah Biglow (Cayelle Publishing), *Haunting You*, by Molly Zenk (Intrigue Publishing); *The Beekeeper*, by Robert E. Hoxie (Six Gun Pictures); *All The Glittering Bones*, by Anna Snow (Entangled Publishing); *Devon's Choice*, by Cathy Bennett (Clean Reads); *Molly's Folly*, by Denise Gwen (Clean Reads); *In Deep*, by Laurie Albano (Solstice Publishing); *The Trouble with Charlie*, by Cathy Bennett (Clean Reads); *The Fairy Godmother Files: Cinderella Complex*, by Rebekah L. Purdy (Clean Reads).

**WRITERS CONFERENCES** The Sell More Books Show, Chicago, Illinois; Annual Conference of Romance Writers of America, Orlando, Florida; Lori Foster's Readers and Authors' Get-Together, West Chester, Ohio; A Weekend with the Authors, Nashville, Tennessee; Willamette Writers' Conference, Portland, Oregon.

**TIPS** "The best writing advice I ever got came from a fellow writer, who wrote, 'Learn how to edit yourself,' when signing her book to me."

## THE BENT AGENCY

145 Lyme Rd., Suite 206, Hanover NH 03755. **E-mail:** info@thebentagency.com. **E-mail:** Please see website. **Website:** www.thebentagency.com. **Contact:** Jenny Bent. Estab. 2009. Member of AAR.

**MEMBER AGENTS** Jenny Bent (adult fiction, including women's fiction, romance, and crime/suspense; she particularly likes novels with magical or fantasy elements that fall outside of genre fiction; young adult and middle-grade fiction; memoir; humor); Molly Ker Hawn (young adult and middle-grade fiction and nonfiction); Nicola Barr (literary and commercial fiction for adults and children, and nonfiction in the areas of sports, popular science, popular culture, and social and cultural history); Victoria Cappello (commercial and literary adult fiction as well as narrative nonfiction); Gemma Cooper (all ages of children's and young adult books, including picture books); Claire Draper (graphic novels for all ages, middle-grade and young adult fiction, feminist memoir and essay collections); Louise Fury (picture books, literary middle-grade, and all young adult; adult fiction: speculative fiction, suspense/thriller, commercial fiction, and all subgenres of romance; nonfiction: cookbooks and pop culture); Sarah Hornsley (commercial and accessible literary adult fiction and nonfiction in the area of memoir, lifestyle, and narrative nonfiction); James Mustelier (literary and commercial adult, young adult, and middle-grade fiction); Zoë Plant (adult fiction (sci-fi/fantasy, horror) as well as middle-grade and young adult fiction); John Silbersack (adult fiction (mystery/thriller, literary fiction, sci-fi/fantasy), adult nonfiction (history, current events, politics, biography, memoir, science and pop culture) as well as some young adult and middle-grade); Laurel Symonds (children's fiction and nonfiction, from picture books to young adult); Desiree Wilson (commercial and literary fiction for middle grade, young adult, and adults, graphic novels for all ages, and memoir).

**REPRESENTS** Nonfiction, fiction, novels, short story collections, juvenile books. **Considers these nonfiction areas:** animals, cooking, creative nonfiction, foods, juvenile nonfiction, popular culture, women's issues, young adult. **Considers these fiction areas:** adventure, commercial, crime, erotica, fantasy, feminist, historical, horror, humor, juvenile, literary, mainstream, middle grade, multicultural, mystery, new adult, picture books, romance, short story collections, suspense, thriller, women's, young adult.

**HOW TO CONTACT** "Tell us briefly who you are, what your book is, and why you're the one to write it. Then include the first 10 pages of your material in the body of your e-mail. We respond to all queries; please resend your query if you haven't had a response within 4 weeks." Please check agency website to see which agents are accepting submissions. Accepts simultaneous submissions.

## VICKY BIJUR LITERARY AGENCY

27 W. 20th St., Suite 1003, New York NY 10011. **E-mail:** queries@vickybijuragency.com. **Website:** www.vickybijuragency.com. Estab. 1988. Member of AAR.

Vicky Bijur worked at Oxford University Press and with the Charlotte Sheedy Literary Agency. Books she represents have appeared on *The New York Times* bestseller list, in the *New York Times* Notable Books of the Year, *Los Angeles Times* Best Fiction of the Year, *Washington Post* Book World Rave Reviews of the Year.

**MEMBER AGENTS** Vicky Bijur; Alexandra Franklin.

**REPRESENTS** Nonfiction, novels. **Considers these nonfiction areas:** memoirs. **Considers these fiction areas:** commercial, literary, mystery, new adult, thriller, women's, young adult, Campus novels, coming-of-age.

"We are not the right agency for screenplays, picture books, poetry, self-help, science fiction, fantasy, horror, or romance."

**HOW TO CONTACT** "Please send a query letter of no more than 3 paragraphs on what makes your book special and unique, a very brief synopsis, its length and genre, and your biographical information, along with the first 10 pages of your manuscript. Please let us know in your query letter if it is a multiple submission, and kindly keep us informed of other agents' interest and offers of representation. If sending electronically, paste the pages in an e-mail as we don't open attachments from unfamiliar senders. If sending by hard copy, please include an SASE for our response. If you want your material returned, include an SASE large enough to contain pages and enough postage to send back to you." Accepts simultaneous submissions. "We generally respond to all queries within 8 weeks of receipt."

**RECENT SALES** *That Darkness*, by Lisa Black; *Long Upon the Land*, by Margaret Maron; *Daughter of Ashes*, by Marcia Talley.

## DAVID BLACK LITERARY AGENCY

335 Adams St., Suite 2707, Brooklyn NY 11201. (718)-852-5500. **Fax:** (718)852-5539. **Website:** www.david-blackagency.com. **Contact:** David Black, owner. Estab. 1989. Member of AAR. Represents 150 clients.

**MEMBER AGENTS** David Black; Jenny Herrera; Gary Morris; Joy E. Tutela (narrative nonfiction, memoir, history, politics, self-help, investment, business, science, women's issues, LGBT issues, parenting, health and fitness, humor, craft, cooking and wine, lifestyle and entertainment, commercial fiction, literary fiction, MG, YA); Susan Raihofer (commercial fiction and nonfiction, memoir, pop culture, music, inspirational, thrillers, literary fiction); Sarah Smith (memoir, biography, food, music, narrative history, social studies, literary fiction); Rica Allanic; Ayla Zuraw-Friedland.

**REPRESENTS** Nonfiction, novels. **Considers these nonfiction areas:** biography, business, cooking, crafts, gay/lesbian, health, history, humor, inspirational, memoirs, music, parenting, popular culture, politics, science, self-help, sociology, sports, women's issues. **Considers these fiction areas:** commercial, literary, middle grade, thriller, young adult.

**HOW TO CONTACT** "To query an individual agent, please follow the specific query guidelines outlined in the agent's profile on our website. Not all agents are currently accepting unsolicited queries. To query the agency, please send a 1-2 page query letter describing your book, and include information about any previously published works, your audience, and your platform." Do not e-mail your query unless an agent specifically asks for an e-mail. Accepts simultaneous submissions. Responds in 2 months to queries.

**RECENT SALES** Some of the agency's best-selling authors include: Erik Larson, Stuart Scott, Jeff Hobbs, Mitch Albom, Gregg Olsen, Jim Abbott, and John Bacon.

## BOALS, WINNETT & ASSOCIATES

1411 Broadway, 16th Floor, New York NY 10018. (212)500-1424. **Fax:** (212)500-1426. **E-mail:** info@ boalswinnett.com. **Website:** www.judyboals.com. **Contact:** Judy Boals.

**MEMBER AGENTS** Katie Lynch, Jenna Winnett, Judy Boals.

**HOW TO CONTACT** Query by referral or invitation only. Accepts simultaneous submissions.

## BOND LITERARY AGENCY

201 Milwaukee St., Suite 200, Denver CO 80206. (303)781-9305. **E-mail:** sandra@bondliteraryagency.com; becky@bondliteraryagency.com; patrick@ bondliteraryagency.com. **Website:** www.bondliteraryagency.com. **Contact:** Sandra Bond.

○ Prior to her current position, Ms. Bond worked with agent Jody Rein and was the program administrator at the University of Denver's Publishing Institute.

**MEMBER AGENTS** Sandra Bond, agent (fiction: adult commercial and literary, mystery/thriller/suspense, women's, historical, young adult; nonfiction: narrative, history, science, business); Becky LeJeune, associate agent (fiction: horror, mystery/thriller/suspense, science fiction/fantasy, historical, general fiction, young adult); Patrick Munnelly (horror, fantasy, political science, current affairs, health & wellness, fitness, and graphic novels).

**REPRESENTS** Nonfiction, fiction, novels, juvenile books. **Considers these nonfiction areas:** business, history, juvenile nonfiction, popular culture, science, young adult. **Considers these fiction areas:** commercial, crime, detective, family saga, fantasy, historical, horror, juvenile, literary, mainstream, middle grade, multicultural, mystery, police, science fiction, suspense, thriller, urban fantasy, women's, young adult.

☛ Agency does not represent romance, poetry, young reader chapter books, children's picture books, or screenplays.

**HOW TO CONTACT** Please submit query by e-mail (absolutely no attachments unless requested). No unsolicited mss. "They will let you know if they are interested in seeing more material. No phone calls, please." Accepts simultaneous submissions.

**RECENT SALES** *The Past is Never*, by Tiffany Quay Tyson; *Cold Case: Billy the Kid*, by W.C. Jameson; *Women in Film: The Truth and the Timeline*, by Jill S. Tietjen and Barbara Bridges; Books 7 & 8 in the Hiro Hattori Mystery Series, by Susan Spann.

## BOOK CENTS LITERARY AGENCY, LLC

121 Black Rock Turnpike, Suite #499, Redding Ridge CT 06876. **Website:** www.bookcentsliteraryagency.com. **Contact:** Christine Witthohn. Estab. 2005. Member of AAR, RWA, MWA, SinC, KOD.

**REPRESENTS** Novels. **Considers these nonfiction areas:** cooking, gardening, travel, women's issues. **Considers these fiction areas:** commercial, mainstream, multicultural, mystery, paranormal, romance, suspense, thriller, women's, young adult.

☛ Actively seeking upmarket fiction, commercial fiction (particularly if it has crossover appeal), women's fiction (emotional and layered), romance (single title or category), mainstream mystery/suspense, thrillers (particularly psychological), and young adult. For a detailed list of what this agency is currently searching for, visit the website. Does not want to receive third party submissions, previously published titles, short stories/novellas, erotica, inspirational, historical, science fiction/fantasy, horror/pulp/ slasher thrillers, middle-grade, children's picture books, poetry, or screenplays. Does not want stories with priests/nuns, religion, abuse of children/animals/elderly, rape, or serial killers.

**HOW TO CONTACT** Submit via agency website. Does not accept mail or e-mail submissions.

**TIPS** Sponsors the International Women's Fiction Festival in Matera, Italy. See www.womensfictionfestival.com for more information. Ms. Witthohn is also the U.S. rights and licensing agent for leading French publisher Bragelonne, German publisher Egmont, and Spanish publisher Edebe.

## BOOKENDS LITERARY AGENCY

**Website:** www.bookendsliterary.com. **Contact:** Jessica Faust, Kim Lionetti, Jessica Alvarez, Moe Ferrara, Tracy Marchini, Rachel Brooks, Naomi Davis, Amanda Jain, James McGowan, Emily Forney. Estab. 1999. Member of AAR, MWA, SCBWI, SFWA, ITW. Represents 50+ clients.

**MEMBER AGENTS** Jessica Faust (women's fiction, upmarket, literary, mysteries, thrillers, suspense); Kim Lionetti (romance, women's fiction, young adult, cozy mystery, suspense); Jessica Alvarez (romance, women's fiction, mystery, nonfiction); Moe Ferrara (picture book, middle-grade, young adult, adult: graphic novels, LGBT-centric, contemporary, romance/romantic comedy, light horror, magical realism, re-tellings, light science fiction, fantasy, humorous (picture book)); Tracy Marchini (picture book, middle-grade, children's illustration, and young adult: fiction and nonfiction); Rachel Brooks (adult romance, young adult, upmarket and commercial women's fiction, mysteries); Naomi Davis (science fiction, fantasy, young adult, romance, middle grade, picture book); Amanda Jain (nonfiction and adult: mystery, romance, women's fiction, upmarket, historical fiction); James McGowan (picture book fiction and nonfiction, upmarket, mystery, suspense, thriller, crime, illustrators); Emily Forney (picture book, middle-grade, young adult, historical fiction, adult romance).

**REPRESENTS** Nonfiction, fiction, novels, juvenile books. **Considers these nonfiction areas:** art, business, creative nonfiction, current affairs, economics, ethnic, how-to, inspirational, juvenile nonfiction, money, self-help, true crime, women's issues, young adult, picture book, middle grade. **Considers these fiction areas:** adventure, comic books, commercial, crime, detective, erotica, family saga, fantasy, feminist, gay, historical, horror, humor, juvenile, lesbian, literary, mainstream, middle grade, multicultural, mystery, paranormal, picture books, police, romance, science fiction, supernatural, suspense, thriller, urban fantasy, women's, young adult.

☛    "BookEnds is currently accepting queries from published and unpublished writers in the areas of romance, mystery, suspense, science fiction and fantasy, horror, women's fiction, picture books, middle-grade, and young adult. In nonfiction we represent titles in the following areas: current affairs, reference, business and career, parenting, pop culture, coloring books, general nonfiction, and nonfiction for children and teens." BookEnds does not represent short fiction, poetry, screenplays, or techno-thrillers.

**HOW TO CONTACT** Visit website for the most up-to-date guidelines and current preferences. BookEnds agents accept all submissions through their personal Query Manager forms. These forms are accessible on the agency website under Submissions. Accepts simultaneous submissions. "Our response time goals are 6 weeks for queries and 12 weeks on requested partials and fulls."

## THE BOOK GROUP

20 W. 20th St., Suite 601, New York NY 10011. (212)803-3360. **E-mail:** submissions@thebookgroup.com. **Website:** www.thebookgroup.com. Estab. 2015. Member of AAR. Signatory of WGA.

**MEMBER AGENTS** Julie Barer; Faye Bender; Brettne Bloom (fiction: literary and commercial fiction, select young adult; nonfiction, including cookbooks, lifestyle, investigative journalism, history, biography, memoir, and psychology); Elisabeth Weed (upmarket fiction, especially plot-driven novels with a sense of place); Dana Murphy (story-driven fiction with a strong sense of place, narrative nonfiction/essays with a pop-culture lean, and YA with an honest voice); Brenda Bowen; Jamie Carr; Nicole Cunningham; DJ Kim.

**REPRESENTS** **Considers these nonfiction areas:** biography, cooking, history, investigative, memoirs, psychology. **Considers these fiction areas:** commercial, literary, mainstream, women's, young adult.

☛    Please do not send poetry or screenplays.

**HOW TO CONTACT** Send a query letter and 10 sample pages to submissions@thebookgroup.com, with the first and last name of the agent you are querying in the subject line. All material must be in the body of the e-mail, as the agents do not open attachments. "If we are interested in reading more, we will get in touch with you as soon as possible." Accepts simultaneous submissions.

**RECENT SALES** *This Is Not Over*, by Holly Brown; *Perfect Little World*, by Kevin Wilson; *City of Saints & Thieves*, by Natalie C. Anderson; *The Runaway Midwife*, by Patricia Harman; *Always*, by Sarah Jio; *The Young Widower's Handbook*, by Tom McAllister.

## BOOKS & SUCH LITERARY MANAGEMENT

52 Mission Circle, Suite 122, PMB 170, Santa Rosa CA 95409. **E-mail:** representation@booksandsuch.com. **Website:** www.booksandsuch.com. **Contact:** Janet Kobobel Grant, Wendy Lawton, Rachel Kent, Cynthia Ruchti, Barb Roose, Mary DeMuth. Estab. 1996. CBA, American Christian Fiction Writers. Represents 250 clients.

○ Prior to founding the agency, Ms. Grant was an editor for Zondervan and managing editor for Focus on the Family. Ms. Lawton was an author, sculptor, and designer of porcelain dolls and became an agent in 2005. Ms. Ruchti has written 21 books—both fiction and nonfiction—and was president of ACFW. Now she serves as ACFW's professional relations liaison (since 2011) and became an agent in 2017. Ms. Kent has worked as an agent for ten years and is a graduate of UC Davis majoring in English. Ms. Roose has written five books with workbooks and video curriculum to accompany them. She speaks at multiple conferences throughout the year and utilizes her sales experience with a major pharmaceutical company as a literary agent. She's been agenting since 2020. Mary DeMuth brought her experience as an author of more than 40 books, writing coach, and successful podcaster to her role as literary agent starting in January 2021.

**REPRESENTS** Nonfiction, fiction, novels, juvenile books. **Considers these nonfiction areas:** autobiography, biography, business, cooking, creative nonfiction, cultural interests, current affairs, foods, health, inspirational, juvenile nonfiction, memoirs, parenting, popular culture, religious, self-help, spirituality, true crime, women's issues, young adult. **Considers these fiction areas:** adventure, commercial, crime, family saga, frontier, historical, inspirational, juvenile, middle grade, mystery, picture books, religious, romance, spiritual, suspense, women's.

☞ This agency specializes in general and inspirational fiction and nonfiction, and in the Christian booksellers market. Actively seeking well-crafted material that presents Judeo-Christian values, even if only subtly. Science fiction, fantasy, erotica.

**HOW TO CONTACT** Query via e-mail only; no attachments. Accepts simultaneous submissions. Responds in 1 month to queries. "If you don't hear from us asking to see more of your writing within 30 days after you have sent your e-mail, please know that we have read and considered your submission but determined that it would not be a good fit for us." Obtains most new clients through recommendations from others, conferences.

**TERMS** Agent receives 15% commission on domestic sales; 20% commission on foreign sales. Offers written contract; two-month notice must be given to terminate contract. No additional charges.

**RECENT SALES** A full list of this agency's clients (and the awards they have won) is on the agency website.

**WRITERS CONFERENCES** The Declare Conference, The Why Conference, She Speaks, American Christian Fiction Writers Conference, West Coast Christian Writers Conference, People of Color Conference.

**TIPS** "Our agency highlights personal attention to individual clients that includes coaching on how to thrive in a rapidly changing publishing climate, grow a career, and get the best publishing offers possible."

## BOOKSTOP LITERARY AGENCY

(925)254-2664. **E-mail:** info@bookstopliterary.com. **Website:** www.bookstopliterary.com. Estab. 1984.

**MEMBER AGENTS** Kendra Marcus; Minju Chang; Karyn Fischer.

**REPRESENTS** Juvenile books, fiction and nonfiction for children and young adults. **Considers these nonfiction areas:** juvenile nonfiction, young adult. **Considers these fiction areas:** juvenile, middle grade, picture books, young adult, all genres in children's and YA.

☞ Please see agent bios on our website for more information about our individual areas of interest. Please see agent bios on our website for more information about our individual areas of interest. We do not accept books for the general adult audience or screenplays.

**HOW TO CONTACT** Please look at the agent bios on our website and address your submission to the appropriate agent via Query Manager. Accepts simultaneous submissions.

**TERMS** Agent receives 15% commission on domestic sales. Offers written contract, binding for 1 year.

## ⃠ GEORGES BORCHARDT, INC.

136 E. 57th St., New York NY 10022. (212)753-5785.
**Website:** www.gbagency.com. Estab. 1967. Member
of AAR. Represents 200+ clients.

**MEMBER AGENTS** Valerie Borchardt; Samantha
Shea; Cora Markowitz; Cassie Gross.

**REPRESENTS** Nonfiction, fiction, novels, short story collections, novellas. **Considers these nonfiction
areas:** art, biography, creative nonfiction, current affairs, history, investigative, literature, memoirs, philosophy, politics, religious, science, true crime, wom-
en's issues.

☞     This agency specializes in literary fiction and
      outstanding nonfiction.

**HOW TO CONTACT** No unsolicited submissions.
Obtains most new clients through recommendations
from others.

**TERMS** Agent receives 15% commission on domestic
sales; 20% commission on foreign sales. Offers written contract.

**RECENT SALES** *The Relive Box and Other Sto-
ries*, by T.C. Boyle; *Nutshell*, by Ian McEwan; *What
It Means When a Man Falls From the Sky*, by Lesley
Nneka Arimah.

## BRADFORD LITERARY AGENCY

5694 Mission Center Rd., #347, San Diego CA 92108.
(619)521-1201. **E-mail:** queries@bradfordlit.com.
**Website:** www.bradfordlit.com. **Contact:** Laura Brad-
ford, Natalie Lakosil, Sarah LaPolla, Kari Sutherland,
Jennifer Chen Tran. Estab. 2001. Member of AAR,
RWA, SCBWI, ALA. Represents 130 clients.

**MEMBER AGENTS** Laura Bradford (romance
[historical, romantic suspense, paranormal, category, contemporary, erotic], mystery, women's fiction, thrillers/suspense, middle grade & YA); Kari
Sutherland (children's literature, middle grade, YA,
upmarket women's fiction, magical realism, historical dramas, light-hearted contemporary fiction, biography, humor, and parenting); Jennifer Chen Tran
(women's fiction, YA, middle grade, graphic novels,
narrative nonfiction, parenting, culinary, lifestyle,
business, memoir, parenting, psychology); Katherine Wessbecher.

**REPRESENTS** Nonfiction, fiction, novels, juvenile
books. **Considers these nonfiction areas:** biography,
cooking, creative nonfiction, cultural interests, foods,
history, humor, juvenile nonfiction, memoirs, parenting, popular culture, politics, psychology, self-help,

women's issues, women's studies, young adult. **Considers these fiction areas:** commercial, crime, ethnic, gay, historical, juvenile, lesbian, literary, mainstream, middle grade, multicultural, mystery, new
adult, paranormal, picture books, romance, science
fiction, thriller, women's, young adult.

☞     Laura Bradford does not want to receive poet-
      ry, screenplays, short stories, westerns, horror,
      new age, religion, crafts, cookbooks, gift books.
      Natalie Lakosil does not want to receive inspi-
      rational novels, memoir, romantic suspense,
      adult thrillers, poetry, screenplays. Jennifer
      Chen Tran does not want to receive picture
      books, sci-fi/fantasy, urban fantasy, westerns,
      erotica, poetry, or screenplays.

**HOW TO CONTACT** Accepts e-mail queries only;
For submissions to Laura Bradford, send to queries@
bradfordlit.com. For submissions to Kari Sutherland,
send to kari@bradfordlit.com. For submissions to Jennifer Chen Tran, send to jen@bradfordlit.com. The
entire submission must appear in the body of the e-
mail and not as an attachment. The subject line should
begin as follows: "QUERY: (the title of the ms or any
short message that is important should follow)." For
fiction: e-mail a query letter along with the first chapter of ms and a synopsis. Include the genre and word
count in your query letter. Nonfiction: e-mail full
nonfiction proposal including a query letter and a
sample chapter. Accepts simultaneous submissions.
Responds in 4 weeks to queries; 10 weeks to mss. Obtains most new clients through queries.

**TERMS** Agent receives 15% commission on domestic
sales; 25% commission on foreign sales. Offers written
contract. Charges for extra copies of books for foreign
submissions.

**RECENT SALES** Sold 80 titles in the last year, in-
cluding *Vox* by Christina Dalcher (Berkley); *The Last
8*, by Laura Pohl (Sourcebooks Fire); *You'll Miss Me
When I'm Gone*, by Rachel Solomon (Simon Pulse);
*Monday's Not Coming*, by Tiffany Jackson (Harper
Collins); *Where She Fell*, by Kaitlin Ward (Adaptive);
*Into the Nightfell Wood*, by Kristin Bailey (Katherine
Tegen Books); *Yasmin the Explorer*, by Saadia Faruqi
(Capstone); *Fix Her Up*, by Tessa Bailey (Entangled);
*The Protector*, by HelenKay Dimon (Avon); *The Spitfire
Girls*, by Soraya Lane (St. Martins); *Highland Wrath*,
by Madeline Martin (Diversion); *Everybody's Favor-
ite Book*, by Mike Allegra (Macmillan); *The Hook Up*,
by Erin McCarthy (PRH); *Next Girl to Die*, by Dea

Poirier (Thomas & Mercer); *The Fearless King*, by Katee Robert (Entangled); *Noble Hops*, by Layla Reyne (Carina Press); *The Rogue of Fifth Avenue*, by Joanna Shupe (Kensington).

**WRITERS CONFERENCES** RWA National Conference, Romantic Times Booklovers Convention.

## BRANDT & HOCHMAN LITERARY AGENTS, INC.

1501 Broadway, Suite 2605, New York NY 10036. (212)840-5760. **Fax:** (212)840-5776. **Website:** brandthochman.com. **Contact:** Gail Hochman or individual agent best suited for the submission. Estab. over a century ago. Member of AAR. Represents 200 clients.

**MEMBER AGENTS** Gail Hochman (works of literary fiction, idea-driven nonfiction, literary memoir and children's books); Marianne Merola (fiction, nonfiction and children's books with strong and unique narrative voices); Bill Contardi (voice-driven young adult and middle grade fiction, commercial thrillers, psychological suspense, quirky mysteries, high fantasy, commercial fiction and memoir); Emily Forland (voice-driven literary fiction and nonfiction, memoir, narrative nonfiction, history, biography, food writing, cultural criticism, graphic novels, and young adult fiction); Emma Patterson (fiction from dark, literary novels to upmarket women's and historical fiction; narrative nonfiction that includes memoir, investigative journalism, and popular history; young adult fiction); Jody Kahn (literary and upmarket fiction; narrative nonfiction, particularly books related to sports, food, history, science and pop culture—including cookbooks, and literary memoir and journalism); Henry Thayer (nonfiction on a wide variety of subjects and fiction that inclines toward the literary). The e-mail addresses and specific likes of each of these agents is listed on the agency website.

**REPRESENTS** Nonfiction, novels. **Considers these nonfiction areas:** biography, cooking, current affairs, foods, health, history, memoirs, music, popular culture, science, sports, narrative nonfiction, journalism. **Considers these fiction areas:** fantasy, historical, literary, middle grade, mystery, suspense, thriller, women's, young adult.

☞ No screenplays or textbooks.

**HOW TO CONTACT** "We accept queries by e-mail and regular mail; however, we cannot guarantee a response to e-mailed queries. For queries via regular mail, be sure to include a SASE for our reply. Query letters should be no more than 2 pages and should include a convincing overview of the book project and information about the author and his or her writing credits. Address queries to the specific Brandt & Hochman agent whom you would like to consider your work. Agent e-mail addresses and query preferences may be found at the end of each agent profile on the 'Agents' page of our website." Accepts simultaneous submissions. Obtains most new clients through recommendations from others.

**TERMS** Agent receives 15% commission on domestic sales; 20% commission on foreign sales.

**RECENT SALES** This agency sells 40-60 new titles each year. A full list of their hundreds of clients is on the agency website.

**TIPS** "Write a letter which will give the agent a sense of you as a professional writer—your long-term interests as well as a short description of the work at hand."

## THE BRATTLE AGENCY

P.O. Box 380537, Cambridge MA 02238. **E-mail:** christopher.vyce@thebrattleagency.com. **E-mail:** submissions@thebrattleagency.com. **Website:** thebrattleagency.com. **Contact:** Christopher Vyce. Member of AAR. Signatory of WGA.

○ Prior to being an agent, Mr. Vyce worked for the Beacon Press in Boston as an acquisitions editor.

**REPRESENTS** Nonfiction, fiction, scholarly books. **Considers these nonfiction areas:** art, biography, creative nonfiction, cultural interests, current affairs, environment, film, history, literature, metaphysics, music, philosophy, popular culture, politics, regional, sports, war, race studies, American studies. **Considers these fiction areas:** literary.

**HOW TO CONTACT** Query by e-mail. Include cover letter, brief synopsis, brief CV. Accepts simultaneous submissions. Responds to queries in 72 hours. Responds to approved submissions in 6-8 weeks.

## BRESNICK WEIL LITERARY AGENCY

30 Deep Six Dr., East Hampton NY 11937. (631)324-1177. **E-mail:** paul@bresnickagency.com; susan@bresnickagency.com. **Website:** bresnickagency.com. **Contact:** Paul Bresnick.

○ Prior to becoming an agent, Mr. Bresnick spent 25 years as a trade book editor.

**MEMBER AGENTS** Paul Bresnick; Susan Duff (women's health, food and wine, fitness, humor, memoir).

**REPRESENTS** Nonfiction, novels. **Considers these nonfiction areas:** foods, health, history, humor, memoirs, music, popular culture, politics, science, sports, women's issues, fitness, pop/alternative culture, video games. **Considers these fiction areas:** commercial, literary.

**HOW TO CONTACT** Electronic submissions only. For fiction, submit query and 2 chapters. For nonfiction, submit query with proposal. Accepts simultaneous submissions.

## ⊘ M. COURTNEY BRIGGS

Derrick & Briggs, LLP, Banc First Tower, Suite 2700, 100 N. Broadway Ave., 28th Floor, Oklahoma City OK 73102. (405)235-1900. **Fax:** (405)235-1995. **Website:** www.derrickandbriggs.com. "M. Courtney Briggs combines her primary work as a literary agent with expertise in intellectual property, entertainment law, and estates and probate. Her clients are published authors (exclusively), theaters, and a variety of small businesses and individuals."

## ◑ RICK BROADHEAD & ASSOCIATES LITERARY AGENCY

47 St. Clair Ave. W., Suite 501, Toronto ON M4V 3A5 Canada. (416)929-0516. **E-mail:** info@rbaliterary.com. **E-mail:** submissions@rbaliterary.com. **Website:** www.rbaliterary.com. **Contact:** Rick Broadhead, president. Estab. 2002. Membership includes Authors Guild. Represents 125 clients.

◑ With an MBA from the Schulich School of Business, one of the world's leading business schools, Rick Broadhead is one of the few literary agents in the publishing industry with a business and entrepreneurial background, one that benefits his clients at every step of the book development and contract negotiation process.

**REPRESENTS** Nonfiction. **Considers these nonfiction areas:** biography, business, current affairs, environment, health, history, humor, medicine, military, popular culture, politics, science, self-help, relationships, pop science, security/intelligence, natural history.

⌐ The agency is actively seeking compelling proposals from experts in their fields, journalists, and authors with relevant credentials and an established media platform (TV, web, radio, print experience/exposure). Does not want to receive fiction, screenplays, children's or poetry at this time.

**HOW TO CONTACT** Query with e-mail. Include a brief description of your project, your credentials, and contact information. Accepts simultaneous submissions.

**TIPS** "Books rarely sell themselves these days, so I look for authors who have a 'platform' (media exposure/experience, university affiliation, recognized expertise, etc.). Remember that a literary agent has to sell your project to an editor, and then the editor has to sell your project internally to his/her colleagues (including the marketing and sales staff), and then the publisher has to sell your book to the book buyers at the chains and bookstores. You're most likely to get my attention if you write a succinct and persuasive query letter that demonstrates your platform/credentials, the market potential of your book, and why your book is different."

## CURTIS BROWN, LTD.

228 East 45th St., New York NY 10017. (212)473-5400. **Website:** www.curtisbrown.com. Estab. 1914. Member of AAR. Signatory of WGA.

**MEMBER AGENTS** Ginger Clark (science fiction, fantasy, paranormal romance, literary horror, and young adult and middle grade fiction); Kerry D'Agostino (literary and commercial fiction, as well as narrative nonfiction and memoir); Katherine Fausset (literary fiction, upmarket commercial fiction, journalism, memoir, popular science, and narrative nonfiction); Sarah Gerton (fiction and nonfiction for middle grade and young adult in all genres); Holly Frederick; Peter Ginsberg, president; Elizabeth Harding, vice president (represents authors and illustrators of juvenile, middle-grade and young adult fiction); Ginger Knowlton, executive vice president (authors and illustrators of children's books in all genres—picture book, middle grade, young adult fiction and nonfiction); Timothy Knowlton, CEO; Jonathan Lyons (biographies, history, science, pop culture, sports, general narrative nonfiction, mysteries, thrillers, science fiction and fantasy, and young adult fiction); Laura Blake Peterson, vice president (memoir and biography, natural history, literary fiction, mystery, suspense, women's fiction, health and fitness, young adult, faith issues and popular culture); Steven Salpeter (literary fiction, fantasy, graphic novels, historical fiction, mysteries, thrillers, young adult, narrative nonfiction, gift books, history, humor, and popular science).

**REPRESENTS** Nonfiction, fiction, novels, short story collections, juvenile books. **Considers these nonfiction areas:** animals, biography, business, computers, cooking, creative nonfiction, current affairs, ethnic, gardening, health, history, humor, juvenile nonfiction, memoirs, money, popular culture, psychology, religious, science, self-help, spirituality, sports, young adult. **Considers these fiction areas:** contemporary issues, ethnic, fantasy, feminist, gay, historical, horror, humor, juvenile, lesbian, literary, mainstream, middle grade, mystery, paranormal, picture books, religious, romance, spiritual, sports, suspense, thriller, urban fantasy, women's, young adult.

**HOW TO CONTACT** Please refer to the "Agents" page on the website for each agent's submission guidelines. Accepts simultaneous submissions. Responds in 4-8 weeks to queries; 8 weeks to mss (but do see Agent page on website for more information). Obtains most new clients through recommendations from others, solicitations, conferences.

**TERMS** Agent receives 15% commission on domestic sales; 20% on foreign sales. Offers written contract. 75-day notice must be given to terminate contract. Charges for some postage (overseas, etc.).

**RECENT SALES** This agency prefers not to share information on specific sales.

## ANDREA BROWN LITERARY AGENCY, INC.

**E-mail:** andrea@andreabrownlit.com; caryn@andreabrownlit.com; lauraqueries@gmail.com; jennifer@andreabrownlit.com; kelly@andreabrownlit.com; jennL@andreabrownlit.com; jamie@andreabrownlit.com; jmatt@andreabrownlit.com; kathleen@andreabrownlit.com; lara@andreabrownlit.com; soloway@andreabrownlit.com; jemiscoe@andreabrownlit.com; saritza@andreabrownlit.com; paige@andreabrownlit.com. **Website:** www.andreabrownlit.com. Estab. 1981. Member of AAR.

○ Prior to opening her agency, Ms. Brown served as an editorial assistant at Random House and Dell Publishing and as an editor with Knopf.

**MEMBER AGENTS** Andrea Brown (president); Laura Rennert (executive agent); Caryn Wiseman (senior agent); Jennifer Laughran (senior agent); Jennifer Rofé (senior agent); Kelly Sonnack (senior agent); Jamie Weiss Chilton (senior agent); Jennifer Mattson (agent); Kathleen Rushall (agent); Lara Perkins (agent); Saritza Hernandez (agent); Jennifer March Soloway (associate agent); Jemiscoe Chambers-Black (associate agent); Paige Terlip (associate agent).

**REPRESENTS** Juvenile books. **Considers these nonfiction areas:** juvenile nonfiction, popular culture, young adult, narrative. **Considers these fiction areas:** crime, fantasy, feminist, gay, horror, juvenile, middle grade, multicultural, picture books, romance, science fiction, suspense, thriller, women's, young adult, middle-grade, all juvenile genres.

☞ Specializes in all kinds of children's books—illustrators and authors. 98% juvenile books. Considers: nonfiction, fiction, picture books, young adult.

**HOW TO CONTACT** Writers should review the large agent bios on the agency website to determine which agent to contact. Please choose only one agent to query. The agents share queries, so a no from one agent at Andrea Brown Literary Agency is a no from all. (Note that Jennifer Laughran and Kelly Sonnack only receive queries by querymanager—please visit the agency's website for information.) For picture books, submit a query letter and complete ms in the body of the e-mail. For fiction, submit a query letter and the first 10 pages in the body of the e-mail. For nonfiction, submit proposal, first 10 pages in the body of the e-mail. Illustrators: submit a query letter and 2-3 illustration samples (in jpeg format), link to online portfolio, and text of picture book, if applicable. "We only accept queries via e-mail. No attachments, with the exception of jpeg illustrations from illustrators." Visit the agents' bios on our website and choose only one agent to whom you will submit your e-query. Send a short e-mail query letter to that agent with "QUERY" in the subject field. Accepts simultaneous submissions. If we are interested in your work, we will certainly follow up by e-mail or by phone. However, if you haven't heard from us within 12-16 weeks, please assume that we are passing on your project. Obtains most new clients through queries and referrals from editors, clients, and agents. Check website for guidelines and information.

**TERMS** Agent receives 15% commission on domestic sales; 25% commission on foreign sales. Offers written contract. No fees.

**RECENT SALES** Supriya Kelkar's middle grade novel *American As Paneer Pie* to Jennifer Ung at Aladdin, at auction, by Kathleen Rushall. Mitali Perkins's *You Bring the Distant Near* sold at auction, in a two-book deal, to Grace Kendall at Farrar, Straus Children's, by Laura Rennert. Cynthia Salaysay's YA novel *Private Lessons* to Kate Fletcher at Candlewick, by Jennifer March Soloway. Dev Petty's picture book text, *The Bear Must Go On* to Talia Benamy at Philomel, by Jennifer Rofe. Carrie Pearson's nonfiction picture book text *A Girl Who Leaped, A Woman Who Soared* to Simon Boughton at Norton Children's by Kelly Sonnack. K. C. Johnson's YA novel, *This is My America* to Chelsea Eberly at Random House Children's in a two-book deal by Jennifer March Soloway. Nancy Castaldo's nonfiction YA, *Water* to Elise Howard at Algonquin Young Readers by Jennifer Laughran. Kate Messner's picture book text, *The Next President* to Melissa Manlove at Chronicle Children's, in a two book deal by Jennifer Laughran. Amber Lough's YA novel, *Summer of War* to Amy Fitzgerald at Carolrhoda Lab by Laura Rennert and Jennifer March Soloway. Andrea Zimmerman and David Clemesha's picture book *All Buckled Up* to Jeffrey Salane at Little Simon, in a two-book deal by Jamie Weiss Chilton. Jennifer Berne's picture book *Dinosaur Doomsday* to Melissa Manlove at Chronicle Children's by Caryn Wiseman. Tami Charles's *Serena Williams—G.O.A.T.: Making the Case for the Greatest of All Time*, a sports biography of Serena Williams to Ada Zhang at Sterling Children's by Lara Perkins. Katy Loutzenhiser's YA *If You're Out There* to Donna Bray at Balzer & Bray in a two-book deal by Jennifer Mattson. Barry Eisler's *The Killer Collective,* as well as a John Rain prequel, and two more in the Livia Lone series, to Gracie Doyle at Thomas & Mercer, in a major deal by Laura Rennert. Maggie Stiefvater's The Raven Cycle series to Universal Cable Productions by Laura Rennert.

**WRITERS CONFERENCES** SCBWI, Asilomar; Maui Writers' Conference, Southwest Writers' Conference, San Diego State University Writers' Conference, Big Sur Children's Writing Workshop, William Saroyan Writers' Conference, Columbus Writers' Conference, Willamette Writers' Conference, La Jolla Writers' Conference, San Francisco Writers' Conference, Hilton Head Writers' Conference, Pacific Northwest Conference, Pikes Peak Conference.

## CURTIS BROWN (AUST) PTY LTD

P.O. Box 19, Paddington NSW 2021 Australia. (+61)(2)9361-6161. **Fax:** (+61)(2)9360-3935. **E-mail:** sub-

mission@curtisbrown.com.au. **Website:** www.curtisbrown.com.au.

○ "Prior to joining Curtis Brown, most of our agents worked in publishing or the film/theatre industries in Australia and the United Kingdom."

**MEMBER AGENTS** Fiona Inglis (managing director/agent); Tara Wynne (agent); Pippa Masson (agent); Clare Foster (agent); Benjamin Paz (agent); Caitlan Cooper-Trent (agent).

☛ "We are Australia's oldest and largest literary agency representing a diverse range of Australian and New Zealand writers and Estates."

**HOW TO CONTACT** "Please refer to our website for information regarding ms submissions, permissions, theatre rights requests, and the clients and Estates we represent. We are not currently looking to represent poetry, short stories, stage/screenplays, picture books, or translations. We do not accept e-mailed or faxed submissions. No responsibility is taken for the receipt or loss of mss." Accepts simultaneous submissions.

## BROWNE & MILLER LITERARY ASSOCIATES

52 Village Place, Hinsdale IL 60521. (312)922-3063. **E-mail:** mail@browneandmiller.com. **Website:** www.browneandmiller.com. **Contact:** Danielle Egan-Miller, president. Estab. 1971. Member of AAR, RWA, MWA, Authors Guild.

○ Prior to joining the agency as Jane Jordan Browne's partner, Danielle Egan-Miller worked as an editor.

**REPRESENTS** Nonfiction, fiction.

☛ Browne & Miller is most interested in literary and commercial fiction, women's fiction, women's historical fiction, literary-leaning crime fiction, dark suspense/domestic suspense, romance, and Christian/inspirational fiction by established authors, and a wide range of platform-driven nonfiction by nationally recognized author-experts. "We do not represent children's books of any kind or young adult; no adult memoirs; we do not represent horror, science fiction or fantasy, short stories, poetry, original screenplays, or articles."

**HOW TO CONTACT** Query via e-mail only; no attachments. Do not send unsolicited mss. Accepts simultaneous submissions.

## SHEREE BYKOFSKY ASSOCIATES, INC.

P.O. Box 706, Brigantine NJ 08203. **E-mail:** shereebee@aol.com. **Website:** www.shereebee.com. **Contact:** Sheree Bykofsky. Estab. 1991. Member of AAR. Represents 1,000+ clients.

**REPRESENTS** Nonfiction. **Considers these nonfiction areas:** anthropology, child guidance, history. **Considers these script areas:** Dramatic rights represented by Joel Gotler.

☛ Does not want to receive poetry, children's, screenplays, westerns, science fiction, or horror.

**HOW TO CONTACT** Query via e-mail to shereebee@aol.com. "We only accept e-queries. We respond only to those queries in which we are interested. No attachments, snail mail, or phone calls, please. We do not open attachments." Responds in 1 month to requested mss. Obtains most new clients through referrals.

**TERMS** Agent receives 15% commission on domestic sales. Agent receives 15% commission on foreign sales, plus international co-agent receives another 10%. Offers written contract, binding for 1 year. Charges for international postage.

**RECENT SALES** *A Tangled Web* by Leslie Rule (Kensington), *Sneaky Uses for Everyday Things*, 2nd Edition by Cy Tymony (Andrews McMeel), *Gamer Nation* by Eric Geissinger (Prometheus Books), *Virtual Billions: The Genius, the Drug Lord, and the Ivy League Twins Behind the Rise of Bitcoin*.

**WRITERS CONFERENCES** Truckee Meadow Community College Keynote, Southwest Florida Writers Conference, Philadelphia Writer's Conference, Push to Publish, Lewes Writers Conference, Pennwriters, League of Vermont Writers, Asilomar, Florida Suncoast Writers' Conference, Whidbey Island Writers' Conference, Florida First Coast Writers' Festival, Agents and Editors Conference, Columbus Writers' Conference, Southwest Writers' Conference, Willamette Writers' Conference, Dorothy Canfield Fisher Conference, Pacific Northwest Writers' Conference, IWWG.

## KIMBERLEY CAMERON & ASSOCIATES

1550 Tiburon Blvd., #704, Tiburon CA 94920. (415)789-9191. **Website:** www.kimberleycameron. com. **Contact:** Kimberley Cameron. Member of AAR. Signatory of WGA.

Kimberley Cameron & Associates (formerly The Reece Halsey Agency) has had an illustrious client list of established writers, including Aldous Huxley, Upton Sinclair, William Faulkner, and Henry Miller.

**MEMBER AGENTS** Kimberley Cameron; Elizabeth Kracht (nonfiction: memoir, self-help, spiritual, investigative, creative / fiction: women's, literary, historical, mysteries, thrillers); Amy Cloughley (literary and upmarket fiction, women's, historical, narrative nonfiction, travel or adventure memoir); Mary C. Moore (fantasy, science fiction, upmarket "book club," genre romance, thrillers with female protagonists, and stories from marginalized voices); Lisa Abellera (currently closed to unsolicited submissions); Dorian Maffei (only open to submissions requested through Twitter pitch parties, conferences, or #MSWL).

**REPRESENTS** Nonfiction, fiction, novels. **Considers these nonfiction areas:** animals, creative nonfiction, cultural interests, current affairs, environment, ethnic, gay/lesbian, health, history, how-to, humor, investigative, literature, memoirs, metaphysics, psychology, science, self-help, sex, spirituality, travel, true crime, women's issues, women's studies, narrative nonfiction. **Considers these fiction areas:** action, adventure, commercial, confession, crime, detective, gay, historical, literary, mainstream, military, mystery, police, romance, science fiction, spiritual, thriller, women's, young adult, LGBTQ.

☛ "We are looking for a unique and heartfelt voice that conveys a universal truth."

**HOW TO CONTACT** Prefers queries via site. Only query one agent at a time. For fiction, fill out the correct submissions form for the individual agent and attach the first 50 pages and a synopsis (if requested) as a Word doc or PDF. For nonfiction, fill out the correct submission form of the individual agent and attach a full book proposal and sample chapters (includes the first chapter and no more than 50 pages) as a Word doc or PDF. Accepts simultaneous submissions. Obtains new clients through recommendations from others, solicitations.

## CYNTHIA CANNELL LITERARY AGENCY

54 W. 40th St., New York NY 10018. (212)396-9595. **E-mail:** info@cannellagency.com. **Website:** www. cannellagency.com. **Contact:** Cynthia Cannell. Estab. 1997. Member of AAR, Women's Media Group and the Authors Guild.

○ Prior to forming the Cynthia Cannell Literary Agency, Ms. Cannell was the vice president of Janklow & Nesbit Associates for 12 years.

**REPRESENTS** Nonfiction, fiction. **Considers these nonfiction areas:** biography, current affairs, memoirs, self-help, spirituality.

☛ Does not represent screenplays, children's books, illustrated books, cookbooks, romance, category mystery, or science fiction.

**HOW TO CONTACT** "Please query us with an e-mail or letter. If querying by e-mail, send a brief description of your project with relevant biographical information including publishing credits (if any) to info@cannellagency.com. Do not send attachments. If querying by conventional mail, enclose an SASE." Responds if interested. Accepts simultaneous submissions.

**RECENT SALES** Check the website for an updated list of authors and sales.

## CAPITAL TALENT AGENCY

419 S. Washington St., Alexandria VA 22314. (703)349-1649. **E-mail:** literary.submissions@capitaltalentagency.com. **Website:** capitaltalentagency.com/html/literary.shtml. **Contact:** Cynthia Kane. Estab. 2014. Member of AAR. Signatory of WGA.

○ Prior to joining CTA, Ms. Kane was involved in the publishing industry for more than 10 years. She has worked as a development editor for different publishing houses and individual authors and has seen more than 100 titles to market.

**MEMBER AGENTS** Cynthia Kane; Shaheen Qureshi.

**REPRESENTS** Nonfiction, fiction, movie scripts, stage plays.

**HOW TO CONTACT** "We accept submissions only by e-mail. We do not accept queries via postal mail or fax. For fiction and nonfiction submissions, send a query letter in the body of your e-mail. Please note that while we consider each query seriously, we are unable to respond to all of them. We endeavor to respond within 6 weeks to projects that interest us." Accepts simultaneous submissions.

## CHALBERG & SUSSMAN

115 W. 29th St., Third Floor, New York NY 10001. (917)261-7550. **Website:** www.chalbergsussman.com. Member of AAR. Signatory of WGA.

○ Prior to her current position, Ms. Chalberg held a variety of editorial positions, and was an agent with The Susan Golomb Literary Agency. Ms. Sussman was an agent with Zachary Shuster Harmsworth.

**MEMBER AGENTS** Terra Chalberg; Rachel Sussman (narrative journalism, memoir, psychology, history, humor, pop culture, literary fiction).

**REPRESENTS** Nonfiction, fiction, novels. **Considers these nonfiction areas:** history, humor, memoirs, popular culture, psychology, self-help, narrative journalism. **Considers these fiction areas:** erotica, fantasy, horror, literary, middle grade, romance, science fiction, suspense, young adult, contemporary realism, speculative fiction.

**HOW TO CONTACT** To query by e-mail, please contact one of the following: terra@chalbergsussman.com, rachel@chalbergsussman.com. Accepts simultaneous submissions.

**RECENT SALES** The agents' sales and clients are listed on their website.

## CHASE LITERARY AGENCY

11 Broadway, Suite 1010, New York NY 10004. (212)477-5100. **E-mail:** farley@chaseliterary.com. **Website:** www.chaseliterary.com. **Contact:** Farley Chase. Member of AAR.

**MEMBER AGENTS** Farley Chase.

**REPRESENTS** Nonfiction, fiction, novels. **Considers these nonfiction areas:** agriculture, Americana, animals, anthropology, archeology, architecture, autobiography, biography, business, creative nonfiction, cultural interests, current affairs, design, education, environment, ethnic, film, foods, gay/lesbian, health, history, how-to, humor, inspirational, investigative, juvenile nonfiction, language, law, literature, medicine, memoirs, metaphysics, military, money, multicultural, music, philosophy, popular culture, politics, recreation, regional, satire, science, sex, sociology, sports, technology, translation, travel, true crime, war, women's issues, women's studies. **Considers these fiction areas:** commercial, historical, literary, mystery.

☛ No romance, science fiction, or young adult.

**HOW TO CONTACT** E-query farley@chaseliterary.com. If submitting fiction, please include the first few pages of the ms with the query. "I do not response to queries not addressed to me by name. I'm keenly interested in both fiction and nonfiction. In fiction, I'm looking for both literary or commercial projects in either contemporary or historical settings. I'm open to anything with a strong sense of place, voice, and, especially plot. I don't handle science fiction, romance, supernatural or young adult. In nonfiction, I'm especially interested in narratives in history, memoir, journalism, natural science, military history, sports, pop culture, and humor. Whether by first-time writers or long time journalists, I'm excited by original ideas, strong points of view, detailed research, and access to subjects which give readers fresh perspectives on things they think they know. I'm also interested in visually-driven and illustrated books. Whether they involve photography, comics, illustrations, or art I'm taken by creative storytelling with visual elements, four-color or black and white." Accepts simultaneous submissions.

**RECENT SALES** *Devil in the Grove: Thurgood Marshall, the Groveland Boys, and the Dawn of a New America* by Gilbert King (Harper); *Heads in Beds: A Reckless Memoir of Hotels, Hustles, and So-Called Hospitality,* by Jacob Tomsky (Doubleday); *And Every Day Was Overcast,* by Paul Kwiatowski (Black Balloon); *The Badlands Saloon,* by Jonathan Twingley (Scribner).

## CHENEY ASSOCIATES, LLC

39 W. 14th St., Suite 403, New York NY 10011. (212)277-8007. **Fax:** (212)614-0728. **E-mail:** submissions@cheneyliterary.com. **Website:** www.cheneyliterary.com. **Contact:** Elyse Cheney; Adam Eaglin; Alex Jacobs; Alice Whitwham.

○ Prior to her current position, Ms. Cheney was an agent with Sanford J. Greenburger Associates.

**MEMBER AGENTS** Elyse Cheney; Adam Eaglin (literary fiction and nonfiction, including history, politics, current events, narrative reportage, biography, memoir, and popular science); Allison Devereux (narrative nonfiction, memoir, cultural history, natural history, sports, philosophy, and literary fiction); Danny Hertz; Claire Gillepsie (literary fiction, memoir, cutlural criticism, upmarket fiction, and audio); Isabel Mendia (cultural criticism, narrative reportage, politics, history); Alice Whitwham (literary and commercial fiction, as well as voice-driven narrative nonfiction, cultural criticism, and journalism).

**REPRESENTS** Nonfiction, novels. **Considers these nonfiction areas:** biography, cultural interests, current affairs, history, memoirs, politics, science, narrative nonfiction, narrative reportage. **Considers these fiction areas:** commercial, crime, family saga, historical, literary, short story collections, suspense, women's.

**HOW TO CONTACT** Query by e-mail or snail mail. For a snail mail responses, include a SASE. Include up to 3 chapters of sample material. Do not query more than one agent. Accepts simultaneous submissions.

**RECENT SALES** *The Love Affairs of Nathaniel P.,* by Adelle Waldman (Henry Holt & Co.); *This Town,* by Mark Leibovich (Blue Rider Press); *Thunder & Lightning,* by Lauren Redniss (Random House).

## THE CHUDNEY AGENCY

72 N. State Rd., Suite 501, Briarcliff Manor NY 10510. (914)465-5560. **E-mail:** steven@thechudneyagency.com. **Website:** www.thechudneyagency.com. **Contact:** Steven Chudney. Estab. 2001. Member of SCBWI.

○ Prior to becoming an agent, Mr. Chudney held various marketing and sales positions with major publishers.

**REPRESENTS** Novels, juvenile books. **Considers these nonfiction areas:** humor. **Considers these fiction areas:** commercial, family saga, gay, historical, juvenile, lesbian, literary, middle grade, mystery, picture books, regional, suspense, thriller, young adult. **Considers these script areas:** detective, family saga, gay, juvenile, mystery.

☛ "At this time, the agency is only looking for author/illustrators (one individual), who can both write and illustrate wonderful picture books. The author/illustrator must really know and understand the prime audience's needs and wants of the child reader! Storylines should be engaging, fun, with a hint of a life lesson and cannot be longer than 700 words. With chapter books, middle grade and teen novels, I'm primarily looking for quality, contemporary literary fiction: novels that are exceedingly well-written, with wonderful settings and developed, unforgettable characters. I'm looking for historical fiction that will excite me, young readers, editors, and reviewers, and will introduce us to unique characters in settings and situations, countries, and eras we haven't encountered too often yet in children's and teen literature." Does not want most fantasy and no science fiction.

**HOW TO CONTACT** No snail mail submissions for fiction/novels. Queries only. Please do not send any text for novels. Submission package info from us to follow should we be interested in your project. For children's picture books, we only want author/illustrator projects. Submit a pdf with full text and at least 5-7 full-color illustrations. Accepts simultaneous submissions. Responds if interested in 2-3 weeks to queries.

## WM CLARK ASSOCIATES

54 W. 21st St., Suite 809, New York NY 10010. (212)675-2784. **E-mail:** general@wmclark.com. **Website:** www.wmclark.com. **Contact:** William Clark. Estab. 1997. Member of AAR. Member, Board of Directors, Association of American Literary Agents; Director, Literary Agents of Change.

**REPRESENTS** Nonfiction, novels. **Considers these nonfiction areas:** architecture, art, autobiography, biography, creative nonfiction, cultural interests, current affairs, dance, design, economics, ethnic, film, foods, history, inspirational, interior design, literature, memoirs, music, popular culture, politics, religious, science, sociology, technology, theater, translation, travel. **Considers these fiction areas:** historical, literary.

☞ Agency does not represent screenplays or respond to screenplay pitches.

**HOW TO CONTACT** Accepts queries via online query form only. "We will endeavor to respond as soon as possible as to whether or not we'd like to see a proposal or sample chapters from your manuscript." Responds in 1-2 months to queries.

**TERMS** Agent receives 15% commission on domestic sales; 20% commission on foreign sales. Offers written contract.

**WRITERS CONFERENCES** London Book Fair, Frankfurt Book Fair.

## FRANCES COLLIN, LITERARY AGENT

Sarah Yake, Literary Agent, P.O. Box 33, Wayne PA 19087-0033. **E-mail:** queries@francescollin.com. **Website:** www.francescollin.com. Estab. 1948. Member of AAR. Represents 50 clients.

**REPRESENTS** Nonfiction, fiction, novels, short story collections. **Considers these nonfiction areas:** architecture, art, autobiography, biography, creative nonfiction, cultural interests, dance, environment, history, literature, memoirs, popular culture, science, sociology, travel, women's issues, women's studies. **Considers these fiction areas:** adventure, commer-

cial, experimental, feminist, gay, historical, juvenile, literary, middle grade, multicultural, science fiction, short story collections, women's, young adult.

☞ Actively seeking authors who are invested in their unique visions and who want to set trends not chase them. "I'd like to think that my authors are unplagiarizable by virtue of their distinct voices and styles." Does not want previously self-published work. Query with new mss only, please.

**HOW TO CONTACT** "We periodically close to queries, so please check our Publishers Marketplace account or other social media accounts before querying. When we are open to queries, we ask that writers send a traditional query e-mail describing the project and copy and paste the first 5 pages of the manuscript into the body of the e-mail. We look forward to hearing from you at queries@francescollin.com. Please send queries to that e-mail address. Any queries sent to another e-mail address within the agency will be deleted unread." Accepts simultaneous submissions. Responds in 1-4 weeks for initial queries, longer for full mss.

## ⊘ COMPASS TALENT

729 7th Ave., New York NY 10019. (646)822-4691. **Website:** www.compasstalent.com. **Contact:** Heather Schroder. Member of AAR. Signatory of WGA.

**REPRESENTS Considers these nonfiction areas:** cooking, creative nonfiction, foods, memoirs. **Considers these fiction areas:** commercial, literary, mainstream.

**HOW TO CONTACT** This agency is currently closed to unsolicited submissions. Accepts simultaneous submissions.

**RECENT SALES** A full list of agency clients is available on the website.

## DON CONGDON ASSOCIATES INC.

110 William St., Suite 2202, New York NY 10038. (212)645-1229. **Fax:** (212)727-2688. **E-mail:** dca@doncongdon.com. **Website:** doncongdon.com. Estab. 1983. Member of AAR.

**MEMBER AGENTS** Cristina Concepcion (crime fiction, narrative nonfiction, political science, journalism, history, books on cities, classical music, biography, science for a popular audience, philosophy, food and wine, iconoclastic books on health and human relationships, essays, and arts criticism); Michael Congdon (commercial and literary fiction, suspense, mystery, thriller, history, military history, biography, memoir, current affairs, and narrative nonfiction [adventure, medicine, science, and nature]); Katie Grimm (literary fiction, historical, women's fiction, short story collections, graphic novels, mysteries, young adult, middle-grade, memoir, science, academic); Katie Kotchman (business [all areas], narrative nonfiction [particularly popular science and social/cultural issues], self-help, success, motivation, psychology, pop culture, women's fiction, realistic young adult, literary fiction, and psychological thrillers); Maura Kye-Casella (narrative nonfiction, cookbooks, women's fiction, young adult, self-help, and parenting); Susan Ramer (literary fiction, upmarket commercial fiction [contemporary and historical], narrative nonfiction, social history, cultural history, smart pop culture [music, film, food, art], women's issues, psychology and mental health, and memoir).

**REPRESENTS** Nonfiction, novels, short story collections. **Considers these nonfiction areas:** art, biography, business, cooking, creative nonfiction, cultural interests, current affairs, film, foods, history, humor, literature, medicine, memoirs, military, multicultural, music, parenting, philosophy, popular culture, politics, psychology, science, self-help, sociology, sports, women's issues, young adult. **Considers these fiction areas:** crime, hi-lo, historical, literary, middle grade, mystery, short story collections, suspense, thriller, women's, young adult.

☛ Susan Ramer: "Not looking for romance, science fiction, fantasy, espionage, mysteries, politics, health/diet/fitness, self-help, or sports." Katie Kotchman: "Please do not send her screenplays or poetry."

**HOW TO CONTACT** "We are currently accepting queries from new and established authors via email only. A query letter consists of a one-page description or synopsis of your work and your relevant background information. We ask that you paste the first chapter into the body of your email following your query letter. We do not accept unsolicited manuscripts. Due to the volume of queries we receive, we regret that we are unable to reply to each one. We will only respond if we are requesting additional material. You must include the word "Query" and the agent's full name in your subject heading. Please include your query, sample chapter, your full name, and complete email address in the body of the email, as we do not open unsolicited attachments for security reasons.

Please query only one agent within the agency at a time. For a listing of specific agent interests, please see our Agents section." Accepts simultaneous submissions.

**RECENT SALES** This agency represents many bestselling clients such as David Sedaris and Kathryn Stockett.

## ○⊘ COOKE MCDERMID LITERARY MANAGEMENT

320 Front St. W., Suite 1105, Toronto ON M5V 3B6 Canada. (647)788-4010. **E-mail:** info@cookemcdermid.com. **Website:** www.mcdermidagency.com. **Contact:** Anne McDermid. Estab. 1996.

**MEMBER AGENTS** Anne McDermid; Martha Webb; Dean Cooke; Sally Harding; Suzanne Brandreth; Ron Eckel; Rachel Letofsky; Stephanie Sinclair; Paige Sisley.

**REPRESENTS** Novels.

☛ The agency represents literary novelists and commercial novelists of high quality, and also writers of nonfiction in the areas of memoir, biography, history, literary travel, narrative science, and investigative journalism. "We also represent a certain number of children's and YA writers and writers in the fields of science fiction and fantasy."

**HOW TO CONTACT** Query via e-mail or mail with a brief bio, description, and first 5 pages of project only. Accepts simultaneous submissions. *No unsolicited manuscripts.* Obtains most new clients through recommendations from others.

## THE DOE COOVER AGENCY

P.O. Box 668, Winchester MA 01890. (781)721-6000. **Fax:** (781)721-6727. **E-mail:** info@doecooveragency.com. **Website:** www.doecooveragency.com. Represents 150+ clients.

**MEMBER AGENTS** Doe Coover (general nonfiction, including business, cooking/food writing, history, biography, health, and science); Colleen Mohyde (literary fiction and commercial fiction, general nonfiction).

**REPRESENTS** Nonfiction, novels. **Considers these nonfiction areas:** creative nonfiction. **Considers these fiction areas:** commercial, literary.

☛ The agency specializes in narrative nonfiction, particularly biography, business, cooking and food writing, health, history, popular science, social issues, gardening, and humor; literary and commercial fiction. The agency does not represent poetry, screenplays, romance, fantasy, science fiction, or unsolicited children's books.

**HOW TO CONTACT** Accepts queries by e-mail only. Check website for submission guidelines. No unsolicited mss. Accepts simultaneous submissions. Responds within 6 weeks. Responds only if additional material is required. Obtains most new clients through solicitation and recommendation.

**TERMS** Agent receives 15% commission on domestic sales, 10% of original advance commission on foreign sales. No reading fees.

**RECENT SALES** *Lessons from a Grandfather* by Jacques Pépin (Houghton Mifflin Harcourt), *Lift Off* by Donovan Livingston (Speigel & Grau), *World Food* by James Oseland (Ten Speed Press), *Biography of Garry Trudeau* by Steven Weinberg (St. Martin's Press), *A Welcome Murder* by Robin Yocum (Prometheus Books).

## CREATIVE MEDIA AGENCY, INC.

(212)812-1494. **E-mail:** paige@cmalit.com. **Website:** www.cmalit.com. **Contact:** Paige Wheeler. Estab. 1997. Member of AAR, WMG, RWA, MWA, Authors Guild, AALA, Agents Roundtable. Represents about 30 clients.

After starting out as an editor for Harlequin Books in NY and Euromoney Publications in London, Paige repped writers, producers, and celebrities as an agent with Artists Agency, until she formed Creative Media Agency in 1997. In 2006 she co-created Folio Literary Management and grew that company for 8 years into a successful mid-sized agency. In 2014 she decided to once again pursue a boutique approach, and she relaunched CMA.

**REPRESENTS** Nonfiction, fiction, novels, juvenile books. **Considers these nonfiction areas:** biography, business, child guidance, creative nonfiction, decorating, diet/nutrition, health, inspirational, interior design, memoirs, money, parenting, popular culture, self-help, travel, women's issues, young adult, prescriptive nonfiction, narrative nonfiction, some memoir. **Considers these fiction areas:** commercial, crime, detective, ethnic, historical, inspirational, juvenile, literary, mainstream, middle grade, mystery, new adult, New Age, romance, suspense, thriller, women's, young adult, general fiction.

Fiction: All commercial and upscale (think book club) fiction, as well as women's fiction, romance (all types), mystery, thrillers, inspirational/Christian and psychological suspense. I enjoy both historical fiction as well as contemporary fiction, so do keep that in mind. I seem to be especially drawn to a story if it has a high concept and a fresh, unique voice. Nonfiction: I'm looking for both narrative nonfiction and prescriptive nonfiction. I'm looking for books where the author has a huge platform and something new to say in a particular area. Some of the areas that I like are lifestyle, relationship, parenting, business/entrepreneurship, food-subsistence-homesteading topics, wish fulfillment memoir, popular/trendy reference projects and women's issues. I'd like books that would could be a Hello Sunshine Book Club pick. Does not want to receive children's picture books, science fiction, fantasy, poetry or academic nonfiction.

**HOW TO CONTACT** E-query. Write "query" in your e-mail subject line. For fiction, paste in the first 5 pages of the ms after the query. For nonfiction, paste in an extended author bio as well as the marketing section of your book proposal after the query. Accepts simultaneous submissions. Responds in 4-6 weeks.

## RICHARD CURTIS ASSOCIATES, INC.

200 E. 72nd St., Suite 28J, New York NY 10021. (212)772-7363. **Website:** www.curtisagency.com. Member of AAR, RWA, MWA, ITW, SFWA. Represents 100 clients.

Prior to becoming an agent, Mr. Curtis authored blogs, articles, and books on the publishing business and help for authors.

**REPRESENTS** Nonfiction, fiction, novels, juvenile books. **Considers these nonfiction areas:** biography, business, current affairs, dance, gay/lesbian, health, history, how-to, investigative, literature, military, music, politics, psychology, science, sports, theater, true crime, war, women's issues, young adult. **Considers these fiction areas:** adventure, commercial, fantasy, romance, science fiction, suspense, thriller, translation, women's, young adult.

Actively seeking nonfiction (but no memoir), women's fiction (especially contemporary), thrillers, science fiction, middle-grade, and young adult. Does not want screenplays.

**HOW TO CONTACT** Use submission procedure on website. "We also read one-page query letters accompanied by SASE." Accepts simultaneous submissions.

**TERMS** Agent receives 15% commission on domestic sales; 25% commission on foreign sales. Offers written contract. Charges for photocopying, express mail, international freight, book orders.

**RECENT SALES** Sold 50 titles in the last year, including *Safecracker*, by Dave McOmie; Champions series, by Janet Dailey; and *Taking Mr. Exxon*, by Philip Jett.

## D4EO LITERARY AGENCY

7 Indian Valley Rd., Weston CT 06883. (203)544-7180. **Fax:** (203)544-7160. **Website:** www.d4eoliteraryagency.com. **Contact:** Bob Diforio. Estab. 1990.

○ Prior to opening his agency, Mr. Diforio was a publisher.

**MEMBER AGENTS** Bob Diforio; Joyce Holland; Pam Pho; Julie Dinneen; Katelyn Uplinger; Megan Manzano; Mariah Nichols; Vanessa Campos; Julie Dinnesen.

**REPRESENTS** Nonfiction, novels. **Considers these nonfiction areas:** biography, business, health, history, humor, money, psychology, science, sports. **Considers these fiction areas:** adventure, detective, erotica, juvenile, literary, mainstream, middle grade, mystery, new adult, romance, sports, thriller, young adult.

**HOW TO CONTACT** Each of these agents has a different submission e-mail and different tastes regarding how they review material. See all on their individual agent pages on the agency website. Responds in 1 week to queries if interested. Obtains most new clients through recommendations from others.

**TERMS** Offers written contract, binding for 2 years; automatic renewal unless 60 days notice given prior to renewal date. Charges for photocopying and submission postage.

## LAURA DAIL LITERARY AGENCY, INC.

121 W. 27th St., Suite 1201, New York NY 10001. (212)239-7477. **Website:** www.ldlainc.com. Member of AAR.

**MEMBER AGENTS** Laura Dail; Carrie Pestritto; Elana Roth Parker.

**REPRESENTS** Nonfiction, fiction, novels, juvenile books. **Considers these nonfiction areas:** biography, cooking, creative nonfiction, current affairs, government, history, investigative, juvenile nonfic-

tion, memoirs, multicultural, popular culture, politics, psychology, sociology, true crime, war, women's studies, young adult. **Considers these fiction areas:** commercial, contemporary issues, crime, detective, ethnic, fantasy, feminist, gay, historical, juvenile, lesbian, mainstream, middle grade, multicultural, mystery, picture books, thriller, women's, young adult.

☛ Specializes in women's fiction, literary fiction, young adult fiction, as well as both practical and idea-driven nonfiction. "Due to the volume of queries and mss received, we apologize for not answering every e-mail and letter. None of us handles children's picture books or chapter books. No New Age. We do not handle screenplays or poetry."

**HOW TO CONTACT** Accepts queries via Query Manager only. Check website for individual links. Accepts simultaneous submissions. Responds in 2-4 weeks.

## DANIEL LITERARY GROUP

601 Old Hickory Blvd., #56, Brentwood TN 37027. **E-mail:** greg@danielliterarygroup.com. **Website:** www.danielliterarygroup.com. **Contact:** Greg Daniel. Represents 45 clients.

○ Prior to becoming an agent, Mr. Daniel spent 10 years in publishing—6 at the executive level at Thomas Nelson Publishers.

**REPRESENTS** Nonfiction. **Considers these nonfiction areas:** autobiography, biography, business, child guidance, cultural interests, current affairs, economics, environment, film, health, history, how-to, humor, inspirational, medicine, memoirs, parenting, popular culture, religious, satire, self-help, spirituality, sports, theater, travel, true crime, women's issues, women's studies.

☛ "We take pride in our ability to come alongside our authors and help strategize about where they want their writing to take them in both the near and long term. Forging close relationships with our authors, we help them with such critical factors as editorial refinement, branding, audience, and marketing." The agency is no longer accepting unsolicited queries.

**HOW TO CONTACT** This agency is no longer accepting unsolicited queries.

## DARHANSOFF & VERRILL LITERARY AGENTS

529 11th St., Third Floor, Brooklyn NY 11215. (917) 305-1300. **E-mail:** submissions@dvagency.com. **Website:** www.dvagency.com. Member of AAR.

**MEMBER AGENTS** Liz Darhansoff; Chuck Verrill; Michele Mortimer; Eric Amling.

**REPRESENTS** Nonfiction, fiction, novels, short story collections. **Considers these nonfiction areas:** current affairs, gay/lesbian, history, investigative, juvenile nonfiction, literature, memoirs, money, multicultural, science, true crime. **Considers these fiction areas:** crime, literary, thriller.

☛ "We are readers of literary fiction, narrative nonfiction, memoir, contemporary young adult, graphic novels, and all manner of crime and mystery. Our nonfiction interests range from art and design to food and cooking to yoga and mindfulness to animal welfare and environmental causes to feminism and progressive causes. While we lean into dystopian and speculative fiction, we rarely match up to fantasy, science fiction, or paranormal work."

**HOW TO CONTACT** Please see our website for submission guidelines. Accepts simultaneous submissions. If we are interested in reading your work, we will be in touch. If you have not heard from us within 6-8 weeks, it is safe to assume that we have passed on the opportunity. We are currently pursuing new talent to add to our roster.

## LIZA DAWSON ASSOCIATES

121 W. 27th St., Suite 1201, New York NY 10001. (212)465-9071. **Website:** www.lizadawsonassociates.com. **Contact:** Caitie Flum. Member of AAR, MWA, Women's Media Group. Represents 50+ clients.

💬 Prior to becoming an agent, Ms. Dawson was an editor for 20 years, spending 11 years at William Morrow as vice president and 2 years at Putnam as executive editor. Ms. Blasdell was a senior editor at HarperCollins and Avon. Ms. Johnson-Blalock was an assistant at Trident Media Group. Ms. Flum was the coordinator for the Children's Book of the Month club.

**MEMBER AGENTS** Liza Dawson, queryliza@lizadawsonassociates.com (plot-driven literary and popular fiction, historical, thrillers, suspense, history, psychology [both popular and clinical], politics, narrative nonfiction, and memoirs); Caitlin Blasdell,

querycaitlin@lizadawsonassociates.com (science fiction, fantasy [both adult and young adult], parenting, business, thrillers, and women's fiction); Hannah Bowman, queryhannah@lizadawsonassociates.com (commercial fiction [especially science fiction and fantasy, young adult] and nonfiction in the areas of mathematics, science, and spirituality); Caitie Flum, querycaitie@lizadawsonassociates.com (commercial fiction, especially historical, women's fiction, mysteries, crossover fantasy, young adult, and middle-grade; nonfiction in the areas of theater, current affairs, and pop culture); Rachel Beck, queryrachel@lizadawson.com; Tom Miller, querytom@lizadawson.com.

**REPRESENTS** Nonfiction, novels. **Considers these nonfiction areas:** agriculture, Americana, animals, anthropology, archeology, architecture, art, autobiography, biography, business, computers, cooking, creative nonfiction, cultural interests, current affairs, environment, ethnic, film, gardening, gay/lesbian, history, humor, investigative, juvenile nonfiction, memoirs, multicultural, parenting, popular culture, politics, psychology, religious, science, sex, sociology, spirituality, theater, travel, true crime, women's issues, women's studies, young adult. **Considers these fiction areas:** action, adventure, commercial, contemporary issues, crime, detective, ethnic, family saga, fantasy, feminist, gay, historical, horror, humor, juvenile, lesbian, mainstream, middle grade, multicultural, mystery, new adult, police, romance, science fiction, supernatural, suspense, thriller, urban fantasy, women's, young adult.

☛ This agency specializes in readable literary fiction, thrillers, mainstream historicals, women's fiction, young adult, middle-grade, academics, historians, journalists, and psychology.

**HOW TO CONTACT** Query by e-mail only. No phone calls. Each of these agents has their own specific submission requirements, which you can find online at the agency's website. Obtains most new clients through recommendations from others, conferences, and queries.

**TERMS** Agent receives 15% commission on domestic sales; 20% commission on foreign sales. Offers written contract.

## THE JENNIFER DE CHIARA LITERARY AGENCY

245 Park Ave., 39th Floor, New York NY 10167. (212) 372-8989. **E-mail:** jenndec@aol.com. **Website:** www.jdlit.com. **Contact:** Jennifer De Chiara. Estab. 2001.

**MEMBER AGENTS** Jennifer De Chiara, Stephen Fraser, Marie Lamba, Roseanne Wells, Savannah Brooks, Erin Clyburn, Megan Barnard, Marlo Berliner, Zabe Ellor, Tara Gilbert, Amy Giuffrida, Stefanie Molina, Tori Sharp.

**REPRESENTS** Nonfiction, fiction, novels, juvenile books. **Considers these nonfiction areas:** art, autobiography, biography, child guidance, cooking, creative nonfiction, cultural interests, current affairs, dance, decorating, diet/nutrition, education, environment, film, foods, gay/lesbian, government, health, history, humor, investigative, juvenile nonfiction, literature, memoirs, multicultural, music, parenting, philosophy, popular culture, politics, psychology, religious, science, self-help, sex, spirituality, sports, technology, theater, travel, true crime, war, women's issues, women's studies, young adult. **Considers these fiction areas:** commercial, contemporary issues, crime, ethnic, family saga, fantasy, feminist, gay, historical, horror, humor, inspirational, juvenile, lesbian, literary, mainstream, middle grade, multicultural, mystery, new adult, New Age, paranormal, picture books, science fiction, suspense, thriller, urban fantasy, women's, young adult.

**HOW TO CONTACT** Each agent has their own e-mail submission address and submission instructions; check the website for the current updates, as policies do change. Only query one agent at a time. Accepts simultaneous submissions. Obtains most new clients through recommendations from others, conferences, query letters.

**TERMS** Agent receives 15% commission on domestic sales. Offers written contract.

**RECENT SALES** Middle-Grade Fiction: *The Lost Language* by Claudia Mills (Holiday House); Children's Graphic Novel: *Vampires Don't Wear Polka Dots* and *Frankenstein Doesn't Plant Petunias* by Debbie Dadey and Marcia Thornton Jones (Graphix, Scholastic); Children's Graphic Novel: *The Secret of the Ravens* by Joanna Cacao (Etch, Houghton Mifflin Harcourt); Middle-Grade Fiction: *Frances and the Monster* by Refe Tuma (Harper Children's); Young Adult Fiction: *The Other Side of the Tracks* by Charity Alyse (Denene Millner Books, Simon & Schuster); Adult Fiction/Mystery/Crime: *The Department of Rare Books and Special Collections* by Eva Jurczyk (Sourcebooks); Young Adult Graphic Novel: *Trans History: A Graphic Novel* by Alex Combs (Candlewick); Nonfic-

tion Pop Culture: *The Definitive Golden Girls Reference Guide* by Matt Browning (Rowman & Littlefield); Young Adult Fiction: *White Rose* by Kip Wilson (Versify, Houghton Mifflin Harcourt); Young Adult Fiction: *It Will End Like This* by Kyra Leigh (Delacorte); Children's Picture Book: *The Fog Catcher's Daughter* by Marianne McShane (Candlewick); Children's Picture Book: *How to Ride a Dragonfly* by Kitty Donohoe (Schwartz & Wade); Celebrity Memoir: *My West Side Story* by George Chakiris (Rowman & Littlefield); Celebrity Memoir: *Nothing General About It: How Love (and Lithium) Saved Me On and Off General Hospital* by Maurice Benard (HarperCollins); Nonfiction Cookbook: *Botanical* by Thalia Ho (Harper Design).

## DEFIORE & COMPANY

47 E. 19th St., 3rd Floor, New York NY 10003. (212)925-7744. **Fax:** (212)925-9803. **E-mail:** info@defliterary.com, submissions@defliterary.com. **Website:** www.defliterary.com. Member of AAR. Signatory of WGA.

○ Prior to becoming an agent, Mr. DeFiore was publisher of Villard Books (1997-1998), editor-in-chief of Hyperion (1992-1997), editorial director of Delacorte Press (1988-1992), and an editor at St. Martin's Press (1984-88).

**MEMBER AGENTS** Brian DeFiore (popular nonfiction, business, pop culture, parenting, commercial fiction); Laurie Abkemeier (memoir, parenting, business, how-to/self-help, popular science); Matthew Elblonk (young adult, popular culture, narrative nonfiction); Caryn Karmatz-Rudy (popular fiction, self-help, narrative nonfiction); Adam Schear (commercial fiction, humor, young adult, smart thrillers, historical fiction, quirky debut literary novels, popular science, politics, popular culture, current events); Meredith Kaffel Simonoff (smart upmarket women's fiction, literary fiction [especially debut], literary thrillers, narrative nonfiction, nonfiction about science and tech, sophisticated pop culture/humor books); Rebecca Strauss (literary and commercial fiction, women's fiction, urban fantasy, romance, mystery, young adult, memoir, pop culture, select nonfiction); Lisa Gallagher (fiction and nonfiction); Miriam Altshuler (adult literary and commercial fiction, narrative nonfiction, middle-grade, young adult, memoir, narrative nonfiction, self-help, family sagas, historical novels); Reiko Davis (adult literary and upmarket fiction, narrative nonfiction, young adult, middle-grade, memoir); Linda

Kaplan; Chris Park; Tanusri Prasanna; Parik Kostan; Emma Haviland-Blunk.

**REPRESENTS** Nonfiction, novels, short story collections, juvenile books, poetry books. **Considers these nonfiction areas:** autobiography, biography, business, child guidance, cooking, economics, foods, gay/lesbian, how-to, inspirational, money, multicultural, parenting, photography, popular culture, politics, psychology, religious, science, self-help, sex, sports, technology, travel, women's issues, young adult. **Considers these fiction areas:** comic books, commercial, ethnic, feminist, gay, lesbian, literary, mainstream, middle grade, mystery, paranormal, picture books, poetry, romance, short story collections, suspense, thriller, urban fantasy, women's, young adult.

☞ "Please be advised that we are not considering dramatic projects at this time."

**HOW TO CONTACT** Query with SASE or e-mail to submissions@defliterary.com. "Please include the word 'query' in the subject line. All attachments will be deleted; please insert all text in the body of the e-mail. For more information about our agents, their individual interests, and their query guidelines, please visit our 'About Us' page on our website." Accepts simultaneous submissions. Obtains most new clients through recommendations from others.

**TERMS** Agent receives 15% commission on domestic sales; 20% commission on foreign sales. Offers written contract; 10-day notice must be given to terminate contract. Charges clients for photocopying and overnight delivery (deducted only after a sale is made).

## JOELLE DELBOURGO ASSOCIATES, INC.

101 Park St., Montclair NJ 07042. (973)773-0836. **E-mail:** joelle@delbourgo.com. **E-mail:** submissions@delbourgo.com. **Website:** www.delbourgo.com. **Contact:** Joelle Delbourgo. Estab. 1999. Member of AAR. Represents more than 500 clients.

○ Prior to becoming an agent, Ms. Delbourgo was an editor and senior publishing executive at HarperCollins and Random House. She began her editorial career at Bantam Books where she discovered the Choose Your Own Adventure series. Joelle Delbourgo brings more than three decades of experience as an editor and agent. Prior to joining the agency, Jacqueline Flynn was Executive Editor at Amacom for more than 15 years.

**MEMBER AGENTS** Joelle Delbourgo; Jacqueline Flynn.

**REPRESENTS** Nonfiction, fiction, novels. **Considers these nonfiction areas:** Americana, animals, anthropology, archeology, autobiography, biography, business, child guidance, cooking, creative nonfiction, current affairs, dance, decorating, diet/nutrition, design, economics, education, environment, film, gardening, gay/lesbian, government, health, history, how-to, humor, inspirational, interior design, investigative, juvenile nonfiction, literature, medicine, memoirs, military, money, multicultural, music, parenting, philosophy, popular culture, politics, psychology, science, self-help, sex, sociology, spirituality, sports, translation, travel, true crime, war, women's issues, women's studies, young adult. **Considers these fiction areas:** adventure, commercial, contemporary issues, crime, detective, fantasy, feminist, juvenile, literary, mainstream, middle grade, military, mystery, new adult, New Age, romance, science fiction, thriller, urban fantasy, women's, young adult.

☞ "We are former publishers and editors with deep knowledge and an insider perspective. We have a reputation for individualized attention to clients, strategic management of authors' careers, and creating strong partnerships with publishers for our clients." We are looking for strong narrative and prescriptive nonfiction including science, history, health and medicine, business and finance, sociology, parenting, women's issues. We prefer books by credentialed experts and seasoned journalists, especially ones that are research-based. We are taking on very few memoir projects. In fiction, you can send mystery and thriller, commercial women's fiction, book club fiction and literary fiction. Do not send scripts, picture books, poetry.

**HOW TO CONTACT** E-mail queries only are accepted. Query one agent directly, not multiple agents at our agency. No attachments. Put the word "Query" in the subject line. If you have not received a response in 60 days you may consider that a pass. Do not send us copies of self-published books. For nonfiction, send your query only once you have a completed proposal. For fiction and memoir, embed the first 10 pages of ms into the e-mail after your query letter. Please no attachments. If we like your first pages, we may ask to see your synopsis and more manuscript. Accepts simultaneous submissions. Our clients come via referral, and occasionally over the transom.

**TERMS** Agent receives 15% commission on domestic sales and 20% commission on foreign sales as well as television/film adaptation when a co-agent is involved. Offers written contract. Standard industry commissions. Charges clients for postage and photocopying.

**RECENT SALES** *Big Time,* Ben H. Winters (Mulholland); *Enslaved: The Sunken History of the Transatlantic Slave Trade*, Simcha Jacobovici and Sean Kinglsey (Pegasus); *Reclaiming Body Trust*, Hilary Kinavey and Dana Sturtevant (TarcherPerigee); *Crazy to Leave You*, Marilyn Simon Rothstein (Lake Union); *We Share the Same Sky*, Rachael Cerrotti (Blackstone); *Julian,* Philip Freeman (Yale University Press); *Go Big Now,* Julia Pimsleur (New World Library); *The Rule of St. Benedict*, Philip Freeman (St. Martins Essentials).

**WRITERS CONFERENCES** Jewish Writer's Conference (sponsored by the Jewish Book Council).

**TIPS** "Do your homework. Do not cold call. Read and follow submission guidelines before contacting us. Do not call to find out if we received your material. No e-mail queries. Treat agents with respect, as you would any other professional, such as a doctor, lawyer or financial advisor."

## SANDRA DIJKSTRA LITERARY AGENCY

1155 Camino del Mar, PMB 515, Del Mar CA 92014. **E-mail:** queries@dijkstraagency.com. **Website:** www.dijkstraagency.com. Member of AAR, Authors Guild, Organization of American Historians, RWA. Represents 200+ clients.

**MEMBER AGENTS** President: Sandra Dijkstra (adult only). Acquiring associate agents: Elise Capron (adult only); Jill Marr (adult only); Thao Le (adult and YA); Jessica Watterson (subgenres of adult romance, and women's fiction); Suzy Evans (adult and YA); Jennifer Kim (adult and YA).

**REPRESENTS** Nonfiction, fiction, novels, short story collections, juvenile books, scholarly books. **Considers these nonfiction areas:** Americana, animals, anthropology, art, biography, business, creative nonfiction, cultural interests, current affairs, design, economics, environment, ethnic, gardening, government, health, history, juvenile nonfiction, literature, memoirs, multicultural, parenting, popular culture, politics, psychology, science, self-help, sports, true crime, women's issues, women's studies, young adult, narrative. **Considers these fiction areas:** commercial,

contemporary issues, detective, family saga, fantasy, feminist, historical, horror, juvenile, literary, mainstream, middle grade, multicultural, mystery, new adult, romance, science fiction, short story collections, sports, suspense, thriller, urban fantasy, women's, young adult.

**HOW TO CONTACT** "Please see guidelines on our website, www.dijkstraagency.com. Please note that we only accept e-mail submissions. Due to the large number of unsolicited submissions we receive, we are only able to respond to those submissions in which we are interested." Accepts simultaneous submissions. Responds to queries of interest within 6 weeks.

**TERMS** Works in conjunction with foreign and film agents. Agent receives 15% commission on domestic sales and 20% commission on foreign sales. Offers written contract. No reading fee.

**TIPS** "Remember that publishing is a business. Do your research and present your project in as professional a way as possible. Only submit your work when you are confident that it is polished and ready for prime-time. Make yourself a part of the active writing community by getting stories and articles published, networking with other writers, and getting a good sense of where your work fits in the market."

## DONAGHY LITERARY GROUP

(647)527-4353. **E-mail:** stacey@donaghyliterary.com. **Website:** www.donaghyliterary.com. **Contact:** Stacey Donaghy.

Prior to opening her agency, Ms. Donaghy served as an agent at the Corvisiero Literary Agency. And before this, she worked in training and education; acquiring and editing academic materials for publication and training. Ms. Noble interned for Jessica Sinsheimer of Sarah Jane Freymann Literary Agency. Ms. Miller previously worked in children's publishing with Scholastic Canada and also interned with Bree Ogden during her time at the D4EO Agency.

**MEMBER AGENTS** Stacey Donaghy (women's fiction, LGBTQ, diverse and #OwnVoices, psychological thrillers, domestic suspense, contemporary romance, and YA); Valerie Noble (historical, science fiction and fantasy [think Kristin Cashore and Suzanne Collins] for young adults and adults); Sue Miller (YA, urban fantasy, contemporary romance).

**REPRESENTS** Fiction, novels, juvenile books. **Considers these fiction areas:** commercial, contemporary issues, crime, ethnic, family saga, fantasy, feminist, gay, historical, horror, juvenile, lesbian, literary, mainstream, middle grade, multicultural, mystery, paranormal, psychic, romance, science fiction, sports, supernatural, suspense, thriller, urban fantasy, women's, young adult.

**HOW TO CONTACT** Visit agency website for "new submission guidelines." Do not e-mail agents directly. This agency only accepts submissions through the QueryManager database system. Accepts simultaneous submissions. Time may vary depending on the volume of submissions.

**TERMS** Agent receives 15% commission on domestic sales; 20% commission on foreign sales. Offers written contract, 30-day notice must be given to terminate contract.

**WRITERS CONFERENCES** Romantic Times Booklovers Convention, Windsor International Writers Conference, OWC Ontario Writers Conference, SoCal Writers Conference, WD Toronto Writer's Conference.

**TIPS** "Only submit to one DLG agent at a time, we work collaboratively and often share projects that may be better suited to another agent at the agency."

### JIM DONOVAN LITERARY

5635 SMU Blvd., Suite 201, Dallas TX 75206. **E-mail:** jdliterary@sbcglobal.net. **Website:** www.jimdonovanliterary.com. **Contact:** Melissa Shultz, agent. Estab. 1993. Signatory of WGA. Represents 34 clients.

○ I was a bookstore assistant manager for a few years, then a bookstore chain buyer for four years, then a book editor for four years.

**MEMBER AGENTS** Jim Donovan (history—particularly American, military and Western; biography; sports; popular reference; popular culture; fiction—literary, thrillers and mystery); Melissa Shultz (all subjects listed above [like Jim], along with parenting and women's issues).

**REPRESENTS** Nonfiction, fiction, novels. **Considers these nonfiction areas:** biography, current affairs, health, history, investigative, literature, military, parenting, popular culture, science, sports, war, women's issues. **Considers these fiction areas:** action, adventure, commercial, crime, detective, frontier, historical, mainstream, multicultural, mystery, police, suspense, thriller, war, westerns.

○— This agency specializes in commercial fiction and nonfiction. "Does not want to receive poetry, children's, sci-fi, fantasy, short stories, memoir, inspirational or anything else not listed above."

**HOW TO CONTACT** "For nonfiction, I need a well-thought-out query letter telling me about the book: What it does, how it does it, why it's needed now, why it's better or different than what's out there on the subject, and why the author is the perfect writer for it. For fiction, the novel has to be finished, of course; a short (2- to 5-page) synopsis—not a teaser, but a summary of all the action, from first page to last—and the first 30-50 pages is enough. This material should be polished to as close to perfection as possible." Accepts simultaneous submissions. Responds in 2 weeks to queries; 1 month to mss. Obtains most new clients through recommendations from others.

**TERMS** Agent receives 15% commission on domestic sales. Agent receives 20% commission on foreign sales. Offers written contract, binding for 1 year; 30-day notice must be given to terminate contract. This agency charges for things such as overnight delivery and manuscript copying. Charges are discussed beforehand.

**RECENT SALES** *The Undiscovered Country*, by Paul Andrew Hutton; *The Road to Jonestown*, by Jeff Guinn (S&S); *The Earth Is All That Lasts*, by Mark Gardner (HarperCollins); *As Good as Dead*, by Stephen Moore (NAL); *James Monroe*, by Tim McGrath (NAL); *The Greatest Fury*, by William C. Davis (NAL); *Rogues' Gallery*, by John Oller (Dutton); *The Hamilton Affair*, by Elizabeth Cobbs (Arcade); *Resurrection Pass*, by Kurt Anderson (Kensington).

**TIPS** "Get published in short form—magazine reviews, journals, etc.—first. This will increase your credibility considerably, and make it much easier to sell a full-length book."

### DUNHAM LITERARY, INC.

487 Hardscrabble Road, North Salem NY 10560. **E-mail:** query@dunhamlit.com. **Website:** www.dunhamlit.com. **Contact:** Jennie Dunham. Estab. 2000. Member of AAR, SCBWI. Represents 50 clients.

○ Prior to opening her agency, Ms. Dunham worked as a literary agent for Russell & Volkening. The Rhoda Weyr Agency is now a division of Dunham Literary, Inc.

**MEMBER AGENTS** Jennie Dunham, Leslie Zampetti.

**REPRESENTS** Nonfiction, fiction, novels, short story collections, juvenile books. **Considers these nonfiction areas:** anthropology, art, biography, creative nonfiction, cultural interests, environment, gay/lesbian, health, history, language, literature, medicine, memoirs, multicultural, parenting, popular culture, politics, psychology, science, sociology, technology, women's issues, women's studies, young adult. **Considers these fiction areas:** family saga, fantasy, feminist, gay, historical, humor, juvenile, lesbian, literary, mainstream, middle grade, multicultural, mystery, picture books, science fiction, short story collections, sports, urban fantasy, women's, young adult.

☛ "We are not looking for Westerns, genre romance, poetry, or individual short stories."

**HOW TO CONTACT** We accept queries by email only.

☛ Please include a brief description of the project, brief author bio, and the first 5 pages with the query.

☛ Attachments will not be opened.

☛ Paper queries NOT accepted. Accepts simultaneous submissions. Responds in 4 weeks to queries; 3 months to mss. Obtains most new clients through recommendations from others.

**TERMS** Agent receives 15% commission on domestic sales; 20% commission on foreign sales.

**RECENT SALES** The Bad Kitty series, by Nick Bruel (Macmillan); *Believe*, by Robert Sabuda (Candlewick); *The Gollywhopper Games* and sequels, by Jody Feldman (HarperCollins); *Show Me a Sign* by Ann LeZotte, *The Low Desert*, by Tod Goldberg (Counterpoint).

## DUNOW, CARLSON, & LERNER AGENCY

27 W. 20th St., Suite 1107, New York NY 10011. (212)645-7606. **E-mail:** mail@dclagency.com. **Website:** www.dclagency.com. Member of AAR.

**MEMBER AGENTS** Jennifer Carlson (narrative nonfiction writers and journalists covering current events and ideas and cultural history, as well as literary and upmarket commercial novelists); Henry Dunow (quality fiction—literary, historical, strongly written commercial—and with voice-driven nonfiction across a range of areas—narrative history, biography, memoir, current affairs, cultural trends and criticism, science, sports); Betsy Lerner (nonfiction

writers in the areas of psychology, history, cultural studies, biography, current events, business; fiction: literary, dark, funny, voice driven); Yishai Seidman (broad range of fiction: literary, postmodern, and thrillers; nonfiction: sports, music, and pop culture); Amy Hughes (nonfiction in the areas of history, cultural studies, memoir, current events, wellness, health, food, pop culture, and biography; also literary fiction); Eleanor Jackson (literary, commercial, memoir, art, food, science and history); Julia Kenny (fiction—adult, middle grade and YA—and is especially interested in dark, literary thrillers and suspense); Edward Necarsulmer IV (strong new voices in teen & middle grade as well as picture books); Stacia Decker; Rachel Vogel (nonfiction, including photography, humor, pop culture, history, memoir, investigative journalism, current events, science, and more); Arielle Datz (fiction—adult, YA, or middle-grade—literary and commercial, nonfiction—essays, unconventional memoir, pop culture, and sociology).

**REPRESENTS** Nonfiction, fiction, novels, short story collections. **Considers these nonfiction areas:** art, biography, creative nonfiction, cultural interests, current affairs, foods, health, history, memoirs, music, popular culture, psychology, science, sociology, sports. **Considers these fiction areas:** commercial, literary, mainstream, middle grade, mystery, picture books, thriller, young adult.

**HOW TO CONTACT** Query via snail mail with SASE, or by e-mail. E-mail preferred, paste 10 sample pages below query letter. No attachments. Will respond only if interested. Accepts simultaneous submissions. Responds in 4-6 weeks if interested.

**RECENT SALES** A full list of agency clients is on the website.

## DYSTEL, GODERICH & BOURRET LLC

1 Union Square W., Suite 904, New York NY 10003. (212)627-9100. **Fax:** (212)627-9313. **Website:** www.dystel.com. Estab. 1994. Member of AAR. Other membership includes SCBWI. Represents 600+ clients.

**MEMBER AGENTS** Jane Dystel; Miriam Goderich, miriam@dystel.com (literary and commercial fiction as well as some genre fiction, narrative nonfiction, pop culture, psychology, history, science, art, business books, and biography/memoir); Stacey Glick, sglick@dystel.com (adult narrative nonfiction including memoir, parenting, cooking and food, psychology, science, health and wellness, lifestyle, current events, pop culture, YA, middle grade, children's nonfiction, and select adult contemporary fiction); Michael Bourret, mbourret@dystel.com (middle grade and young adult fiction, commercial adult fiction, and all sorts of nonfiction, from practical to narrative; he's especially interested in food and cocktail related books, memoir, popular history, politics, religion (though not spirituality), popular science, and current events); Jim McCarthy, jmccarthy@dystel.com (literary women's fiction, underrepresented voices, mysteries, romance, paranormal fiction, narrative nonfiction, memoir, and paranormal nonfiction); Jessica Papin, jpapin@dystel.com (plot-driven literary and smart commercial fiction, and narrative nonfiction across a range of subjects, including history, medicine, science, economics and women's issues); Lauren Abramo, labramo@dystel.com (humorous middle grade and contemporary YA on the children's side, and upmarket commercial fiction and well-paced literary fiction on the adult side; adult narrative nonfiction, especially pop culture, psychology, pop science, reportage, media, and contemporary culture; in nonfiction, has a strong preference for interdisciplinary approaches, and in all categories she's especially interested in underrepresented voices); John Rudolph, jrudolph@dystel.com (picture book author/illustrators, middle grade, YA, select commercial fiction, and narrative nonfiction—especially in music, sports, history, popular science, "big think," performing arts, health, business, memoir, military history, and humor); Sharon Pelletier, spelletier@dystel.com (smart commercial fiction, from upmarket women's fiction to domestic suspense to literary thrillers, and strong contemporary romance novels; compelling nonfiction projects, especially feminism and religion); Amy Bishop, abishop@dystel.com (commercial and literary women's fiction, fiction from diverse authors, historical fiction, YA, personal narratives, and biographies); Michaela Whatnall, mwatnall@dystel.com; Cat Hosch, chosch@dystel.com; Andrew Dugan, adugan@dystel.com; Melissa Melo, mmelo@dystel.com.

**REPRESENTS Considers these nonfiction areas:** animals, art, autobiography, biography, business, cooking, cultural interests, current affairs, ethnic, foods, gay/lesbian, health, history, humor, inspirational, investigative, medicine, memoirs, metaphysics, military, New Age, parenting, popular culture, politics, psychology, religious, science, sports, women's issues, women's studies. **Considers these fiction ar-**

eas: commercial, ethnic, gay, lesbian, literary, mainstream, middle grade, mystery, paranormal, romance, suspense, thriller, women's, young adult.

☛ "We are actively seeking fiction for all ages, in all genres." No plays, screenplays, or poetry.

**HOW TO CONTACT** Query via e-mail and put "Query" in the subject line. "Synopses, outlines or sample chapters (say, one chapter or the first 25 pages of your manuscript) should either be included below the cover letter or attached as a separate document. We won't open attachments if they come with a blank e-mail." Accepts simultaneous submissions. Responds in 6 to 8 weeks to queries; within 8 weeks to mss. Obtains most new clients through recommendations from others, solicitations, conferences.

**TERMS** Agent receives 15% commission on domestic sales; 19% commission on foreign sales. Offers written contract.

**WRITERS CONFERENCES** Backspace Writers' Conference, Pacific Northwest Writers' Association, Pike's Peak Writers' Conference, Writers League of Texas, Love Is Murder, Surrey International Writers Conference, Society of Children's Book Writers and Illustrators, International Thriller Writers, Willamette Writers Conference, The South Carolina Writers Workshop Conference, Las Vegas Writers Conference, Writer's Digest, Seton Hill Popular Fiction, Romance Writers of America, Geneva Writers Conference.

**TIPS** "DGLM prides itself on being a full-service agency. We're involved in every stage of the publishing process, from offering substantial editing on mss and proposals, to coming up with book ideas for authors looking for their next project, negotiating contracts and collecting monies for our clients. We follow a book from its inception through its sale to a publisher, its publication, and beyond. Our commitment to our writers does not, by any means, end when we have collected our commission. This is one of the many things that makes us unique in a very competitive business."

## EBELING & ASSOCIATES

898 Pioneer Rd., Lyons CO 80540. (303)823-6963. **E-mail:** michael@ebelingagency.com. **Website:** www.ebelingagency.com. **Contact:** Michael Ebeling. Estab. 2000. Represents 30 clients.

○ Prior to becoming an agent, Mr. Ebeling established a career in the publishing industry through long-term author management. He has expertise in sales, platform building, publicity and marketing. "Our mission at The Ebeling Agency is to work with individuals who inspire positive change in the world through their writing, speaking and vision. We are inspired to promote author's work that encourage people to find their passions and fulfill their dreams."

**REPRESENTS** Nonfiction. **Considers these nonfiction areas:** business, health, New Age, parenting, self-help, spirituality, commercial.

➤ The Ebeling Agency assists authors in building their promotional platform. Services include developing comprehensive strategies involving branding, website and e-newsletter development, speaking engagements, traditional media, social media and the latest platform-building techniques. Authors that want to use their books to spread their messages. The money is no longer in the book, it is in the author's message. We help authors build book funnels that take people from a quiz, into an e-mail sequence and ultimately to a program that is built around the author's message. Does not want to receive fiction, poetry or children's lit.

**HOW TO CONTACT** Accepts e-mail submissions and proposals only. Include a brief statement of the purpose and premise of your book, your contact information, proposal, 1-2 page description of the book, biography, promotion plan, TOC, significant aspects of your platform, introduction and 1-2 sample chapters, current status of ms, and any other relevant information. Accepts simultaneous submissions. Responds in 6-8 weeks to queries.

**RECENT SALES** A partial list of clients and recent sales is available on their website.

### EDEN STREET LITERARY

P.O. Box 30, Billings NY 12510. **E-mail:** info@edenstreetlit.com. **E-mail:** submissions@edenstreetlit.com. **Website:** www.edenstreetlit.com. **Contact:** Liza Voges. Member of AAR. Signatory of WGA. Represents over 40 clients.

**REPRESENTS** Nonfiction, fiction, novels, juvenile books. **Considers these fiction areas:** juvenile, middle grade, picture books, young adult.

**HOW TO CONTACT** E-mail a picture book ms or dummy; a synopsis and 3 chapters of a MG or YA novel; a proposal and 3 sample chapters for nonfiction. Accepts simultaneous submissions. Responds only to submissions of interest.

**RECENT SALES** *Dream Dog*, by Lou Berger; *Biscuit Loves the Library*, by Alyssa Capucilli; *The Scraps Book*, by Lois Ehlert; *Two Bunny Buddies*, by Kathryn O. Galbraith; *Between Two Worlds*, by Katherine Kirkpatrick.

### JUDITH EHRLICH LITERARY MANAGEMENT, LLC

146 Central Park W., 20E, New York NY 10023. (646)505-1570. **Fax:** (646)505-1570. **Website:** www.judithehrlichliterary.com. Estab. 2002. Member of the Author's Guild and the American Society of Journalists and Authors.

○ Prior to her current position, Ms. Ehrlich was a senior associate at the Linda Chester Agency and is an award-winning journalist; she is the co-author of *The New Crowd: The Changing of the Jewish Guard on Wall Street* (Little, Brown).

**MEMBER AGENTS** Judith Ehrlich, jehrlich@judithehrlichliterary.com (upmarket, literary and quality commercial fiction, nonfiction: narrative, women's, business, prescriptive, medical and health-related topics, history, and current events).

**REPRESENTS** Nonfiction, fiction, novels, short story collections, juvenile books. **Considers these nonfiction areas:** animals, art, autobiography, biography, business, creative nonfiction, cultural interests, current affairs, diet/nutrition, health, history, how-to, humor, inspirational, investigative, juvenile nonfiction, memoirs, parenting, photography, popular culture, politics, psychology, science, self-help, sociology, true crime, women's issues, young adult. **Considers these fiction areas:** adventure, commercial, contemporary issues, crime, detective, family saga, historical, humor, juvenile, literary, middle grade, mystery, picture books, short story collections, suspense, thriller, women's, young adult.

➤ Does not want to receive novellas, poetry, textbooks, plays, or screenplays.

**HOW TO CONTACT** E-query, with a synopsis and some sample pages. The agency will respond only if interested. Accepts simultaneous submissions.

**RECENT SALES** Fiction: *The Bicycle Spy*, by Yona Zeldis McDonough (Scholastic); *The House on Primrose Pond*, by Yona McDonough (NAL/Penguin); *You Were Meant for Me*, by Yona McDonough (NAL/Penguin); *Echoes of Us: The Hybrid Chronicles*, Book 3 by Kat Zhang (HarperCollins); *Once We Were: The Hybrid Chronicles* Book 2, by Kat Zhang (HarperCollins). Nonfiction: *Listen to the Echoes: The Ray Bradbury Interviews (Deluxe Edition)*, by Sam Weller (Hat & Beard Press); *What are The Ten Commandments?*, by Yona McDonough (Grosset & Dunlap); *Little Author in the Big Woods: A Biography of Laura Ingalls Wilder*, by Yona McDonough (Christy Ottaviano Books/Henry Holt); *Ray Bradbury: The Last Interview: And Other Conversations*, by Sam Weller (Melville House); *Who Was Sojourner Truth?*, by Yona McDonough (Grosset & Dunlap); *Power Branding: Leveraging the Success of the World's Best Brands*, by Steve McKee (Palgrave Macmillan); *Confessions of a Sociopath: A Life Spent Hiding in Plain Sight*, by M.E. Thomas (Crown); *Luck and Circumstance: A Coming of Age in Hollywood, New York, and Points Beyond*, by Michael Lindsay-Hogg (Knopf).

## EINSTEIN LITERARY MANAGEMENT

27 W. 20th St., No. 1003, New York NY 10011. (212)221-8797. **E-mail:** info@einsteinliterary.com. **E-mail:** submissions@einsteinliterary.com. **Website:** http://einsteinliterary.com. **Contact:** Susanna Einstein. Estab. 2015. Member of AAR. Signatory of WGA.

- Prior to her current position, Ms. Einstein was with LJK Literary Management and the Einstein Thompson Agency.

**MEMBER AGENTS** Susanna Einstein, Susan Graham, Paloma Hernando.

**REPRESENTS** Nonfiction, fiction, novels, short story collections, juvenile books. **Considers these nonfiction areas:** cooking, creative nonfiction, memoirs, blog-to-book projects. **Considers these fiction areas:** comic books, commercial, crime, fantasy, historical, juvenile, literary, middle grade, mystery, picture books, romance, science fiction, suspense, thriller, women's, young adult.

- "As an agency we represent a broad range of literary and commercial fiction, including upmarket women's fiction, crime fiction, historical fiction, romance, and books for middle-grade children and young adults, including picture books and graphic novels. We also handle nonfiction including cookbooks, memoir and narrative, and blog-to-book projects. Please see agent bios on the website for specific

information about what each of ELM's agents represents." Does not want poetry, textbooks, or screenplays.

**HOW TO CONTACT** Please submit a query letter and the first 10 double-spaced pages of your manuscript in the body of the e-mail (no attachments). Does not respond to mail queries or telephone queries or queries that are not specifically addressed to this agency. Accepts simultaneous submissions. Responds in 6 weeks if interested.

## THE LISA EKUS GROUP, LLC

57 North St., Hatfield MA 01038. (413)247-9325. **Fax:** (413)247-9873. **E-mail:** info@lisaekus.com. **Website:** www.lisaekus.com. **Contact:** Sally Ekus. Estab. 1982. Member of AAR.

**MEMBER AGENTS** Lisa Ekus; Sally Ekus.

**REPRESENTS** Nonfiction. **Considers these nonfiction areas:** cooking, diet/nutrition, foods, health, how-to, humor, women's issues, occasionally health/well-being and lifestyle.

- "Please note that we do not handle fiction, poetry, or children's books. If we receive a query for titles in these categories, please understand that we do not have the time or resources to respond."

**HOW TO CONTACT** "For more information about our literary services, visit http://lisaekus.com/services/literary-agency. Submit a query via e-mail or through our contact form on the website. You can also submit complete hard copy proposal with title page, proposal contents, concept, bio, marketing, TOC, etc. Include SASE for the return of materials." Accepts simultaneous submissions. Responds in 4-6 weeks.

**RECENT SALES** "Please see the regularly updated client listing on our website."

**TIPS** "Please do not call. No phone queries."

## ETHAN ELLENBERG LITERARY AGENCY

155 Suffolk St., No. 2R, New York NY 10002. (212)431-4554. **E-mail:** agent@ethanellenberg.com. **Website:** http://ethanellenberg.com. **Contact:** Ethan Ellenberg. Estab. 1984. Member of AAR, Science Fiction and Fantasy Writers of America, SCBWI, RWA, and MWA.

**MEMBER AGENTS** Ethan Ellenberg, president; Evan Gregory, senior agent; Ezra Ellenberg; Bibi Lewis.

**REPRESENTS** Nonfiction, fiction, scholarly books. **Considers these nonfiction areas:** archeology, biography, cooking, creative nonfiction, current affairs, health, history, juvenile nonfiction, literature, memoirs, military, New Age, philosophy, popular culture, psychology, science, spirituality, true crime, war, young adult, adventure. **Considers these fiction areas:** commercial, crime, detective, ethnic, fantasy, historical, horror, juvenile, literary, middle grade, military, mystery, new adult, paranormal, picture books, romance, science fiction, suspense, thriller, women's, young adult, general.

☛ "We specialize in commercial fiction and children's books. In commercial fiction we want to see science fiction, fantasy, romance, mystery, thriller, women's fiction; all genres welcome. In children's books, we want to see everything: picture books, early reader, middle grade and young adult. We do some nonfiction: history, biography, military, popular science, and cutting-edge books about any subject." Does not want to receive poetry, short stories, or screenplays.

**HOW TO CONTACT** Query by e-mail. Paste all of the material in the order listed. Fiction: query letter, synopsis, first 50 pages. Nonfiction: query letter, book proposal. Picture books: query letter, complete ms, 4-5 sample illustrations. Illustrators: query letter, 4-5 sample illustrations, link to online portfolio. Will not respond unless interested. Accepts simultaneous submissions. Responds in 2 weeks.

### EMPIRE LITERARY

115 W. 29th St., 3rd Floor, New York NY 10001. (917)213-7082. **E-mail:** abarzvi@empireliterary.com. **E-mail:** queries@empireliterary.com. **Website:** www.empireliterary.com. Estab. 2013. Member of AAR. Signatory of WGA.

**MEMBER AGENTS** Andrea Barzvi.

**REPRESENTS** Nonfiction, novels. **Considers these nonfiction areas:** diet/nutrition, health, memoirs, popular culture. **Considers these fiction areas:** literary, middle grade, women's, young adult.

**HOW TO CONTACT** Please only query one agent at a time. "If we are interested in reading more we will get in touch with you as soon as possible." Accepts simultaneous submissions.

### FELICIA ETH LITERARY REPRESENTATION

555 Bryant St., Suite 350, Palo Alto CA 94301-1700. **E-mail:** feliciaeth.literary@gmail.com. **Website:** eth-literary.com. **Contact:** Felicia Eth. Member of AAR.

☛ Worked as agent in NY at Writers House Inc. Prior to that worked in the movie business, Warner Bros NY. and Palomar Pictures for Story Dept.

**REPRESENTS** Nonfiction, fiction, novels. **Considers these nonfiction areas:** animals, creative nonfiction, cultural interests, current affairs, foods, history, investigative, memoirs, parenting, popular culture, psychology, science, sociology, travel, women's issues. **Considers these fiction areas:** contemporary issues, historical, literary, mainstream, suspense.

☛ This agency specializes in high-quality fiction (preferably mainstream/contemporary) and provocative, intelligent, and thoughtful nonfiction on a wide array of commercial subjects. "The agency does not represent genre ficiton, including romance novels, sci fi and fantasy, westerns, anime and graphic novels, mysteries."

**HOW TO CONTACT** For fiction: Please write a query letter introducing yourself, your book, your writing background. Don't forget to include degrees you may have, publishing credits, awards and endorsements. Please wait for a response before including sample pages. "We only consider material where the manuscript for which you are querying is complete, unless you have previously published." For nonfiction: A query letter is best, introducing idea and what you have written already (proposal, manuscript?). "For writerly nonfiction (narratives, bio, memoir) please let us know if you have a finished manuscript. Also it's important you include information about yourself, your background and expertise, your platform and notoriety, if any. We do not ask for exclusivity in most instances but do ask that you inform us if other agents are considering the same material." Accepts simultaneous submissions. Responds in ideally 2 weeks for query, a month if more.

**TERMS** Agent receives 15% commission on domestic sales; 20% commission on foreign and film sales. Charges clients for photocopying and express mail service

**RECENT SALES** *Bumper Sticker Philosophy*, by Jack Bowen (Random House); *Boys Adrift*, by Leonard Sax (Basic Books); *The Memory Thief*, by Emily Colin (Ballantine Books); *The World is a Carpet*, by Anna Bad-khen (Riverhead).

**WRITERS CONFERENCES** "Wide array—from Squaw Valley to Mills College."

## MARY EVANS INC.

P.O. Box 44, Hudson NY 12534. (518)828-0132. **E-mail:** info@maryevansinc.com. **Website:** maryevansinc.com. Member of AAR.

**MEMBER AGENTS** Mary Evans (progressive politics, alternative medicine, science and technology, social commentary, American history and culture); Leslie Meredith (memoir, science, psychology, health, nature, animals, spirituality, mind-body-spirit practices).

**REPRESENTS** Nonfiction, novels. **Considers these nonfiction areas:** creative nonfiction, cultural interests, history, medicine, politics, science, technology, social commentary, journalism. **Considers these fiction areas:** literary, upmarket.

☛ No screenplays or stage plays.

**HOW TO CONTACT** Query by mail or e-mail. If querying by mail, include a SASE. If querying by e-mail, put "Query" in the subject line. For fiction: Include the first few pages, or opening chapter of your novel as a single Word attachment. For nonfiction: Include your book proposal as a single Word attachment. Accepts simultaneous submissions. Responds within 4-8 weeks.

## FAIRBANK LITERARY REPRESENTATION

Post Office Box Six, Hudson NY 12534-0006. (617)576-0030. **E-mail:** queries@fairbankliterary.com. **Website:** www.fairbankliterary.com; www.publishersmarketplace.com/members/SorcheFairbank/. **Contact:** Sorche Elizabeth Fairbank. Estab. 2002. Member of AAR. Author's Guild, the Agents Round Table, and Grub Street's Literary Advisory Council.

**MEMBER AGENTS** Sorche Fairbank (narrative nonfiction, commercial and literary fiction, memoir, food and wine); Matthew Frederick, matt@fairbankliterary.com (scout for sports nonfiction, architecture, design).

**REPRESENTS** Nonfiction, fiction, novels, short story collections, juvenile books. **Considers these nonfiction areas:** agriculture, animals, architecture, art, autobiography, biography, cooking, crafts, creative nonfiction, cultural interests, current affairs, decorating, diet/nutrition, design, environment, ethnic, foods, gardening, gay/lesbian, government, history,

hobbies, horticulture, how-to, humor, interior design, investigative, juvenile nonfiction, law, literature, memoirs, photography, popular culture, politics, science, sociology, sports, technology, true crime, women's issues, women's studies. **Considers these fiction areas:** cartoon, commercial, contemporary issues, ethnic, feminist, juvenile, literary, mainstream, middle grade, mystery, new adult, picture books, short story collections, women's, international voices, Southern voices.

☛ "I tend to gravitate toward literary fiction and narrative nonfiction, with a strong interest in women's issues and women's voices, international voices, class and race issues, and projects that simply teach me something new about the greater world and society around us. We work closely and developmentally with our authors, and love what we do." Actively seeking literary fiction, international and culturally diverse voices, narrative nonfiction, topical subjects (politics, current affairs), history, sports, humor, architecture/design, and humor/pop culture. Also looking for picture books by illustrator authors only and illustrated middle grade. Does not want to receive romance, screenplays, poetry, science fiction or fantasy, or children's works unless by an illustrator author.

**HOW TO CONTACT** No phone queries please! By e-mail: queries@fairbankliterary.com. Please paste the first five pages of your work below your query. No attachments. Given the work constraints caused by the pandemic, we temporarily are only responding to works in which we're interested. If you haven't received a request for more material within eight or so weeks after submitting, it's likely a pass from us. We expect to gradually return to our policy of responding to queries via e-mail and SASE. Thank you for your understanding. Accepts simultaneous submissions. Obtains most new clients through recommendations from others, solicitations, conferences, ideas generated in-house.

**TERMS** Agent receives 15% commission on domestic sales; 20% commission on foreign sales. Offers written contract, binding for 12 months; 60-day notice must be given to terminate contract.

**RECENT SALES** Literary fiction about the British partition of India, by Shilpi Suneja to Milkweed Editions; photo-heavy, fun book about opossums by Ally Burguieres to Quirk Books; 2-book deal for children's picture books (biographies) by Katie Mazeika to Beach Lane Books (Simon & Schuster); 3-book deal for Lisa Currie's doodle journals to TarcherPerigee (Penguin Random House); A new issue of Angie Bailey's *Texts From Mittens* to Hanover Square (Harlequin/HarperCollins); 3-book deal for Terry Border for picture books to Philomel; scratch & sniff spin-off and an early reader adaptation of Terry Border's bestselling *Peanut Butter & Cupcake* to Grosset and Dunlap/Penguin; 10-book deal for Matthew Frederick for his bestselling *101 Things I Learned* series to Crown (Penguin Random House).

**TIPS** "Show me that you know your audience—and your competition. Have the writing and/or proposal at the very, very best it can be before starting the querying process. Don't assume that if someone likes it enough they'll 'fix' it. The biggest mistake new writers make is starting the querying process before they—and the work—are ready. Take your time and do it right."

## LEIGH FELDMAN LITERARY

**E-mail:** assistant@lfliterary.com. **E-mail:** query@lfliterary.com. **Website:** http://lfliterary.com. **Contact:** Leigh Feldman. Estab. 2014. Member of AAR. Signatory of WGA.

○ During her 25 years as a literary agent based in New York City, Leigh Feldman has established herself as an invaluable partner to the writers she represents, and is highly respected by her peers in the industry. Her agency, Leigh Feldman Literary, is the culmination of experiences and lessons learned from her 20-plus years at Darhansoff, Verrill, Feldman Literary Agency and Writer's House. In that time, Feldman has represented National Book Award winners and bestsellers of literary fiction, historical fiction, memoir, middle grade, and young adult. No matter the writer or the category, Feldman only represents books she believes in, that captivate her, and that she can best serve with her passion and tenacity. Leigh Feldman Literary is a full service literary agency.

**REPRESENTS** Nonfiction, fiction, novels, short story collections. **Considers these nonfiction areas:** creative nonfiction, memoirs. **Considers these fiction areas:** commercial, contemporary issues, family saga, feminist, gay, historical, lesbian, literary, mainstream,

multicultural, short story collections, women's, young adult.

☛ Does not want mystery, thriller, romance, paranormal, sci-fi.

**HOW TO CONTACT** E-query. "Please include 'query' in the subject line. Due to large volume of submissions, we regret that we cannot respond to all queries individually. Please include the first chapter or the first 10 pages of your manuscript (or proposal) pasted after your query letter. I'd love to know what led you to query me in particular, and please let me know if you are querying other agents as well." Accepts simultaneous submissions.

**RECENT SALES** List of recent sales and best known sales are available on the agency website.

## FINEPRINT LITERARY MANAGEMENT

207 W. 106th St., Suite 1D, New York NY 10025. (212)279-1412. **E-mail:** info@fineprintlit.com. **Website:** www.fineprintlit.com. **Contact:** Peter Rubie. Estab. 2007. Member of AAR, Authors Guild.

○ Peter Rubie was a journalist in Fleet Street, London, and for BBC Radio News and ITN television news. In America he was the editor in chief of a local newspaper in Manhattan, before becoming a freelance editor and book doctor, and then an in-house editor at Walker & Co., for 6 years. He became an agent in the mid 1990s and became the CEO of FinePrint in 2007. He considers himself an editorially inclined agent. He is also a published novelist and author of a number of nonfiction books and articles.

**MEMBER AGENTS** To submit to FinePrint agents send a query and sample material to submissions@fineprintlit.com, and address the email to the particular agent you are hoping to get your material to. Peter Rubie, CEO, (nonfiction interests include narrative nonfiction, popular science, spirituality, history, biography, pop culture, business, technology, parenting, health, self help, music, and food; fiction interests include literate thrillers, crime fiction, science fiction and fantasy, military fiction and literary fiction, middle grade and boy-oriented YA fiction); Laura Wood, (serious nonfiction, especially in the areas of science and nature, along with substantial titles in business, history, religion, and other areas by academics, experienced professionals, and journalists; select genre fiction only (no poetry, literary fiction or memoir) in the categories of science fiction & fantasy and mystery); Lauren Bieker, (Lauren is looking for commercial and upmarket women's fiction and some well-crafted and differentiated YA novels. She is also open to select science fiction, as well as high concept and literary fiction works. She appreciates great storytelling and is a "sucker" for outstanding writing and convincing characters. While primarily interested in fiction, she will consider nonfiction proposals. She is looking for #ownvoices stories, Feminist lit/#MeToo stories, and LGBTQIA+ authors in both fiction and nonfiction. Her goal is to "hold the mic" for authors to tell their stories and be a helpful support system). Bobby O'Neil (Bobby is looking for middle grade and young adult fiction across the board ranging from the grounded to the fantastic. In adult fiction, he is primarily interested in fantasy and speculative fiction that push the conventions of the genre, and character-driven commercial fiction. For nonfiction, he loves a strong narrative and is especially partial to memoir and historical. He is drawn to powerful voices and unique points of view that tell the stories from underrepresented communities, and LGBTQIA+ authors in both fiction and nonfiction).

**REPRESENTS** Nonfiction, fiction, novels, juvenile books. **Considers these nonfiction areas:** biography, business, cooking, cultural interests, current affairs, diet/nutrition, environment, foods, health, history, how-to, humor, inspirational, investigative, juvenile nonfiction, medicine, memoirs, multicultural, music, parenting, philosophy, popular culture, psychology, science, self-help, spirituality, technology, travel, true crime, women's issues, women's studies, young adult, fitness, lifestyle. **Considers these fiction areas:** action, adventure, commercial, crime, detective, fantasy, feminist, frontier, historical, literary, mainstream, middle grade, military, multicultural, multimedia, mystery, police, romance, science fiction, suspense, thriller, translation, urban fantasy, war, women's, young adult. **Considers these script areas:** mystery, police, science fiction.

**HOW TO CONTACT** E-query. For fiction, send a query, synopsis, bio, and 30 pages. For nonfiction, send a query only; proposal requested later if the agent is interested. Send to submissions@fineprintlit.com and address the email to the appropriate FP agent. Accepts simultaneous submissions. We aim to get back to authors within 12 weeks, but Covid has made that a tough bar to clear sometimes. Obtains most new clients through recommendations from others, solicitations.

**TERMS** Agent receives 15% commission on domestic sales; 20% commission on foreign sales.

## FLANNERY LITERARY

1140 Wickfield Ct., Naperville IL 60563. **E-mail:** jennifer@flanneryliterary.com. **Website:** flanneryliterary.com. **Contact:** Jennifer Flannery. Estab. 1992. Represents 40 clients.

**REPRESENTS** Juvenile books. **Considers these nonfiction areas:** juvenile nonfiction, young adult. **Considers these fiction areas:** juvenile, middle grade, new adult, picture books, young adult.

⊶   This agency specializes in middle grade and young adult fiction and nonfiction, we also represent picturebook, text only. 100% juvenile books. Actively seeking middle grade and young adult novels. No rhyming picture books nor bodily function topics, please. Also I do not open attachments unless instructed.

**HOW TO CONTACT** Query by e-mail only. "Multiple queries are fine, but please inform us. Please no attachments. If you're sending a query about a novel, please embed in the e-mail the first 5-10 pages; if it's a picture book, please embed the entire text in the e-mail. We do not open attachments unless they have been requested." Accepts simultaneous submissions. Responds in 2-4 weeks to queries; 1 month to mss. Obtains new clients through referrals and queries.

**TERMS** Agent receives 15% commission on domestic sales; 20% commission on foreign sales. Offers written contract, binding for life of book in print.

**TIPS** "Write an engrossing, succinct query describing your work. We are always looking for a fresh new voice."

## FLETCHER & COMPANY

78 Fifth Ave., 3rd Floor, New York NY 10011. **E-mail:** info@fletcherandco.com. **Website:** www.fletcherandco.com. **Contact:** Christy Fletcher. Estab. 2003. Member of AAR.

**MEMBER AGENTS** Christy Fletcher (referrals only); Melissa Chinchillo (select list of her own authors); Rebecca Gradinger (literary fiction, up-market commercial fiction, narrative nonfiction, self-help, memoir, Women's studies, humor, and pop culture); Gráinne Fox (literary fiction and quality commercial authors, award-winning journalists and food writers, American voices, international, literary crime, upmarket fiction, narrative nonfiction); Lisa Grub-ka (fiction—literary, upmarket women's, and young adult; and nonfiction—narrative, food, science, and more); Eric Lupfer; Sarah Fuentes; Veronica Goldstein; Eve MacSweeney; Peter Steinberg.

**REPRESENTS** Nonfiction, novels. **Considers these nonfiction areas:** biography, business, creative nonfiction, current affairs, foods, history, humor, investigative, memoirs, popular culture, politics, science, self-help, sports, women's studies. **Considers these fiction areas:** commercial, crime, literary, women's, young adult.

**HOW TO CONTACT** Send queries to info@fletcherandco.com. Please do not include e-mail attachments with your initial query, as they will be deleted. Address your query to a specific agent. No snail mail queries. Accepts simultaneous submissions.

**RECENT SALES** *The Profiteers*, by Sally Denton; *The Longest Night*, by Andria Williams; *Disrupted: My Misadventure in the Start-Up Bubble*, by Dan Lyons; *Free Re-Fills: A Doctor Confronts His Addiction*, by Peter Grinspoon, M.D.; *Black Man in a White Coat: A Doctor's Reflections on Race and Medicine*, by Damon Tweedy, M.D.

## FOLIO LITERARY MANAGEMENT, LLC

The Film Center Building, 630 Ninth Ave., Suite 1101, New York NY 10036. (212)400-1494. **Fax:** (212)967-0977. **Website:** www.foliolit.com. Member of AAR. Represents 100+ clients.

○ Prior to creating Folio Literary Management, Mr. Hoffman worked for several years at another agency; Mr. Kleinman was an agent at Graybill & English.

**MEMBER AGENTS** Claudia Cross (romance novels, commercial women's fiction, cooking and food writing, serious nonfiction on religious and spiritual topics); Jeff Kleinman (bookclub fiction (not genre commercial, like mysteries or romances), literary fiction, thrillers and suspense novels, narrative nonfiction, memoir); Dado Derviskadic (nonfiction: cultural history, biography, memoir, pop science, motivational self-help, health/nutrition, pop culture, cookbooks; fiction that's gritty, introspective, or serious); Frank Weimann (biography, business/investing/finance, history, religious, mind/body/spirit, health, lifestyle, cookbooks, sports, African-American, science, memoir, special forces/CIA/FBI/mafia, military, prescriptive nonfiction, humor, celebrity; adult and children's

fiction); Michael Harriot (commercial nonfiction (both narrative and prescriptive) and fantasy/science fiction); Erin Harris (book club, historical fiction, literary, narrative nonfiction, psychological suspense, young adult); Katherine Latshaw (blogs-to-books, food/cooking, middle grade, narrative and prescriptive nonfiction); Erin Niumata (fiction: commercial women's fiction, romance, historical fiction, mysteries, psychological thrillers, suspense, humor; nonfiction: self-help, women's issues, pop culture and humor, pet care/pets, memoirs, and anything blogger); Marcy Posner (adult: commercial women's fiction, historical fiction, mystery, biography, history, health, and lifestyle, commercial novels, thrillers, narrative nonfiction; children's: contemporary YA and MG, mystery series for boys, select historical fiction and fantasy); Steve Troha; Emily van Beek (YA, MG, picture books), Melissa White (general nonfiction, literary and commercial fiction, MG, YA); John Cusick (middle grade, picture books, YA); Jamie Chambliss; Roger Freet; Jan Baumer; Sonali Chanchani; Will Murphy; Rachel Ekstrom; Karen Gormandy; Katherine Odom-Tomehin; Adriann Ranta Zurhellen; Margaret Sutherland Brown.

**REPRESENTS** Nonfiction, novels. **Considers these nonfiction areas:** animals, art, biography, business, cooking, creative nonfiction, economics, environment, foods, health, history, how-to, humor, inspirational, memoirs, military, parenting, popular culture, politics, psychology, religious, satire, science, self-help, technology, war, women's issues, women's studies. **Considers these fiction areas:** commercial, fantasy, horror, literary, middle grade, mystery, picture books, religious, romance, thriller, women's, young adult.

☛ No poetry, stage plays, or screenplays.

**HOW TO CONTACT** Query via e-mail only (no attachments). Read agent bios online for specific submission guidelines and e-mail addresses, and to check if someone is closed to queries. "All agents respond to queries as soon as possible, whether interested or not. If you haven't heard back from the individual agent within the time period that they specify on their bio page, it's possible that something has gone wrong, and your query has been lost–in that case, please e-mail a follow-up."

**TIPS** "Please do not submit simultaneously to more than one agent at Folio. If you're not sure which of us is exactly right for your book, don't worry. We work closely as a team, and if one of our agents gets a query that might be more appropriate for someone else, we'll always pass it along. It's important that you check each agent's bio page for clear directions as to how to submit, as well as when to expect feedback."

## FOX LITERARY

110 W. 40th St., Suite 2305, New York NY 10018. E-mail: submissions@foxliterary.com. **Website:** foxliterary.com. Estab. 2007.

**MEMBER AGENTS** Diana Fox, Isabel Kaufman.

**REPRESENTS** Nonfiction, fiction, novels, short story collections, novellas, juvenile books, scholarly books, graphic novels. **Considers these nonfiction areas:** autobiography, biography, cooking, creative nonfiction, cultural interests, film, foods, gay/lesbian, health, history, juvenile nonfiction, language, law, literature, medicine, memoirs, multicultural, parenting, philosophy, popular culture, psychology, recreation, science, self-help, sex, sociology, spirituality, women's issues, women's studies, young adult, mind/body/spirit. **Considers these fiction areas:** action, adventure, comic books, commercial, confession, contemporary issues, crime, detective, erotica, fantasy, feminist, gay, historical, horror, juvenile, lesbian, literary, mainstream, middle grade, multicultural, mystery, new adult, paranormal, romance, science fiction, short story collections, spiritual, suspense, thriller, urban fantasy, women's, young adult, general.

☛ Fox Literary is actively seeking the following: young adult fiction (all genres), science fiction/fantasy, romance, historical fiction, literary fiction, thrillers, horror, and graphic novels. We're always interested in books that cross genres and reinvent popular concepts with an engaging new twist (especially when there's a historical and/or speculative element involved). On the nonfiction side, we're interested in memoirs, biography, and smart narrative nonfiction; Diana particularly enjoys memoirs and other nonfiction about sex work, addiction and recovery, popular science, and pop culture. Isabel is especially interested in narratives focused on travel, food, and the science of beauty, as well as microhistories of all things decadent and frivolous, screenplays, category Westerns, Christian/inspirational, or children's picture books.

**HOW TO CONTACT** Please email query and first 5 pages in body of email, and include the name of the agent to whom the submission is directed in the salutation of the email. No email attachments or hard copy submissions. Authors may query more than one agent within the agency at the same time, but if doing so author must send separate queries to each agent rather than a single query addressed to multiple agents. With all submissions, agents may jointly review and determine which agent will be the best fit. Accepts simultaneous submissions.

## JEANNE FREDERICKS LITERARY AGENCY, INC.

221 Benedict Hill Rd., New Canaan CT 06840. (203)972-3011. **Fax:** (203)972-3011. **E-mail:** jeanne.fredericks@gmail.com. **Website:** www.jeannefredericks.com. **Contact:** Jeanne Fredericks. Estab. 1997. Member of AAR. Other memberships include Authors Guild. Represents 100+ clients.

○ Prior to opening her agency in 1997, Ms. Fredericks was an agent and acting director with the Susan P. Urstadt, Inc. Agency. Previously she was the editorial director of Ziff-Davis Books and managing editor and acquisitions editor at Macmillan Publishing Company.

**REPRESENTS** Nonfiction. **Considers these nonfiction areas:** Americana, animals, autobiography, biography, child guidance, cooking, decorating, diet/nutrition, environment, foods, gardening, health, history, how-to, interior design, medicine, parenting, photography, psychology, self-help, women's issues.

☛ This agency specializes in quality adult nonfiction by authorities in their fields. "We do not handle: fiction, true crime, juvenile, textbooks, poetry, essays, screenplays, short stories, science fiction, pop culture, guides to computers and software, politics, horror, pornography, books on overly depressing or violent topics, romance, teacher's manuals, or memoirs."

**HOW TO CONTACT** The agency is currently considering submissions from existing clients only. Query first by e-mail, then send outline/proposal, 1-2 sample chapters, if requested and after you have consulted the submission guidelines on the agency website. If you do send requested submission materials, include the word "Requested" in the subject line. Accepts simultaneous submissions. Responds in 3-5 weeks to queries; 2-4 months to mss. Obtains most new clients through recommendations from others, solicitations, conferences.

**TERMS** Agent receives 15% commission on domestic sales; 25% commission on foreign sales with co-agent. Offers written contract, binding for 9 months; 2-month notice must be given to terminate contract. Charges client for photocopying of whole proposals and mss, overseas postage, expedited mail services. Almost all submissions are made electronically so these charges rarely apply.

**RECENT SALES** *Brave Boundaries*, by Sasha Shill-cutt, M.D. (Health Communications); *Yoga Nidra Meditations,* by Julie Lusk (Llewellyn); *A Naturalist's Book of Wildflowers,* by Laura Martin (Countryman); *Between Grit and Grace*, by Sasha Shillcutt, M.D. (Health Communications); *Shaken Brain*, by Elizabeth Sandel, M.D. (Harvard University Press); *Go by Boat*, by Chuck Radis (Down East); *Ill-Fated Frontier,* by Sam Forman (Lyons); *The Autoimmune Disease Handbook*, by Julius Birnbaum, M.D. (Johns Hopkins University Press); *The Secret Language of Cells*, by Jonathan Lieff, M.D. (BenBella Books); *How to Build Your Own Tiny Home*, by Roger Marshall (Taunton Press); *Yoga Therapy*, by Larry Payne, PH.D.,Terra Gold, D.O.M., and Eden Goldman, D.C. (Basic Health/Turner); *The Creativity Cure*, by Carrie Alton, M.D. and Alton Barron, M.D. (Scribner); *Storm of the Century*, by Willie Drye (Lyons); *Lilias! Yoga*, by Lilias Folan (Skyhorse).

**WRITERS CONFERENCES** Harvard Medical School CME Course in Publishing, Connecticut Authors and Publishers Association-University Conference, ASJA Writers' Conference, BookExpo America, Garden Writers' Association Annual Symposium.

**TIPS** "Be sure to research competition for your work and be able to justify why there's a need for your book. I enjoy building an author's career, particularly if he/she is professional, hardworking, and courteous, and actively involved in establishing a marketing platform. Aside from 25 years of agenting experience, I've had 10 years of editorial experience in adult trade book publishing that enable me to help an author polish a proposal so that it's more appealing to prospective editors. My MBA in marketing also distinguishes me from other agents."

### FRESH BOOKS LITERARY AGENCY

**E-mail:** matt@fresh-books.com. **Website:** www.fresh-books.com. **Contact:** Matt Wagner. Estab. 2005.

Prior to starting his own agency Mr. Wagner was an agent with Waterside Productions from 1989 through 2004.

**REPRESENTS** Nonfiction. **Considers these nonfiction areas:** art, business, computers, cooking, creative nonfiction, diet/nutrition, design, education, health, hobbies, how-to, photography, recreation, satire, science, self-help, true crime, popular science, technology, fitness, gadgets, social media, career development, leadership, personal finance.

"I'm looking for new and established authors writing narrative nonfiction, lifestyle and reference titles, including: popular science, technology, health, fitness, photography, design, computing, gadgets, social media, career development, education, business, leadership, personal finance, how-to, and humor." Does not want fiction, children's books, poetry, or screenplays.

**HOW TO CONTACT** Plain text e-mail query (with no attachments) to matt@fresh-books.com. Accepts simultaneous submissions.

**TERMS** Agent receives 15% commission on domestic sales; 20% commission on foreign sales.

**RECENT SALES** *The Myth of Multitasking 2e*, by Dave Crenshaw (Mango); *Bread Making For Dummies*, by Wendy Jo Peterson (Wiley); *Creative Garden Photography*, by Harold Davis (Rocky Nook); *Machine Learning For Dummies, 2e*, by John Paul Mueller and Luca Massaron (Wiley); *The Computer Book*, by Simson Garfinkel and Rachel Grunspan (Sterling); *How to Get a Meeting with Anyone*, by Stu Heinecke (Ben Bella); *Born to Eat*, by Wendy Jo Peterson and Leslie Schilling (Skyhorse).

### SARAH JANE FREYMANN LITERARY AGENCY

(212)362-9277. **E-mail:** sarah@sarahjanefreymann.com; submissions@sarahjanefreymann.com. **Website:** www.sarahjanefreymann.com. **Contact:** Sarah Jane Freymann, Steve Schwartz.

**MEMBER AGENTS** Sarah Jane Freymann (nonfiction: spiritual, psychology, self-help, women's/men's issues, books by health experts [conventional and alternative], cookbooks, narrative nonfiction, natural science, nature, memoirs, cutting-edge journalism, travel, multicultural issues, parenting, lifestyle, fiction: literary, mainstream YA); Steven Schwartz, steve@sarahjanefreymann.com (popular fiction [crime, thrillers, and historical novels], world and national affairs, business books, self-help, psychology, humor, sports and travel).

**REPRESENTS** Nonfiction, fiction, novels. **Considers these nonfiction areas:** business, cooking, creative nonfiction, current affairs, health, humor, memoirs, multicultural, parenting, psychology, science, self-help, spirituality, sports, travel, women's issues, men's issues, nature, journalism, lifestyle. **Considers these fiction areas:** crime, historical, literary, mainstream, thriller, young adult, popular fiction.

**HOW TO CONTACT** Query via e-mail. No attachments. Below the query, please paste the first 10 pages of your work. Accepts simultaneous submissions.

**TERMS** Charges clients for long distance, overseas postage, photocopying. 100% of business is derived from commissions on ms sales.

## FREDRICA S. FRIEDMAN AND CO., INC.

857 Fifth Ave., New York NY 10065. (212)639-9455. **E-mail:** info@fredricafriedman.com; submissions@fredricafriedman.com. **Website:** www.fredricafriedman.com. **Contact:** Ms. Chandler Smith.

○ Prior to establishing her own literary management firm, Ms. Friedman was the Editorial Director, Associate Publisher and Vice President of Little, Brown & Co., a division of Time Warner, and the first woman to hold those positions.

**REPRESENTS** Nonfiction, fiction.

✎ Does not want poetry, plays, screenplays, children's picture books, sci-fi/fantasy, or horror.

**HOW TO CONTACT** Submit e-query, synopsis; be concise, and include any pertinent author information, including relevant writing history. If you are a fiction writer, submit the first 10 pages of your manuscript. Keep all material in the body of the e-mail. Accepts simultaneous submissions. Responds in 6 weeks.

## REBECCA FRIEDMAN LITERARY AGENCY

**E-mail:** queries@rfliterary.com. **Website:** www.rfliterary.com. Estab. 2013. Member of AAR. Signatory of WGA.

○ Prior to opening her own agency in 2013, Ms. Friedman was with Sterling Lord Literistic from 2006 to 2011, then with Hill Nadell Agency.

**MEMBER AGENTS** Rebecca Friedman (commercial and literary fiction with a focus on literary novels of suspense, women's fiction, contemporary romance,

and young adult, as well as journalistic nonfiction and memoir); Susan Finesman, susan@rfliterary.com (fiction, cookbooks, and lifestyle); Abby Schulman, abby@rfliterary.com (YA and nonfiction related to health, wellness, and personal development).

**REPRESENTS** Nonfiction, fiction, novels. **Considers these nonfiction areas:** cooking, crafts, creative nonfiction, cultural interests, decorating, foods, health, humor, interior design, investigative, memoirs, parenting, women's issues, young adult, journalistic nonfiction. **Considers these fiction areas:** commercial, family saga, fantasy, feminist, gay, historical, juvenile, lesbian, literary, mystery, science fiction, suspense, thriller, women's, young adult.

**HOW TO CONTACT** Please submit your brief query letter and first chapter (no more than 15 pages, double-spaced). No attachments. Accepts simultaneous submissions. Tries to respond in 6-8 weeks.

**RECENT SALES** A complete list of agency authors is available online.

## THE FRIEDRICH AGENCY

New York NY (212)317-8810. **E-mail:** mfriedrich@friedrichagency.com; lcarson@friedrichagency.com; hcarr@friedrichagency.com; hbrattesani@friedrichagency.com. **Website:** www.friedrichagency.com. **Contact:** Molly Friedrich; Lucy Carson; Heather Carr; Hannah Brattesani. Estab. 2006. Member of AAR. Represents 50+ clients.

○ Prior to her current position, Ms. Friedrich was an agent at the Aaron Priest Literary Agency.

**MEMBER AGENTS** Molly Friedrich, founder and agent (open to queries); Lucy Carson, TV/film rights director and agent (open to queries); Hannah Brattesani, foreign rights director and agent (open to queries); Heather Carr, contracts director and agent (open to queries).

**REPRESENTS** Nonfiction, fiction, novels, short story collections. **Considers these nonfiction areas:** autobiography, biography, creative nonfiction, memoirs, multicultural, true crime, women's issues, young adult. **Considers these fiction areas:** commercial, detective, family saga, feminist, gay, horror, lesbian, literary, multicultural, mystery, science fiction, short story collections, suspense, thriller, women's, young adult.

**HOW TO CONTACT** Query by e-mail only. Please query only 1 agent at this agency. Accepts simultaneous submissions. Responds in 2-4 weeks.

**RECENT SALES** *W Is for Wasted*, by Sue Grafton; *Olive Kitteridge*, by Elizabeth Strout. Other clients include Frank McCourt, Jane Smiley, Esmeralda Santiago, Terry McMillan, Cathy Schine, Ruth Ozeki, Karen Joy Fowler, and more.

## FULL CIRCLE LITERARY, LLC

3268 Governor Dr., #323, San Diego CA 92122. **E-mail:** Submissions by Query Manager only please see links on website. **Website:** www.fullcircleliterary.com. **Contact:** Stefanie Von Borstel. Estab. 2005. Member of AAR, Society of Children's Books Writers & Illustrators, Authors Guild. Represents 100+ clients.

**MEMBER AGENTS** Stefanie Sanchez Von Borstel; Adriana Dominguez; Taylor Martindale Kean; Lilly Ghahremani, Nicole Geiger.

**REPRESENTS Considers these nonfiction areas:** how-to, multicultural. **Considers these fiction areas:** multicultural.

☞ Actively seeking nonfiction and fiction projects that offer new and diverse viewpoints, and literature with a global or multicultural perspective. "We are particularly interested in books with a Latino or Middle Eastern angle."

**HOW TO CONTACT** Online submissions only via Query Manager (links on website fullcircleliterary. com). Please note agency wishlists and areas of representation. Illustrators please include link to your online portfolio or website. Accepts simultaneous submissions. "Due to the high volume of submissions, please keep in mind we are no longer able to personally respond to every submission. However, we read every submission with care and often share for a second read within the office. If we are interested, we will contact you by email to request additional materials (such as a complete manuscript or additional manuscripts). Please keep us updated if there is a change in the status of your project, such as an offer of representation or book contract. If you have not heard from us in 6-8 weeks, your project is not right for our agency at the current time and we wish you all the best with your writing. Thank you for considering Full Circle Literary, we look forward to reading!" Obtains most new clients through recommendations from others and conferences.

**TERMS** Agent receives 15% commission on domestic sales; 25% commission on foreign sales. Offers written contract which outlines responsibilities of the author and the agent.

## FUSE LITERARY

Foreword Literary, Inc. dba Fuse Literary, P.O. Box 258, La Honda CA 94020. **E-mail:** info@fuseliterary. com. **Website:** www.fuseliterary.com. **Contact:** info@ fuseliterary.com. Estab. 2013. Member of RWA, SCB-WI, MWA, ITWA. Represents 180+ clients.

○ Each agent at Fuse had a specific set of interests and jobs prior to becoming a member of Team Fuse. Laurie ran a multi-million dollar publicity agency. Michelle was an editor at a Big Five publisher. Emily worked in the contracts department at Simon & Schuster. Gordon ran a successful independent editing business. Tricia worked in the video game industry. Connor worked in talent management. Carlisle is a youth librarian. Ernie is a graphic designer. Veronica is a brand expert. Check each agent's bio on our website for more specific information.

**MEMBER AGENTS** Laurie McLean, genre fiction for adults, young adults and middle grade; Gordon Warnock, fiction: high-concept commercial fiction, literary fiction (adults through YA), graphic novels (adults through MG); nonfiction: memoir (adult, YA, NA, graphic), cookbooks/food narrative/food studies, illustrated/art/photography (especially graphic nonfiction), political and current events, pop science, pop culture (especially punk culture and geek culture), self-help, how-to, humor, pets, business and career); Connor Goldsmith, books by and about people from marginalized perspectives, such as LGBT people and/or racial minorities; nonfiction (from recognized experts with established platforms): history (particularly of the ancient world), theater, cinema, music, television, mass media, popular culture, feminism and gender studies, LGBT issues, race relations, and the sex industry; Michelle Richter, primarily seeking fiction, specifically book club reads, literary fiction, and mystery/suspense/thrillers; for nonfiction, seeking fashion, pop culture, science/medicine, sociology/social trends, and economics); Emily S. Keyes, picture books, middle grade and young adult children's books, plus select commercial fiction, including fantasy & science fiction, women's fiction, new adult fiction, pop culture and humor); Tricia Skinner, romance, science fiction, fantasy; Carlisle Webber, high-concept commercial fiction in middle grade, young adult, and adult; dark thrillers, mystery, horror, dark women's fiction, dark pop/mainstream fiction; especially interested in diverse authors and their stories; Veronica Park, specializes in nonfiction (the more creatively structured your narrative, the better), women's fiction, and romance for all ages. Darker subject matter and wry humor are encouraged, even if they go hand in hand; Karly Dizon, represents picture books, middle grade and young adult fiction and nonfiction; Ernie Chiara, specializes in adult fantasy, science fiction, and magical realism, as well as young adult fantasy and graphic novels.

**REPRESENTS** Nonfiction, fiction, novels, juvenile books, scholarly books, poetry books. **Considers these nonfiction areas:** autobiography, biography, business, child guidance, computers, cooking, crafts, creative nonfiction, cultural interests, current affairs, dance, decorating, diet/nutrition, design, economics, education, environment, ethnic, film, foods, gardening, gay/lesbian, government, health, history, hobbies, horticulture, how-to, humor, inspirational, interior design, investigative, juvenile nonfiction, language, law, literature, medicine, memoirs, metaphysics, money, multicultural, music, New Age, parenting, philosophy, photography, popular culture, politics, psychology, recreation, regional, satire, science, self-help, sex, sociology, software, spirituality, sports, technology, theater, travel, true crime, women's issues, women's studies, young adult, celebrity. **Considers these fiction areas:** action, adventure, cartoon, comic books, commercial, confession, contemporary issues, crime, detective, erotica, ethnic, experimental, family saga, fantasy, feminist, frontier, gay, glitz, hi-lo, historical, horror, humor, inspirational, juvenile, lesbian, literary, mainstream, metaphysical, middle grade, multicultural, multimedia, mystery, new adult, New Age, occult, paranormal, picture books, plays, poetry, poetry in translation, police, psychic, regional, romance, satire, science fiction, spiritual, sports, supernatural, suspense, thriller, urban fantasy, westerns, women's, young adult. **Considers these script areas:** We do not represent scripts. "We are committed to expanding storytelling into a wide variety of formats other than books, including video games, movies, television shows, streaming videos, enhanced e-books, VR, etc."

**HOW TO CONTACT** E-query an individual agent. Check the website to see if any individual agent has closed themselves to submissions, as well as for a description of each agent's individual submission prefer-

ences. (You can find these details by clicking on each agent's photo.) Accepts simultaneous submissions. Usually responds in 6-8 weeks, but sometimes more if an agent is exceptionally busy. Check each agent's bio/submissions page on the website. Only accepts e-mailed queries that follow our online guidelines.

**TERMS** "We earn 15% on negotiated deals for books and with our co-agents earn 20-25% on foreign translation deals depending on the territory; 20% on TV/Movies/Plays; other multimedia deals are so new there is no established commission rate. The author has the last say, approving or not approving all deals." After the initial 90-day period, there is a 30-day termination of the agency agreement clause. No fees.

**RECENT SALES** Seven-figure and six-figure deals for *NYT* bestseller Julie Kagawa (YA); six-figure deal for debut Melissa D. Savage (MG); seven-figure and six-figure deals for Kerry Lonsdale (suspense); two six-figure audio deals for fantasy author Brian D. Anderson; *First Watch*, by Dale Lucas (fantasy); *This Is What a Librarian Looks Like*, by Kyle Cassidy (photo essay); *A Big Ship at the Edge of the Universe*, by Alex White (sci-fi); Runebinder Chronicles, by Alex Kahler (YA); *Perceptual Intelligence*, by Dr. Brian Boxler Wachler (science); *The Night Child*, by Anna Quinn (literary); *Hollywood Homicide*, by Kellye Garrett (mystery); Breakup Bash Series, by Nina Crespo (romance); *America's Next Reality Star*, by Laura Heffernan (women's fiction); *Losing the Girl*, by MariNaomi (graphic novel); *Maggie and Abby's Neverending Pillow Fort*, by Will Taylor (MG); *Idea Machine*, by Jorjeana Marie (how-to); six-figure deal for Ebony Gate series by Ken Bebelle & Julia Vee (fantasy); six-figure deal for *The Honeys* by Ryan La Sala (YA).

**WRITERS CONFERENCES** Agents from this agency attend many conferences. A full list of their appearances is available on the agency website.

### GALLT AND ZACKER LITERARY AGENCY

273 Charlton Ave., South Orange NJ 07079. **Website:** www.galltzacker.com. **Contact:** Nancy Gallt, Marietta Zacker. Estab. 2000. Represents 100+ clients.

Ms. Gallt was subsidiary rights director of the children's book division at Morrow, Harper and Viking. Ms. Zacker started her career as a teacher, championing children's and YA books, then worked in the children's book world, bookselling, marketing, and editing.

Ms. Camacho held positions in foreign rights, editorial, marketing, and operations at Penguin Random House, Dorchester, Simon & Schuster, and Writers House literary agency before venturing into agenting at Prospect Agency. Ms. Phelan got her start at Scott Waxman Agency and Morhaim Literary then spent four years as an agent with The Bent Agency.

**MEMBER AGENTS** Nancy Gallt; Marietta Zacker; Linda Camacho; Beth Phelan; Ellan K. Greenberg; Erin Casey.

**REPRESENTS** Nonfiction, fiction, novels, juvenile books, scholarly books, poetry books. **Considers these fiction areas:** juvenile, middle grade, picture books, young adult.

☛ Books for children and young adults. Actively seeking author, illustrators, author/illustrators who create books for young adults and younger readers.

**HOW TO CONTACT** Submission guidelines on our website: http://galltzacker.com/submissions.html. No e-mail queries, please. Accepts simultaneous submissions. We endeavor to respond to all queries within 4 weeks. Obtains new clients through submissions, conferences and recommendations from others.

**TERMS** Agent receives 15% commission on domestic sales; 20% commission on foreign sales. Offers written contract; 30-day notice must be given to terminate contract.

**RECENT SALES** Rick Riordan's Books (Hyperion); *Trace*, by Pat Cummings (Harper); *I Got Next*, by Daria Peoples-Riley (Bloomsbury); *Gondra's Treasure*, illustrated by Jennifer Black Reinhardt (Clarion/HMH); *Caterpillar Summer*, by Gillian McDunn (Bloomsbury); *It Wasn't Me*, by Dana Alison Levy (Delacorte/Random House); *Five Midnights*, by Ann Dávila Cardinal (Tor/Macmillan); *Patron Saints of Nothing*, by Randy Ribay (Kokila/Penguin); *Rot*, by Ben Clanton (Simon & Schuster). *The Year They Fell*, by David Kreizman (Imprint/Macmillan); *Manhattan Maps*, by Jennifer Thermes (Abrams); *The Moon Within*, by Aida Salazar (Scholastic); *Artist in Space*, by Dean Robbins (Scholastic); *Where Are You From?*, by Yamile Saied Méndez (Harper); *The Girl King*, by Mimi Yu (Bloomsbury); *Narwhal and Jelly*, by Ben Clanton (Tundra/Penguin Random House Canada).

**TIPS** "Writing and illustrations stand on their own, so submissions should tell the most compelling stories possible—whether visually, in narrative, or both."

## THE GARAMOND AGENCY, INC.

**E-mail:** query@garamondagency.com. **Website:** www.garamondagency.com. Memberships include Author's Guild.

**MEMBER AGENTS** Lisa Adams; David Miller.

**REPRESENTS** Nonfiction. **Considers these nonfiction areas:** anthropology, archeology, biography, business, creative nonfiction, current affairs, economics, environment, government, history, law, medicine, parenting, politics, psychology, science, sociology, sports, technology, women's issues.

☛ No proposals for children's or young adult books, fiction, poetry, or memoir.

**HOW TO CONTACT** "Queries sent by e-mail may not make it through the spam filters on our server. Please e-mail a brief query letter only, we do not read unsolicited manuscripts submitted by e-mail under any circumstances. See our website." Accepts simultaneous submissions.

**RECENT SALES** *The Lincoln Miracle* by Edward Achorn (Grove Atlantic), *Renegade at Law* by Shaun Ossei-Owusu (Liveright), *Framers* by Kenneth Cukier, Viktor Mayer Schoenberger and Francis de Vericourt, *Coming Out Republican* by Neil J. Young (University of Chicago Press), *Halfway Home* by Reuben Miller (Little Brown), *Unexampled Courage* by Richard Gergel (Sarah Crichton Books/FSG), *Firepower* by Paul Lockhart (Basic Books), *The Emancipation of Priscilla Joyner* by Carole Emberton (W. W. Norton). See website for other clients.

**TIPS** "Query us first if you have any questions about whether we are the right agency for your work."

## MAX GARTENBERG LITERARY AGENCY

912 N. Pennsylvania Ave., Yardley PA 19067. (215)295-9230. **Website:** www.maxgartenberg.com. **Contact:** Anne Devlin (nonfiction). Estab. 1954. Represents 100 clients.

**MEMBER AGENTS** Anne G. Devlin (current events, education, politics, true crime, women's issues, sports, parenting, biography, environment, narrative nonfiction, health, lifestyle, and celebrity).

**REPRESENTS** Nonfiction, juvenile books, scholarly books, textbooks. **Considers these nonfiction areas:**

animals, art, biography, business, current affairs, education, environment, film, gardening, government, health, history, how-to, military, money, music, psychology, science, sports, true crime, women's issues.

**HOW TO CONTACT** Writers desirous of having their work handled by this agency may query by e-mail to agdevlin@aol.com. Accepts simultaneous submissions. Responds in 2 weeks to queries; 6 weeks to mss.

**TERMS** Agent receives 15% commission on sales.

**RECENT SALES** *The Enlightened College Applicant*, by Andrew Belasco (Rowman and Littlefield); *Beethoven for Kids: His Life and Music*, by Helen Bauer (Chicago Review Press); *Portrait of a Past Life Skeptic*, by Robert L. Snow (Llewellyn Books); *Beyond Your Baby's Checkup*, by Luke Voytas, MD (Sasquatch Books); *Unorthodox Warfare: The Chinese Experience*, by Ralph D. Sawyer (Westview Press); *Encyclopedia of Earthquakes and Volcanoes*, by Alexander E. Gates (Facts on File); *Pandas!: Step Into Reading*, by David Salomon (Random House Children's Books).

**TIPS** "We have recently expanded to allow more access for new writers."

## GELFMAN SCHNEIDER/ICM PARTNERS

850 7th Ave., Suite 903, New York NY 10019. **E-mail:** mail@gelfmanschneider.com. **Website:** www.gelfmanschneider.com. **Contact:** Jane Gelfman, Deborah Schneider. Member of AAR. Represents 300+ clients.

**MEMBER AGENTS** Deborah Schneider (all categories of literary and commercial fiction and nonfiction); Jane Gelfman; Heather Mitchell (particularly interested in narrative nonfiction, historical fiction and young debut authors with strong voices); Penelope Burns, penelope.gsliterary@gmail.com (literary and commercial fiction and nonfiction, as well as a variety of young adult and middle grade).

**REPRESENTS** Nonfiction, fiction, juvenile books. **Considers these nonfiction areas:** creative nonfiction, popular culture. **Considers these fiction areas:** commercial, fantasy, historical, literary, mainstream, middle grade, mystery, science fiction, suspense, women's, young adult.

☛ "Among our diverse list of clients are novelists, journalists, playwrights, scientists, activists & humorists writing narrative nonfiction, memoir, political & current affairs, popular science and popular culture nonfiction, as well as literary & commercial fiction, women's fiction, and

historical fiction." Does not currently accept screenplays or scripts, poetry, or picture book queries.

**HOW TO CONTACT** Query. Check Submissions page of website to see which agents are open to queries and further instructions. Accepts simultaneous submissions.

**TERMS** Agent receives 15% commission on domestic sales; 20% commission on foreign sales; 15% commission on film sales. Offers written contract. Charges clients for photocopying and messengers/couriers.

## THE GERNERT COMPANY

136 E. 57th St., New York NY 10022. (212)838-7777. **E-mail:** info@thegernertco.com. **Website:** www.thegernertco.com. West Coast Office: 8440 Warner Dr., Culver City CA 90232. Estab. 1996. "Our client list is as broad as the market; we represent equal parts fiction and nonfiction."

**MEMBER AGENTS** Sarah Burnes (literary fiction and nonfiction; children's fiction); Chris Parris-Lamb (nonfiction, literary fiction); Seth Fishman (looking for the new voice, the original idea, the entirely breathtaking creative angle in both fiction and nonfiction); Will Roberts (smart, original thrillers with distinctive voices, compelling backgrounds, and fast-paced narratives); Erika Storella (nonfiction projects that make an argument, narrate a history, and/or provide a new perspective); Sarah Bolling (literary fiction, smart genre fiction—particularly sci-fi—memoir, pop culture, and style); Anna Worrall (smart women's literary and commercial fiction, psychological thrillers, and narrative nonfiction); Ellen Coughtrey (women's literary and commercial fiction, historical fiction, narrative nonfiction and smart, original thrillers, plus well-written Southern Gothic anything); Jack Gernert (stories about heroes—both real and imagined); Joy Fowlkes; Nora Gonzalez; Sophie Pugh-Sellers; Nicole Tourtelot. At this time, Courtney Gatewood and Rebecca Gardner are closed to queries. See the website to find out the tastes of each agent.

**REPRESENTS** Nonfiction, novels. **Considers these fiction areas:** commercial, crime, fantasy, historical, literary, middle grade, science fiction, thriller, women's, young adult.

**HOW TO CONTACT** Please send us a query letter by e-mail to info@thegernertco.com describing the work you'd like to submit, along with some information about yourself and a sample chapter if appropriate. Please indicate in your letter which agent you are querying. Please do not send e-mails directly to individual agents. It's our policy to respond to your query only if we are interested in seeing more material, usually within 4-6 weeks. See company website for more instructions. Accepts simultaneous submissions. Obtains most new clients through recommendations from others, solicitations.

**RECENT SALES** *Partners*, by John Grisham; *The River Why*, by David James Duncan; *The Thin Green Line*, by Paul Sullivan; *A Fireproof Home for the Bride*, by Amy Scheibe; *The Only Girl in School*, by Natalie Standiford.

## GHOSH LITERARY

P.O. Box 765, 2000 Allston Way, Berkeley CA 94704-9998. **E-mail:** annaghosh@ghoshliterary.com. **E-mail:** submissions@ghoshliterary.com. **Website:** www.ghoshliterary.com. **Contact:** Anna Ghosh. Member of AAR. Signatory of WGA.

Prior to opening her own agency, Ms. Ghosh was previously a partner at Scovil Galen Ghosh.

**REPRESENTS** Nonfiction, fiction, novels, short story collections, novellas, juvenile books.

"Anna's literary interests are wide and eclectic and she is known for discovering and developing writers. She is particularly interested in literary narratives and books that illuminate some aspect of human endeavor or the natural world. Anna does not typically represent genre fiction but is drawn to compelling storytelling in most guises."

**HOW TO CONTACT** E-query. Please send an e-mail briefly introducing yourself and your work. Although no specific format is required, it is helpful to know the following: your qualifications for writing your book, including any publications and recognition for your work; who you expect to buy and read your book; similar books and authors. Accepts simultaneous submissions.

## GLASS LITERARY MANAGEMENT

138 W. 25th St., 10th Floor, New York NY 10001. (646)237-4881. **E-mail:** alex@glassliterary.com. **Website:** www.glassliterary.com. **Contact:** Alex Glass. Estab. 2014. Member of AAR. Signatory of WGA.

**MEMBER AGENTS** Alex Glass.

**REPRESENTS** Nonfiction, novels.

Represents general fiction, mystery, suspense/thriller, juvenile fiction, biography, history,

mind/body/spirit, health, lifestyle, cookbooks, sports, literary fiction, memoir, narrative nonfiction, pop culture. "We do not represent picture books for children."

**HOW TO CONTACT** "Please send your query letter in the body of an e-mail and if we are interested, we will respond and ask for the complete manuscript or proposal. No attachments." Accepts simultaneous submissions.

**RECENT SALES** *100 Days of Cake*, by Shari Goldhagen; *The Red Car*, by Marcy Dermansky; *The Overnight Solution*, by Dr. Michael Breus; *So That Happened: A Memoir*, by Jon Cryer; *Bad Kid*, by David Crabb; *Finding Mr. Brightside*, by Jay Clark; *Strange Animals*, by Chad Kultgen.

## BARRY GOLDBLATT LITERARY LLC

c/o Industrious Brooklyn, 594 Dean St., 2nd Floor, Brooklyn NY 11238. **Website:** www.bgliterary.com. **Contact:** Barry Goldblatt. Estab. 2000. Member of AAR. Signatory of WGA.

**REPRESENTS** Fiction. **Considers these fiction areas:** fantasy, middle grade, mystery, romance, science fiction, thriller, young adult.

"Please see our website for specific submission guidelines and information on our particular tastes."

**HOW TO CONTACT** Query via online submission form. Accepts simultaneous submissions. Obtains clients through referrals, queries, and conferences.

**TERMS** Agent receives 15% commission on domestic sales; 20% on foreign and dramatic sales. Offers written contract. 60 days notice must be given to terminate contract.

**RECENT SALES** *Trolled*, by Bruce Coville; *Grim Tidings*, by Caitlin Kittredge; *Max at Night*, by Ed Vere.

**TIPS** "We're a hands-on agency, focused on building an author's career, not just making an initial sale. We don't care about trends or what's hot; we just want to sign great writers."

## FRANCES GOLDIN LITERARY AGENCY, INC.

214 W. 29th St., Suite 410, New York NY 10001. (212)777-0047. **Fax:** (212)228-1660. **Website:** www.goldinlit.com. Estab. 1977. Member of AAR.

**MEMBER AGENTS** Ellen Geiger, vice president/principal (nonfiction: history, biography, progressive politics, photography, science and medicine, women, religion and serious investigative journalism; fiction: literary thriller, and novels in general that provoke and challenge the status quo, as well as historical and multicultural works. Please no New Age, romance, how-to or right-wing politics); Matt McGowan, agent/rights director, mm@goldinlit.com (literary fiction, essays, history, memoir, journalism, biography, music, popular culture & science, sports [particularly soccer], narrative nonfiction, cultural studies, as well as literary travel, crime, food, suspense and sci-fi); Sam Stoloff, vice president/principal, (literary fiction, memoir, history, accessible sociology and philosophy, cultural studies, serious journalism, narrative and topical nonfiction with a progressive orientation); Ria Julien, agent/counsel; Caroline Eisenmann, associate agent; Roz Foster; Jade Wong-Baxter; Sulamita Garbuz.

**REPRESENTS** Nonfiction, novels. **Considers these nonfiction areas:** biography, creative nonfiction, cultural interests, foods, history, investigative, medicine, memoirs, music, philosophy, photography, popular culture, politics, science, sociology, sports, travel, women's issues, crime. **Considers these fiction areas:** historical, literary, mainstream, multicultural, suspense, thriller.

🔖 "We are hands on and we work intensively with clients on proposal and manuscript development." "Please note that we do not handle screenplays, romances or most other genre fiction, and hardly any poetry. We do not handle work that is racist, sexist, ageist, homophobic, or pornographic."

**HOW TO CONTACT** There is an online submission process you can find online. Responds in 4-6 weeks to queries.

## IRENE GOODMAN LITERARY AGENCY

27 W. 24th St., Suite 804, New York NY 10010. **E-mail:** miriam.queries@irenegoodman.com, barbara.queries@irenegoodman.com, kim.queries@irenegoodman.com, victoria.queries@irenegoodman.com, irene.queries@irenegoodman.com, whitney.queries@irenegoodman.com, pam.queries@irenegoodman.com, maggie.queries@irenegoodman.com, margaret.queries@irenegoodman.com, lee.queries@irenegoodman.com. **E-mail:** submissions@irenegoodman.com. **Website:** www.irenegoodman.com. **Contact:** Maggie Kane. Estab. 1978. Member of AAR. Represents 150 clients.

**MEMBER AGENTS** Irene Goodman, Miriam Kriss, Barbara Poelle, Kim Perel, Victoria Marini, Whitney Ross, Pam Gruber, Maggie Kane, Margaret Danko, Lee O'Brien; Natalie Lakosil; Danny Baror; Heather Baror-Shapiro.

**REPRESENTS** Nonfiction, fiction, novels, juvenile books. **Considers these nonfiction areas:** animals, autobiography, cooking, creative nonfiction, cultural interests, current affairs, decorating, diet/nutrition, design, foods, health, history, how-to, humor, interior design, juvenile nonfiction, memoirs, parenting, politics, science, self-help, women's issues, young adult, parenting, social issues, Francophilia, Anglophilia, Judaica, lifestyles, cooking, memoir. **Considers these fiction areas:** action, crime, detective, family saga, fantasy, feminist, historical, horror, middle grade, mystery, romance, science fiction, suspense, thriller, urban fantasy, women's, young adult.

🔖 Commercial and literary fiction and nonfiction. No screenplays, poetry, or inspirational fiction.

**HOW TO CONTACT** Query. Submit synopsis, first 10 pages pasted into the body of the email. E-mail queries only! See the website submission page. No e-mail attachments. Query 1 agent only. Accepts simultaneous submissions. Responds in 2 months to queries. Consult website for each agent's submission guidelines.

**TERMS** 15% commission.

**TIPS** "We are receiving an unprecedented amount of e-mail queries. If you find that the mailbox is full, please try again in two weeks. E-mail queries to our personal addresses will not be answered. E-mails to our personal inboxes will be deleted."

## DOUG GRAD LITERARY AGENCY, INC.

156 Prospect Park West, #3L, Brooklyn NY 11215. **E-mail:** query@dgliterary.com. **Website:** www.dgliterary.com. **Contact:** Doug Grad. Estab. 2008. Represents 50+ clients.

🔾 Prior to being an agent, Doug Grad spent 22 years as an editor at imprints at 4 major publishing houses—Simon & Schuster, Random House, Penguin, and HarperCollins.

**MEMBER AGENTS** Doug Grad (narrative nonfiction, military, sports, celebrity memoir, thrillers, mysteries, cozies, historical fiction, music, style, business, home improvement, food, science and theater).

**REPRESENTS** Nonfiction, fiction, novels. **Considers these nonfiction areas:** Americana, autobiography, biography, business, cooking, creative nonfiction, current affairs, diet/nutrition, design, film, government, history, humor, investigative, language, military, music, popular culture, politics, science, sports, technology, theater, travel, true crime, war. **Considers these fiction areas:** action, adventure, commercial, crime, detective, historical, horror, literary, mainstream, military, mystery, police, romance, science fiction, suspense, thriller, war.

☞ Does not want fantasy, young adult, or children's picture books.

**HOW TO CONTACT** Query by e-mail first. No sample material unless requested; no printed submissions by mail. Accepts simultaneous submissions. Due to the volume of queries, it's impossible to give a response time.

**RECENT SALES** *Net Force* series created by Tom Clancy and Steve Pieczenik, written by Jerome Preisler (Hanover Square); *A Serial Killer's Daughter* by Kerri Rawson (Thomas Nelson); *The Next Greatest Generation*, by Joseph L. Galloway and Marvin J. Wolf (Thomas Nelson); *All Available Boats* by L. Douglas Keeney (Lyons Press); *Here Comes the Body*, Book 1 in the Catering Hall mystery series, by Agatha Award-winner Ellen Byron writing as Maria DiRico (Kensington); *Please Don't Feed the Mayor* and *Alaskan Catch*, by Sue Pethick (Kensington).

### ➰ GRAHAM MAW CHRISTIE LITERARY AGENCY

37 Highbury Place, London England N5 1QP United Kingdom. **E-mail:** enquiries@grahammawchristie.com. **E-mail:** submissions@grahammawchristie.com. **Website:** www.grahammawchristie.com. Estab. 2005. Association of Authors' Agents. Represents 50 clients.

◯ Jane Graham Maw was a publishing director at HarperCollins, where she worked in rights, publicity and editorial. She later worked as a ghostwriter. She therefore has an insider knowledge of both the publishing industry and the pleasures and pitfalls of authorships. Jennifer Christie has been a literary agent for 13 years. She previously worked in advertising, PR and journalism, giving her a keen marketing focus and honed editorial skills. She has also worked as a ghostwriter and a child counselor.

**MEMBER AGENTS** Jane Graham Maw; Jennifer Christie; Maddy Belton; Meg Davis; Rebecca Winfield.

**REPRESENTS** Nonfiction. **Considers these nonfiction areas:** biography, business, child guidance, cooking, crafts, cultural interests, current affairs, diet/nutrition, foods, gardening, health, history, hobbies, how-to, humor, inspirational, memoirs, parenting, philosophy, popular culture, psychology, science, self-help, sex, women's issues.

☞ "We aim to make the publishing process easier and smoother for authors. We work hard to ensure that publishing proposals are watertight before submission. We aim for collaborative relationships with publishers so that we provide the right books to the right editor at the right time. We represent ghostwriters as well as authors." Does not want to receive fiction, poetry, plays or screenwriters.

**HOW TO CONTACT** E-queries only. This agency only accepts nonfiction. Query with a one-page summary of the topic, a detailed chapter-by-chapter outline, your qualifications for writing the book, your social media and online profile, a note on the market and competing titles, how you could help promote and sell the book, a sample chapter, your contact details. Aims to respond within 3-4 weeks to queries. Recommendations, approaches, and submissions.

**TERMS** Agent receives 15% commission on domestic sales; 20% commission on foreign sales. Offers written contract; 90-day notice must be given to terminate contract.

**WRITERS CONFERENCES** London Book Fair, Frankfurt Book Fair.

**TIPS** "UK clients only!"

### SANFORD J. GREENBURGER ASSOCIATES, INC.

55 Fifth Ave., New York NY 10003. (212)206-5600. **Fax:** (212)463-8718. **Website:** www.greenburger.com. Member of AAR. Represents 500 clients.

**MEMBER AGENTS** Matt Bialer, querymb@sjga.com (fantasy, science fiction, thrillers, and mysteries as well as a select group of literary writers, and also loves smart narrative nonfiction including books about current events, popular culture, biography, history, music, race, and sports); Faith Hamlin, fhamlin@sjga.com (receives submissions by referral); Heide Lange, queryhl@sjga.com (receives submissions by referral); Daniel Mandel, querydm@sjga.com (literary and commercial fiction, as well as memoirs and nonfiction about business, art, history, politics, sports, and popular culture); Rachael Dillon Fried, rfried@sjga.com (both fiction and nonfiction authors, with a keen interest in unique literary voices, women's fiction, narrative nonfiction, memoir, and comedy); Stephanie Delman, sdelman@sjga.com (literary/upmarket contemporary fiction, psychological thrillers/suspense, and atmospheric, near-historical fiction); Ed Maxwell, emaxwell@sjga.com (expert and narrative nonfiction authors, novelists and graphic novelists, as well as children's book authors and illustrators); Wendi Gu, wgu@sjga.com; Sarah Phair, sphair@sjga.com; Abigail Frank, afrank@sjga.com; Iwalani Kim, ikim@sjga.com; Bailey Tamayo, btamayo@sjga.com.

**REPRESENTS** Nonfiction, fiction, novels, juvenile books. **Considers these nonfiction areas:** art, biography, business, creative nonfiction, current affairs, ethnic, history, humor, memoirs, music, popular culture, politics, sports. **Considers these fiction areas:** commercial, crime, family saga, fantasy, feminist, historical, literary, middle grade, multicultural, mystery, picture books, romance, science fiction, thriller, women's, young adult.

☞ **No screenplays.**

**HOW TO CONTACT** E-query. "Please look at each agent's profile page for current information about what each agent is looking for and for the correct email address to use for queries to that agent. Please be sure to use the correct query e-mail address for each agent." Agents may not respond to all queries; will respond within 6-8 weeks if interested. Obtains most new clients through recommendations from others.

**TERMS** Agent receives 15% commission on domestic sales; 20% commission on foreign sales. Charges for photocopying and books for foreign and subsidiary rights submissions.

**RECENT SALES** *Origin*, by Dan Brown; *Sweet Pea and Friends: A Sheepover*, by John Churchman and Jennifer Churchman; *Code of Conduct*, by Brad Thor.

### KATHRYN GREEN LITERARY AGENCY, LLC

157 Columbus Ave., Suite 508, New York NY 10023. (212)245-4225. **E-mail:** query@kgreenagency.com. **Website:** www.kathryngreenliteraryagency.com. **Contact:** Kathy Green. Estab. 2004. Other memberships include Women's Media Group.

○ Prior to becoming an agent, Ms. Green was a book and magazine editor.

**REPRESENTS** Nonfiction, fiction, novels, short story collections, juvenile books. **Considers these nonfiction areas:** autobiography, biography, business, cooking, cultural interests, current affairs, diet/nutrition, foods, history, how-to, humor, inspirational, investigative, memoirs, parenting, popular culture, psychology, satire, science, spirituality, sports, true crime, women's issues, young adult. **Considers these fiction areas:** commercial, crime, detective, family saga, historical, humor, juvenile, literary, mainstream, middle grade, multicultural, mystery, police, romance, satire, suspense, thriller, women's, young adult.

☞ "Considers all types of fiction but particularly like historical fiction, cozy mysteries, young adult and middle grade. For nonfiction, I am interested in memoir, parenting, humor with a pop culture bent, and history. Quirky nonfiction is also a particular favorite." Does not want to receive science fiction, fantasy, children's picture books, screenplays, or poetry.

**HOW TO CONTACT** Query by e-mail. Send no attachments unless requested. Do not send queries via regular mail. Responds in 4 weeks. "Queries do not have to be exclusive; however if further material is requested, please be in touch before accepting other representation." Accepts simultaneous submissions. Obtains most new clients through recommendations from others, solicitations, conferences.

**TERMS** Agent receives 15% commission on domestic sales; 20% commission on foreign sales.

**RECENT SALES** *The Last Secret I Ever Told* by Laurie Stolarz, *The Thing I'm Most Afraid Of* by Kristin Levine, *Deliberate Evil* by Edward Renehan, *Where I Belong* by Marcia Arqueta Mickelson, *A Place to Hang the Moon* by Kate Albus, *The Franklin Avenue Rookery for Wayward Babies* by Laura Newman, *When We Die* by Kenneth Doka, PhD.

### THE GREENHOUSE LITERARY AGENCY

**E-mail:** submissions@greenhouseliterary.com. **Website:** www.greenhouseliterary.com. **Contact:** Sarah Davies. Estab. 2008. Member of AAR. Other memberships include SCBWI. Represents 70 clients.

○ Before launching Greenhouse, Sarah Davies had an editorial and management career in children's publishing spanning 25 years; for 5 years prior to launching the Greenhouse she was Publishing Director of Macmillan Children's Books in London, and published leading authors from both sides of the Atlantic.

**MEMBER AGENTS** Sarah Davies, vice president (fiction and nonfiction by North American authors, chapter books through to middle grade and young adult); Chelsea Eberly; Kristin Ostby.

**REPRESENTS** Juvenile books. **Considers these nonfiction areas:** juvenile nonfiction, young adult. **Considers these fiction areas:** juvenile, young adult.

➛ "We represent authors writing fiction and nonfiction for children and teens. The agency has offices in both the US and UK, and the agency's commission structure reflects this—taking 15% for sales to both US and UK, thus treating both as 'domestic' market." All genres of children's and YA fiction. Occasionally, a nonfiction proposal will be considered. Does not want to receive picture books texts (ie, written by writers who aren't also illustrators) or short stories, educational or religious/inspirational work, pre-school/novelty material, screenplays. Represents novels and some nonfiction.

**HOW TO CONTACT** Query 1 agent only. Put the target agent's name in the subject line. Paste the first 5 pages of your story after the query. Please see our website for up-to-date information as occasionally we close to queries for short periods of time. Accepts simultaneous submissions.

**TERMS** Agent receives 15% commission on domestic sales; 25% commission on foreign sales. Offers written contract. This agency occasionally charges for submission copies to film agents or foreign publishers.

**RECENT SALES** *Agents of the Wild*, by Jennifer Bell & Alice Lickens (Walker UK); *Bookshop Girl in Paris*, by Chloe Coles (Hot Key); *Votes for Women*, by Winifred Conkling (Algonquin); *The Monster Catchers*, by George Brewington (Holt); *City of the Plague God*, by Sarwat Chadda (Disney-Hyperion); *Whiteout*, by Gabriel Dylan (Stripes); *The Lying Woods*, by Ashley Elston (Disney-Hyperion); *When You Trap a Tiger*, by Tae Keller (Random House); *We Speak in Storms*, by Natalie Lund (Philomel); *When We Wake*, by Elle Cosimano (HarperCollins); *Carpa Fortuna*, by Lindsay Eagar (Candlewick); *Instructions Not Included*, by Tami Lewis Brown & Debbie Loren Dunn (Disney-Hyperion); *Fake*, by Donna Cooner (Scholastic); *Unicorn Academy*, by Julie Sykes (Nosy Crow); *The Girl*

*Who Sailed the Stars*, by Matilda Woods (Scholastic UK/Philomel US).

**WRITERS CONFERENCES** Bologna Children's Book Fair, ALA and SCBWI conferences, BookExpo America.

**TIPS** "Before submitting material, authors should visit the Greenhouse Literary Agency website and carefully read all submission guidelines."

## GREYHAUS LITERARY

3021 20th St., Pl. SW, Puyallup WA 98373. **E-mail:** scott@greyhausagency.com. **E-mail:** submissions@greyhausagency.com. **Website:** www.greyhausagency.com. **Contact:** Scott Eagan, member RWA. Estab. 2003. Member of AAR. Signatory of WGA.

**REPRESENTS** Novels. **Considers these fiction areas:** new adult, romance, women's.

➛ Greyhaus only focuses on romance and women's fiction. Please review submission information found on the website to know exactly what Greyhaus is looking for. Stories should be 75,000-120,000 words in length or meet the word count requirements for Harlequin found on its website. Greyhaus does not deviate from these genres. Does not want fantasy, single title inspirational, young adult or middle grade, picture books, memoirs, biographies, erotica, urban fantasy, science fiction, screenplays, poetry, authors interested in only e-publishing or self-publishing.

**HOW TO CONTACT** Submissions to Greyhaus can be done in one of three ways: 1) A standard query letter via e-mail. If using this method, do not attach documents or send anything else other than a query letter. 2) Use the Submission Form found on the website on the Contact page. Or 3) send a query, the first 3 pages and a synopsis of no more than 3-5 pages (and a SASE), using a snail mail submission. Do not submit anything more than asked. Please also understand Greyhaus does not consider queries through social media sites. Accepts simultaneous submissions. Responds in up to 3 months.

**TERMS** Agent receives 15% commission.

**WRITERS CONFERENCES** Scott Eagan is available to assist writing chapters and organizations through conference attendance, teaching workshops, guest blogging, judging contest final rounds, online workshops and certainly listening to pitches. The agency does not make it a practice of just showing up. If you want Scott to help out, please reach out to the agency.

## JILL GRINBERG LITERARY MANAGEMENT, LLC

392 Vanderbilt Avenue, Brooklyn NY 11238. (212)620-5883. **E-mail:** info@jillgrinbergliterary.com. **Website:** www.jillgrinbergliterary.com. Estab. 2007. Member of AAR.

○ Prior to her current position, Ms. Grinberg was a partner at Anderson Grinberg Literary Management.

**MEMBER AGENTS** Jill Grinberg; Katelyn Detweiler; Sophia Seidner; Sam Farkas; Larissa Melo Pienkowski; Jessica Saint Jean.

**REPRESENTS** Nonfiction, fiction, novels, juvenile books. **Considers these nonfiction areas:** biography, creative nonfiction, current affairs, history, language, literature, memoirs, parenting, popular culture, politics, science, sociology, spirituality, travel, women's issues, young adult. **Considers these fiction areas:** fantasy, feminist, historical, juvenile, literary, mainstream, middle grade, multicultural, picture books, romance, science fiction, women's, young adult.

☛ "We do not accept unsolicited queries for screenplays."

**HOW TO CONTACT** Please send your query to info@jillgrinbergliterary.com. Your e-mail subject line should follow this general format: QUERY: Title of Project by Your Name / Your Book's Age Category and Genre / ATTN: Name of Agent. Paste your query letter in the body of the e-mail, addressed to the agent of your choice, and attach your materials as a docx file. Do not attach zip folders, Pages files, links to Google Docs, or links to download materials from file sharing sites. You will receive an auto-response confirming your submission was received. For fiction submissions, please send a query letter and the first fifty (50) pages of your manuscript. If we are interested in reading more, we will reach out to request the full manuscript. For nonfiction submissions, please send a query letter and proposal. Your nonfiction proposal should include a project overview or outline, proposed chapter summaries, comparable titles, a sample chapter, your biography, and a bibliography of any additional works. Picture book submissions should include the full text, which can either be attached as a docx. file or pasted in the body of the email below your query. If you are an author-illustrator, please provide a sketch dummy (as a lo-res PDF). We no longer accept or consider mailed hard copy submissions, and any materials received will be discarded unread. Accepts simultaneous submissions.

**TIPS** Please refer to our website, www.jillgrinbergliterary.com, for the most up-to-date agency information and submission guidelines.

## JILL GROSJEAN LITERARY AGENCY

1390 Millstone Rd., Sag Harbor NY 11963. (631)725-7419. **E-mail:** jilllit310@aol.com. **Contact:** Jill Grosjean. Estab. 1999.

○ Prior to becoming an agent, Ms. Grosjean managed an independent bookstore. She also worked in publishing and advertising.

**REPRESENTS** Novels. **Considers these fiction areas:** historical, literary, mainstream, mystery, women's.

☛ Actively seeking literary novels and mysteries. Does not want serial killer, science fiction or YA novels.

**HOW TO CONTACT** E-mail queries preferred, no attachments. No cold calls, please. Accepts simultaneous submissions, though when manuscript requested, requires exclusive reading time. Accepts simultaneous submissions. Responds in 1 week to queries; 1 month to mss.

**TERMS** Agent receives 15% commission on domestic sales; 20% commission on foreign and film sales.

**RECENT SALES** *Murder in Old Bombay* by Nev March (St. Martin's Minotaur); *Shadows in Time* by Julie McElwain (Pegasus Books); *The Gold Pawn*, by L.A. Chandlar (Kensington Books); *Caught in Time*, by Julie McElwain (Pegasus Books); *A Murder in Time*, by Julie McElwain (Pegasus Books); *A Twist in Time*, by Julie McElwain (Pegasus Books); *The Silver Gun*, by L.A. Chandlar (Kensington Books); *The Edison Effect*, by Bernadette Pajer (Poison Pen Press); *Threading the Needle*, by Marie Bostwick (Kensington Publishing); *Tim Cratchit's Christmas Carol: A Novel of Scrooge's Legacy*, by Jim Piecuch (Simon & Schuster); *The Lighterman's Curse*, by Loretta Marion (Crooked Lane Books); *Betrayal in Time*, by Julie McElwain (Pegasus Books); *The Strange Case of Eliza Doolittle*, by Timothy Miller (Prometheus Books).

**WRITERS CONFERENCES** Thrillerfest, Texas Writer's League, Book Passage Mystery Writer's Conference, Writer's Market Conference.

## ⊘ LAURA GROSS LITERARY AGENCY

**E-mail:** assistant@lg-la.com. **Website:** www.lg-la.com. Estab. 1988. Represents 30 clients.

○ Prior to becoming an agent, Ms. Gross was an editor and ran a reading series.

**MEMBER AGENTS** Laura Gross; Lauren Scovel; Will Morningstar.

**REPRESENTS** Nonfiction, novels.

☞ "I represent a broad range of both fiction and nonfiction writers. I am particularly interested in history, politics, and current affairs, and also love beautifully written literary fiction and intelligent thrillers."

**HOW TO CONTACT** Currently closed to submissions. Check website for updates.

**TERMS** Agent receives 15% commission on domestic sales; 20% commission on foreign sales. Offers written contract.

## THE JOY HARRIS LITERARY AGENCY, INC.

1501 Broadway, Suite 2605, New York NY 10036. (212)924-6269. **Fax:** (212)540-5776. **E-mail:** contact@joyharrisliterary.com. **Website:** joyharrisliterary.com. **Contact:** Joy Harris. Estab. 1990. Member of AAR. Represents 100+ clients.

**MEMBER AGENTS** Joy Harris (literary fiction, strongly-written commercial fiction, narrative nonfiction across a broad range of topics, memoir and biography); Adam Reed (literary fiction, science and technology, and pop culture); Alice Fugate.

**REPRESENTS** Nonfiction, fiction. **Considers these nonfiction areas:** art, biography, creative nonfiction, memoirs, popular culture, science, technology. **Considers these fiction areas:** commercial, literary.

☞ "We are not accepting poetry, screenplays, genre fiction, or self-help submissions at this time."

**HOW TO CONTACT** Please e-mail all submissions, comprised of a query letter, outline or sample chapter, to submissions@joyharrisliterary.com. Accepts simultaneous submissions. Obtains most new clients through recommendations from clients and editors.

**TERMS** Agent receives 15% commission on domestic sales; 20% commission on foreign sales. Charges clients for some office expenses.

**RECENT SALES** *Smash Cut*, by Brad Gooch; *The Other Paris*, by Luc Sante; *The Past*, by Tessa Hadley; *In A Dark Wood*, by Joseph Luzzi.

## HARTLINE LITERARY AGENCY

123 Queenston Dr., Pittsburgh PA 15235-5429. (412)829-2483. **E-mail:** jim@hartlineliterary.com. **Website:** www.hartlineliterary.com. **Contact:** James D. Hart. Estab. 1992. Member of ACFW. Represents 400 clients.

○ Jim Hart was a production journalist for 20 years; Joyce Hart was the Vice President of Marketing at Whitaker House Publishing.

**MEMBER AGENTS** Jim Hart, principal agent (jim@hartlineliterary.com); Joyce Hart, founder (joyce@hartlineliterary.com); Linda Glaz (linda@hartlineliterary.com); Cyle Young (cyle@hartlineliterary.com).

**REPRESENTS** Nonfiction, fiction, novels, novellas, scholarly books. **Considers these nonfiction areas:** Americana, animals, autobiography, biography, business, child guidance, cooking, crafts, creative nonfiction, cultural interests, current affairs, diet/nutrition, foods, health, history, hobbies, how-to, humor, inspirational, investigative, juvenile nonfiction, memoirs, military, multicultural, music, parenting, philosophy, popular culture, politics, psychology, recreation, religious, self-help, spirituality, travel, true crime, women's issues, young adult. **Considers these fiction areas:** action, adventure, commercial, contemporary issues, crime, detective, family saga, fantasy, frontier, historical, humor, inspirational, literary, mainstream, military, mystery, new adult, police, religious, romance, science fiction, suspense, thriller, urban fantasy, westerns, women's.

☞ "This agency specializes in the Christian bookseller market." We also represent general market, but no graphic sex or language. Actively seeking adult fiction, all genres, self-help, social issues, Christian living, parenting, marriage, business, biographies, narrative nonfiction, creative nonfiction. Does not want to receive erotica, horror, graphic violence or graphic language.

**HOW TO CONTACT** E-mail submissions are preferred. Target one agent only. Each agent has specific interests, please refer to our web page for that information. All e-mail submissions sent to Hartline Agents should be sent as a MS Word doc attached to an e-mail with 'submission: title, author's name and word count' in the subject line. A proposal is a single document, not a collection of files. Place the query letter in the email itself. Do not send the entire proposal in the body of the e-mail. Further guidelines online. Accepts simultaneous submissions. Responds in 2 months to queries; 3 months to mss. Obtains most new clients through recommendations from others, and at conferences.

**TERMS** Agent receives 15% commission on domestic sales. Offers written contract.

**RECENT SALES** *The Beautiful Ashes of Gomez Gomez*, by Buck Storm (Kregel); *The Mr. Rogers Effect*, by Dr. Anita Knight (Baker Books); *People Can Change*, by Dr. Mark W. Baker (Fortress); *Obedience Over Hustle*, by Malinda Fuller (Barbour); *Keller's Heart*, by John Gray, Illustrations Shanna Oblenus (Paraclete); *Create Your Yes*, by Angela Marie Hutchinson (Source Books); *Simply Spirit Filled*, by Dr. Andrew K. Gabriel (Thomas Nelson).

**WRITERS CONFERENCES** ACFW; Mt. Hermon Christian Writers Conference, Oregon Christian Writers; Realm Makers; Blue Ridge Mountain Christian Writers; Florida Christian Writers; Write to Publish; Mount Hermon Conference; Taylor's Professional Writing Conference; Maranatha Christian Writers Conference; Write His Answer Christian Conferences (Colorado and Philadelphia), St. Davids Christian Writers Conference.

**TIPS** Please follow the guidelines on our website www.hartlineliterary for the fastest response to your proposal. E-mail proposals only.

### 🙩 ANTONY HARWOOD LIMITED

103 Walton St., Oxford OX2 6EB United Kingdom. (44)(018)6555-9615. **E-mail:** mail@antonyharwood.com. **Website:** www.antonyharwood.com. **Contact:** Antony Harwood; James Macdonald Lockhart; Jo Williamson. Estab. 2000. Represents 52 clients.

○ Prior to starting this agency, Mr. Harwood and Mr. Lockhart worked at publishing houses and other literary agencies.

**MEMBER AGENTS** Antony Harwood, James Macdonald Lockhart, Jo Williamson (children's); Jonathan Gregory.

**REPRESENTS** Nonfiction, novels. **Considers these nonfiction areas:** Americana, animals, anthropology, archeology, architecture, art, autobiography, biography, business, child guidance, computers, cooking, current affairs, design, economics, education, environment, ethnic, film, gardening, gay/lesbian, government, health, history, horticulture, how-to, humor,

language, memoirs, military, money, multicultural, music, parenting, philosophy, photography, popular culture, psychology, recreation, regional, science, self-help, sex, sociology, software, spirituality, sports, technology, translation, travel, true crime, war, women's issues, women's studies. **Considers these fiction areas:** action, adventure, cartoon, comic books, confession, crime, detective, erotica, ethnic, experimental, family saga, fantasy, feminist, frontier, gay, hi-lo, historical, horror, humor, lesbian, literary, mainstream, military, multicultural, multimedia, mystery, occult, picture books, plays, police, regional, religious, romance, satire, science fiction, spiritual, sports, suspense, thriller, translation, war, westerns, young adult, gothic.

**HOW TO CONTACT** "We are happy to consider submissions of fiction and nonfiction in every genre and category except for screenwriting and poetry. If you wish to submit your work to us for consideration, please send a covering letter, brief outline and the opening 50 pages by e-mail. If you want to post your material to us, please be sure to enclose an SAE or the cost of return postage." Replies if interested. Accepts simultaneous submissions. Responds in 2 months to queries.

**TERMS** Agent receives 15% commission on domestic sales; 20% commission on foreign sales.

### JOHN HAWKINS & ASSOCIATES, INC.

80 Maiden Ln., Suite 1503, New York NY 10038. (212)807-7040. **E-mail:** jha@jhalit.com. **Website:** www.jhalit.com. **Contact:** Moses Cardona (rights and translations); Anne Hawkins (permissions); Warren Frazier, literary agent; Anne Hawkins, literary agent; William Reiss, literary agent. Estab. 1893. Member of AAR, The Author Guild. Represents 100+ clients.

**MEMBER AGENTS** Moses Cardona, moses@jhalit.com (commercial fiction, suspense, business, science, and multicultural fiction); Warren Frazier, frazier@jhalit.com (fiction; nonfiction, specifically technology, history, world affairs and foreign policy); Anne Hawkins, ahawkins@jhalit.com (thrillers to literary fiction to serious nonfiction; interested in science, history, public policy, medicine and women's issues).

**REPRESENTS** Nonfiction, fiction, novels, short story collections, novellas, juvenile books. **Considers these nonfiction areas:** biography, business, history, medicine, politics, science, technology, women's issues. **Considers these fiction areas:** commercial, historical, literary, multicultural, mystery, suspense, thriller, women's, young adult.

**HOW TO CONTACT** Query. Include the word "Query" in the subject line. For fiction, include 1-3 chapters of your book as a single Word attachment. For nonfiction, include your proposal as a single attachment. E-mail a particular agent directly if you are targeting one. Accepts simultaneous submissions. Responds in 1 month to queries. Obtains most new clients through recommendations from others.

**TERMS** Agent receives 15% commission on domestic sales; 20% commission on foreign sales. Charges clients for photocopying.

**RECENT SALES** *The Charmed Wife*, by Olga Grushin; *Breathe*, by Joyce Carol Oates; *Fierce Little Thing*, by Miranda Beverly-Whittemore; *The Heron's Cry*, by Ann Cleeves; *Hold Fast* by J.H. Gelernter; *Old Lovegood Girls*, by Gail Godwin.

## ◎ HELEN HELLER AGENCY INC.

4-216 Heath St. W., Toronto ON M5P 1N7 Canada. (416)489-0396. **E-mail:** info@helenhelleragency.com. **Website:** www.helenhelleragency.com. **Contact:** Helen Heller. Represents 30+ clients.

◯ Prior to her current position, Ms. Heller worked for Cassell & Co. (England), was an editor for Harlequin Books, a senior editor for Avon Books, and editor-in-chief for Fitzhenry & Whiteside.

**MEMBER AGENTS** Helen Heller, helen@helenhelleragency.com (thrillers and front-list general fiction); Sarah Heller, sarah@helenhelleragency.com (front list commercial YA and adult fiction, with a particular interest in high concept historical fiction); Barbara Berson, barbara@helenhelleragency.com (literary fiction, nonfiction, and YA).

**REPRESENTS** Nonfiction, novels. **Considers these fiction areas:** commercial, crime, historical, literary, mainstream, thriller, young adult.

**HOW TO CONTACT** E-mail info@helenhelleragency.com. Submit a brief synopsis, publishing history, author bio, and writing sample, pasted in the body of the e-mail. No attachments with e-queries. Accepts simultaneous submissions. Responds within 3 months if interested. Accepts simultaneous submissions. Obtains most new clients through recommendations from others, solicitations.

**TIPS** "Whether you are an author searching for an agent, or whether an agent has approached you, it is in your best interest to first find out who the agent represents, what publishing houses that agent has sold to recently and what foreign sales have been made. You should be able to go to the bookstore, or search online and find the books the agent refers to. Many authors acknowledge their agents in the front or back of their books."

## HERMAN AGENCY

350 Central Park W., Apt. 41, New York NY 10025. (212)749-4907. **E-mail:** ronnie@hermanagencyinc.com. **Website:** www.hermanagencyinc.com. **Contact:** Ronnie Ann Herman. Estab. 1999. Member of SCBWI. Represents 19 clients.

◯ Ronnie Ann Herman was the art director, associate publisher and V.P. at Random House and Grosset & Dunlap/Penguin. Ronnie is also an author of numerous picture books, under the name R.H. Herman.

**MEMBER AGENTS** Ronnie Ann Herman, Katia Herman.

**REPRESENTS** Juvenile books. **Considers these nonfiction areas:** juvenile nonfiction. **Considers these fiction areas:** juvenile, middle grade, picture books.

☛ Specializes in children's books of all genres. We only want author/artist projects.

**HOW TO CONTACT** Submit via e-mail only. Accepts simultaneous submissions. Responds in 8 weeks. If you have not had a response from us within this period, please understand that that means we are not able to represent your work. Obtains extremely few new clients.

**TERMS** Agent receives 15% commission. Exclusive contract.

**TIPS** "Check our website to see if you belong with our agency." Remember only author/artist works.

## THE JEFF HERMAN AGENCY, LLC

P.O. Box 1522, Stockbridge MA 01262. (413)298-0077. **E-mail:** jeff@jeffherman.com. **Website:** www.jeffherman.com. **Contact:** Jeffrey H. Herman. Estab. 1987. Member of AAR. Represents 100 clients.

◯ Prior to opening his agency, Mr. Herman served as a public relations executive.

**MEMBER AGENTS** Deborah Levine, vice president (nonfiction book doctor); Jeff Herman.

**REPRESENTS** Nonfiction, scholarly books, textbooks. **Considers these nonfiction areas:** Americana, animals, biography, business, child guidance, computers, cooking, creative nonfiction, cultural interests, current affairs, diet/nutrition, economics, education, environment, ethnic, film, foods, gardening, government, health, history, hobbies, how-to, humor, inspirational, investigative, language, law, medicine, memoirs, metaphysics, military, money, multicultural, New Age, parenting, popular culture, politics, psychology, recreation, regional, religious, satire, science, self-help, sex, sociology, software, spirituality, technology, theater, translation, travel, true crime, war, women's issues, women's studies, popular reference.

☞ This agency specializes in adult nonfiction.

**HOW TO CONTACT** Query by e-mail. Accepts simultaneous submissions.

**TERMS** Agent receives 15% commission on domestic sales. Offers written contract.

**RECENT SALES** Have agented more than 1,000 titles.

## HG LITERARY

37 W. 28th St., 8th Floor, New York NY 10001. **Website:** www.hgliterary.com. **Contact:** Carrie Hannigan; Josh Getzler; Soumeya Roberts; Julia Kardon; Rhea Lyons; Victoria Wells Arms. Estab. 2011. Member of AAR. Signatory of WGA.

○ Prior to opening HG Literary, Carrie Hannigan and Josh Getzler were agents at Russell & Volkening. For more information on individual agents at HG, please see https://www.hgliterary.com/our-team.

**MEMBER AGENTS** Carrie Hannigan, Josh Getzler, Soumeya Roberts, Julia Kardon, Rhea Lyons, Victoria Wells Arms.

**REPRESENTS** Nonfiction, fiction, novels, short story collections, juvenile books. **Considers these nonfiction areas:** animals, business, cooking, creative nonfiction, cultural interests, current affairs, diet/nutrition, design, education, environment, ethnic, foods, gardening, gay/lesbian, health, history, hobbies, humor, literature, memoirs, money, multicultural, music, parenting, photography, popular culture, politics, psychology, science, self-help, sociology, spirituality, sports, true crime, women's issues, women's studies, young adult. **Considers these fiction areas:** adventure, commercial, contemporary issues, crime, detective, ethnic, experimental, family saga, fantasy, feminist, gay, historical, humor, juvenile, lesbian, literary, mainstream, middle grade, multicultural, mystery,

picture books, science fiction, short story collections, suspense, thriller, translation, women's, young adult.

☞ Please note that we do not represent screenplays, romance fiction, or religious fiction.

**HOW TO CONTACT** HG Literary only accepts electronic submissions. Unless another method is specified below, please send a query letter and the first five pages of your manuscript (within the email–no attachments please!) to the appropriate agent for your book. If it is a picture book, please include the entire manuscript. If you were referred to us, please mention it in the first line of your query. We generally respond to queries within 6-8 weeks, although we do get behind occasionally. You can check out our agent bios for more information on each agent's particular interests. We're not able to respond to each query with detailed feedback, but we do appreciate all of your efforts and wish you the best of success with your writing career! Carrie Hannigan: http://QueryMe.Online/Hannigan. Josh Getzler: http://QueryMe.Online/Getzler. Victoria Well Arms: submissions@wellsarms.com. Note: If no response in three months, please assume it is not for us. Soumeya Bendimerad Roberts: https://QueryManager.com/SBR (Note: Due to the volume of queries Soumeya receives, she will only respond to those in which she's interested); Julia Kardon: https://querymanager.com/query/JuliaKardon (Note: Due to the volume of queries Julia receives, she will only respond to those in which she's interested); Rhea Lyons: Rhea is currently closed to queries; Jon Cobb: http://QueryMe.Online/Cobb. All agents except Rhea Lyons are open to new clients.

**RECENT SALES** Some recent sales are *Resident Aliens*, by K-Ming Chang (One World); the third book in the *Vera Kelly* series by Rosalie Knecht (Tin House); *When Carrot Met Cookie* by Erica Perl and Jonathan Fenske (Penguin Workshop); *Let Me Be Frank* by Tracy Dawson (Harper Design); and *The Necklace* by Matt Witten (Oceanview).

## ◉ DAVID HIGHAM ASSOCIATES

Incorporating Gregory & Gregory, 6th Floor, Waverley House, 7-12 Noel St., London W1F 8GQ UK. **E-mail:** dha@davidhigham.co.uk; submissions@davidhigham.co.uk; childrenssubmissions@davidhigham.co.uk. **Website:** www.davidhigham.co.uk. Estab. 1956. Member of AAR. Signatory of WGA.

**MEMBER AGENTS** Veronique Baxter; Nicola Chang; Elise Dillsworth; Jemima Forrester; Georgia

Glover; Anthony Goff; Andrew Gordon; Jane Gregory; Lizzy Kremer; Harriet Moore; Caroline Walsh; Jessica Woollard; Laura West; Camille Burns; Maddalena Cavaciuti; David Evans; Sara Langham; Christabel McKinley; Stephanie Glencross.

**REPRESENTS** Nonfiction, fiction, novels, short story collections, juvenile books. **Considers these nonfiction areas:** animals, art, autobiography, biography, business, child guidance, cooking, creative nonfiction, cultural interests, current affairs, environment, film, government, humor, inspirational, investigative, juvenile nonfiction, literature, memoirs, money, music, popular culture, politics, psychology, science, self-help, travel. **Considers these fiction areas:** action, adventure, commercial, crime, fantasy, historical, horror, humor, literary, mainstream, middle grade, mystery, romance, science fiction, suspense, thriller, young adult.

**HOW TO CONTACT** Accepts simultaneous submissions.

## JULIE A. HILL AND ASSOCIATES

12997 Caminito Del Pasaje, Del Mar CA 92014. **Fax:** (858)259-2777. **E-mail:** hillagent@aol.com. **Website:** www.publishersmarketplace/members/hillagent. **Contact:** Julie Hill.

**MEMBER AGENTS** Julie Hill, agent and principal.
**REPRESENTS** Nonfiction. **Considers these nonfiction areas:** architecture, art, biography, cooking, gardening, health, metaphysics, New Age, self-help, translation, travel, women's issues, technology books, both for professionals and laypersons. **Considers these script areas:** psychic.

☞ Specialties of the house are memoir, health, self-help, art, architecture, business/technology, both literary and reference travel. NOTE: We also do contract and sale consulting for authors who are working unagented. Consulting inquiries welcome.

**HOW TO CONTACT** E-query or query via snail mail with SASE. Accepts simultaneous submissions. Responds in 4-6 weeks to queries. Obtains most new clients through recommendations from authors, editors, and agents.

## HILL NADELL LITERARY AGENCY

6442 Santa Monica Blvd., Suite 200A, Los Angeles CA 90038. (310)860-9605. **Website:** www.hillnadell.com. Represents 100 clients.

**MEMBER AGENTS** Bonnie Nadell (nonfiction books include works on current affairs and food as well as memoirs and other narrative nonfiction; in fiction, she represents thrillers along with upmarket women's and literary fiction); Dara Hyde (literary and genre fiction, narrative nonfiction, graphic novels, memoir and the occasional young adult novel).

**REPRESENTS** Nonfiction, novels. **Considers these nonfiction areas:** biography, current affairs, environment, government, health, history, language, literature, medicine, popular culture, politics, science, technology, biography; government/politics, narrative. **Considers these fiction areas:** literary, mainstream, thriller, women's, young adult.

**HOW TO CONTACT** Send a query and SASE. If you would like your materials returned, please include adequate postage. To submit electronically: Send your query letter and the first 5-10 pages via online form. Due to the high volume of submissions the agency receives, it cannot guarantee a response to all queries. Accepts simultaneous submissions.

**TERMS** Agent receives 15% commission on domestic and film sales; 20% commission on foreign sales. Charges clients for photocopying and foreign mailings.

## HOLLOWAY LITERARY

P.O. Box 771, Cary NC 27512. **E-mail:** submissions@hollowayliteraryagency.com. **Website:** hollowayliteraryagency.com. **Contact:** Nikki Terpilowski. Estab. 2011. Member of AAR. Signatory of WGA. Also member of International Thriller Writers and Romance Writers of America. Represents 26 clients.

**MEMBER AGENTS** Nikki Terpilowski (romance, women's fiction, Southern fiction, historical fiction, cozy mysteries, lifestyle nonfiction (minimalism, homesteading, southern, etc.) commercial, upmarket/book club fiction, African-American fiction of all types, literary).

**REPRESENTS** Nonfiction, fiction, movie scripts, feature film. **Considers these nonfiction areas:** Americana, environment, humor, narrative nonfiction, New Journalism, essays. **Considers these fiction areas:** action, adventure, commercial, contemporary issues, crime, detective, ethnic, family saga, fantasy, glitz, historical, inspirational, literary, mainstream, metaphysical, middle grade, military, multicultural, mystery, new adult, New Age, regional, romance, short story collections, spiritual, suspense, thriller, urban fantasy, war, women's, young adult. **Considers these script areas:** action, adventure, biography, contemporary issues, ethnic, romantic comedy, romantic drama, teen, thriller, TV movie of the week.

☞ "Note to self-published authors: While we are happy to receive submissions from authors who have previously self-published novels, we do not represent self-published works. Send us your unpublished manuscripts only." Nikki is open to submissions and is selectively reviewing queries for cozy mysteries with culinary, historical or book/publishing industry themes written in the vein of Jaclyn Brady, Laura Childs, Julie Hyzy and Lucy Arlington; women's fiction with strong magical realism similar to Meena van Praag's *The Dress Shop of Dreams*, Sarah Addison Allen's *Garden Spells, Season of the Dragonflies* by Sarah Creech and Mary Robinette Kowal's Glamourist Series. She would love to find a wine-themed mystery series similar to Nadia Gordon's Sunny McCoskey series or Ellen Crosby's Wine County Mysteries that combine culinary themes with lots of great Southern history. Nikki is also interested in seeing contemporary romance set in the southern US or any wine county or featuring a culinary theme, dark, edgy historical romance, gritty military romance or romantic suspense with sexy Alpha heroes and lots of technical detail. She is also interested in acquiring historical fiction written in the vein of Alice Hoffman, Lalita Tademy and Isabel Allende. Nikki is also interested in espionage, military, political and AI thrillers similar to Tom Clancy, Robert Ludlum, Steve Berry, Vince Flynn, Brad Thor and Daniel Silva. Nikki has a special interest in nonfiction subjects related to governance, politics, military strategy and foreign relations; food and beverage, mindfulness, southern living and lifestyle. Does not want horror, true crime or novellas.

**HOW TO CONTACT** Send query and first 15 pages of ms pasted into the body of e-mail to submissions@hollowayliteraryagency.com. In the subject header write: (Insert Agent's Name)/Title/Genre. Holloway Literary does accept submissions via mail (query letter and first 50 pages). Expect a response time of at least 3 months. Include e-mail address, phone number, social media accounts, and mailing address on your query letter. Accepts simultaneous submissions. Responds in 6-8 weeks. If the agent is interested, he/she'll respond with a request for more material.

**RECENT SALES** A list of recent sales are listed on the agency website's "news" page.

## HORNFISCHER LITERARY MANAGEMENT

Austin TX **E-mail:** queries@hornfischerlit.com. **Website:** www.hornfischerlit.com. **Contact:** Jim Hornfischer, president. Estab. 2001. Represents 55 clients.

○ Prior to becoming a literary agent in 1993, Mr. Hornfischer held editorial positions at HarperCollins and McGraw-Hill in New York.

**REPRESENTS** Nonfiction. **Considers these nonfiction areas:** autobiography, creative nonfiction, current affairs, government, history, medicine, memoirs, military, popular culture, politics, science, war. **Considers these fiction areas:** commercial, historical, military.

☞ Hornfischer Literary Management, L.P., is a literary agency with a strong track record handling a broad range of serious and commercial nonfiction and select fiction.

**HOW TO CONTACT** E-mail queries only. Responds if interested. Accepts simultaneous submissions.

**TERMS** Agent receives 15% commission on domestic sales; 25% commission on foreign sales. Offers written contract.

**RECENT SALES** *Top Secret Umbra*, by Peter Pesavento; *Save or Avenge*, by Daniel Wasserbly; *Blindfold*, by Theo Padnos; *Sutherland Springs*, by Joe Holley; *The Last Stand of Payne Stewart*, by Kevin Robbins.

**TIPS** "When you query agents and send out proposals, present yourself as someone who's in command of his material and comfortable in his own skin. Too many writers have a palpable sense of anxiety and insecurity. Take a deep breath and realize that—if you're good—someone in the publishing world will want you."

## ⊘ HUDSON AGENCY

3 Travis Lane, Montrose New York 10548. (914)737-1475. **E-mail:** sue@hudsonagency.net. **Website:** www.hudsonagency.net. **Contact:** Sue Giordano. Estab. 25. Signatory of WGA. Represents 20+ clients.

**MEMBER AGENTS** Sue Giordano (partner/agent); Pat Giordano (partner/producer); Leif Giordano (agent/creative consultant); Michele Dickinson (agent).

**REPRESENTS** TV scripts, TV movie of the week, animation.

☞ Only handles writers for children's TV.

**HOW TO CONTACT** "We are no longer taking on any new clients."

## ⊘ ICM PARTNERS

65 E. 55th St., New York NY 10022. (212)556-5600. **E-mail:** careersny@icmpartners.com. **Website:** www.icmtalent.com. **Contact:** Literary Department. Member of AAR. Signatory of WGA.

**REPRESENTS** Nonfiction, fiction, novels.

**HOW TO CONTACT** Accepts simultaneous submissions.

## INKWELL MANAGEMENT, LLC

521 Fifth Ave., Suite 2600, New York NY 10175. (212)922-3500. **Fax:** (212)922-0535. **E-mail:** info@inkwellmanagement.com. **E-mail:** submissions@inkwellmanagement.com. **Website:** www.inkwell-management.com. Represents 500 clients.

**MEMBER AGENTS** Stephen Barbara (select adult fiction and nonfiction); William Callahan (nonfiction of all stripes, especially American history and memoir, pop culture and illustrated books, as well as voice-driven fiction that stands out from the crowd); Michael V. Carlisle; Catherine Drayton (bestselling authors of books for children, young adults and women readers); David Forrer (literary, commercial, historical and crime fiction to suspense/thriller, humorous nonfiction and popular history); Alexis Hurley (literary and commercial fiction, memoir, narrative nonfiction and more); Nathaniel Jacks (memoir, narrative nonfiction, social sciences, health, current affairs, business, religion, and popular history, as well as fiction—literary and commercial, women's, young adult, historical, short story, among others); Richard Pine; Eliza Rothstein (literary and commercial fiction, narrative nonfiction, memoir, popular science, and food writing); David Hale Smith; Kimberly Witherspoon; Jenny Witherell; Charlie Olson; George Lucas; Lyndsey Blessing; Claire Friedman; Michael Mungiello; Jessica Mileo; Maria Whelan; Namoi Eisenbeiss; Laura Hill; Hannah Lehmkuhl; Tizom Pope; Jessie Thorsted; Kristin van Ogtrop.

**REPRESENTS** Novels. **Considers these nonfiction areas:** biography, business, cooking, creative nonfiction, current affairs, foods, health, history, humor, memoirs, popular culture, religious, science. **Consid-**ers these fiction areas: commercial, crime, historical, literary, middle grade, picture books, romance, short story collections, suspense, thriller, women's, young adult.

**HOW TO CONTACT** "In the body of your e-mail, please include a query letter and a short writing sample (1-2 chapters). We currently accept submissions in all genres except screenplays. Due to the volume of queries we receive, our response time may take up to 2 months. Feel free to put 'Query for [Agent Name]: [Your Book Title]' in the e-mail subject line." Accepts simultaneous submissions. Obtains most new clients through recommendations from others.

**TERMS** Agent receives 15% commission on domestic sales; 20% commission on foreign sales. Offers written contract.

**TIPS** "We will not read mss before receiving a letter of inquiry."

## INTERNATIONAL TRANSACTIONS, INC.

P.O. Box 97, Gila NM 88038-0097. (845)373-9696. **E-mail:** Info@internationaltransactions.us. **Website:** www.intltrans.com. **Contact:** Peter Riva. Estab. 1975. Represents 120+ clients.

**MEMBER AGENTS** Peter Riva (principle).

**REPRESENTS** Nonfiction, fiction, novels, short story collections, juvenile books, scholarly books. illustrated books, anthologies. **Considers these nonfiction areas:** Americana, anthropology, archeology, architecture, art, autobiography, biography, business, computers, cooking, cultural interests, current affairs, diet/nutrition, environment, ethnic, film, foods, gay/lesbian, government, health, history, humor, inspirational, investigative, juvenile nonfiction, language, law, literature, medicine, memoirs, military, multicultural, music, popular culture, politics, religious, satire, science, self-help, sports, technology, translation, true crime, war, women's issues, women's studies, young adult. **Considers these fiction areas:** action, adventure, commercial, crime, detective, feminist, gay, historical, humor, juvenile, lesbian, literary, mainstream, middle grade, military, multicultural, mystery, new adult, police, religious, satire, science fiction, short story collections, sports, suspense, thriller, translation, war, westerns, women's, young adult, chick lit.

☞ "We specialize in large and small projects, helping qualified authors perfect material for publication." Seeking intelligent, well-written innovative material that breaks new ground.

Authors of nonfiction must have an active and wide-reaching platform to help promote their work (since publishers rarely work at that any more). Does not want to receive material influenced by TV (too much dialogue); a rehash of previous successful novels' themes, or poorly prepared material. Does not want to be sent any material being reviewed by others.

**HOW TO CONTACT** In the changing publishing world, we will have to be increasingly and extremely selective of new projects. First, e-query with an outline or synopsis. E-queries only. Put "Query: [Title]" in the e-mail subject line. Submissions or emails received without these conditions being met are automatically discarded. Responds in 3 weeks to queries if interested; 5 weeks for ms but only after follow-up request. Obtains most new clients through recommendations from others.

**TERMS** Agent receives 15% (25%+ on illustrated books) commission on domestic sales; 20% commission on foreign sales and media rights. Offers written contract; 100-day notice must be given to terminate contract. No additional fees, ever.

**RECENT SALES** Averaging 20+ book placements per year.

**TIPS** "'Book'—a published work of literature. That last word is the key. Not a string of words, not a book of (TV or film) 'scenes,' and never a stream of consciousness unfathomable by anyone outside of the writer's coterie. A writer should only begin to get 'interested in getting an agent' if the work is polished, literate and ready to be presented to a publishing house. Anything less is either asking for a quick rejection or is a thinly disguised plea for creative assistance—which is often given but never fiscally sound for the agents involved. Writers, even published authors, have difficulty in being objective about their own work. Friends and family are of no assistance in that process either. Writers should attempt to get their work read by the most unlikely and stern critic as part of the editing process, months before any agent is approached. In another matter: the economics of our job have changed as well. As the publishing world goes through the transition to e-books (much as the music industry went through the change to downloadable music)—a transition we expect to see at 95% within 10 years—everyone is nervous and wants 'assured bestsellers' from which to eke out a living until they know what the new e-world will continue to bring. This makes the sales rate and, especially, the advance royalty rates, plummet. Hence, our ability to take risks and take on new clients' work is increasingly perilous financially for us and all agents."

## J DE S ASSOCIATES, INC.

9 Shagbark Rd., Norwalk CT 06854. (203)838-7571. **Fax:** (203)866-2713. **E-mail:** jdespoel@aol.com. **Website:** www.jdesassociates.com. **Contact:** Jacques de Spoelberch. Estab. 1975.

◐ Prior to opening his agency, Mr. de Spoelberch was an editor with Houghton Mifflin. And launched International Literary Management for the International Management Group.

**REPRESENTS** Novels. **Considers these nonfiction areas:** biography, business, cultural interests, current affairs, economics, ethnic, government, health, history, law, medicine, metaphysics, military, New Age, politics, self-help, sociology, sports, translation. **Considers these fiction areas:** crime, detective, frontier, historical, juvenile, literary, mainstream, mystery, New Age, police, suspense, westerns, young adult.

**HOW TO CONTACT** "Brief queries by regular mail and e-mail are welcomed for fiction and nonfiction, but kindly do not include sample proposals or other material unless specifically requested to do so." Accepts simultaneous submissions. Responds in 2 months to queries. Obtains most new clients through recommendations from authors and other clients.

**TERMS** Agent receives 15% commission on domestic sales; 20% commission on foreign sales. Charges clients for foreign postage and photocopying.

**RECENT SALES** Joshilyn Jackson's novel *A Grown-Up Kind of Pretty* (Grand Central); Margaret George's final Tudor historical *Elizabeth I* (Penguin); the fifth in Leighton Gage's series of Brazilian thrillers *A Vine in the Blood* (Soho); Genevieve Graham's romance *Under the Same Sky* (Berkley Sensation); Hilary Holladay's biography of the early Beat Herbert Huncke, *American Hipster* (Magnus); Ron Rozelle's *My Boys and Girls Are In There: The 1937 New London School Explosion* (Texas A&M); the concluding novel in Dom Testa's YA science fiction series, *The Galahad Legacy* (Tor); and Bruce Coston's new collection of animal stories *The Gift of Pets* (St. Martin's Press).

## JABBERWOCKY LITERARY AGENCY

49 W. 45th St., 12th Floor, New York NY 10036. **Website:** www.awfulagent.com. **Contact:** Joshua Bilmes.

Estab. 1990. Other memberships include SFWA. Represents 120 clients.

**MEMBER AGENTS** Joshua Bilmes, Eddie Schneider, Lisa Rodgers, Brady McReynolds, Bridget Smith.

**REPRESENTS** Nonfiction, fiction, novels, novellas, juvenile books. **Considers these nonfiction areas:** autobiography, biography, business, cooking, current affairs, economics, ethnic, film, foods, gay/lesbian, government, health, history, humor, investigative, language, law, literature, medicine, memoirs, money, multicultural, music, popular culture, politics, psychology, satire, science, sociology, sports, technology, theater, war, women's issues, women's studies, young adult. **Considers these fiction areas:** action, adventure, commercial, contemporary issues, crime, detective, ethnic, family saga, fantasy, feminist, gay, glitz, historical, horror, humor, juvenile, lesbian, literary, mainstream, middle grade, multicultural, mystery, new adult, paranormal, psychic, regional, romance, satire, science fiction, sports, supernatural, suspense, thriller, urban fantasy, women's, young adult.

☛ This agency represents quite a lot of genre fiction (science fiction & fantasy), romance, and mystery; and is actively seeking to increase the amount of nonfiction projects. Select agents represent young adult and middle-grade projects. Book-length material and novellas only —no poetry, articles, or short fiction.

**HOW TO CONTACT** We are currently open to unsolicited queries. No phone or fax queries, please; we only accept queries to our query inboxes. Please check our website, as there may be times during the year when we are not accepting queries. Query letter only; no manuscript material unless requested. Accepts simultaneous submissions. Responds in 3-6 weeks to queries. Obtains most new clients through solicitations, recommendation by current clients.

**TERMS** Agent receives 15% commission on domestic sales; 20% commission on foreign sales. Offers written contract, binding for 1 year. Charges clients for book purchases, photocopying, international book/ms mailing.

**RECENT SALES** *Rhythm of War* by Brandon Sanderson; *Mexican Gothic* by Silvia Moreno-Garcia; *The Russian Cage* by Charlaine Harris; *The Kingdom of Liars* by Nick Martell; *The Desert Prince* by Peter V. Brett; *Ophie's Ghosts* by Justina Ireland; *The Southern Book Club's Guide to Slaying Vampires* by Grady Hendrix; *Son of the Storm* by Suyi Davies Okungbowa. Other clients include Lilliam Rivera, Tanya Huff, Simon Green, Jack Campbell, Marie Brennan, K. Eason, T. Frohock, Michael Mammay, Jim Hines, Mark Hodder, Toni Kelner, Ari Marmell, Emma Mills, C.M. Waggoner, Ellery Queen, Erin Lindsey, Mallory O'Meara, and Walter Jon Williams.

**TIPS** "In approaching with a query, the most important things to us are your credits and your biographical background to the extent it's relevant to your work. I (and most agents) will ignore the adjectives you may choose to describe your own work."

## JANKLOW & NESBIT ASSOCIATES

285 Madison Ave., 21st Floor, New York NY 10017. (212)421-1700. **Fax:** (212)355-1403. **E-mail:** info@janklow.com. **E-mail:** submissions@janklow.com. **Website:** www.janklowandnesbit.com. Estab. 1989.

**MEMBER AGENTS** Morton L. Janklow; Anne Sibbald; Lynn Nesbit; Luke Janklow; PJ Mark (interests are eclectic, including short stories and literary novels. His nonfiction interests include journalism, popular culture, memoir/narrative, essays and cultural criticism); Paul Lucas (literary and commercial fiction, focusing on literary thrillers, science fiction and fantasy; also seeks narrative histories of ideas and objects, as well as biographies and popular science); Emma Parry (nonfiction by experts, but will consider outstanding literary fiction and upmarket commercial fiction); Kirby Kim (formerly of WME); Marya Spence; Allison Hunter; Melissa Flashman; Stefanie Lieberman.

**REPRESENTS** Nonfiction, fiction.

**HOW TO CONTACT** Be sure to address your submission to a particular agent. For fiction submissions, send an informative cover letter, a brief synopsis and the first 10 pages. "If you are sending an e-mail submission, please include the sample pages in the body of the e-mail below your query. For nonfiction submissions, send an informative cover letter, a full outline, and the first 10 pages of the ms. If you are sending an e-mail submission, please include the sample pages in the body of the e-mail below your query. For picture book submissions, send an informative cover letter, full outline, and include a picture book dummy and at least one full-color sample. If you are sending an e-mail submission, please attach a picture book dummy as a PDF and the full-color samples as JPEGs or PDFs." Accepts simultaneous submissions. Due to the volume of submissions received, please note that we cannot respond to every query. We shall contact you if we wish to pursue your submission. Obtains most new clients through recommendations from others.

**TIPS** "Please send a short query with first 10 pages or artwork."

## THE CAROLYN JENKS AGENCY

30 Cambridge Park Dr. Unit 3140, Cambridge MA 02140. (617)233-9130. **Website:** www.carolynjenksagency.com. **Contact:** Carolyn Jenks. Estab. 1987. Signatory of WGA. Represents 39 clients.

○ Began publishing career working at Scribner's Subsidiary Rights Dept., managing editor Ballantine Books, Literary agent subcontractor William Morris Agency, Partner Kurt Hellmer Literary Agency. Established Jenks Agency in NYC in the 1970s.

**MEMBER AGENTS** Carolyn Jenks, carolyn@carolynjenksagency.com; Becca Crandall, becca@carolynjenksagency.com; Brenna Girard, brenna@carolynjenksagency.com; Kwaku Acheampong, kwaku@carolynjenksagency.com.

**REPRESENTS** Nonfiction, fiction, novels, short story collections, novellas, feature film, TV movie of the week, documentary, miniseries. **Considers these nonfiction areas:** animals, autobiography, biography, creative nonfiction, cultural interests, current affairs, education, environment, film, gay/lesbian, literature, memoirs, politics, theater, true crime, women's studies. **Considers these fiction areas:** contemporary issues, crime, detective, family saga, feminist, gay, historical, literary, mainstream, mystery, short story collections, thriller. **Considers these script areas:** autobiography, biography, contemporary issues, detective, documentary, family saga, feature film, gay, historical, lesbian, mainstream, romantic drama, suspense, thriller, TV movie of the week.

**HOW TO CONTACT** Please submit a one page query including a brief bio via the form on the agency website. Queries are reviewed on a rolling basis, and we will follow up directly with the author if there is interest. No cold calls.

**TERMS** Offers written contract, 1-3 years depending on the project. Standard agency commissions. No fees.

**RECENT SALES** *Snafu*, *The Land of Forgotten Girls*, by Erin Kelly, HarperCollins; *The Christos Mosaic*, by

Vincent Czyz, Blank Slate Press; *A Tale of Two Maidens*, by Anne Echols, Bagwyn Books; *Esther, Magnolia City*, by Duncan Alderson, Kensington Books; *Create My Heart*, Pamela Rivers; *Silo*, by Kate McCamy; *New Circle Theatre, Until The Iris Bloom*, Tina Olton; *American Ghosts*, Edward Santella; *The Ostermann House*, John R. Klein.

**WRITERS CONFERENCES** Book Club appearances Womens' Writing and *The Red Tent*, by Anita Diamant, The Villages, Florida.

**TIPS** E-mail contact only. Do not query for more than one property at a time. Response within two weeks unless otherwise notified.

## JERNIGAN LITERARY AGENCY

P.O. Box 741624, Dallas TX 75374. (972)722-4838. **E-mail:** jerniganliterary@gmail.com. **Contact:** Barry Jernigan. Estab. 2010. Represents 45 clients.

○ Prior to becoming an agent, spent many years in the book department at the William Morris Agency.

**MEMBER AGENTS** Barry Jernigan (eclectic tastes in nonfiction and fiction; nonfiction interests include women's issues, gay/lesbian, ethnic/cultural, memoirs, true crime; fiction interests include mystery, suspense and thriller).

**REPRESENTS** Nonfiction, fiction, novels, movie scripts, feature film. **Considers these nonfiction areas:** biography, business, child guidance, current affairs, education, ethnic, health, history, how-to, memoirs, military, psychology, self-help, true crime. **Considers these fiction areas:** historical, mainstream, mystery, romance, thriller.

**HOW TO CONTACT** E-mail your query with a synopsis, brief bio and the first few pages embedded (no attachments). "We do not accept unsolicited manuscripts. We accept submissions via e-mail only. No snail mail accepted." Accepts simultaneous submissions. Responds in 2 weeks to queries; 6 weeks to mss. Obtains new clients through conferences and word of mouth.

**TERMS** Agent receives 15% commission.

## JET LITERARY ASSOCIATES

941 Calle Mejia, #507, Santa Fe NM 87501. (505)780-0721. **E-mail:** etp@jetliterary.com. **Website:** www.jetliterary.wordpress.com. **Contact:** Liz Trupin-Pulli. Estab. 1975.

**MEMBER AGENTS** Liz Trupin-Pulli (adult fiction/nonfiction; romance, mysteries, parenting); Jim Trupin (adult fiction/nonfiction, military history, pop culture).

**REPRESENTS** Nonfiction, fiction, novels, short story collections.

☛ "JET was founded in New York in 1975, so we bring a wealth of knowledge and contacts, as well as quite a bit of expertise to our representation of writers." JET represents a wide range of adult fiction and nonfiction. Does not want to receive YA, sci-fi, fantasy, horror, poetry, children's, how-to, memoirs, illustrated or religious books.

**HOW TO CONTACT** Only an e-query should be sent at first. Accepts simultaneous submissions. Responds in 1 week to queries; 8-12 weeks to mss. Obtains most new clients through recommendations from others, solicitations, conferences.

**TERMS** Agent receives 15% commission on domestic sales; 10% commission on foreign sales, while foreign agent receives 10%. Offers written agency contract, binding for 3 years. This agency charges for reimbursement of mailing and any photocopying.

**TIPS** "Do not write cute queries; stick to a straightforward message that includes the title and what your book is about, why you are suited to write this particular book, and what you have written in the past (if anything), along with a bit of a bio."

## KELLER MEDIA INC.

578 Washington Blvd., No. 745, Marina del Rey CA 90292. (800)278-8706. **Website:** www.kellermedia.com. **Contact:** Wendy Keller, senior agent; Will Reichert, executive assistant; Elise Howard, query manager. Estab. 1989. Member of the National Speakers Association.

○ Prior to becoming an agent, Ms. Keller was an award-winning journalist and worked for PR Newswire. Prior to her agenting career, Ms. Close Zavala read, reviewed, edited, rejected, and selected thousands of book and script projects for agencies, film companies, and publishing companies. She uses her background in entertainment and legal affairs in negotiating the best deals for her clients and in helping them think outside of the box.

**REPRESENTS** Nonfiction. **Considers these nonfiction areas:** archeology, autobiography, biography, business, child guidance, crafts, creative nonfiction, current affairs, diet/nutrition, economics, environment, film, foods, gardening, health, history, hobbies, how-to, inspirational, investigative, literature, money, music, parenting, popular culture, politics, psychology, science, self-help, sociology, technology, true crime, women's issues, relationships, pop culture, pop psychology, management, career, entrepreneurship, and personal finance.

☛ "All of our authors are highly credible experts, who have or want to create a significant platform in media, academia, politics, paid professional speaking, syndicated columns, and/or regular appearances on radio/TV." Does not want (and absolutely will not respond to) scripts, teleplays, screenplays, poetry, juvenile, science fiction, fantasy, anything religious or overtly political, picture books, illustrated books, young adult, science fiction, fantasy, first-person stories of mental or physical illness, wrongful incarceration, abduction by aliens, books channeled by aliens, demons, or dead celebrities ("we wish we were kidding!").

**HOW TO CONTACT** "We look forward to working with talented writers who are offering something new and exciting and/or fresh takes on pre-existing subject matter. To query, please review our current screening criteria on our website. Please do not mail us anything unless requested to do so by a staff member." Accepts simultaneous submissions. Responds in 7 days or less. Obtains most new clients through referrals.

**TERMS** Agent receives 15% commission on domestic sales; 20% commission on foreign, dramatic, sponsorship, appearance fees, audio, and merchandising deals; 30% on speaking engagements we book for the author.

**RECENT SALES** Check online for latest sales.

**TIPS** "Don't send a query to any agent (including us) unless you're certain they handle the type of book you're writing. 90% of all rejections happen because what someone offered us doesn't fit our established, advertised, printed, touted and shouted guidelines. Be organized! Have your proposal in order before you query. Never make apologies for 'bad writing' or sloppy content. Please just get it right before you waste your 1 shot with us. Have something new, different or interesting to say and be ready to dedicate your whole heart to marketing it. Marketing is everything in publishing these days."

## ⊘ NATASHA KERN LITERARY AGENCY

White Salmon WA 98672. **E-mail:** via website. **Website:** www.natashakernliterary.com. **Contact:** Natasha Kern. Estab. 1986. Memberships include RWA, MWA, SinC, The Authors Guild, and American Society of Journalists and Authors. Represents 40 clients.

🔾 Prior to opening her agency, Ms. Kern worked in publishing in New York. This agency has sold more than 1,500 books.

**REPRESENTS** Fiction, novels. **Considers these nonfiction areas:** investigative journalism. **Considers these fiction areas:** commercial, historical, inspirational, mainstream, multicultural, mystery, romance, suspense, women's, only inspirational fiction in these genres.

☛ "This agency specializes in inspirational fiction." Inspirational fiction in a broad range of genres including: suspense and mysteries, historicals, romance, and contemporary novels. By referral only. Does not represent horror, true crime, erotica, children's books, short stories or novellas, poetry, screenplays, technical, photography or art/craft books, cookbooks, travel, or sports books.

**HOW TO CONTACT** This agency is currently closed to unsolicited fiction and nonfiction submissions. Submissions only via referral. Obtains new clients by referral only.

**TERMS** Agent receives 15% commission on domestic sales; 20% commission on foreign sales; 15% commission on film sales.

**WRITERS CONFERENCES** RWA National Conference; ACFW Conference.

**TIPS** "Your chances of being accepted for representation will be greatly enhanced by going to our website first. Our idea of a dream client is someone who participates in a mutually respectful business relationship, is clear about needs and goals, and communicates about career planning. If we know what you need and want, we can help you achieve it. A dream client has a storytelling gift, a commitment to a writing career, a desire to learn and grow, and a passion for excellence. We want clients who are expressing their own unique voice and truly have something of their own to communicate. This client understands that many people have to work together for a book to succeed and that everything in publishing takes far longer than one imagines. Trust and communication are truly essential."

## HARVEY KLINGER, INC.

300 W. 55th St., Suite 11V, New York NY 10019. (212)581-7068. **E-mail:** queries@harveyklinger.com. **Website:** www.harveyklinger.com. **Contact:** Harvey Klinger. Estab. 1977. Member of AAR, PEN. Represents 100 clients.

**MEMBER AGENTS** Harvey Klinger, harvey@harveyklinger.com; David Dunton, david@harveyklinger.com (popular culture, music-related books, literary fiction, young adult, fiction, and memoirs); Andrea Somberg, andrea@harveyklinger.com (literary fiction, commercial fiction, romance, sci-fi/fantasy, mysteries/thrillers, young adult, middle grade, quality narrative nonfiction, popular culture, how-to, self-help, humor, interior design, cookbooks, health/fitness); Wendy Silbert Levinson, wendy@harveyklinger.com (literary and commercial fiction, occasional children's YA or MG, wide variety of nonfiction); Rachel Ridout, rachel@harveyklinger.com (children's, MG and YA), Cate Hart, cate@harveyklinger.com (women's fiction, historicals, MG and YA), Analieze Cervantes, analieze@harveyklinger.com (primarily MG and YA in all categories), Jennifer Herrington, jennifer@harveyklinger.com (MG and YA in all categories, adult women's fiction).

**REPRESENTS** Nonfiction, fiction, novels, juvenile books. **Considers these nonfiction areas:** anthropology, autobiography, biography, business, child guidance, cooking, crafts, creative nonfiction, cultural interests, current affairs, diet/nutrition, foods, gay/lesbian, health, history, how-to, investigative, juvenile nonfiction, literature, medicine, memoirs, money, music, popular culture, psychology, science, self-help, sociology, spirituality, sports, technology, true crime, women's issues, women's studies, young adult. **Considers these fiction areas:** action, adventure, commercial, contemporary issues, crime, detective, erotica, family saga, fantasy, gay, glitz, historical, horror, juvenile, lesbian, literary, mainstream, middle grade, mystery, new adult, police, romance, suspense, thriller, women's, young adult.

This agency specializes in big, mainstream, contemporary fiction and nonfiction. Great debut or established novelists and in nonfiction, authors with great ideas and a national platform already in place to help promote one's book. No screenplays, poetry, textbooks or anything too technical.

**HOW TO CONTACT** Use online e-mail submission form on the website, or query with SASE via snail mail. No phone or fax queries. Don't send unsolicited mss or e-mail attachments. Make submission letter to the point and as brief as possible. A bit of biographical information is always welcome, particularly with nonfiction submissions where one's national platform is vitally important. Accepts simultaneous submissions. Responds in 2-4 weeks to queries, if interested. Obtains most new clients through recommendations from others.

**TERMS** Agent receives 15% commission on domestic sales; 25% commission on foreign sales. Offers written contract. Charges for photocopying mss and overseas postage for mss.

**RECENT SALES** *The Dearly Beloved*, by Cara Wall; *Other People's Children*, by R.J. Hoffmann; *I Me, Myself and Us*, by Brian Little; *The Secret of Magic*, by Deborah Johnson; *Children of the Mist*, by Paula Quinn. Other clients include George Taber, Terry Kay, Scott Mebus, Jacqueline Kolosov, Jonathan Skariton, Tara Altebrando, Alex McAuley, Eva Nagorski, Greg Kot, Justine Musk, Ashley Kahn, Barbara De Angelis, Robert Patton, Augusta Trobaugh, Deborah Blum, Andy Aledort, Alan Paul.

### KNEERIM & WILLIAMS

90 Canal St., Boston MA 02114. **Website:** www.kwlit. com. Also located in Santa Fe, NM, with affiliated office in NYC. Estab. 1990.

○ Prior to becoming an agent, Mr. Williams was a lawyer; Ms. Kneerim was a publisher and editor; Ms. Flynn was pursuing a Ph.D. in history; Ms. Savarese was a publishing executive.

**MEMBER AGENTS** Katherine Flynn, kflynn@ kwlit.com (history, biography, politics, current affairs, adventure, nature, pop culture, science, and psychology for nonfiction and particularly loves exciting narrative nonfiction; literary and commercial fiction with urban or foreign locales, crime novels, insight into women's lives, biting wit, and historical settings); Jill Kneerim, jill@kwlit.com (narrative history; big ideas; sociology; psychology and anthropology; biography; women's issues; and good writing); John Taylor ("Ike") Williams, jtwilliams@kwblit.com (biography, history, politics, natural science, and anthropology); Carol Franco, carolfranco@comcast.net (business; nonfiction; distinguished self-help/how-to); Lucy Cleland, lucy@kwlit.com (literary/commercial fiction, YA novels, history, narrative); Carolyn Savarese, carolyn@kwlit.com (riveting narratives in science, technology and medicine; unknown history; big think subjects; memoir; lifestyle and design, literary fiction and short stories); Sarah Khalil; Elaine Rogers; Matthew Valentinas.

Actively seeking distinguished authors, experts, professionals, intellectuals, and serious writers.

**HOW TO CONTACT** E-query an individual agent. Send no attachments. Put "Query" in the subject line. Accepts simultaneous submissions. Obtains most new clients through recommendations from others.

### THE KNIGHT AGENCY

232 W. Washington St., Madison GA 30650. **E-mail:** deidre.knight@knightagency.net. **E-mail:** submissions@knightagency.net. **Website:** http://knightagency.net/. **Contact:** Deidre Knight. Estab. 1996. Member of AAR, SCWBI, WFA, SFWA, RWA. Represents 200+ clients.

**MEMBER AGENTS** Deidre Knight (romance, women's fiction, erotica, commercial fiction, inspirational, m/m fiction, memoir and nonfiction narrative, personal finance, true crime, business, popular culture, self-help, religion, and health); Pamela Harty (romance, women's fiction, young adult, business, motivational, diet and health, memoir, parenting, pop culture, and true crime); Elaine Spencer (romance (single title and category), women's fiction, commercial "book-club" fiction, cozy mysteries, young adult and middle grade material); Lucienne Diver (fantasy, science fiction, romance, suspense and young adult); Nephele Tempest (literary/commercial fiction, women's fiction, fantasy, science fiction, romantic suspense, paranormal romance, contemporary romance, historical fiction, young adult and middle grade fiction); Melissa Jeglinski (romance [contemporary, category, historical, inspirational], young adult, middle grade, women's fiction and mystery); Kristy Hunter (romance, women's fiction, commercial fiction, young adult and middle grade material), Travis Pennington (young adult, middle grade, mysteries, thrillers, commercial fiction, and romance [nothing paranormal/fantasy in any genre for now]); Janna Bonikowski (romance, women's fiction, young adult, cozy mystery, upmarket fiction); Jackie Williams.

**REPRESENTS** Nonfiction, fiction, novels. **Considers these nonfiction areas:** autobiography, business, creative nonfiction, cultural interests, current affairs, diet/nutrition, design, economics, ethnic, film, foods, gay/lesbian, health, history, how-to, inspirational, interior design, investigative, juvenile nonfiction, literature, memoirs, military, money, multicultural, parenting, popular culture, politics, psychology, self-help, sociology, technology, travel, true crime, women's issues, young adult. **Considers these fiction areas:** commercial, crime, erotica, fantasy, gay, historical, juvenile, lesbian, literary, mainstream, middle grade, multicultural, mystery, new adult, paranormal, psychic, romance, science fiction, thriller, urban fantasy, women's, young adult.

☞ Actively seeking romance in all subgenres, including romantic suspense, paranormal romance, historical romance (a particular love of mine), LGBT, contemporary, and also category romance. Occasionally I represent new adult. I'm also seeking women's fiction with vivid voices and strong concepts (think *Me Before You*). Further seeking YA and MG, and select nonfiction in the categories of personal development, self-help, finance/business, memoir, parenting and health. Does not want to receive screenplays, short stories, poetry, essays, or children's picture books.

**HOW TO CONTACT** E-queries only. "Your submission should include a one-page query letter and the first five pages of your manuscript. All text must be contained in the body of your e-mail. Attachments will not be opened nor included in the consideration of your work. Queries must be addressed to a specific agent. Please do not query multiple agents." Accepts simultaneous submissions. Responds in 1-2 weeks on queries, 6-8 weeks on submissions.

**TERMS** 15% Simple agency agreement with open-ended commitment. 15% commission on all domestic sales, 20% on foreign and film.

## LINDA KONNER LITERARY AGENCY

10 W. 15th St., Suite 1918, New York NY 10011. **E-mail:** ldkonner@cs.com. **Website:** www.lindakonnerliteraryagency.com. **Contact:** Linda Konner. Estab. 1996. Member of AAR. Other memberships include ASJA and Authors Guild. Represents 50 clients.

**REPRESENTS** Nonfiction. **Considers these nonfiction areas:** business, child guidance, cooking, diet/nutrition, foods, health, how-to, inspirational, investigative, medicine, money, parenting, popular culture, psychology, science, self-help, true crime, women's issues, celebrity memoir, African American and Latino issues, relationships, popular science.

☞ This agency specializes in health, self-help, and how-to books. Authors/co-authors must be top experts in their field with a substantial media and/or social media platform. Prescriptive (self-help) books written by recognized experts in their field with a large social media following and/or national profile via traditional media and large/frequent speaking engagements. Does not want fiction, children's, YA, religious.

**HOW TO CONTACT** Query by e-mail with synopsis and author bio, including size of social media following, size of website following (your own and bigger ones you blog for regularly), appearances in traditional media (print/TV/radio), podcasts and frequency/size of speaking engagements. Prefers to read materials exclusively for 2 weeks. Accepts simultaneous submissions. Responds within 2 weeks. Obtains most new clients through recommendations from others, occasional solicitation among established authors/journalists.

**TERMS** Agent receives 15% commission on domestic sales; 25% commission on foreign sales. Offers written contract. Charges one-time fee for domestic expenses; additional expenses may be incurred for foreign sales.

**RECENT SALES** *What to Eat When You Want to Get Pregnant* by Nicole Avena, PhD (Kensington); *Unblocked* by Margaret Lynch Raniere & David Raniere, PhD (Hay House); *What to Do with Everything You Own to Leave the Legacy You Want* by Marni Jameson (The Experiment); *Raising Resilient Kids* by Rhonda Spencer-Hwang, DrPH, MPH (Tyndale); *Changemaker Playbook* by Henry De Sio Jr. (Nicholas Brealey/Hachette).

**WRITERS CONFERENCES** ASJA Writers Conference, Harvard Medical School's "Publishing Books,

Memoirs, and Other Creative Nonfiction" Annual Conference.

## STUART KRICHEVSKY LITERARY AGENCY, INC.

6 E. 39th St., Suite 500, New York NY 10016. (212)725-5288. **Fax:** (212)725-5275. **Website:** www.skagency.com. Member of AAR.

**MEMBER AGENTS** Stuart Krichevsky, query@skagency.com (emphasis on narrative nonfiction, literary journalism and literary and commercial fiction); Ross Harris, rhquery@skagency.com (voice-driven humor and memoir, books on popular culture and our society, narrative nonfiction and literary fiction); David Patterson, dpquery@skagency.com (writers of upmarket narrative nonfiction and literary fiction, historians, journalists and thought leaders); Mackenzie Brady Watson, mbwquery@skagency.com (narrative nonfiction, science, history, sociology, investigative journalism, food, business, memoir, and select upmarket and literary YA fiction); Hannah Schwartz, hsquery@skagency; Laura Usselman, luquery@skagency.com; Melissa Danaczko; Laura Usselman; Aemilia Phillips.

**REPRESENTS** Nonfiction, novels. **Considers these nonfiction areas:** business, creative nonfiction, foods, history, humor, investigative, memoirs, popular culture, science, sociology, memoir. **Considers these fiction areas:** commercial, contemporary issues, literary, young adult.

**HOW TO CONTACT** Please send a query letter and the first few (up to 10) pages of your ms or proposal in the body of an e-mail (not an attachment) to one of the e-mail addresses. No attachments. Responds if interested. Accepts simultaneous submissions. Obtains most new clients through recommendations from others, solicitations.

## KT LITERARY, LLC

9249 S. Broadway, #200-543, Highlands Ranch CO 80129. **E-mail:** contact@ktliterary.com. **Website:** www.ktliterary.com. **Contact:** Kate Schafer Testerman, Sara Megibow, Renee Nyen, Hannah Fergesen, Hilary Harwell. Estab. 2008. Member of AAR, SCBWI, YALSA, ALA, SFWA and RWA. Represents 75 clients.

**MEMBER AGENTS** Kate Testerman (middle grade and young adult); Renee Nyen (middle grade and young adult); Sara Megibow (middle grade, young adult, romance, science fiction and fantasy); Hannah Fergesen (middle grade, young adult and speculative fiction); and Hilary Harwell (middle grade and young adult); Kelly Van Sant; Jas Perry; Chelsea Hensley; Aida Z. Lilly; Kate Linnea Walsh. Always LGBTQ and diversity friendly!

**REPRESENTS** Fiction. **Considers these fiction areas:** fantasy, middle grade, romance, science fiction, young adult.

Kate is looking only at young adult and middle grade fiction, especially #OwnVoices, and selective nonfiction for teens and tweens. Sara seeks authors in middle grade, young adult, romance, science fiction, and fantasy. Renee is looking for young adult and middle grade fiction only. Hannah is interested in speculative fiction in young adult, middle grade, and adult. Hilary is looking for young adult and middle grade fiction only. "We're thrilled to be actively seeking new clients with great writing, unique stories, and complex characters, for middle grade, young adult, and adult fiction. We are especially interested in diverse voices." Does not want adult mystery, thrillers, or adult literary fiction.

**HOW TO CONTACT** Check website for which agents are open to submissions. "To query us, please select one of the agents at KT Literary at a time. If we pass, you can feel free to submit to another. Please e-mail your query letter and the first 3 pages of your manuscript in the body of the e-mail to either Kate at katequery@ktliterary.com, Sara at saraquery@ktliterary.com, Renee at reneequery@ktliterary.com, Hannah at hannahquery@ktliterary.com, or Hilary at hilaryquery@ktliterary.com. The subject line of your e-mail should include the word 'Query' along with the title of your manuscript. Queries should not contain attachments. Attachments will not be read, and queries containing attachments will be deleted unread. We aim to reply to all queries within 4 weeks of receipt. For examples of query letters, please feel free to browse the About My Query archives on the KT Literary website. In addition, if you're an author who is sending a new query, but who previously submitted a novel to us for which we requested chapters but ultimately declined, please do say so in your query letter. If we like your query, we'll ask for the first 5 chapters and a complete synopsis. For our purposes, the synopsis should include the full plot of the book including the conclusion. Don't tease us. Thanks! We are not accepting snail mail queries or queries by phone at this time. We also do not accept pitches on social media." Accepts simultaneous submissions. Responds in 2-4 weeks to queries; 2 months to mss. Obtains most new clients through query slush pile.

**TERMS** Agent receives 15% commission on domestic sales; 20% commission on foreign sales. Offers written contract; 30-day notice must be given to terminate contract.

**RECENT SALES** *Most Likely*, by Sarah Watson, *All of Us With Wings*, by Michelle Ruiz Keil, *Postcards for a Songbird*, by Rebekah Crane, *The Tourist Trap*, by Sarah Morgenthaler, *The Last Year of James and Kat*, by Amy Spalding, and many more. A full list of clients and most recent sales are available on the agency website and some recent sales are available on Publishers Marketplace.

**WRITERS CONFERENCES** Various SCBWI conferences, ALA, BookExpo, Bologna, RWA, Wonder-Con, ComicCon.

## PETER LAMPACK AGENCY, INC.

The Empire State Building, 350 Fifth Ave., Suite 5300, New York NY 10118. (212) 687-9106. **Fax:** (212) 687-9109. **E-mail:** andrew@peterlampackagency.com. **Website:** www.peterlampackagency.com. **Contact:** Andrew Lampack. Estab. 1977.

**REPRESENTS** Nonfiction, fiction, novels. **Considers these fiction areas:** action, adventure, commercial, crime, detective, literary, mainstream, mystery, police, suspense, thriller.

- "This agency specializes in commercial fiction, and nonfiction by recognized experts." Actively seeking literary and commercial fiction in the following categories: adventure, action, thrillers, mysteries, suspense, and psychological thrillers. Does not want to receive horror, romance, science fiction, westerns, historical literary fiction, or academic material.

**HOW TO CONTACT** The Peter Lampack Agency no longer accepts material through conventional mail. E-queries only. When submitting, you should include a cover letter, author biography and a 1- or 2-page synopsis. Please do not send more than 1 sample chapter of your ms at a time. "Due to the extremely high volume of submissions, we ask that you allow 4-6 weeks

for a response." Obtains most new clients through referrals made by clients.

**TERMS** Agent receives 15% commission on domestic sales; 20% commission on foreign sales.

**RECENT SALES** *Clive Cussler's Untitled Oregon Files #16*, by Mike Maden; *Clive Cussler's Untitled NUMA Files #16*, by Graham Brown; *Clive Cussler's The Saboteurs*, by Justin Scott; *Clive Cussler's The Devil's Sea*, by Dirk Cussler; *Clive Cussler's Serpent's Eye*, by Robin Burcell; *Blood On The Table*, by Gerry Spence; *The Death of Jesus*, by J.M. Coetzee.

**WRITERS CONFERENCES** BookExpo America; Mystery Writers of America.

**TIPS** "Submit only your best work for consideration. Have a very specific agenda of goals you wish your prospective agent to accomplish for you. Provide the agent with a comprehensive statement of your credentials—educational and professional accomplishments."

## THE STEVE LAUBE AGENCY

24 W. Camelback Rd., A-635, Phoenix AZ 85013. **E-mail:** info@stevelaube.com. **Website:** www.stevelaube.com. Estab. 2004. Represents 330+ clients.

- Prior to becoming an agent, Mr. Laube worked over a decade as a Christian bookseller (honored as bookstore of the year in the industry) and 11 years as editorial director of nonfiction with Bethany House Publishers (named editor of the year). Also named Agent of the Year in 2009. Mrs. Murray was an accomplished novelist before becoming an agent. She was also named Agent of the Year in 2017. Mr. Hostetler is also an accomplished author with over 50 books in print. Mr. Balow has over three decades of marketing experience and is an expert in brand management (he was the marketing director for the Left Behind series while at Tyndale Publishers). Combined the agency has over 120 years of experience in the industry.

**MEMBER AGENTS** Steve Laube (president), Tamela Hancock Murray, Bob Hostetler, Dan Balow.

**REPRESENTS** Nonfiction, fiction, novels. **Considers these nonfiction areas:** inspirational, religious, spirituality, Christian. **Considers these fiction areas:** inspirational, religious, Christian.

- Primarily serves the Christian market (CBA). Actively seeking Christian fiction and Christian nonfiction. Does not want to receive poetry or cookbooks.

**HOW TO CONTACT** Consult the website for guidelines because queries are sent to assistants, and the assistants' e-mail addresses may change. Submit proposal package, outline, 3 sample chapters, SASE. For e-mail submissions, attach a Word doc or PDF. Accepts simultaneous submissions. Responds in 8-12 weeks to queries. Obtains most new clients through recommendations from others, solicitations, conferences.

**TERMS** Agent receives 15% commission on domestic sales; 20% commission on foreign sales. Offers written contract; 30-day notice must be given to terminate contract.

**RECENT SALES** Averages closing a new book deal every two business days, often for multiple titles in a contract. Clients include Dallas & Amanda Jenkins (The Chosen TV), Lisa Bergren, Lynette Eason, Susy Larson, Deborah Raney, Vannetta Chapman, Robert Lesslie, Stephen M. Miller, Nancy Pearcey, William Lane Craig, Elizabeth Goddard, Kim Vogel Sawyer, Nadine Brandes, Mesu Andrews, Hugh Ross, Kathy Tyers, Virginia Vaughan, Roseanna White, Bill & Pam Farrel, Carla Laureano, Stan Jantz, Ronie Kendig, and Kyle Mann (Babylon Bee).

**WRITERS CONFERENCES** Blue Ridge Christian Writers' Conference; RealmMakers; American Christian Fiction Writers' Conference (ACFW), and others.

**TIPS** Please follow the guidelines on our website. Many fail to take this small step.

## LAUNCHBOOKS LITERARY AGENCY

**E-mail:** david@launchbooks.com. **Website:** www.launchbooks.com. **Contact:** David Fugate. Estab. 2005. Represents 45 clients.

○ David Fugate has been an agent for over 25 years and has successfully represented more than 1,000 book titles. He left another agency to found LaunchBooks in 2005.

**REPRESENTS** Nonfiction, fiction, novels. **Considers these nonfiction areas:** animals, anthropology, autobiography, biography, business, computers, creative nonfiction, current affairs, diet/nutrition, economics, environment, film, health, history, how-to, humor, investigative, language, literature, medicine, memoirs, money, music, parenting, popular culture, politics, psychology, recreation, science, self-help, sex, sociology, sports, technology, travel. **Considers these fiction areas:** action, adventure, commercial, crime,

fantasy, horror, humor, mainstream, military, paranormal, satire, science fiction, sports, suspense, thriller, urban fantasy, war, westerns.

☞ "We're looking for genre-breaking fiction. Do you have the next *The Martian*? Or maybe the next *Red Rising*, *Ready Player One*, or *Dark Matter*? We're on the lookout for fun, engaging, contemporary novels that appeal to a broad audience. In nonfiction, we're interested in a broad range of topics. Check www.launchbooks.com/submissions for a complete list."

**HOW TO CONTACT** Query via e-mail. Accepts simultaneous submissions. Responds in 1 week to queries; 4 weeks to mss. Obtains most new clients through recommendations from others, solicitations.

**TERMS** Agent receives 15% commission on domestic sales; 25% commission on foreign sales. Offers written contract; 30-day notice to terminate contract. Charges occur very seldom. This agency's agreement limits any charges to $50 unless the author gives a written consent.

**RECENT SALES** *Project Hail Mary*, *Artemis* and *The Martian*, by Andy Weir (Ballantine); *The Fold*, by Peter Clines (Crown); *Cues* and *Captivate*, by Vanessa Van Edwards (Portfolio); *Side Hustle* (Crown) and *The Money Tree* (Portfolio), by Chris Guillebeau; *The Art of Invisibility*, by Kevin Mitnick (Little, Brown); the Hell Divers series, by Nicholas Smith (Blackstone); *It's OK That You're Not OK*, by Megan Devine (Sounds True); *She Builds*, by Jadah Sellner (Harper Business); *The Children of Red Peak*, by Craig DiLouie (Orbit).

## 🜨 SUSANNA LEA ASSOCIATES

331 W. 20th St., New York New York 10011. (646)638-1435. **E-mail:** ny@susannalea.com; london@susannalea.com; paris@susannalea.com. **Website:** www.susannalea.com. **Contact:** Submissions Department. South Wing, Somerset House, Strand, London, WC2R 1LA. Estab. Paris: 2000; New York: 2004; London: 2007. Member of Association of Authors' Agents.

**REPRESENTS** Nonfiction, fiction, novels.

☞ "Keeps list small; prefers to focus energies on a limited number of projects rather than spreading themselves too thinly. The company is currently developing new international projects—selective, yet broad in their reach, their slogan is: 'Published in Europe, Read by the World.'" Does not want to receive poetry, plays, screenplays, educational text books, short stories or illustrated works.

**HOW TO CONTACT** To submit your work, please send the following by e-mail: a concise query letter, including your e-mail address, telephone number, any relevant information about yourself (previous publications, etc.), a brief synopsis, and the first 3 chapters and/or proposal. Please check the website for information on which office you should submit to. Accepts simultaneous submissions.

**TIPS** "Your query letter should be concise and include any pertinent information about yourself, relevant writing history, etc."

## ⊘ THE NED LEAVITT AGENCY

70 Wooster St., Suite 4F, New York NY 10012. (212)334-0999. **Website:** www.nedleavittagency. com. **Contact:** Ned Leavitt; Jillian Sweeney. Member of AAR. Represents 40+ clients.

**MEMBER AGENTS** Ned Leavitt, founder and agent; Britta Alexander, agent; Jillian Sweeney, agent.

**REPRESENTS** Novels.

➤ "We are small in size, but intensely dedicated to our authors and to supporting excellent and unique writing."

**HOW TO CONTACT** This agency now only takes queries/submissions through referred clients. Do not cold query. Accepts simultaneous submissions.

**TIPS** "Look online for this agency's recently changed submission guidelines."

## ROBERT LECKER AGENCY

4055 Melrose Ave., Montreal QC H4A 2S5 Canada. **E-mail:** robert.lecker@gmail.com. **Website:** www.leckeragency.com. **Contact:** Robert Lecker. Estab. 2003. Member of PACLA. Represents 50 clients.

○ Prior to becoming an agent, Mr. Lecker was the cofounder and publisher of ECW Press and professor of English literature at McGill University. He has 30 years of experience in book and magazine publishing.

**MEMBER AGENTS** Robert Lecker (popular culture, music); Mary Williams (travel, food, popular science).

**REPRESENTS** Nonfiction, novels, syndicated material. **Considers these nonfiction areas:** autobiography, biography, cooking, cultural interests, dance, diet/nutrition, ethnic, film, foods, how-to, language, literature, music, popular culture, science, technology, theater. **Considers these fiction areas:** action, adventure, crime, detective, erotica, literary, mainstream, mystery, police, suspense, thriller.

➤ RLA specializes in books about popular culture, popular science, music, entertainment, food, and travel. The agency responds to articulate, innovative proposals within 2 weeks. Nonfiction titles related to politics, history, popular culture, popular science, music-related titles. We do not represent children's literature, screenplays, poetry, self-help books, or spiritual guides.

**HOW TO CONTACT** E-query. In the subject line, write: "New Submission QUERY." Accepts simultaneous submissions. Responds in 2 weeks to queries; 1 month to mss. Obtains most new clients through recommendations from others, conferences, interest in website.

**TERMS** Agent receives 15% commission on domestic sales; 15-20% commission on foreign sales. Offers written contract, binding for 1 year; 6-month notice must be given to terminate contract.

## THE LESHNE AGENCY

New York NY. **E-mail:** submissions@leshneagency. com. **Website:** www.leshneagency.com. **Contact:** Lisa Leshne, agent and owner. Estab. 2011. Member of AAR, Women's Media Group.

○ Lisa Leshne has been in the media and entertainment business for over 25 years. Lisa's experience spans the broadest range of the industry. In 1991, she co-founded *The Prague Post*, the largest English-language newspaper in Central Europe, along with its book division and website, PraguePost.com. Lisa worked in Prague as the newspaper's Publisher for almost a decade. In 1999, she moved to Manhattan to work for Accenture as a Senior Consultant in the Entertainment & Media Group. She later worked in strategy and business development for Dow Jones, and was Executive Director, International, for WSJ.com, *The Wall Street Journal* online, responsible for digital business operations in Europe and Asia, where she oversaw advertising, marketing and circulation. Lisa also served as VP, Strategy and Business Development, for Ink2, an industry leader in the print-on-demand industry and the owner of Cardstore.com. Lisa worked for a year after 9/11 at the Partnership for New York City's Financial Recovery Fund, evaluating grant applications and providing strategic advice to small businesses destroyed in the World Trade Center attacks. Prior to founding The Leshne Agency in 2011, she was a literary agent at LJK Literary.

**MEMBER AGENTS** Lisa Leshne, agent and owner; Sandy Hodgman, director of foreign rights; Samantha Morrice; Yvette Greenwald; Christine J. Lee.

**REPRESENTS** Nonfiction, fiction, novels. **Considers these nonfiction areas:** business, creative nonfiction, cultural interests, health, how-to, humor, inspirational, memoirs, parenting, politics, science, self-help, sports, women's issues. **Considers these fiction areas:** commercial, middle grade, young adult.

☛ An avid reader of blogs, newspapers and magazines in addition to books, Lisa is most interested in narrative and prescriptive nonfiction, especially on social justice, sports, health, wellness, business, political and parenting topics. She loves memoirs that transport the reader into another person's head and give a voyeuristic view of someone else's extraordinary experiences. Lisa also enjoys literary and commercial fiction and some young adult and middle-grade books that take the reader on a journey and are just plain fun to read. Wants "authors across all genres. We are interested in narrative, memoir, and prescriptive nonfiction, with a particular interest in sports, wellness, business, political and parenting topics. We will also look at truly terrific commercial fiction and young adult and middle grade books."

**HOW TO CONTACT** The Leshne Agency is seeking new and existing authors across all genres. "We are especially interested in narrative; memoir; prescriptive nonfiction, with a particular interest in sports, health, wellness, business, political and parenting topics; and truly terrific commercial fiction, young adult and middle-grade books. We are not interested in screenplays; scripts; poetry; and picture books. If your submission is in a genre not specifically listed here, we are still open to considering it, but if your submission is for a genre we've mentioned as not being interested in, please don't bother sending it to us. All submissions should be made through the Authors.me portal by clicking on this link: https://app.authors.me/#submit/the-leshne-agency." Accepts simultaneous submissions.

## LEVINE GREENBERG ROSTAN LITERARY AGENCY, INC.

307 Seventh Ave., Suite 2407, New York NY 10001. (212)337-0934. **E-mail:** submit@lgrliterary.com. **Website:** www.lgrliterary.com. Member of AAR. Represents 250 clients.

○ Prior to opening his agency, Mr. Levine served as vice president of the Bank Street College of Education.

**MEMBER AGENTS** Jim Levine (nonfiction, including business, science, narrative nonfiction, social and political issues, psychology, health, spirituality, parenting); Stephanie Rostan (adult and YA fiction; nonfiction, including parenting, health & wellness, sports, memoir); Daniel Greenberg (nonfiction: popular culture, narrative nonfiction, memoir, and humor; literary fiction); Victoria Skurnick; Danielle Svetcov (nonfiction); Lindsay Edgecombe (narrative nonfiction, memoir, lifestyle and health, illustrated books, as well as literary fiction); Monika Verma (nonfiction: humor, pop culture, memoir, narrative nonfiction and style and fashion titles; some young adult fiction (paranormal, historical, contemporary)); Kerry Sparks (young adult and middle grade; select adult fiction and occasional nonfiction); Tim Wojcik (nonfiction, including food narratives, humor, pop culture, popular history and science; literary fiction); Arielle Eckstut (no queries); Sarah Bedingfield (literary and upmarket commercial fiction, epic family dramas, literary novels with notes of magical realism, darkly gothic stories, psychological suspense); Courtney Pagenelli; Rebecca Rodd.

**REPRESENTS** Nonfiction, novels. **Considers these nonfiction areas:** business, creative nonfiction, health, history, humor, memoirs, parenting, popular culture, science, spirituality, sports. **Considers these fiction areas:** commercial, literary, mainstream, middle grade, suspense, young adult.

**HOW TO CONTACT** E-query to submit@lgrliterary.com, or online submission form. "If you would like to direct your query to one of our agents specifically, please feel free to name them in the online form or in the email you send." Cannot respond to submissions by mail. Do not attach more than 50 pages. "Due to the volume of submissions we receive, we are unable to respond to each individually. If we would like more information about your project, we'll contact you within 3 weeks (though we do get backed up on occasion!)." Accepts simultaneous submissions. Obtains most new clients through recommendations from others.

**TERMS** Agent receives 15% commission on domestic sales; 20% commission on foreign sales. Offers written contract. Charges clients for out-of-pocket expenses—telephone, fax, postage, photocopying—directly connected to the project.

**RECENT SALES** *Notorious RBG*, by Irin Carmon and Shana Knizhnik; *Pogue's Basics: Life*, by David Pogue; *Invisible City*, by Julia Dahl; *Gumption*, by Nick Offerman; *All the Bright Places*, by Jennifer Niven.

**WRITERS CONFERENCES** ASJA Writers' Conference.

**TIPS** "We focus on editorial development, business representation, and publicity and marketing strategy."

## PAUL S. LEVINE LITERARY AGENCY

1054 Superba Ave., Venice CA 90291. (310)450-6711. **Fax:** (310)450-0181. **E-mail:** paul@paulslevinelit.com. **Website:** www.paulslevinelit.com. **Contact:** Paul S. Levine. Estab. 1992. Member of the State Bar of California. Represents over 100 clients.

**MEMBER AGENTS** Paul S. Levine (children's and young adult fiction and nonfiction, adult fiction and nonfiction except sci-fi, fantasy, and horror); Loren R. Grossman (archeology, art/photography, architecture, child guidance/parenting, coffee table books,gardening, education/academics, health/medicine/science/technology, law, religion, memoirs, sociology).

**REPRESENTS** Nonfiction, fiction, novels, TV movie of the week, episodic drama, sitcom, animation, documentary, miniseries, syndicated material, variety show, comic books; graphic novels. **Considers these nonfiction areas:** architecture, art, autobiography, biography, business, child guidance, cooking, crafts, creative nonfiction, current affairs, decorating, diet/nutrition, design, education, foods, gardening, gay/lesbian, health, history, how-to, humor, inspirational, interior design, investigative, juvenile nonfiction, law, medicine, memoirs, money, music, New Age, parenting, philosophy, photography, popular culture, politics, psychology, recreation, religious, satire, science, self-help, sex, sociology, spirituality, sports, technology, travel, true crime, women's issues, women's studies, young adult. **Considers these fiction areas:** adventure, ethnic, mainstream, mystery, romance, thriller, young adult.

☛ Does not want to receive science fiction, fantasy, or horror.

**HOW TO CONTACT** E-mail preferred; "snail mail" with SASE is also acceptable. Send a 1-page, single-spaced query letter. In your query letter, note your target market, with a summary of specifics on how your work differs from other authors' previously published work. Accepts simultaneous submissions. Responds in 1 day to queries; 6-8 weeks to mss. Obtains most new clients through conferences, referrals, giving classes and seminars, and listings on various websites and in directories.

**TERMS** Agent receives 15% commission on domestic sales. Offers written contract. Charges for postage and actual, out-of-pocket costs only.

**WRITERS CONFERENCES** Willamette Writers Conference; San Francisco Writers Conference; Santa Barbara Writers Conference; Chicago Writers Conference; Atlanta Writers Conference; West Coast Writers Conferences; and many others.

**TIPS** "Write good, sellable books."

## ⊚ LIMELIGHT CELEBRITY MANAGEMENT LTD.

10 Filmer Mews, 75 Filmer Rd., London SW6 7JF United Kingdom. (44)(0)207-384-9950. **E-mail:** mail@limelightmanagement.com. **Website:** www.limelightmanagement.com. **Contact:** Fiona Lindsay. Estab. 1991. Member AAA.

◯ Prior to becoming an agent, Ms. Lindsay was a public relations manager at the Dorchester and was working on her law degree.

**MEMBER AGENTS** Fiona Lindsay.

**REPRESENTS** Nonfiction and selected fiction. **Considers these nonfiction areas:** art, autobiography, business, foods, gardening, health, history, politics, science, self-help, travel, antiques, drink, entertainment. **Considers these fiction areas:** crime, historical, literary, mystery, suspense, thriller, women's.

☛ "We are always looking for exciting new authors and read all work submitted. We endeavour to respond within 8 to 10 weeks of receipt, but this time scale is not always possible due to the volume of submissions we receive." This agency will consider women's fiction, as well.

**HOW TO CONTACT** All work should be typed with double spacing. Ensure that the word "Submission" is clearly marked in the subject line and that any attachments include the title of your work. E-mail a brief synopsis and the first 3 chapters only as a Word or Open Document attachment. Only handles film and TV scripts for existing clients. Accepts simultaneous submissions. Obtains most new clients through recommendations from others.

**TERMS** Agent receives 15% commission on domestic sales; 25% commission on foreign sales; 10-20% commission on TV and radio deals.

## LITERARY MANAGEMENT GROUP, INC.

150 Young Way, Richmond Hill GA 31324. (615)812-4445. **E-mail:** brucebarbour@literarymanagement-group.com. **Website:** literarymanagementgroup.com. **Contact:** Bruce R. Barbour. Estab. 1996. Represents 100+ clients.

- Prior to becoming an agent, Mr. Barbour held executive positions at several publishing houses, including Revell, Barbour Books, Thomas Nelson, and Random House.

**REPRESENTS** Nonfiction. **Considers these nonfiction areas:** business, child guidance, current affairs, diet/nutrition, health, history, how-to, inspirational, money, parenting, psychology, religious, self-help, spirituality, Christian living; spiritual growth; women's and men's issues; prayer; devotional; meditational; Bible study; marriage; business; family/parenting.

- Does not want to receive gift books, poetry, children's books, short stories, or juvenile/ young adult fiction. No unsolicited mss or proposals from unpublished authors.

**HOW TO CONTACT** E-mail proposal as an attachment. Consult website for submission guidelines. Accepts simultaneous submissions. "We acknowledge receipt and review proposals within 4 weeks."

**TERMS** Agent receives 15% commission on domestic sales.

## LITERARY SERVICES, INC.

P.O. Box 888, Barnegat NJ 08005. **E-mail:** jwlitagent@msn.com; john@literaryservicesinc.com. **Website:** www.literaryservicesinc.com. **Contact:** John Willig. Estab. 1991. Represents 150 clients.

- "I started working in publishing in 1977 as a sales representative ('college traveler') in academic publishing and then marketing manager before becoming an editor in 1982 for Harper & Row; shifted to professional/subscription-based publishing as a senior editor and then became an executive editor for business professional and trade books for Prentice Hall/Simon & Schuster. During this time I was fortunate to work with world-class authors including Henry Mintzberg, Philip Kotler, and Jim Collins. In 1976 I graduated from Brown University. I have always been an avid reader with a broad range of interests and have admired leading thought and research throughout my career i.e. in 1982 I initiated an Artificial Intelligence and Expert Systems series; in the 1990s I advocated for Sustainable Development as an editor for environmental journals and launched a new management journal in Design Management."

**MEMBER AGENTS** John Willig (business, personal growth, history, health, wellness and lifestyle, science and technology, politics, psychology, true crime, current events and global issues, finance, food and travel, reference and gift books).

**REPRESENTS** Nonfiction, scholarly books. **Considers these nonfiction areas:** Americana, architecture, art, autobiography, biography, business, cooking, crafts, creative nonfiction, current affairs, decorating, diet/nutrition, design, economics, environment, foods, gardening, health, history, hobbies, how-to, humor, inspirational, interior design, language, law, literature, medicine, military, money, parenting, popular culture, politics, psychology, recreation, regional, science, self-help, sex, sociology, spirituality, sports, technology, travel, true crime, war, women's issues.

- Works primarily with nonfiction authors. "Our publishing experience and 'inside' knowledge of how companies and editors really work sets us apart from many agencies; our specialties are noted above, but we are open to unique research, creative and contrarian approaches, and fresh presentations with expert advice in all nonfiction topic area. I'm especially interested in writers 'shining a light' on new research, perspectives, events or stories or 'connecting the dots' in thought-provoking ways. Actively seeking science, history, current events and global issues, health/wellness, lifestyle topics, psychology, true crime, business and finance, food and travel, sports, hobbies and gardening, research-driven narratives. Does not want to receive fiction, children's books, science fiction, religion, or memoirs.

**HOW TO CONTACT** Query with SASE. For starters, a one-page outline sent via e-mail is acceptable. See our website(www.LiteraryServicesInc.com) and our

Submissions section to learn more about our questions. Please do not send a manuscript unless requested. Accepts simultaneous submissions. Thankfully, obtains most new clients through recommendations from others, solicitations, writer's conferences.

**TERMS** Agent receives 15% commission on domestic sales; 15% commission on foreign sales. Offers written contract. This agency charges an administrative fee for copying, postage, etc.

**RECENT SALES** Sold 20+ titles in the past year including: *Reimagining Investing* by Prusad Pulak; *The Bullied Brain* by Jennifer Fraser, PhD; *A Living Time Machine* by David Guggenheim, PhD; *The Connected Leader* by Karen Hardwick; *The Threat* by Walter Pickut and Kay Haas: *Tractor Wars* by Neil Dahlstrom; *Overcoming Toxic Emotions Now* by Leah Guy; *Coach: Life Lessons for the All Time Best Coaches* by Justin Spizman.

**WRITERS CONFERENCES** ASJA; Writer's Digest Conferences.

**TIPS** "Be focused and targeted. In all likelihood, your work is not going to be of interest to 'a very broad audience' or 'every parent,' so I appreciate when writers research and do some homework, i.e., positioning, special features and benefits of your work. Be a marketer. How have you tested your ideas and writing (beyond your inner circle of family and friends)? Have you received any key awards for your work or endorsements from influential persons in your field? What steps, especially social media and speaking, have you taken to increase your presence and community in the marketplace?"

## LKG AGENCY

134 West 83rd St., 3rd Floor, New York NY 10024. **E-mail:** query@lkgagency.com; mgya@lkgagency.com (MG/YA); nonfiction@lkgagency.com (nonfiction). **Website:** lkgagency.com. **Contact:** Lauren Galit. Estab. 2005.

**MEMBER AGENTS** Lauren Galit (nonfiction, middle grade, young adult); Caitlen Rubino-Bradway (middle grade and young adult, some nonfiction).

**REPRESENTS** Nonfiction, juvenile books. **Considers these nonfiction areas:** animals, child guidance, creative nonfiction, diet/nutrition, design, health, how-to, humor, juvenile nonfiction, memoirs, parenting, popular culture, psychology, women's issues,

young adult. **Considers these fiction areas:** middle grade, young adult.

⌐ "The LKG Agency specializes in nonfiction, both practical and narrative, as well as middle grade and young adult fiction." Actively seeking parenting, beauty, celebrity, dating & relationships, entertainment, fashion, health, diet & fitness, home & design, lifestyle, memoir, narrative, pets, psychology, women's focused, middle grade & young adult fiction. Does not want history, biography, true crime, religion, picture books, spirituality, screenplays, poetry any fiction other than middle grade or young adult.

**HOW TO CONTACT** For nonfiction submissions, please send a query letter to nonfiction@lkgagency.com, along with a TOC and 2 sample chapters. The TOC should be fairly detailed, with a paragraph or 2 overview of the content of each chapter. Please also make sure to mention any publicity you have at your disposal. For middle grade and young adult submissions, please send a query, synopsis, and the three (3) chapters, and address all submissions to mgya@lkgagency.com. Please note: due to the high volume of submissions, we are unable to reply to every one. If you do not receive a reply, please consider that a rejection. Accepts simultaneous submissions.

## STERLING LORD LITERISTIC, INC.

115 Broadway, New York NY 10006. (212)780-6050. **Fax:** (212)780-6095. **E-mail:** info@sll.com. **Website:** www.sll.com. Estab. 1987. Member of AAR. Signatory of WGA.

**MEMBER AGENTS** Philippa Brophy (represents journalists, nonfiction writers and novelists, and is most interested in current events, memoir, science, politics, biography, and women's issues); Laurie Liss (represents authors of commercial and literary fiction and nonfiction whose perspectives are well developed and unique); Peter Matson (abiding interest in storytelling, whether in the service of history, fiction, the sciences); Douglas Stewart (primarily fiction for all ages, from the innovatively literary to the unabashedly commercial); Neeti Madan (memoir, journalism, popular culture, lifestyle, women's issues, multicultural books and virtually any intelligent writing on intriguing topics); Robert Guinsler (literary and commercial fiction (including YA), journalism, narrative nonfiction with an emphasis on pop culture, science and current events, memoirs and biographies); Jim Rutman; Mary Krienke (literary fiction, memoir, and narrative nonfiction, including psychology, popular science, and cultural commentary); Jenny Stephens (nonfiction: cookbooks, practical lifestyle projects, transportive travel and nature writing, and creative nonfiction; fiction: contemporary literary narratives strongly rooted in place); Elizabeth Bewley; Jessica Friedman; Sarah Landis; Danielle Bukowski; Chris Combemale; Nell Pierce.

**REPRESENTS** Nonfiction, fiction. **Considers these nonfiction areas:** biography, business, cooking, creative nonfiction, current affairs, economics, education, foods, gay/lesbian, history, humor, memoirs, multicultural, parenting, popular culture, politics, psychology, science, technology, travel, women's issues, fitness. **Considers these fiction areas:** commercial, juvenile, literary, middle grade, picture books, science fiction, young adult.

**HOW TO CONTACT** Submit via online submission form. Accepts simultaneous submissions.

**TERMS** Agent receives 15% commission on domestic sales; 20% commission on foreign sales. Offers written contract.

## LOWENSTEIN ASSOCIATES INC.

115 E. 23rd St., Floor 4, New York NY 10010. (212)206-1630. **E-mail:** assistant@bookhaven.com. **Website:** www.lowensteinassociates.com. **Contact:** Barbara Lowenstein. Member of AAR.

**MEMBER AGENTS** Barbara Lowenstein, president (nonfiction interests include narrative nonfiction, health, money, finance, travel, multicultural, popular culture, and memoir; fiction interests include literary fiction and women's fiction); Ronald Gerber, agent and rights manager (areas represented include contemporary and historical fiction, literary fiction, domestic and psychological thrillers, horror, grounded science-fiction, romance/romantic comedy, biography and memoir, narrative nonfiction, true crime, middle grade, and #OwnVoices stories across all genres).

**REPRESENTS** Nonfiction, fiction, novels, short story collections. **Considers these nonfiction areas:** autobiography, biography, film, humor, literature, memoirs, multicultural, music, popular culture, true crime, women's issues, women's studies. **Considers these fiction areas:** commercial, crime, feminist, gay, historical, horror, humor, literary, middle grade, mystery, romance, science fiction, short story collections, suspense, thriller, women's.

☛ Does not want textbooks, religious fiction/nonfiction, erotica, high fantasy, new adult, picture books, or books in need of translation.

**HOW TO CONTACT** "Barbara Lowenstein is not currently open to queries. To query Ronald Gerber, please send a query letter in the body of the email, along with the first chapter attached, to assistant@bookhaven.com. Please put the word 'QUERY' and the title of your project in the subject field of your email. Please do not mail us queries or manuscripts, all submission mail will be discarded unopened." Accepts simultaneous submissions. Will respond if interested. If you do not receive a response within 6 weeks, please consider it a pass from the agency. Obtains most new clients through recommendations from others, solicitations, conferences.

**TERMS** Agent receives 15% commission on domestic sales; 20% commission on foreign sales. Offers written contract. Charges for large photocopy batches, messenger service, international postage.

**TIPS** "Know the genre you are working in and read!"

## 🗨 ANDREW LOWNIE LITERARY AGENCY, LTD.

36 Great Smith St., London SW1P 3BU United Kingdom. (44)(207)222-7574. **Fax:** (44)(207)222-7576. **E-mail:** lownie@globalnet.co.uk. **Website:** www.andrewlownie.co.uk. **Contact:** Andrew Lownie, nonfiction. Estab. 1988. Member of Society of Authors. Represents 200 clients.

◯ Prior to becoming an agent, Mr. Lownie was a journalist, bookseller, publisher and a former director of the Curtis Brown Agency. He is a critically acclaimed writer and President of the Biographers Club, a judge of several nonfiction prizes and regularly speaks at festivals around the world.

**REPRESENTS** Nonfiction. **Considers these nonfiction areas:** autobiography, biography, current affairs, government, history, humor, investigative, law, memoirs, military, popular culture, politics, true crime, war.

☛ This agent has wide publishing experience, extensive journalistic contacts, and a specialty in showbiz/celebrity memoir. Actively seeking showbiz memoirs, narrative histories, and biographies. No fiction, poetry, short stories, children's, academic, or scripts.

**HOW TO CONTACT** Query by e-mail only. For nonfiction, submit outline and one sample chapter. Accepts simultaneous submissions. Responds in 1 week to queries; 1 month to mss. Obtains most new clients through recommendations from others and unsolicited through website.

**TERMS** Agent receives 15% commission on domestic sales; 20% commission on foreign sales. Offers written contract; 30-day notice must be given to terminate contract.

**RECENT SALES** Sells about 50 books a year, with over a dozen top 10 bestsellers including many number ones, as well as the memoirs of Queen Elizabeth II's press officer Dickie Arbiter, Lance Armstrong's masseuse Emma O'Reilly, actor Warwick Davis, Multiple Personality Disorder sufferer Alice Jamieson, round-the-world yachtsman Mike Perham, poker player Dave 'Devilfish' Ulliott, David Hasselhoff, Sam Faiers and Kirk Norcross from *TOWIE*, Spencer Matthews from *Made in Chelsea*, singer Kerry Katona. Other clients: Juliet Barker, Guy Bellamy, Joyce Cary estate, Roger Crowley, Patrick Dillon, Duncan Falconer, Cathy Glass, Timothy Good, Robert Hutchinson, Lawrence James, Christopher Lloyd, Sian Rees, Desmond Seward, Daniel Tammet, Casey Watson.

## DONALD MAASS LITERARY AGENCY

1000 Dean St., Suite 252, Brooklyn NY 11238. (212)727-8383. **E-mail:** query.dmaass@maassagency.com. **Website:** www.maassagency.com. Estab. 1980. Member of AAR, SFWA, MWA, RWA. Represents more than 200 clients.

Prior to opening his agency, Mr. Maass worked as an editor at Dell Publishing (New York) and as a reader at Gollancz (London). He is a past president of the Association of Authors' Representatives, Inc. (AAR).

**MEMBER AGENTS** Donald Maass (mainstream, literary, mystery/suspense, science fiction, romance, women's fiction); Jennifer Jackson (science fiction, fantasy, and horror for both adult and YA markets, thrillers that mine popular and controversial issues, YA that challenges traditional thinking); Cameron McClure (fantasy and science-fiction, literary, mystery/suspense, projects with multicultural, international, and environmental themes, gay/lesbian); Michael Curry (literary science fiction, fantasy, near

future thrillers). Paul Stevens (science fiction, fantasy, horror, mystery, suspense, and humorous fiction, LBGT a plus); Jennie Goloboy (fun, innovative, diverse, and progressive science fiction and fantasy for adults; history for a popular, adult audience (no memoir)); Caitlin McDonald (fantasy, science fiction, and horror for Adult/YA/MG/GN, genre-bending/cross-genre fiction, diversity); Kiana Nguyen (women's fiction/book club, edgy/dark, realistic/contemporary YA, SF/F—adult/YA, horror—Adult/YA, domestic suspense, thrillers Adult/YA, contemporary romance—Adult/YA); Kat Kerr; Anne Tibbets.

**REPRESENTS** Nonfiction, fiction, novels, short story collections, novellas, juvenile books. **Considers these nonfiction areas:** autobiography, biography, creative nonfiction, memoirs, popular culture, science. **Considers these fiction areas:** commercial, contemporary issues, crime, detective, ethnic, family saga, fantasy, feminist, frontier, gay, historical, horror, humor, inspirational, juvenile, lesbian, literary, mainstream, middle grade, military, multicultural, mystery, new adult, occult, paranormal, police, psychic, regional, religious, romance, satire, science fiction, short story collections, spiritual, supernatural, suspense, thriller, urban fantasy, war, westerns, women's, young adult.

This agency specializes in commercial fiction, especially science fiction, fantasy, thrillers, suspense, women's fiction—for both the adult and YA markets. All types of fiction, including YA and MG. Does not want poetry, screenplays, picture books.

**HOW TO CONTACT** Query via e-mail only. All the agents have different submission addresses and instructions. See the website and each agent's online profile for exact submission instructions. Accepts simultaneous submissions.

**TERMS** Agency receives 15% commission on domestic sales; 20% commission on foreign sales.

**RECENT SALES** *Battle Ground* by Jim Butcher (Penguin Random House); *Foundryside* by Robert Jackson Bennett (Crown); *Gideon the Ninth* by Tamsyn Muir (Macmillan); *Treachery at Lancaster Gate* by Anne Perry (Random House); *Crowbones* by Anne Bishop (Penguin Random House); *We Are the Ants*, by Shaun David Hutchinson (Simon & Schuster); *Binti* by Nnedi Okorafor (DAW); *Star Eater* by Kerstin Hall (Macmillan); *The Tyrant Baru Cormorant* by Seth Dickinson (Tor); *Nothing But Blackened Teeth* by Cassandra Khaw (Nightfire); *The Space Between Worlds* by Micaiah Johnson (Del Rey); *Machinehood* by S.B. Divya (Saga); *Million Dollar Demon* by Kim Harrison (PRH/Ace); *The Grey Bastards* by Jonathan French (Crown); *A Snake Falls to Earth* by Darcie Little Badger (Levine Querido); *The Conductors*, by Nicole Glover (John Joseph Adams/HMH); *When the Sparrow Falls* by Neil Sharpson (Tor and Rebellion); *The Ones We Burn* by Rebecca Mix (Simon & Schuster); *Hot Copy* by Ruby Barrett (Harlequin); *Fugitive Telemetry* by Martha Wells (Macmillan); *The Midnight Bargain* by C.L. Polk (Erewhon); *The Archive Undying* by Emma Mieko Candon (Macmillan).

**WRITERS CONFERENCES** See each agent's profile page at the agency website for conference schedules.

**TIPS** "We are fiction specialists, also noted for our innovative approach to career planning. We are always open to submissions from new writers." Works with subagents in all principle foreign countries and for film and television.

## GINA MACCOBY LITERARY AGENCY

P.O. Box 60, Chappaqua NY 10514. (914)238-5630. **E-mail:** query@maccobylit.com. **Website:** www.publishersmarketplace.com/members/ginamaccoby/. **Contact:** Gina Maccoby. Estab. 1986. Member of AAR. AAR Board of Directors; Royalties and Ethics and Contracts subcommittees; Authors Guild, SCBWI.

**REPRESENTS** Nonfiction, fiction, novels, juvenile books. **Considers these nonfiction areas:** autobiography, biography, cultural interests, current affairs, ethnic, history, juvenile nonfiction, literature, popular culture, women's issues, women's studies, young adult. **Considers these fiction areas:** crime, detective, family saga, historical, juvenile, literary, mainstream, middle grade, multicultural, mystery, new adult, suspense, thriller, women's, young adult.

**HOW TO CONTACT** Query by e-mail only. Accepts simultaneous submissions. Owing to volume of submissions, may not respond to queries unless interested. Obtains most new clients through recommendations.

**TERMS** Agent receives 15% commission on domestic sales; 20-25% commission on foreign sales, which includes subagents commissions. May recover certain costs, such as purchasing books, shipping books overseas by airmail, legal fees for vetting motion pic-

ture contracts, bank fees for electronic funds transfers, overnight delivery services.

**WRITERS CONFERENCES** ThrillerFest PitchFest, Washington Independent Writers Conference, New England Crime Bake, Ridgefield Writers Conference, CLMP Literary Writers Conference.

## MACGREGOR & LUEDEKE

P.O. Box 1316, Manzanita OR 97130. (503)389-4803. **E-mail:** submissions@macgregorliterary.com. **Website:** www.macgregorliterary.com. **Contact:** Chip MacGregor. Estab. 2006. Member of AAR. Signatory of WGA. Represents 80 clients.

Prior to his current position, Mr. MacGregor was the senior agent with Alive Communications, an agency in Colorado. Most recently, he was an associate publisher with the Time-Warner Book Group (now Hachette Book Group), and helped put together their Center Street imprint.

**MEMBER AGENTS** Chip MacGregor (general nonfiction and memoir, select fiction); Amanda Luedeke (nonfiction, literary fiction, romance, and twenty-something/post college-aged hip lit); Alina Mitchell (memoir, biographies, how-to, elementary and secondary education topics, religion/spirituality, narrative nonfiction, and new perspectives in history, arts and culture).

**REPRESENTS** Nonfiction, fiction. **Considers these nonfiction areas:** business, creative nonfiction, cultural interests, current affairs, history, inspirational, memoirs, parenting, popular culture, politics, religious, self-help, spirituality, sports, true crime, women's issues. **Considers these fiction areas:** action, commercial, crime, detective, family saga, humor, inspirational, literary, mainstream, mystery, new adult, police, religious, romance, suspense, thriller, women's.

"My specialty has been in career planning with authors—finding commercial ideas, then helping authors bring them to market, and in the midst of that assisting the authors as they get firmly established in their writing careers. I'm probably best known for my work with spirituality books and memoir over the years, but I've done a fair amount of general nonfiction as well." Nonfiction from authors with a proven platform. Significant literary and thriller fiction. Does not want screenplays, westerns, erotica, paranormal fiction, children's books, YA fiction, art books, poetry.

**HOW TO CONTACT** MacGregor Literary is not currently accepting submissions except through referrals. Please do not query this agency without an invitation or referral. Accepts simultaneous submissions. Responds in 4-6 weeks to queries. Obtains most new clients through recommendations from others. Not looking to add unpublished authors except through referrals from current clients.

**TERMS** Agent receives 15% commission on domestic sales; 10% commission on foreign sales. Offers written contract.

**RECENT SALES** Fiction includes *New York Times* bestselling authors Rachel Hauck, Vincent Zandri, Davis Bunn, Oprah Network star Evelyn Lozada, thriller writers Susan Sleeman and Maegan Beaumont. Nonfiction includes former Space Shuttle Commander Scott Parazynski, Waylon Jennings' son and memoirist Terry Jennings, marriage author Sheila Wray Gregoire, Olympic Gold Medalist Mark Schultz's *Foxcatcher*, Navy SEAL writer Robert Vera.

**WRITERS CONFERENCES** BEA, RWA, ThrillerFest, Left Coast Crime, several West Coast writing conferences.

**TIPS** "Seriously consider attending a good writers' conference. It will give you the chance to be face-to-face with people in the industry. Also, if you're a novelist, consider joining one of the national writers' organizations. RWA, ACFW, MWA, ITW are wonderful groups for new as well as established writers and will help you make connections and become a better writer."

## CAROL MANN AGENCY

55 Fifth Ave., 18th Floor, New York NY 10003. (212)206-5635. **Fax:** (212)675-4809. **E-mail:** submissions@carolmannagency.com. **Website:** www.carolmannagency.com. **Contact:** Agnes Carlowicz. Member of AAR. Represents roughly 200 clients.

**MEMBER AGENTS** Carol Mann (health/medical, religion, spirituality, self-help, parenting, narrative nonfiction, current affairs); Laura Yorke; Gareth Esersky; Myrsini Stephanides (nonfiction areas of interest: pop culture and music, humor, narrative nonfiction and memoir, cookbooks; fiction areas of interest: offbeat literary fiction, graphic works, and edgy YA fiction); Joanne Wyckoff (nonfiction areas of interest: memoir, narrative nonfiction, personal narrative,

psychology, women's issues, education, health and wellness, parenting, serious self-help, natural history; also accepts fiction); Iris Blasi; Maile Beal; Agnes Carlowicz.

**REPRESENTS** Nonfiction, fiction, novels. **Considers these nonfiction areas:** anthropology, archeology, architecture, art, autobiography, biography, business, child guidance, cultural interests, current affairs, design, ethnic, government, health, history, humor, law, medicine, memoirs, money, music, parenting, popular culture, politics, psychology, self-help, sociology, sports, women's issues, women's studies. **Considers these fiction areas:** commercial, literary, young adult, graphic works. **Considers these script areas:** romantic drama.

☞ Does not want to receive genre fiction (romance, mystery, etc.).

**HOW TO CONTACT** Please see website for submission guidelines. Accepts simultaneous submissions. Responds in 4 weeks to queries.

**TERMS** Agent receives 15% commission on domestic sales; 20% commission on foreign sales. Offers written contract.

## MANSION STREET LITERARY MANAGEMENT

**Website:** mansionstreet.com. **Contact:** Jean Sagendorph; Michelle Witte.

**MEMBER AGENTS** Jean Sagendorph, querymansionstreet@gmail.com (pop culture, gift books, cookbooks, general nonfiction, lifestyle, design, brand extensions), Michelle Witte (young adult, middle grade, early readers, picture books from author-illustrators, juvenile nonfiction).

**REPRESENTS** Nonfiction, novels, juvenile books. **Considers these nonfiction areas:** cooking, design, juvenile nonfiction, popular culture, young adult. **Considers these fiction areas:** humor, juvenile, middle grade, picture books, young adult.

☞ Jean is not interested in memoirs or medical/reference. Typically sports and self-help are not a good fit; also does not represent travel books. Michelle is not interested in fiction or nonfiction for adults.

**HOW TO CONTACT** Mansion Street Literary Management has changed how we accept queries, so we now use a submission form. To query Jean, go to http://QueryMe.Online/mansionstreet. To query Michelle, go to http://QueryMe.Online/michellewitte.

Accepts simultaneous submissions. Responds in up to 6 weeks.

**RECENT SALES** *Shake and Fetch*, by Carli Davidson; *Bleed, Blister, Puke and Purge*, by J. Marin Younker; *Spectrum*, by Ginger Johnson; *I Left You a Present* and *Movie Night Trivia*, by Robb Pearlman; *Open Sesame!*, by Ashley Evanson; *Fox Hunt*, by Nilah Magruder; *ABC Now You See Me*, by Kim Siebold.

**WRITERS CONFERENCES** Maui Writers' Conference; San Diego State University Writers' Conference; Willamette Writers' Conference; BookExpo America; MEGA Book Marketing University.

**TIPS** "Research agents using a variety of sources."

## MARCIL O'FARRELL LITERARY

86 Dennis St., Manhasset NY 11030. (203)327-9970. **E-mail:** annemarie@marcilofarrellagency.com. **Website:** www.denisemarcilagency.com. **Contact:** Anne Marie O'Farrell. Estab. 1977. Member of AAR, Women's Media Group.

**MEMBER AGENTS** Anne Marie O'Farrell (books that convey and promote innovative, practical and cutting-edge information and ideas which help people increase their self-awareness and fulfillment and maximize their potential in whatever area they choose; she is dying to represent a great basketball book).

**REPRESENTS** Nonfiction. **Considers these nonfiction areas:** business, cooking, diet/nutrition, education, health, how-to, New Age, psychology, self-help, spirituality, women's issues.

☛ "In nonfiction we are looking for self-help, personal growth, popular psychology, how-to, business, and popular reference; we want to represent books that help people's lives." Does not want fiction.

**HOW TO CONTACT** Send a query letter of 200 words maximum in the body of the e-mail to annemarie@marcilofarrellagency.com. "Please tell us how you discovered our agency. If you've found our website or listing in various publishing guides or on the Internet, met us at a writer's conference, or have been referred by a specific colleague or friend, please feel free to include that in the beginning of your letter." Anne Marie O'Farrell only represents practical and narrative nonfiction in the areas of business, self-help, health and fitness, spirituality, cooking, gift books, travel, sports and quirky books. "We do not represent fiction, memoirs or screenplays. Your query should contain a succinct and exciting explanation of the book concept, information on why you are the right person to write this book, and your ability to market and publicize the book." Authors seeking representation must have extensive traditional and social media platforms, seminar and/or speaking event schedules. "We may request certain sections of a standard nonfiction book proposal or a proposal in its entirety. The proposal should include an overview of the book concept, your biography, a marketing section, a comparable books section, chapter summaries and a sample chapter." Accepts simultaneous submissions.

**TERMS** Agent receives 15% commission on domestic sales; 20% commission on foreign sales and film sales. Offers written contract, binding for 2 years.

**RECENT SALES** *Lilac Lane*, by Sherryl Woods; *Dr. Knox*, by Peter Spiegelman; *The Baby Book*, by William Sears, M.D. and Martha Sears, R.N.; *Dr. Sears T5 Wellness Plan*, by William Sears, M.D. and Erin Sears Basile; *The Allergy Book*, by Robert W. Sears, M.D. and William Sears, M.D.; *Work that Works*, by Geil Browning, Ph.D.; *Exponential Living*, by Sheri Riley; *The Girls of Ennismore* and *The Yellow House*, by Patricia Falvey; *Irresistible Force* and *Force Of Attraction*, by D.D. Ayres; *The Soldier's Forever Family*, by Gina Wilkins.

## ● MARJACQ SCRIPTS LTD

235 High Holborn, London WC1V 7LE United Kingdom. (44)(207)935-9499. **Fax:** (44)(207)935-9115. **E-mail:** enquiries@marjacq.com. **Website:** www.marjacq.com. **Contact:** Submissions: individual agent whose area of interest may include your work. Business matters: Guy Herbert. Estab. 1974. Member of AAA. Represents 120+ clients.

◯ Ms. Beaumont was an editor at Random House and an agent at UTA; Mr. Patterson was a film, TV, and theatre agent at Curtis Brown and sold rights at HarperCollins; Ms. Pelham worked as assistant to the late Gillon Aitken dealing with his very high-profile clients; Ms. Pellegrino ran her own agency, and before that was at Rogers Coleridge and White; Ms. Sawicka worked as a rights executive in publishing. Ms Middleton was a senior TV agent at Aitken Alexander.

**MEMBER AGENTS** Philip Patterson (thrillers, commercial fiction and nonfiction); Sandra Sawicka (commercial, genre, speculative and upmarket fiction); Diana Beaumont (commercial and accessible literary fiction and nonfiction); Imogen Pelham (literary and upmarket fiction and nonfiction); Catherine Pellegrino (children's, middle grade and young adult, romance); Leah Middleton (Film & TV, commercial fiction, investigative journalism, popular science).

**REPRESENTS** Nonfiction, fiction, novels, short story collections, novellas, juvenile books, scholarly books, movie scripts, feature film, TV scripts, TV movie of the week, episodic drama, sitcom, documentary, miniseries, syndicated material. **Considers these script areas:** Scriptwriting for film & TV. Experience in interactive development.

☛ Actively seeking quality fiction, nonfiction, children's books, and young adult books. New and experienced working screenwriters. Does not want to receive stage plays or poetry.

**HOW TO CONTACT** Email submissions direct to the individual agent who you feel is the best fit. Submit outline, synopsis, 3 sample chapters, bio, covering letter. "Do not bother with fancy bindings and folders. Keep synopses, bio, and covering letter short." Accepts simultaneous submissions. Responds in 4-6 weeks to mss. Don't send queries without sample. Obtains most new clients through recommendations from others, solicitations, conferences.

**TERMS** Agent receives 15% commission on direct book sales; 20% on foreign rights, film, etc. Offers written contract. Services include in-house business affairs consultant. No service fees other than commission. Recharges bank fees for money transfers.

**RECENT SALES** 3-book deal for Stuart MacBride (Transworld) (repeated *Sunday Times* #1 bestseller); *The Whisper Man* and *The Shadow Friend*, by Alex North; book and TV rights for *The Cry*, by Helen Fitzgerald; *Insatiable*, by Daisy Buchanan.

**TIPS** "Keep trying! If one agent rejects you, you can try someone else. Perseverance and self-belief are important, but do listen to constructive criticism, and 'no' does mean no. Be warned, few agents will give you advice as a non-client. We just don't have the time. Be aware of what is being published. If you show awareness of what other writers are doing in your field/genre, you might be able to see how your book fits in and why an editor/agent might be interested in taking it on. But make your book the best you can rather than trying to devise your own marketing—that's what publishers are for. Take care with your submissions. Research the agency and pay atten-

tion to presentation: Always follow the specific agency submission guidelines. Doing so helps the agent assess your work. Join writers groups. Sharing your work is a good way to get constructive criticism. If you know anyone in the industry, use your contacts. A personal recommendation will get more notice than cold calling."

## MARSAL LYON LITERARY AGENCY, LLC

PMB 121, 665 San Rodolfo Dr. 124, Solana Beach CA 92075. **E-mail:** jill@marsallyonliteraryagency.com; kevan@marsallyonliteraryagency.com; patricia@marsallyonliteraryagency.com; deborah@marsallyonliteraryagency.com; shannon@marsallyonliteraryagency.com; jolene@marsallyonliteraryagency.com. **Website:** www.marsallyonliteraryagency.com. Estab. 2009. See agency website for a client listing.

**MEMBER AGENTS** Jill Marsal (all types of women's fiction, book club fiction, stories of family, friendships, relationships, secrets, and stories with strong emotion; historical fiction, mystery, cozy, suspense, psychological suspense, thriller; romance—contemporary, romantic suspense, historical, and category; nonfiction in the areas of current events, business, health, self-help, relationships, psychology, parenting, history, science, and narrative nonfiction); Kevan Lyon (women's fiction of all types, both historical and contemporary); Patricia Nelson (literary fiction and commercial fiction, all types of women's fiction, contemporary and historical romance, young adult and middle grade fiction, LGBTQ fiction for both YA and adult); Deborah Ritchken (lifestyle books, specifically in the areas of food, design and entertaining; pop culture; women's issues; biography; and current events; her niche interest is projects about France, including fiction); Shannon Hassan (upmarket/bookclub fiction, historical fiction, thrillers, young adult fiction, middle grade fiction); Jolene Haley (literary and commercial fiction, all types of women's fiction and all genres of romance, mysteries and thrillers, young adult and middle grade fiction, and select nonfiction).

**REPRESENTS** Nonfiction, fiction, novels, juvenile books. **Considers these nonfiction areas:** animals, biography, business, cooking, creative nonfiction, current affairs, diet/nutrition, environment, foods, health, history, how-to, investigative, memoirs, multicultural, New Age, parenting, popular culture, politics, psychology, science, self-help, sports, true crime, women's issues, women's studies, young adult. **Considers these **fiction areas:** commercial, contemporary issues, crime, detective, ethnic, family saga, feminist, historical, juvenile, literary, mainstream, middle grade, multicultural, mystery, paranormal, romance, suspense, thriller, women's, young adult.

**HOW TO CONTACT** Query by e-mail. Query only one agent at this agency at a time. "Please visit our website to determine who is best suited for your work. Write 'query' in the subject line of your e-mail. Please allow up to several weeks to hear back on your query." Accepts simultaneous submissions. Query response time is generally up to 2 weeks and submission time varies by agent.

**RECENT SALES** All sales are posted on Publishers Marketplace.

**TIPS** "Our agency's mission is to help writers achieve their publishing dreams. We want to work with authors not just for a book but for a career; we are dedicated to building long-term relationships with our authors and publishing partners. Our goal is to help find homes for books that engage, entertain, and make a difference."

## THE EVAN MARSHALL AGENCY

1 Pacio Ct., Roseland NJ 07068-1121. (973)287-6216. **E-mail:** evan@evanmarshallagency.com. **Website:** www.evanmarshallagency.com. **Contact:** Evan Marshall. Estab. 1987. Represents 50+ clients.

○ Prior to becoming an agent, Evan Marshall held senior editorial positions at Houghton Mifflin, Ariel Books, New American Library, Everest House and Dodd, Mead, where he acquired national and international bestsellers.

**REPRESENTS** Fiction, novels. **Considers these fiction areas:** action, adventure, crime, detective, erotica, ethnic, family saga, fantasy, feminist, frontier, gay, glitz, historical, horror, humor, inspirational, lesbian, literary, mainstream, military, multicultural, multimedia, mystery, new adult, New Age, occult, paranormal, police, psychic, regional, religious, romance, satire, science fiction, spiritual, sports, supernatural, suspense, thriller, translation, urban fantasy, war, westerns, women's, young adult, romance (contemporary, gothic, historical, regency).

☛ "We represent all genres of adult and young adult full-length fiction." Does not want articles, children's books, essays, memoirs, nonfiction, novellas, poetry, screenplays, short stories, stage plays.

**HOW TO CONTACT** "We consider new clients by referral only." Accepts simultaneous submissions. Responds in 1 week to queries if interested; 1 month to mss. Considers new clients by referral only.

**TERMS** Agent receives 15% commission on domestic sales; 20% commission on foreign and film/TV sales. Offers written contract.

**RECENT SALES** *The Sculptress*, by V. S. Alexander (Kensington); *A Mother's Promise*, by K. D. Alden (Grand Central); *Pieces of Eight*, by Steve Goble (Seventh Street); *Murder in an Irish Bookshop*, by Carlene O'Connor (Kensington); *The Boyfriend Project*, by Farrah Rochon (Grand Central); *Real Men Knit*, by Kwana Jackson (Berkley); *Tie Die*, by Max Tomlinson (Oceanview).

## THE MARTELL AGENCY

1350 Avenue of the Americas, Suite 1205, New York NY 10019. (212)317-2672. **E-mail:** submissions@themartellagency.com. **Website:** www.themartellagency.com. **Contact:** Alice Martell.

**REPRESENTS** Nonfiction, fiction, novels. **Considers these nonfiction areas:** "big idea" books, business, current affairs, economics, health/diet, history, medicine, memoirs, multicultural, politics, personal finance, psychology, science for the general reader, self-help, women's issues.

☛ Seeks the following subjects in fiction: literary and commercial, including mystery, suspense and thrillers. Does not want to receive romance, genre mysteries, genre historical fiction, science fiction or children's books.

**HOW TO CONTACT** E-query Alice Martell. This should include a summary of the project and a short biography and any information, if appropriate, as to why you are qualified to write on the subject of your book, including any publishing credits. Accepts simultaneous submissions.

## MARTIN LITERARY AND MEDIA MANAGEMENT

914 164th St. SE, Suite B12, #307, Mill Creek WA 98012. **E-mail:** Sharlene@MartinLit.com. **Website:** www.MartinLit.com. **Contact:** Sharlene Martin. Estab. 2002. Member of Producers Guild of America.

○ Prior to becoming an agent, Ms. Martin worked in film/TV production and acquisitions.

**MEMBER AGENTS** Sharlene Martin (nonfiction); Clelia Gore (children's, middle grade, young adult);

Adria Goetz (Christian books, lifestyle books, children's, and YA); Lindsay Guzzardo (adult fiction). **REPRESENTS** Nonfiction. **Considers these nonfiction areas:** autobiography, biography, business, creative nonfiction, current affairs, health, history, how-to, humor, inspirational, investigative, medicine, memoirs, multicultural, parenting, popular culture, psychology, satire, true crime, war, women's issues, women's studies. **Considers these script areas:** Only reps for film/TV books that Martin Lit has sold.

☞ This agency has strong ties to film/TV. See her bio at IMDB.com Actively seeking nonfiction that is highly commercial and that can be adapted to film/television. "We are being inundated with queries and submissions that are wrongfully being submitted to us, which only results in more frustration for the writers. Please review our Submission page on our website and direct your query accordingly."

**HOW TO CONTACT** Query via e-mail with MS Word only. No attachments on queries; place letter in body of e-mail. Accepts simultaneous submissions. Responds in 2 weeks to queries; 3-4 weeks to mss. Obtains most new clients through recommendations from others.

**TERMS** Agent receives 15% commission on domestic sales. We are exclusive for foreign sales to Taryn Fagerness Agency. Offers written contract, binding for 1 year; 1-month notice must be given to terminate contract. 99% of materials are sent electronically to minimize charges to author for postage and copying.

**RECENT SALES** *The Next Everest* by Jim Davidson; *Soles of a Survivor* by Nhi Aronheim; *Taken At Birth* by Jane Blasio; *Victim F*, by Denise Huskins and Aaron Quinn; *Taking My Life Back*, by Rebekah Gregory with Anthony Flacco; *Breakthrough*, by Jack Andraka; *In the Matter of Nikola Tesla: A Romance of the Mind*, by Anthony Flacco; *Honor Bound: My Journey to Hell and Back with Amanda Knox*, by Raffaele Sollecito; *Impossible Odds: The Kidnapping of Jessica Buchanan and Dramatic Rescue by SEAL Team Six*, by Jessica Buchanan, Erik Landemalm and Anthony Flacco; *Walking on Eggshells*, by Lisa Chapman; *Newtown: An American Tragedy*, by Matthew Lysiak; *Publish Your Nonfiction Book*, by Sharlene Martin and Anthony Flacco.

**TIPS** "Have a strong platform for nonfiction. Please don't call. (I can't tell how well you write by the sound of your voice.) I welcome e-mail. I'm very responsive when I'm interested in a query and work hard to get my clients' materials in the best possible shape before submissions. Do your homework prior to submission and only submit your best efforts. Please review our website carefully to make sure we're a good match for your work. If you read my book, *Publish Your Nonfiction Book: Strategies For Learning the Industry, Selling Your Book and Building a Successful Career* (Writer's Digest Books), you'll know exactly how to charm me."

### MASSIE & MCQUILKIN

27 W. 20th St., Suite 305, New York NY 10011. **E-mail:** info@lmqlit.com. **Website:** www.lmqlit.com.

**MEMBER AGENTS** Laney Katz Becker, laney@lmqlit.com (book club fiction, upmarket women's fiction, suspense, thrillers and memoir); Ethan Bassoff, ethan@lmqlit.com (literary fiction, crime fiction, and narrative nonfiction in the areas of history, sports writing, journalism, science writing, pop culture, humor, and food writing); Jason Anthony, jason@lmqlit.com (commercial fiction of all types, including young adult, and nonfiction in the areas of memoir, pop culture, true crime, and general psychology and sociology); Will Lippincott, will@lmqlit.com (narrative nonfiction and nonfiction in the areas of politics, history, biography, foreign affairs, and health); Rob McQuilkin, rob@lmqlit.com (literary fiction; narrative nonfiction and nonfiction in the areas of memoir, history, biography, art history, cultural criticism, and popular sociology and psychology); Rayhane Sanders, rayhane@lmqlit.com (literary fiction, historical fiction, upmarket commercial fiction [including select YA], narrative nonfiction [including essays], and select memoir); Stephanie Abou (literary and upmarket commercial fiction (including select young adult and middle grade), crime fiction, memoir, and narrative nonfiction); Julie Stevenson (literary and upmarket fiction, narrative nonfiction, YA and children's books).

**REPRESENTS** Nonfiction, fiction, novels. **Considers these nonfiction areas:** art, biography, cultural interests, foods, health, history, humor, memoirs, popular culture, politics, psychology, science, sociology, sports, true crime, narrative nonfiction. **Considers these fiction areas:** commercial, contemporary issues, crime, literary, mainstream, middle grade, suspense, thriller, women's, young adult.

☞ "Massie & McQuilkin is a full-service literary agency that focuses on bringing fiction and nonfiction of quality to the largest possible audience."

**HOW TO CONTACT** E-query preferred. Include the word "Query" in the subject line of your e-mail. Review the agency's online page of agent bios (lmqlit. com/contact.html), as some agents want sample pages with their submissions and some do not. If you have not heard back from the agency in 4 weeks, assume they are not interested in seeing more. Accepts simultaneous submissions. Obtains most new clients through recommendations from others, solicitations, conferences.

**TERMS** Agent receives 15% commission on domestic sales; 20% commission on foreign sales. Offers written contract; 30-day notice must be given to terminate contract. Only charges for reasonable business expenses upon successful sale.

**RECENT SALES** Clients include Roxane Gay, Peter Ho Davies, Kim Addonizio, Natasha Trethewey, David Sirota, Katie Crouch, Uwen Akpan, Lydia Millet, Tom Perrotta, Jonathan Lopez, Chris Hayes, Caroline Weber.

## MB ARTISTS

775 Sixth Ave., #6, New York NY 10001. (212)689-7830. **E-mail:** mela@mbartists.com. **Website:** www.mbartists.com. **Contact:** Mela Bolinao. Estab. 1986. Member of SPAR, Society of Illustrators and Graphic Artists Guild. Represents 60+ clients.

**REPRESENTS** Nonfiction, fiction, novels, short story collections, juvenile books, textbooks, poetry books.

☛ Specializes in illustration for juvenile markets. Markets include: advertising agencies; editorial/magazines; publishing/books, board games, stationery, etc.

**HOW TO CONTACT** For first contact, send query letter, direct mail flier/brochure, website address, tearsheets, slides, photographs or color copies and SASE or send website link to mela@mbartists.com. Portfolio should include at least 12 images appropriate for the juvenile market. Accepts simultaneous submissions.

**TERMS** Rep receives 25% commission. No geographic restrictions. Advertising costs are split: 75% paid by talent; 25% paid by representative.

## MARGRET MCBRIDE LITERARY AGENCY

P.O. Box 9128, La Jolla CA 92038. (858)454-1550. **E-mail:** mmla@mcbridelit.com. **Website:** www.mc-brideliterary.com. Estab. 1981. Member of AAR, Authors Guild.

○ Prior to opening her agency, Ms. McBride worked at Random House and Ballantine Books. Later, she became the Director of Publicity at Warner Books, and Director of Publicity, Promotions and Advertising for Pinnacle Books.

**MEMBER AGENTS** Margret McBride; Faye Atchison.

**REPRESENTS** Nonfiction, fiction, novels. **Considers these nonfiction areas:** autobiography, biography, business, cooking, creative nonfiction, cultural interests, current affairs, diet/nutrition, ethnic, foods, gay/lesbian, health, history, hobbies, how-to, inspirational, investigative, juvenile nonfiction, medicine, memoirs, money, multicultural, music, popular culture, psychology, science, self-help, sex, sociology, theater, travel, true crime, women's issues, young adult. **Considers these fiction areas:** action, adventure, comic books, commercial, confession, contemporary issues, crime, detective, family saga, feminist, historical, horror, juvenile, mainstream, multicultural, multimedia, mystery, new adult, paranormal, police, psychic, regional, supernatural, suspense, thriller, young adult.

☛ This agency specializes in mainstream nonfiction and some commercial fiction. Actively seeking commercial nonfiction, business, health, self-help. Does not want screenplays, romance, poetry, or children's.

**HOW TO CONTACT** Please check our website, as instructions are subject to change. Use QueryManager. In your query letter, provide a brief synopsis of your work, as well as any pertinent information about yourself. We recommend that authors look at book jacket copy of professionally published books to get an idea of the style and content that should be included in a query letter. Essentially, you are marketing yourself and your work to us, so that we can determine whether we feel we can market you and your work to publishers. There are detailed nonfiction proposal guidelines on our website, but we recommend authors get a copy of *How to Write a Book Proposal* by Jody Rein and Michael Larsen for further instruction. **Please note: The McBride Agency will not respond to queries sent by mail, and will not be responsible for the return of any material submitted by mail.** Accepts simultaneous submissions. Responds within 8 weeks to queries; 6-8 weeks to requested mss. "You are welcome to follow up by phone or e-mail after 6 weeks if you have not yet received a response."

**TERMS** Agent receives 15% commission on domestic sales; 25% commission on translation rights sales (15% to agency, 10% to sub-agent). Charges for overnight delivery and photocopying.

**RECENT SALES** *Millennial Money*, by Grant Sabatier (Atria/Simon & Schuster); *Nimble*, by Baba Prasad (Perigee/Penguin Random House—US and World rights excluding India); *Carefrontation*, by Dr. Arlene Drake (Regan Arts/Phaidon); *There Are No Overachievers*, by Brian Biro (Crown Business/Penguin Random House); *Cheech Is Not My Real Name*, by Richard Marin (Grand Central Books/Hachette); *Killing It!*, by Sheryl O'Loughlin (Harper Business/HarperCollins); *Scrappy*, by Terri Sjodin (Portfolio/Penguin Random House).

**TIPS** "E-mail queries only. Please don't call to pitch your work by phone."

## E. J. MCCARTHY AGENCY

(415)383-6639. **E-mail:** ejmagency@gmail.com. **Website:** http://www.publishersmarketplace.com/members/ejmccarthy/. Signatory of WGA.

○ Prior to his current position, Mr. McCarthy was a former executive editor with more than 20 years book publishing experience (Bantam Doubleday Dell, Presidio Press, Ballantine/Random House).

**REPRESENTS Considers these nonfiction areas:** biography, history, memoirs, military, sports.

☛ This agency specializes in nonfiction.

**HOW TO CONTACT** Query first by e-mail. Accepts simultaneous submissions.

**RECENT SALES** *One Bullet Away*, by Nathaniel Fick; *The Unforgiving Minute*, by Craig Mullaney; *The Sling And The Stone*, by Thomas X. Hammes; *The Heart and the First*, by Eric Greitens; *When Books Went to War*, by Molly Guptill Manning.

## SEAN MCCARTHY LITERARY AGENCY

**E-mail:** submissions@mccarthylit.com. **Website:** www.mccarthylit.com. **Contact:** Sean McCarthy. Estab. 2013.

○ Prior to his current position, Sean McCarthy began his publishing career as an editorial intern at Overlook Press and then moved over to the Sheldon Fogelman Agency.

**REPRESENTS Considers these nonfiction areas:** juvenile nonfiction, young adult. **Considers these fiction areas:** juvenile, middle grade, picture books, young adult.

☛ Sean is drawn to flawed, multifaceted characters with devastatingly concise writing in YA, and character-driven work or smartly paced mysteries/adventures in MG. In picture books, he looks more for unforgettable characters, offbeat humor, and especially clever endings. He is not currently interested in issue-driven stories or query letters that pose too many questions.

**HOW TO CONTACT** E-query. "Please include a brief description of your book, your biography, and any literary or relevant professional credits in your query letter. If you are a novelist: Please submit the first 3 chapters of your manuscript (or roughly 25 pages) and a 1-page synopsis in the body of the e-mail or as a Word or PDF attachment. If you are a picture book author: Please submit the complete text of your manuscript. We are not currently accepting picture book manuscripts over 1,000 words. If you are an illustrator: Please attach up to 3 JPEGs or PDFs of your work, along with a link to your website." Accepts simultaneous submissions.

## MCCORMICK LITERARY

150 28th St., Suite 903, New York NY 10001. (212)691-9726. **E-mail:** queries@mccormicklit.com. **Website:** mccormicklit.com. Member of AAR. Signatory of WGA.

**MEMBER AGENTS** David McCormick; Bridget McCarthy (literary and commercial fiction, narrative nonfiction, memoir, and cookbooks); Edward Orloff (literary fiction and narrative nonfiction, especially cultural history, politics, biography, and the arts); Leslie Falk.

**REPRESENTS** Nonfiction, novels. **Considers these nonfiction areas:** biography, cooking, history, memoirs, politics. **Considers these fiction areas:** literary, women's.

**HOW TO CONTACT** Snail mail queries or via e-mail. Send an SASE. Accepts simultaneous submissions.

## MCINTOSH & OTIS, INC.

207 E. 37th Street, New York NY 10016. (212)687-7400. **Fax:** (212)687-6894. **E-mail:** info@mcintoshandotis.com. **Website:** www.mcintoshandotis.com. **Contact:**

Elizabeth Winick Rubinstein. Estab. 1928. Member of AAR, SCBWI. Signatory of WGA.

**MEMBER AGENTS** Elizabeth Winick Rubinstein, ewrquery@mcintoshandotis.com (literary fiction, women's fiction, historical fiction, and mystery/suspense, along with narrative nonfiction, spiritual/self-help, history, and current affairs); Christa Heschke, chquery@mcintoshandotis.com (picture books, middle grade, young adult and new adult projects); Adam Muhlig, amquery@mcintoshandotis.com (music—from jazz to classical to punk—popular culture, natural history, travel and adventure, and sports).

**REPRESENTS** Nonfiction, fiction, novels, juvenile books. **Considers these nonfiction areas:** creative nonfiction, current affairs, history, popular culture, self-help, spirituality, sports, travel. **Considers these fiction areas:** fantasy, historical, horror, literary, middle grade, mystery, new adult, paranormal, picture books, romance, science fiction, suspense, urban fantasy, women's, young adult.

☞ Actively seeking "books with memorable characters, distinctive voices, and great plots."

**HOW TO CONTACT** E-mail submissions only. Each agent has their own e-mail address for subs. For fiction: Please send a query letter, synopsis, author bio, and the first 3 consecutive chapters (no more than 30 pages) of your novel. For nonfiction: Please send a query letter, proposal, outline, author bio, and 3 sample chapters (no more than 30 pages) of the ms. For children's & young adult: Please send a query letter, synopsis and the first 3 consecutive chapters (not to exceed 25 pages) of the ms. Accepts simultaneous submissions. Obtains clients through recommendations from others, editors, conferences and queries.

**TERMS** Agent receives 15% commission on domestic sales; 20% on foreign sales.

**WRITERS CONFERENCES** Attends Bologna Book Fair, in Bologna, Italy, in April, SCBWI Conference in New York in February, and regularly attends other conferences and industry conventions.

## MENDEL MEDIA GROUP, LLC

P.O. Box 5032, East Hampton NY 11937. (646)239-9896. **E-mail:** query@mendelmedia.com. **Website:** www.mendelmedia.com. Estab. 2002. Member of AAR.

○ Prior to becoming an agent, Mr. Mendel was an academic. "I taught American literature, Yiddish, Jewish studies, and literary theory at the University of Chicago and the University of Illinois at Chicago while working on my PhD in English. I also worked as a freelance technical writer and as the managing editor of a healthcare magazine. In 1998, I began working for the late Jane Jordan Browne, a long-time agent in the book publishing world."

**REPRESENTS** Nonfiction, fiction, novels. **Considers these nonfiction areas:** Americana, animals, anthropology, architecture, art, biography, business, child guidance, cooking, current affairs, dance, education, environment, ethnic, foods, gardening, gay/lesbian, government, health, history, how-to, humor, investigative, language, medicine, memoirs, military, money, multicultural, music, parenting, philosophy, popular culture, psychology, recreation, regional, religious, science, self-help, sex, sociology, software, spirituality, sports, travel, true crime, war, women's issues, women's studies, all narrative projects, and creative nonfiction. **Considers these fiction areas:** action, adventure, commercial, contemporary issues, crime, detective, erotica, ethnic, family saga, feminist, gay, glitz, historical, humor, inspirational, juvenile, lesbian, literary, mainstream, military, multicultural, mystery, picture books, police, religious, romance, satire, sports, thriller, young adult, commercial and literary fiction.

☞ "I am interested in major works of history, current affairs, biography, business, politics, economics, science, major memoirs, narrative nonfiction, and other sorts of general nonfiction." Actively seeking new, major or definitive work on a subject of broad interest, or a controversial, but authoritative, new book on a subject that affects many people's lives. "I also represent more light-hearted nonfiction projects, such as gift or novelty books, when they suit the market particularly well." Does not want "queries about projects written years ago that were unsuccessfully shopped to a long list of trade publishers by either the author or another agent. I am specifically not interested in considering original plays or original film scripts."

**HOW TO CONTACT** You should e-mail your work to query@mendelmedia.com. We no longer accept or read submissions sent by mail, so please do not send inquiries by any other method. If we want to read more or discuss your work, we will respond to you by e-mail or phone. Fiction queries: If you have a novel you would like to submit, please paste a synopsis and the first twenty pages into the body of your email, below a detailed letter about your publication history and the history of the project, if it has been submitted previously to publishers or other agents. Please do not use attachments, as we will not open them. Nonfiction queries: If you have a completed nonfiction book proposal and sample chapters, you should paste those into the body of an e-mail, below a detailed letter about your publication history and the history of the project, if it has been submitted previously to any publishers or other agents. Please do not use attachments, as we will not open them. If we want to read more or discuss your work, we will call or e-mail you directly. If you do not receive a personal response within a few weeks, we are not going to offer representation. In any case, however, please do not call or email to inquire about your query. Accepts simultaneous submissions. Responds within a few weeks, if interested. Obtains most new clients through referrals.

**TERMS** Agent receives 15% commission on domestic sales; 20% commission on foreign sales.

**WRITERS CONFERENCES** BookExpo America; Frankfurt Book Fair; London Book Fair; RWA National Conference; Modern Language Association Convention; Jerusalem Book Fair.

**TIPS** "While I am not interested in being flattered by a prospective client, it does matter to me that she knows why she is writing to me in the first place. Is one of my clients a colleague of hers? Has she read a book by one of my clients that led her to believe I might be interested in her work? Authors of descriptive nonfiction should have real credentials and expertise in their subject areas, either as academics, journalists, or policy experts, and authors of prescriptive nonfiction should have legitimate expertise and considerable experience communicating their ideas in seminars and workshops, in a successful business, through the media, etc."

## HOWARD MORHAIM LITERARY AGENCY

30 Pierrepont St., Brooklyn NY 11201. (718)222-8400. **Fax:** (718)222-5056. **E-mail:** info@morhaimliterary.com. **Website:** www.morhaimliterary.com. Member of AAR.

**MEMBER AGENTS** Howard Morhaim, howard@morhaimliterary.com; Kate McKean, kmckean@morhaimliterary.com; DongWon Song, dongwon@

morhaimliterary.com; Kim-Mei Kirtland, kimmei@morhaimliterary.com; Laura Southern.

**REPRESENTS Considers these nonfiction areas:** biography, business, cooking, crafts, creative nonfiction, design, economics, foods, health, humor, memoirs, parenting, self-help, sports. **Considers these fiction areas:** fantasy, historical, literary, middle grade, new adult, romance, science fiction, women's, young adult, LGBTQ young adult, magical realism, fantasy should be high fantasy, historical fiction should be no earlier than the 20th century.

☞   Kate McKean is open to many subgenres and categories of YA and MG fiction. Check the website for the most details. Actively seeking fiction, nonfiction, and young adult novels.

**HOW TO CONTACT** Query via e-mail with cover letter and 3 sample chapters. See each agent's listing for specifics. Accepts simultaneous submissions.

## ⃠  WILLIAM MORRIS ENDEAVOR ENTERTAINMENT

11 Madison Ave., New York NY 10010. (212)586-5100. **Website:** wmeentertainment.com. **Contact:** Literary Department Coordinator. Member of AAR.

**REPRESENTS** Novels.

**HOW TO CONTACT** This agency is generally closed to unsolicited literary submissions. Meet an agent at a conference, or query through a referral. Accepts simultaneous submissions.

**TERMS** Agent receives 15% commission on domestic sales; 20% commission on foreign sales.

## MOVEABLE TYPE MANAGEMENT

244 Madison Ave., Suite 334, New York NY 10016. **E-mail:** achromy@movabletm.com. **Website:** www.movabletm.com. **Contact:** Adam Chromy. Estab. 2002.

**REPRESENTS** Nonfiction, fiction, novels. **Considers these nonfiction areas:** Americana, business, creative nonfiction, current affairs, film, foods, gay/lesbian, history, how-to, humor, inspirational, literature, memoirs, military, money, multicultural, music, popular culture, politics, psychology, satire, science, self-help, sex, sociology, sports, technology, theater, true crime, war, women's issues, women's studies. **Considers these fiction areas:** action, commercial, crime, detective, family saga, hi-lo, historical, humor, literary, mainstream, mystery, police, romance, satire, science fiction, sports, suspense, thriller, women's.

☞ Mr. Chromy is a generalist, meaning that he accepts fiction submissions of virtually any kind (except juvenile books aimed for middle grade and younger) as well as nonfiction. He has sold books in the following categories: new adult, women's, romance, memoir, pop culture, young adult, lifestyle, horror, how-to, general fiction, and more.

**HOW TO CONTACT** E-queries only. Responds if interested. For nonfiction: Send a query letter in the body of an e-mail that precisely introduces your topic and approach, and includes a descriptive bio. For journalists and academics, please also feel free to include a CV. Fiction: Send your query letter and the first 10 pages of your novel in the body of an e-mail. Your subject line needs to contain the word "Query" or your message will not reach the agency. No attachments and no snail mail. Accepts simultaneous submissions.

## ⊘ ERIN MURPHY LITERARY AGENCY

824 Roosevelt Trail, #290, Windham ME 04062. **Website:** emliterary.com. **Contact:** Erin Murphy, president; Ammi-Joan Paquette, senior agent; Tricia Lawrence, senior agent; Kevin Lewis, agent; Tara Gonzalez, associate agent; Miranda Paul, associate agent. Estab. 1999.

**REPRESENTS** Juvenile books. **Considers these fiction areas:** middle grade, picture books, young adult.
☞ Specializes in children's books only.

**HOW TO CONTACT** Accepts simultaneous submissions.

**TERMS** Agent receives 15% commission on domestic sales; 20-30% on foreign sales. Offers written contract. 30 days notice must be given to terminate contract.

**TIPS** "Please do not submit to more than one agent at EMLA at a time."

## JEAN V. NAGGAR LITERARY AGENCY, INC.

JVNLA, Inc., 216 E. 75th St., Suite 1E, New York NY 10021. (212)794-1082. **Website:** www.jvnla.com. **Contact:** Jennifer Weltz. Estab. 1978. Member of AAR, Women's Media Group, SCBWI, Pace University's Masters in Publishing Board Member. Represents 450 clients.

**MEMBER AGENTS** Jennifer Weltz (well-researched and original historicals, thrillers with a unique voice, wry dark humor, and magical realism; enthralling narrative nonfiction; voice-driven young adult, middle grade); Alice Tasman (literary, commercial, YA,

middle grade, and nonfiction in the categories of narrative, biography, music or pop culture); Ariana Philips (nonfiction both prescriptive and narrative); Alicia Brooks (fiction, nonfiction and YA).

**REPRESENTS** Nonfiction, fiction, novels, short story collections, novellas, juvenile books, scholarly books, poetry books. **Considers these nonfiction areas:** animals, child guidance, cooking, creative nonfiction, economics, education, environment, ethnic, foods, gardening, gay/lesbian, how-to, humor, literature, medicine, memoirs, multicultural, parenting, popular culture, politics, psychology, satire, science, self-help, sex, travel, true crime, women's issues, women's studies, young adult. **Considers these fiction areas:** action, adventure, cartoon, comic books, commercial, contemporary issues, crime, detective, ethnic, family saga, fantasy, feminist, gay, historical, humor, inspirational, juvenile, lesbian, literary, mainstream, middle grade, multicultural, mystery, picture books, romance, satire, science fiction, suspense, thriller, women's, young adult.
☞ This agency specializes in mainstream fiction and nonfiction and literary fiction with commercial potential as well as young adult, middle grade, and picture books. Does not want to receive screenplays.

**HOW TO CONTACT** "Visit our website to send submissions and see what our individual agents are looking for. No snail mail submissions please!" Accepts simultaneous submissions. Depends on the agent. No responses for queries unless the agent is interested.

**TERMS** Agent receives 15% commission on domestic sales; 20% commission on foreign and film sales. Offers written contract. Charges for overseas mailing, messenger services, book purchases, photocopying—all deductible from royalties received.

**RECENT SALES** *Enola Holmes and the Black Barouche*, by Nancy Springer; *The City of Incurable Women(e)*, by Maud Casey; *Stuck*, by Jennifer Swender; *The Cage*, Bonnie Kistler; *Lucious, Tender, Juicy* by Kathy Hunt; *A Matter of Live and Death*, by Phillip Margolin; *Doomed*, by John Florio and Ouisie Shapiro; *This Book Is Made of Clouds*, by Misha Blaise; *Drop*, by Emily Kate Moon; *The Girl in His Shadow*, by Audrey Blake; *Skip to My Moo*, by Iza Trapani; *America Made Me a Black Man*, by Boyah Farah; *The 3-D Universe: How to Hold the Universe in Your Hand*, by Kimberly Arcand and Megan Watzke; *All* *the Children Are Home*, by Patry Francis; *Those Who Are Saved*, by Alexis Landau; *This Story Will Change*, by Elizabeth Crane.

**TIPS** "We recommend courage, fortitude, and patience: the courage to be true to your own vision, the fortitude to finish a novel and polish it again and again before sending it out, and the patience to accept rejection gracefully and wait for the stars to align themselves appropriately for success."

## NELSON LITERARY AGENCY

1732 Wazee St., Suite 207, Denver CO 80202. (303)292-2805. **E-mail:** We accept queries through QueryManager.com. Find links to our agents' QueryManager forms on our website. **Website:** www.nelsonagency. com. **Contact:** Kristin Nelson, President. Estab. 2002. Member of AAR, RWA, SCBWI, SFWA. Represents 100 clients.

**MEMBER AGENTS** Danielle Burby, Joanna MacKenzie, Quressa Robinson.

**REPRESENTS** Fiction, novels. **Considers these fiction areas:** commercial, crime, ethnic, family saga, fantasy, feminist, gay, historical, horror, humor, lesbian, literary, mainstream, middle grade, multicultural, mystery, romance, science fiction, suspense, thriller, urban fantasy, women's, young adult, book-club fiction, magical realism, romantic comedy.

➤ NLA specializes in representing commercial fiction as well as high-caliber literary fiction. Regardless of genre, we are actively seeking good stories well told. We do not represent scripts/screenplays, short-story collections, prescriptive nonfiction, abuse narratives, political works, or material for the Christian/inspirational market.

**HOW TO CONTACT** Please visit our website to learn about what each agent is currently seeking. Please choose only one agent at NLA to query. We do share queries with each other here at NLA so a pass from one of us is a pass from all. Submit through QueryManager (find links on our website) with the following: a brief bio, including any writing credentials; the title, genre, and word count of your work; your query letter; the first ten pages of your manuscript. Accepts simultaneous submissions. We make best efforts to respond to all queries within three weeks. Response to full manuscripts requested can take up to three months.

**TERMS** Agency charges industry standard commission.

**TIPS** If you would like to learn how to write an awesome pitch paragraph for your query letter or would like any info on how publishing contracts work, please visit Pub Rants, Kristin's popular industry: https://nelsonagency.com/pub-rants/

## NEW LEAF LITERARY & MEDIA, INC.

110 W. 40th St., Suite 2201, New York NY 10018. (646)248-7989. **Fax:** (646)861-4654. **E-mail:** query@ newleafliterary.com. **Website:** www.newleafliterary. com. Estab. 2012. Member of AAR.

**MEMBER AGENTS** Joanna Volpe (women's fiction, thriller, horror, speculative fiction, literary fiction and historical fiction, young adult, middle grade, art-focused picture books); Kathleen Ortiz, Director of Subsidiary Rights and literary agent (new voices in YA and animator/illustrator talent); Suzie Townsend (new adult, young adult, middle grade, romance [all subgenres], fantasy [urban fantasy, science fiction, steampunk, epic fantasy] and crime fiction [mysteries, thrillers]); Pouya Shahbazian, Director of Film and Television (no unsolicited queries); JL Stermer (nonfiction, smart pop culture, comedy/satire, fashion, health & wellness, self-help, and memoir); Jordan Hamessley; Stephanie Kim; Patrice Caldwell; Janna Morishima.

**REPRESENTS** Nonfiction, fiction, novels, novellas, juvenile books, poetry books. **Considers these nonfiction areas:** cooking, crafts, creative nonfiction, science, technology, women's issues, young adult. **Considers these fiction areas:** crime, fantasy, historical, horror, literary, mainstream, middle grade, mystery, new adult, paranormal, picture books, romance, thriller, women's, young adult.

**HOW TO CONTACT** Send query via e-mail. Please do not query via phone. The word "Query" must be in the subject line, plus the agent's name, i.e., Subject: Query, Suzie Townsend. You may include up to 5 double-spaced sample pages within the body of the e-mail. No attachments, unless specifically requested. Include all necessary contact information. You will receive an auto-response confirming receipt of your query. "We only respond if we are interested in seeing your work." All queries read within 1 month.

**RECENT SALES** *Carve the Mark*, by Veronica Roth (HarperCollins); *Red Queen*, by Victoria Aveyard (HarperCollins); *Lobster is the Best Medicine*, by Liz

Climo (Running Press); *Ninth House*, by Leigh Bardugo (Henry Holt); *A Snicker of Magic*, by Natalie Lloyd (Scholastic).

## DANA NEWMAN LITERARY

1800 Avenue of the Stars, 12th Floor, Los Angeles CA 90067. **E-mail:** dananewmanliterary@gmail.com. **Website:** dananewman.com. **Contact:** Dana Newman. Estab. 2009. Member of AAR, California State Bar. Represents 30 clients.

🅞 Prior to becoming an agent, Ms. Newman was an attorney in the entertainment industry for 14 years.

**MEMBER AGENTS** Dana Newman (narrative nonfiction, business, lifestyle, current affairs, parenting, memoir, pop culture, sports, health, literary and upmarket fiction).

**REPRESENTS** Nonfiction, fiction, novels. **Considers these nonfiction areas:** architecture, art, autobiography, biography, business, child guidance, cooking, creative nonfiction, cultural interests, current affairs, diet/nutrition, design, education, environment, ethnic, film, foods, gay/lesbian, government, health, history, how-to, humor, inspirational, interior design, investigative, language, law, literature, medicine, memoirs, money, multicultural, music, New Age, parenting, popular culture, politics, psychology, regional, science, self-help, sociology, spirituality, sports, technology, theater, travel, true crime, women's issues, women's studies. **Considers these fiction areas:** commercial, contemporary issues, family saga, feminist, historical, literary, multicultural, sports, women's.

☞ Ms. Newman has a background as an attorney in contracts, licensing, publishing and intellectual property law. She is experienced in digital content creation and distribution. "We are interested in practical nonfiction (business, health and wellness, psychology, parenting, technology) by authors with smart, unique perspectives and established platforms who are committed to actively marketing and promoting their books. We love compelling, inspiring narrative nonfiction in the areas of memoir, biography, history, pop culture, current affairs/women's interest, sports, and social trends. On the fiction side, we consider a very selective amount of literary fiction and women's upmarket fiction." Does not want religious, children's, poetry, horror, crime, mystery, thriller, romance, or science fiction. Does not represent screenplays.

**HOW TO CONTACT** E-mail queries only. For both nonfiction and fiction, please submit a query letter including a description of your project and a brief biography. "If we are interested in your project, we will contact you and request a full book proposal (nonfiction) or a synopsis and the first 25 pages (fiction)." Accepts simultaneous submissions. "If we have requested your materials after receiving your query, we will use our best efforts to respond within 4 weeks although response time may vary." Obtains new clients through recommendations from others, queries, and submissions.

**TERMS** Obtains 15% commission on domestic sales; 20% on foreign sales. Offers 1-year written contract. Notice must be given 1 month prior to terminate a contract.

**RECENT SALES** *Radiant Rest*, by Tracee Stanley (Shambhala); *Shot Clock* by Caron Butler and Justin A. Reynolds (HarperCollins); *Climate Cure*, by Jack Adam Weber (Llewellyn); *Eat Like a Local: France*, by Lynne Martin and Deborah Scarborough (Countryman Press); *Climbing the Hill*, by Jaime Harrison and Amos Snead (Ten Speed Press); *Nora Murphy's Country House Style*, by Nora Murphy (Vendome Press); *Crawl of Fame*, by Julie Moss and Robert Yehling (Pegasus Books); *Into the Abyss*, by Ginger Lerner-Wren (Beacon Press); *Native Advertising*, by Mike Smith (McGraw-Hill); *Just Add Water*, by Clay Marzo and Robert Yehling (Houghton Mifflin Harcourt); *A Stray Cat Struts*, by Slim Jim Phantom (St. Martin's Press); *Tuff Juice*, by Caron Butler and Steve Springer (Lyons Press).

## HAROLD OBER ASSOCIATES

630 9th Ave., Suite 1101, New York NY 10036. (212)759-8600. **Fax:** (212)759-9428. **E-mail:** contact@haroldober.com. **Website:** www.haroldober.com. **Contact:** Appropriate agent. Member of AAR. Represents 250 clients.

**HOW TO CONTACT** Submit concise query letter addressed to a specific agent with the first 5 pages of the ms or proposal and SASE. No fax or e-mail. Does not handle film scripts or plays. Responds as promptly as possible. Obtains most new clients through recommendations from others.

**TERMS** Agent receives 15% commission on domestic sales; 20% commission on foreign sales. Charges clients for express mail/package services.

## ALLEN O'SHEA LITERARY AGENCY

Weston CT 06883. (203)222-9004; (203)359-9965. E-mail: coleen@allenoshea.com; marilyn@allenoshea.com. **Website:** www.allenoshea.com. Riverside, CT 06878 Member of AAR, Women's Media Group.

○ Prior to becoming agents, both Ms. O'Shea and Ms. Allen held senior positions in publishing.

**MEMBER AGENTS** Coleen O'Shea; Marilyn Allen.

**REPRESENTS** Nonfiction. **Considers these nonfiction areas:** animals, autobiography, biography, business, cooking, crafts, creative nonfiction, cultural interests, current affairs, decorating, diet/nutrition, design, environment, film, foods, gardening, gay/lesbian, health, history, horticulture, how-to, humor, inspirational, interior design, medicine, memoirs, military, money, multicultural, New Age, parenting, popular culture, psychology, regional, science, self-help, spirituality, sports, true crime, women's issues, women's studies.

☛ This agency specializes in practical nonfiction, including health, cooking and cocktails, business, and pop culture. Looks for passionate clients with strong marketing platforms and new ideas coupled with writing talent. Actively seeking narrative nonfiction, health, mind, body, spirit, popular science, cookbooks, food narrative, and history writers; very interested in writers who have large media platforms and interesting topics. Does not want to receive fiction, poetry, textbooks or children's books.

**HOW TO CONTACT** Query via e-mail or mail with SASE. Submit book proposal with sample chapters, competitive analysis, outline, author bio, and marketing page. No phone or fax queries. Accepts simultaneous submissions. Obtains most new clients through recommendations from others; conferences.

**TERMS** Agent receives 15% commission on domestic sales. Offers written contract, binding for 2 years; one-month notice must be given to terminate contract.

**TIPS** "Prepare a strong book proposal that includes an overview, table of contents, sample chapter, author bio and platform, a well-thought-out marketing plan, a competitive analysis. We will consider your project when your proposal is ready. Thanks for the opportunity to review your work."

## ⊘ PARADIGM TALENT AND LITERARY AGENCY

140 Broadway, 46th Floor, New York NY 10005. (212)897-6400. **Fax:** (212)764-8941. **Website:** www.paradigmagency.com.

**REPRESENTS** Theatrical stage play, stage plays.

☛ Paradigm Talent and Literary Agency is an Los-Angeles-based talent agency with additional offices in New York City, Nashville, and Monterey. The firm acquired Writers & Artists Group International in 2004. The acquisition of WAGI added both talent and agents to Paradigm's roster, bolstering its New York office with legit agents, representing playwrights and theater directors.

**HOW TO CONTACT** Accepts simultaneous submissions. Responds only if interested.

## PARK & FINE

50 Broadway, Suite 1601, New York NY 10006. (212)691-3500. **E-mail:** info@parkliterary.com; queries@parkliterary.com. **Website:** www.parkliterary.com. Estab. 2005.

**MEMBER AGENTS** Theresa Park (plot-driven fiction and serious nonfiction); Abigail Koons (popular science, history, politics, current affairs and art, and women's fiction); Peter Knapp (children's and YA); Celeste Fine; Susanna Alvarez; Ema Barnes; Jaidre Braddix; Charlotte Gillies; John Maas; Alison MacKeen; Sarah Passick; Anna Petkovich; Mia Vitale.

**REPRESENTS** Nonfiction, novels. **Considers these nonfiction areas:** art, current affairs, history, politics, science. **Considers these fiction areas:** juvenile, middle grade, suspense, thriller, women's, young adult.

☛ Represents fiction and nonfiction with a boutique approach: an emphasis on servicing a relatively small number of clients, with the highest professional standards and focused personal attention. Does not want to receive poetry or screenplays.

**HOW TO CONTACT** Please specify the first and last name of the agent to whom you are submitting in the subject line of the e-mail. All materials must be in the body of the e-mail. Responds if interested. For fiction submissions, please include a query letter with short synopsis and the first 3 chapters of your work. Accepts simultaneous submissions.

**RECENT SALES** This agency's client list is on their website. It includes bestsellers Nicholas Sparks, Soman Chainani, Emily Giffin, and Debbie Macomber.

## L. PERKINS AGENCY

5800 Arlington Ave., Riverdale NY 10471. (718)543-5344. **E-mail:** submissions@lperkinsagency.com. **Website:** lperkinsagency.com. Estab. 1987. Member of AAR. Represents 150 clients.

○ Ms. Perkins has been an agent for 25 years. She is also the author of *The Insider's Guide to Getting an Agent* (Writer's Digest Books), as well as 3 other nonfiction books. She has edited 25 erotic anthologies, and is also the founder and publisher of Riverdale Avenue Books, an award-winning hybrid publisher with 9 imprints.

**MEMBER AGENTS** Lori Perkins (not currently taking new clients); Leon Husock (science fiction & fantasy, as well as young adult and middle-grade); Maximilian Ximinez (fiction: science fiction, fantasy, horror, thrillers; nonfiction: popular science, true crime, arts and trends in developing fields and cultures); Ben Grange.

**REPRESENTS** Nonfiction, fiction, novels, short story collections. **Considers these nonfiction areas:** autobiography, biography, business, creative nonfiction, cultural interests, current affairs, film, foods, gay/lesbian, history, how-to, humor, literature, memoirs, music, popular culture, psychology, science, sex, theater, true crime, women's issues, women's studies, young adult. **Considers these fiction areas:** commercial, crime, detective, erotica, fantasy, feminist, gay, historical, horror, lesbian, literary, middle grade, mystery, new adult, paranormal, picture books, romance, science fiction, short story collections, supernatural, thriller, urban fantasy, women's, young adult.

☛ "Most of our clients write both fiction and nonfiction. This combination keeps our clients publishing for years. The founder of the agency is also a published author, so we know what it takes to write a good book." Actively seeking erotic romance, romance, young adult, middle grade, science fiction, fantasy, memoir, pop culture, thrillers. Does not want poetry, stand-alone short stories or novellas, scripts, plays, westerns, textbooks.

**HOW TO CONTACT** E-queries only. Include your query, a 1-page synopsis, and the first 5 pages from your novel pasted into the e-mail, or your proposal. No attachments. Submit to only 1 agent at the agency. No snail mail queries. "If you are submitting to one of our agents, please be sure to check the submission status of the agent by visiting their social media accounts listed [on the agency website]." Accepts simultaneous submissions. Obtains most new clients through recommendations from others, solicitations, conferences.

**TERMS** Agent receives 15% commission on domestic sales; 20% commission on foreign sales. No written contract. Charges clients for photocopying.

**RECENT SALES** *Arena*, by Holly Jennings; *Taking the Lead*, by Cecilia Tan; *The Girl with Ghost Eyes*, by M. H. Boroson; *Silent Attraction*, by Lauren Brown.

**WRITERS CONFERENCES** Romantic Times; Romance Writers of America nationals; Rainbow Book Fair; NECON; Killercon; BookExpo America; World Fantasy Convention.

**TIPS** "Research your field and contact professional writers' organizations to see who is looking for what. Finish your novel before querying agents. Read my book, *An Insider's Guide to Getting an Agent*, to get a sense of how agents operate."

## RUBIN PFEFFER CONTENT

648 Hammond St., Chestnut Hill MA 02467. **E-mail:** info@rpcontent.com. **Website:** www.rpcontent.com. **Contact:** Rubin Pfeffer. Estab. 2014. Member of AAR. Signatory of WGA.

○ Rubin has previously worked as the vice-president and publisher of Simon & Schuster Children's Books and as an independent agent at East West Literary Agency.

**REPRESENTS** **Considers these nonfiction areas:** juvenile nonfiction, young adult. **Considers these fiction areas:** juvenile, middle grade, picture books, young adult.

☛ High-quality children's fiction and nonfiction, including picture books, middle-grade, and young adult. No manuscripts intended for an adult audience.

**HOW TO CONTACT** Note: Rubin Pfeffer accepts submissions by referral only. Melissa Nasson is open to queries for picture books, middle-grade, and young adult fiction and nonfiction. To query Melissa, email her at melissa@rpcontent.com, include the query letter in the body of the email, and attach the first 50 pages as a Word doc or PDF. If you wish to query Rubin Pfeffer by referral only, specify the contact information of your reference when submitting. Authors/illustrators should send a query and a 1-3 chapter ms via e-mail (no postal submissions). The query, placed in the body of the e-mail, should include a synopsis of the piece, as well as any relevant information regarding previous publications, referrals, websites, and biographies. The ms may be attached as a .doc or a .pdf file. Specifically for illustrators, attach a PDF of the dummy or artwork to the e-mail. Accepts simultaneous submissions. Strives to respond within 6-8 weeks.

## PIPPIN PROPERTIES, INC.

110 W. 40th St., Suite 1704, New York NY 10018. (212)338-9310. **E-mail:** info@pippinproperties.com. **Website:** www.pippinproperties.com. **Contact:** Holly McGhee. Estab. 1998.

○ Prior to becoming an agent, Ms. McGhee was an editor for 7 years and in book marketing for 4 years.

**MEMBER AGENTS** Holly McGhee; Elena Giovinazzo; Sara Crowe. Although each of the agents take children's books, you can find in-depth preferences for each agent on the Pippin website.

**REPRESENTS** Juvenile books. **Considers these fiction areas:** middle grade, picture books, young adult.

☞ "We are strictly a children's literary agency devoted to the management of authors and artists in all media. We are small and discerning in choosing our clientele."

**HOW TO CONTACT** If you are a writer who is interested in submitting a ms, please query us via e-mail, and within the body of that e-mail please include: the first chapter of your novel with a short synopsis of the work or the entire picture book ms. For illustrators interested in submitting their work, please send a query letter detailing your background in illustration and include links to website with a dummy or other examples of your work. Direct all queries to the agent whom you wish to query and please do not query more than one. No attachments, please. Accepts simultaneous submissions. Obtains most new clients through recommendations from others.

**TERMS** Agent receives 15% commission on domestic sales; 25% commission on foreign sales. Offers written contract; 30-day notice must be given to terminate contract.

**TIPS** "Please do not call after sending a submission."

## PONTAS LITERARY & FILM AGENCY

Sèneca, 31, principal 08006, Barcelona Spain. (34)(93)218-2212. **E-mail:** info@pontas-agency.com; submissions@pontas-agency.com. **Website:** www.pontas-agency.com. Estab. 1992. Represents 70 clients.

**MEMBER AGENTS** Anna Soler-Pont; Richard Domingo; Marc de Gouvenain; Maria Cadona Serra; Carla Briner.

**REPRESENTS** Fiction, novels. **Considers these fiction areas:** action, adventure, commercial, confession, contemporary issues, crime, detective, ethnic, experimental, family saga, feminist, frontier, gay, historical, horror, inspirational, lesbian, literary, mainstream, multicultural, mystery, regional, satire, thriller, translation, women's, young adult.

☞ "At this moment in time, we are only looking for works of adult fiction written in English and French." Please defer to send any materials that do not match this requirement. Does not want original film screenplays, theatre plays, poetry, sci-fi, fantasy, romance, children's, illustrated.

**HOW TO CONTACT** When submitting work, include a brief cover letter with your name and title of your ms in the e-mail subject, a detailed synopsis of your plot, your biography, and the full work in PDF or Word format. Accepts simultaneous submissions. "Due to the enormous and increasing volume of submissions that we receive, we cannot guarantee a reply. If you do not receive a response 6 weeks from the date of your submission, you can assume we're not interested. It's also important to note that we don't provide specific reasons nor editorial feedback on the submissions received."

## PRENTIS LITERARY

PMB 496 6830 NE Bothell Way, Kenmore WA 98028. **Website:** prentisliterary.com. **Contact:** Autumn Frisse, acquisitions; Terry Johnson, business manager. Represents 12-15 clients.

○ Trodayne Northern worked as an English teacher and Academic Advisor prior to being an agent. He also worked as both a fiction and nonfiction freelancer writer and editor. After coming to work for The Literary Group, Mr. Northern started working for Linn Prentis in 2010. Trodayne Northern, Leslie Varney and Terry Johnson took over the agency and rebranded the company after Linn's retirement and eventual passing.

**REPRESENTS** Nonfiction, fiction, novels. **Considers these nonfiction areas:** biography, current affairs, ethnic, gay/lesbian, humor, memoirs, popular culture, women's issues. **Considers these fiction areas:** adventure, ethnic, fantasy, gay, historical, horror, humor, lesbian, literary, mainstream, middle grade, mystery, paranormal, romance, science fiction, supernatural, thriller, urban fantasy, young adult.

☛ Special interest in sci-fi and fantasy, but fiction is what truly interests us. Nonfiction projects have to be something we just can't resist. Actively seeking science fiction/fantasy, POC/intersectional, women's fiction, LBGTQ+, literary fiction, children's fiction, YA, MG, mystery, horror, romance, nonfiction/memoir. Please visit website for comprehensive list. Does not want to "receive books for little kids."

**HOW TO CONTACT** No phone or fax queries. No surface mail. For submission use our submission form posted on our submission page or e-mail acquisitions afrisse@prentisliterary.com. For other business questions e-mail: tjohnson@prentisliterary.com. Accepts simultaneous submissions. Obtains most new clients through recommendations from others, solicitations.

**TERMS** Agent receives 15% commission on domestic sales; 20% commission on foreign sales. Offers written contract; 60-day notice must be given to terminate contract.

**RECENT SALES** Sales include *The Antiquities Hunter: A Gina Miyoko Mystery*, by *NYT* bestselling author Maya Bohnhoff, *Substrate Phantoms*, by Jessica Reisman, *Vienna*, by William Kirby; *Hunting Ground, Frost Burned*, and *Night Broken* titles in two series for *NYT* bestselling author Patricia Briggs (as well as a graphic novel, *Homecoming*) and a story collection, with more coming; a duology of novels for A. M. Dellamonica whose first book, *Indigo Springs*, won Canada's annual award for best fantasy, as well as several books abroad for client Tachyon Publications.

## AARON M. PRIEST LITERARY AGENCY

200 W. 41st St., 21st Floor, New York NY 10036. (212)818-0344. **Fax:** (212)573-9417. **E-mail:** info@aaronpriest.com. **Website:** www.aaronpriest.com. Estab. 1974. Member of AAR.

**MEMBER AGENTS** Aaron Priest, querypriest@aaronpriest.com (thrillers, commercial fiction, biog-raphies); Lisa Erbach Vance, queryvance@aaronpriest.com (contemporary fiction, thrillers/suspense, international fiction, narrative nonfiction); Lucy Childs, querychilds@aaronpriest.com (literary and commercial fiction, memoir, edgy women's fiction); Mitch Hoffman, queryhoffman@aaronpriest.com (thrillers, suspense, crime fiction, and literary fiction, as well as narrative nonfiction, politics, popular science, history, memoir, current events, and pop culture); Arleen Gradinger Priest; Francis Jalet-Miller; Kristen Pini.

**REPRESENTS Considers these nonfiction areas:** biography, current affairs, history, memoirs, popular culture, politics, science. **Considers these fiction areas:** commercial, contemporary issues, crime, literary, middle grade, suspense, thriller, women's, young adult.

☛ Does not want to receive poetry, screenplays, horror or sci-fi.

**HOW TO CONTACT** Query one of the agents using the appropriate e-mail listed on the website. "Please do not submit to more than 1 agent at this agency. We urge you to check our website and consider each agent's emphasis before submitting. Your query letter should be about one page long and describe your work as well as your background. You may also paste the first chapter of your work in the body of the e-mail. Do not send attachments." Accepts simultaneous submissions. Responds in 4 weeks, only if interested.

**TERMS** Agent receives 15% commission on domestic sales.

## PROSPECT AGENCY

551 Valley Rd., PMB 377, Upper Montclair NJ 07043. (718)788-3217. **Fax:** (718)360-9582. **E-mail:** https://www.prospectagency.com/submit.html. **Website:** www.prospectagency.com. Estab. 2005. Member of AAR. Signatory of WGA. Represents 130+ clients.

**MEMBER AGENTS** Emily Sylvan Kim focuses on romance, women's, commercial, young adult, new adult, nonfiction and memoir. She is currently looking for commercial and upmarket women's fiction; self-published authors looking to explore a hybrid career; established and strong debut romance writing, mainstream romance; memoir and high interest nonfiction; literary and commercial YA fiction; and select middle grade and early reader fiction with strong commercial appeal. Rachel Orr focuses on picture books, illustrators, middle grade and young adult. She is currently looking for short, punchy picture books (either in prose or rhyme) that are humorous and have a strong marketing hook; nonfiction picture books (especially biographies or stories with a historical angle); illustrators for the trade market; and literary and commercial middle-grade and YA (all time periods and genres). Ann Rose focuses on middle grade, young adult and commercial adult fiction. She is currently seeking YA of all genres; MG of all genres, especially ones that push the boundaries of middle grade; Swoony romances; Light sci-fi or fantasy; Commercial fiction; Heartwarming (or heart wrenching) contemporaries; any stories with unique voices, diverse perspectives, vivid settings; stories that explore tough topics; and dark and edgy stories with unlikeable characters. Emma Sector focuses on picture books, illustrators, middle grade and young adult. She is currently seeking quirky, character driven chapter books; literary and commercial middle-grade and YA Novels; picture book authors and illustrators; middle-grade graphic novels; and nonfiction middle-grade. Tin Shen; Charlotte Wenger. Please use the agency form to submit your query: https://www.prospectagency.com/submit.html.

**REPRESENTS** Nonfiction, fiction, novels, novellas, juvenile books, scholarly books, textbooks. **Considers these nonfiction areas:** biography, cooking, creative nonfiction, cultural interests, gardening, gay/lesbian, government, health, history, horticulture, inspirational, memoirs, parenting, popular culture, psychology, women's issues. **Considers these fiction areas:** commercial, contemporary issues, crime, ethnic, family saga, fantasy, feminist, gay, hi-lo, historical, horror, humor, juvenile, lesbian, literary, mainstream, middle grade, multicultural, mystery, new adult, picture books, romance, science fiction, suspense, thriller, urban fantasy, women's, young adult.

> ☞ "We're looking for strong, unique voices and unforgettable stories and characters."

**HOW TO CONTACT** All submissions are electronic and must be submitted through the portal at prospectagency.com/submit.html. Query letter, 3 chapters (or first 30 pages), and a brief synopsis. We do not accept any submissions through snail mail. Accepts simultaneous submissions. Obtains new clients through conferences, recommendations, queries, and some scouting.

**TERMS** Agent receives 15% on domestic sales, 20% on foreign sales sold directly and 25% on sales using a subagent. Offers written contract.

## ⟳ P.S. LITERARY AGENCY

2010 Winston Park Dr., 2nd Floor, Oakville ON L6H 5R7 Canada. **E-mail:** info@psliterary.com; query@psliterary.com. **Website:** www.psliterary.com. **Contact:** Curtis Russell, principal agent; Carly Watters, senior agent; Maria Vicente, senior agent; Eric Smith, literary agent; Claire Harris, literary agent; Stephanie Winter, associate agent; Cecilia Lyra, associate agent. Estab. 2005.

**MEMBER AGENTS** Curtis Russell (literary/commercial fiction, mystery, thriller, suspense, romance, young adult, middle grade, picture books, business, history, politics, current affairs, memoirs, health/wellness, sports, humor, pop culture, pop science, pop psychology); Carly Watters (upmarket/commercial fiction, women's fiction, book club fiction, domestic suspense, literary mystery/thrillers, historical fiction, contemporary romance, cookbooks, lifestyle, memoirs, business, pop science, psychology); Maria Vicente (young adult, middle grade, chapter books, illustrated picture books, graphic novels, pop culture, science, lifestyle, design, gift books); Eric Smith (young adult, middle grade, literary/commercial fiction, cookbooks, pop culture, humor, essay collections); Claire Harris (commercial psychological thrillers, mystery/suspense, contemporary fiction, adult rom-coms, lifestyle, pop culture, pop psychology, humor, true crime, illustrated books for adults); Stephanie Winter (adult, young adult, middle grade, graphic novels, adult rom-coms, thrillers, illustrated nonfiction); Cecilia Lyra (literary/commercial fiction, psychology, pop culture, science, business, lifestyles).

**REPRESENTS** Nonfiction, fiction, novels, juvenile books. **Considers these nonfiction areas:** animals, art, autobiography, biography, business, child guidance, computers, cooking, crafts, creative nonfiction, cultural interests, current affairs, dance, decorating, diet/nutrition, design, economics, education, environment, ethnic, film, foods, gardening, gay/lesbian, government, health, history, hobbies, how-to, humor, inspirational, interior design, investigative, juvenile nonfiction, literature, medicine, memoirs, military, money, multicultural, music, New Age, parenting, philosophy, photography, popular culture, politics, psychology, recreation, satire, science, self-help, sex, sociology, spirituality, sports, technology, travel, true crime, war, women's issues, women's studies, young adult. **Considers these fiction areas:** action, adventure, comic books, commercial, crime, detective, erotica, ethnic, experimental, family saga, fantasy, feminist, gay, historical, horror, humor, inspirational, juvenile, lesbian, literary, mainstream, middle grade, multicultural, mystery, new adult, New Age, paranormal, picture books, police, romance, satire, science fiction, sports, supernatural, suspense, thriller, urban fantasy, women's, young adult.

- Actively seeking both fiction and nonfiction. Seeking both new and established writers. Does not want to receive poetry or screenplays.

**HOW TO CONTACT** Query letters should be directed to query@psliterary.com. PSLA does not accept or respond to phone, paper, or social media queries. Responds in 4-6 weeks to queries/proposals. Obtains most new clients through solicitations.

**TERMS** Agent receives 15% commission on domestic sales; 25% commission on foreign sales. "We offer a written contract, with 30-days notice to terminate."

**TIPS** "Please review our website for the most up-to-date submission guidelines. We do not charge reading fees. We do not offer a critique service."

## PUBLICATION RIOT GROUP

**E-mail:** db@priotgroup.com. **Website:** www.priotgroup.com. **Contact:** Donna Bagdasarian. Member of AAR. Signatory of WGA.

- Prior to being an agent, Ms. Bagdasarian worked as an acquisitions editor. Previously, she worked for the William Morris and Maria Carvainis agencies.

**REPRESENTS** Nonfiction, novels. **Considers these nonfiction areas:** memoirs, popular culture, politics, science, sociology. **Considers these fiction areas:** ethnic, historical, literary, mainstream, thriller, women's.

- "The company is a literary management company, representing their authors in all processes of the entertainment trajectory: from book development, to book sales, to subsidiary sales in the foreign market, television and film." Does not want science fiction and fantasy.

**HOW TO CONTACT** Currently closed to all submissions. Accepts simultaneous submissions.

**RECENT SALES** List of sales on agency website.

## JOANNA PULCINI LITERARY MANAGEMENT

**E-mail:** info@jplm.com. **Website:** www.jplm.com. **Contact:** Joanna Pulcini.

**HOW TO CONTACT** Do not query this agency until they open their client list. Accepts simultaneous submissions.

## THE PURCELL AGENCY

**E-mail:** tpaqueries@gmail.com. **Website:** www.thepurcellagency.com. **Contact:** Tina P. Schwartz. Estab. 2012. SCBWI. Represents 50 clients.

**MEMBER AGENTS** Tina P. Schwartz, Catherine Hedrick, Bonnie Swanson.

**REPRESENTS** Nonfiction, fiction, novels, juvenile books. **Considers these nonfiction areas:** biography, child guidance, creative nonfiction, gay/lesbian, juvenile nonfiction, multicultural, parenting, young adult. **Considers these fiction areas:** juvenile, middle grade, women's, young adult.

- This agency also takes juvenile nonfiction for MG and YA markets. At this point, the agency is not considering fantasy, science fiction or picture book submissions.

**HOW TO CONTACT** Check the website to see if agency is open to submissions and for submission guidelines. Accepts simultaneous submissions.

**RECENT SALES** *Man Up*, by Kim Oclon, *Between Safe & Real*, by Dannie Olguin, *Cody Matthis & Me*, by Sarah Kaminski, *Duke & The Lonely Boy*, by Lynn Langan, *Seven Suspects*, by Renee James; *A Kind of Justice*, by Renee James; *Adventures at Hound Hotel*, by Shelley Swanson Sateren; *Adventures at Tabby Towers*, by Shelley Swanson Sateren; *Keys to Freedom*, by Karen Meade.

## SUSAN RABINER LITERARY AGENCY, INC.

**Website:** www.rabinerlit.com. **Contact:** Susan Rabiner.

- Prior to becoming an agent, Ms. Rabiner was editorial director of Basic Books. She is also the co-author of *Thinking Like Your Editor: How to Write Great Serious Nonfiction and Get it Published* (W. W. Norton).

**MEMBER AGENTS** Susan Rabiner, susan@rabiner.net (well-researched, topical books written by fully credentialed academics, journalists, and recognized public intellectuals with the power to stimulate public debate on a broad range of issues including the state of our economy, political discourse, history, science, and the arts); Sydelle Kramer, sydellek@rabiner.net, (represents a diverse group of academics, journalists, sportswriters, and memoirists); Holly Bemiss, hollyb@rabiner.net (clients include graphic novelists, journalists, memoirists, comedians, crafters, and entertainment writers).

☞ "Representing narrative nonfiction and big-idea books by scholars, public intellectuals, and established journalists—work that illuminates the past and the present in current affairs, history, the sciences, and the arts."

**HOW TO CONTACT** Please send all queries by e-mail. Note: "Because of the number of queries we receive, we cannot respond to every one. If your project fits the profile of the agency, we will be in touch within two weeks." Accepts simultaneous submissions. Obtains most new clients through recommendations from others.

**TERMS** Agent receives 15% commission on domestic sales. Agent receives 20% commission on foreign sales. Offers written contract; 1-month notice must be given to terminate contract.

## REES LITERARY AGENCY

One Westinghouse Plaza, Suite A203, Boston MA 02136. (617)227-9014. **E-mail:** lorin@reesagency.com. **Website:** reesagency.com. Estab. 1983. Member of AAR. Represents more than 100 clients.

**MEMBER AGENTS** Ann Collette, agent10702@aol.com (fiction: literary, upscale commercial women's, crime [including mystery, thriller and psychological suspense], upscale western, historical, military and war, and horror; nonfiction: narrative, military and war, books on race and class, works set in Southeast Asia, biography, pop culture, books on film and opera, humor, and memoir); Lorin Rees, lorin@reesagency.com (literary fiction, memoirs, business books, self-help, science, history, psychology, and narrative nonfiction); Rebecca Podos, rebecca@reesagency.com (young adult and middle grade fiction, particularly books about complex female relationships, beautifully written contemporary, genre novels with a strong focus on character, romance with more at stake than "will they/won't they," and LGBTQ books across all genres); Kelly Peterson; Ashley Herring Blake.

**REPRESENTS** Novels. **Considers these nonfiction areas:** biography, business, film, history, humor, memoirs, military, popular culture, psychology, science, war. **Considers these fiction areas:** commercial, crime, historical, horror, literary, middle grade, mystery, suspense, thriller, westerns, women's, young adult.

**HOW TO CONTACT** Consult website for each agent's submission guidelines and e-mail addresses, as they differ. Accepts simultaneous submissions. Obtains most new clients through recommendations from others, conferences, submissions.

**TERMS** Agent receives 15% commission on domestic sales; 20% commission on foreign sales.

## REGAL HOFFMANN & ASSOCIATES LLC

143 West 29th St., Suite 901, New York NY 10001. (212)684-7900. **E-mail:** info@rhaliterary.com. **Website:** www.rhaliterary.com. Estab. 2002. Member of AAR. Represents 70 clients.

**MEMBER AGENTS** Claire Anderson-Wheeler (nonfiction: memoirs and biographies, narrative histories, popular science, popular psychology; adult fiction: primarily character-driven literary fiction, but open to genre fiction, high-concept fiction; all genres of young adult/middle grade fiction); Markus Hoffmann (international and literary fiction, crime, [pop] cultural studies, current affairs, economics, history, music, popular science, and travel literature); Stephanie Steiker (serious and narrative nonfiction, literary fiction, graphic novels, history, philosophy, current affairs, cultural studies, biography, music, international writing); Elianna Kan (Spanish-language fiction and nonfiction writers, literature in translation); Joseph Regal.

**REPRESENTS** Nonfiction, fiction, novels, short story collections, juvenile books, scholarly books. **Considers these nonfiction areas:** biography, creative nonfiction, cultural interests, current affairs, economics, ethnic, gay/lesbian, history, investigative, juvenile nonfiction, literature, memoirs, music, popular culture, psychology, science, translation, travel, women's issues, women's studies, young adult. **Considers these fiction areas:** literary, mainstream, middle grade, short story collections, thriller, women's, young adult.

☞ We represent works in a wide range of categories, with an emphasis on literary fiction, outstanding thriller and crime fiction, and serious narrative nonfiction. Actively seeking literary fiction and narrative nonfiction. Does not want romance, science fiction, poetry, or screenplays.

**HOW TO CONTACT** Query with SASE or via Submittable (https://rhaliterary.submittable.com/submit). No phone calls. Submissions should consist of a 1-page query letter detailing the book in question, as well as the qualifications of the author. For fiction, submissions may also include the first 10 pages of the novel or one short story from a collection. Accepts simultaneous submissions. Responds in 4-8 weeks.

**TERMS** Agent receives 15% commission on domestic sales; 20% commission on foreign sales. We charge no reading fees.

**RECENT SALES** *Wily Snare*, by Adam Jay Epstein; *Perfectly Undone*, by Jamie Raintree; *A Sister in My House*, by Linda Olsson; *This Is How It Really Sounds*, by Stuart Archer Cohen; *Autofocus*, by Lauren Gibaldi; *We've Already Gone This Far*, by Patrick Dacey; *A Fierce and Subtle Poison*, by Samantha Mabry; *The Life of the World to Come*, by Dan Cluchey; *Willful Disregard*, by Lena Andersson; *The Sweetheart*, by Angelina Mirabella.

**TIPS** "We are deeply committed to every aspect of our clients' careers, and are engaged in everything from the editorial work of developing a great book proposal or line editing a fiction manuscript to negotiating state-of-the-art book deals and working to promote and publicize the book when it's published. We are at the forefront of the effort to increase authors' rights in publishing contracts in a rapidly changing commercial environment. We deal directly with co-agents and publishers in every foreign territory and also work directly and with co-agents for feature film and television rights, with extraordinary success in both arenas. Many of our clients' works have sold in dozens of translation markets, and a high proportion of our books have been sold in Hollywood. We have strong relationships with speaking agents, who can assist in arranging author tours and other corporate and college speaking opportunities when appropriate."

### ⊘ THE AMY RENNERT AGENCY

1550 Tiburon Blvd., #302, Tiburon CA 94920. **E-mail:** queries@amyrennert.com. **Website:** www.publishersmarketplace.com/members/amyrennert/. **Contact:** Amy Rennert.

**REPRESENTS** Nonfiction, novels. **Considers these nonfiction areas:** biography, business, creative nonfiction, health, history, memoirs, money, sports. **Considers these fiction areas:** literary, mainstream, mystery.

☛ "The Amy Rennert Agency specializes in books that matter. We provide career management for established and first-time authors, and our breadth of experience in many genres enables us to meet the needs of a diverse clientele."

**HOW TO CONTACT** Amy Rennert is not currently accepting unsolicited submissions. Accepts simultaneous submissions.

**TIPS** "Due to the high volume of submissions, it is not possible to respond to each and every one. Please understand that we are only able to respond to queries that we feel may be a good fit with our agency."

### ☝ THE LISA RICHARDS AGENCY

108 Upper Leeson St., Dublin D04 E3E7 Ireland. (03)(531)637-5000. **E-mail:** info@lisarichards.ie. **Website:** www.lisarichards.ie. Estab. 1989.

**MEMBER AGENTS** Faith O'Grady (literary).

**REPRESENTS** Nonfiction, fiction, juvenile books. **Considers these nonfiction areas:** biography, history, humor, memoirs, popular culture, self-help, sports, travel, narrative, lifestyle. **Considers these fiction areas:** commercial, literary, middle grade, young adult. **Considers these script areas:** comedy, general scripts.

☛ "For fiction, I am always looking for exciting new writing—distinctive voices, original, strong storylines, and intriguing characters." Doesn't handle horror, science fiction, screenplays, or children's picture books.

**HOW TO CONTACT** If sending fiction, please limit your submission to the first three or four chapters, and include a covering letter and an SASE if required. If sending nonfiction, please send a detailed proposal about your book, a sample chapter and a cover letter. Every effort will be made to respond to submissions within 3 months of receipt. Accepts simultaneous submissions.

**RECENT SALES** Clients include Arlene Hunt, Roisin Ingle, Declan Lynch, Kevin Rafter.

### ☼ THE RIGHTS FACTORY

P.O. Box 499, Station C, Toronto ON M6J 3P6 Canada. **Website:** www.therightsfactory.com. Estab. 2004. PACLA Represents ~150 clients.

**MEMBER AGENTS** Sam Hiyate (President: fiction, nonfiction (narrative business, wellness, lifestyle and memoir) and graphic novel); Stacey Kondla (Agent: YA and children's literature of all kinds); Natalie Kimber (Agent: literary and commercial fiction and creative nonfiction in categories such as memoir, cooking, pop-culture, spirituality, and sustainability); Haskell Nussbaum (Associate Agent: literature of all kinds);

Lindsay Leggett (Associate Agent: SFF, horror, own-voices, children's).Kathryn Willms Associate Agent (literary and commercial fiction and creative nonfiction), Karmen Wells Associate Agent, Film and TV (all genres, especially horror), Tasneem Motala Assistant Agent, (character-driven MG and YA by BIPOC authors).

**REPRESENTS** Nonfiction, fiction, novels, short story collections, novellas, juvenile books. **Considers these nonfiction areas:** biography, business, cooking, environment, foods, gardening, gay/lesbian, health, history, inspirational, juvenile nonfiction, memoirs, money, music, parenting, popular culture, politics, science, self-help, spirituality, travel, women's issues, young adult. **Considers these fiction areas:** commercial, crime, family saga, fantasy, gay, hi-lo, historical, horror, juvenile, lesbian, literary, mainstream, middle grade, multicultural, mystery, new adult, paranormal, picture books, romance, science fiction, short story collections, suspense, thriller, urban fantasy, women's, young adult.

☛ Plays, screenplays, textbooks.

**HOW TO CONTACT** There is a submission form on this agency's website. Accepts simultaneous submissions. Responds in 6-12 weeks.

## ANGELA RINALDI LITERARY AGENCY

P.O. Box 7875, Beverly Hills CA 90212-7875. (310)842-7665. **Fax:** (310)837-8143. **E-mail:** info@rinaldiliterary.com. **Website:** www.rinaldiliterary.com. **Contact:** Angela Rinaldi. Member of AAR.

◯ Prior to opening her agency, Ms. Rinaldi was an editor at NAL/Signet, Pocket Books and Bantam, and the manager of book development for the *Los Angeles Times*.

**REPRESENTS** Nonfiction, novels. TV and motion picture rights (for clients only). **Considers these nonfiction areas:** biography, business, cooking, current affairs, health, memoirs, parenting, psychology, self-help, women's issues, women's studies, narrative nonfiction, food narratives, wine, lifestyle, relationships, wellness, personal finance. **Considers these fiction areas:** commercial, historical, literary, mainstream, mystery, suspense, thriller, women's, contemporary, gothic, women's book club fiction.

☛ Actively seeking commercial and literary fiction, as well as nonfiction. For fiction, we do not want to receive humor, CIA espionage, drug thrillers, techno thrillers, category ro-

mances, science fiction, fantasy, horror/occult/paranormal, poetry, film scripts, magazine articles or religion. For nonfiction, please do not send us magazine articles, celebrity bios, or tell-alls.

**HOW TO CONTACT** E-queries only. Include the word "Query" in the subject line. For fiction, please send a brief synopsis and paste the first 10 pages into an e-mail. Nonfiction queries should include a detailed cover letter, your credentials and platform information as well as any publishing history. Tell us if you have a completed proposal. Accepts simultaneous submissions. Responds in 2-4 weeks.

**TERMS** Agent receives 15% commission on domestic sales; 25% commission on foreign sales. Offers written contract.

## ANN RITTENBERG LITERARY AGENCY, INC.

15 Maiden Lane, Suite 206, New York NY 10038. (212)684-6936. **E-mail:** info@rittlit.com. **Website:** www.rittlit.com. **Contact:** Ann Rittenberg, president. Estab. 1992. Member of AAR. Represents 30 clients.

**MEMBER AGENTS** Ann Rittenberg, Rosie Jonker.

**REPRESENTS** Nonfiction, fiction, novels, juvenile books. **Considers these nonfiction areas:** biography, history, literature, memoirs, popular culture, true crime. **Considers these fiction areas:** crime, detective, family saga, literary, mainstream, mystery, suspense, thriller, women's.

☛ "We don't represent screenplays, poetry, plays, or self-help."

**HOW TO CONTACT** Query via e-mail or postal mail (with SASE). Submit query letter with 3 sample chapters pasted into the body of the e-mail. If you query by e-mail, we will only respond if interested. If you are making a simultaneous submission, you must tell us in your query. Accepts simultaneous submissions. Responds in 6-8 weeks. However, as noted above, if you don't receive a response to an emailed query, that means it was a pass. Obtains most new clients through referrals from established writers and editors.

**TERMS** Agent receives 15% commission on domestic sales, and 20% commission on foreign and film deals. This 20% is shared with co-agents. Offers written contract. No charges except for PDFs or finished books for foreign and film submissions.

**RECENT SALES** *Since We Fell*, by Dennis Lehane; *Your First Novel—Revised and Expanded Edition*, by Ann Rittenberg and Laura Whitcomb with Camille

Goldin; *Paradise Valley*, by C.J. Box; *The Field Guide to Dumb Birds of North America*, by Matt Kracht; *Stay Hidden*, by Paul Doiron.

**TIPS** "Refrain from sending enormous bouquets of red roses. Elegant bouquets of peonies, tulips, ranunculus, calla lily, and white roses are acceptable."

## RIVERSIDE LITERARY AGENCY

41 Simon Keets Rd., Leyden MA 01337. (413)772-0067. **Fax:** (413)772-0969. **E-mail:** rivlit@sover.net. **Website:** www.riversideliteraryagency.com. **Contact:** Susan Lee Cohen. Estab. 1990.

○ Worked at Viking Penguin before becoming an agent at Richard Curtis Associates, and then Sterling Lord Literistic. Founded RLA in 1990.

**REPRESENTS** Nonfiction, fiction.

☛ This agency sells adult nonfiction and fiction, and has sold books in the categories of science, psychology, spirituality, health, memoir, pop culture, true crime, parenting, history/politics, and narrative.

**HOW TO CONTACT** E-query. Accepts simultaneous submissions. Obtains most new clients through referrals.

**TERMS** Agent receives 15% commission on domestic sales. Offers written contract. Charges clients for foreign postage, photocopying large mss, express mail deliveries, etc.

## BJ ROBBINS LITERARY AGENCY

5130 Bellaire Ave., North Hollywood CA 91607-2908. **E-mail:** robbinsliterary@gmail.com. **Website:** www.bjrobbinsliterary.com. **Contact:** (Ms.) BJ Robbins. Estab. 1992. Member of AAR.

○ Prior to becoming an agent, Robbins spent 15 years in publishing, starting in publicity at Simon & Schuster and later as Marketing Director and Senior Editor at Harcourt.

**REPRESENTS** Nonfiction, fiction, novels. **Considers these nonfiction areas:** autobiography, biography, creative nonfiction, cultural interests, current affairs, ethnic, film, health, history, investigative, medicine, memoirs, multicultural, music, popular culture, psychology, science, sociology, sports, theater, travel, true crime, women's issues, women's studies. **Considers these fiction areas:** contemporary issues, crime, detective, ethnic, historical, horror, literary, mainstream, multicultural, mystery, suspense, thriller, women's.

☛ "We do not represent screenplays, plays, poetry, science fiction, fantasy, westerns, romance, techno-thrillers, religious tracts, dating books or anything with the word 'unicorn' in the title."

**HOW TO CONTACT** E-query with no attachments. For fiction, okay to include first 10 pages in body of e-mail. Accepts simultaneous submissions. Only responds to projects if interested. Obtains most new clients through conferences, referrals.

**TERMS** Agent receives 15% commission on domestic sales; 20% commission on foreign sales. Offers written contract. No fees.

**RECENT SALES** *My Heart Is a Chainsaw* by Stephen Graham Jones (Saga Press/Gallery); *If You Lived Here You'd be Famous by Now* by Via Bleidner (Flatiron); *The Sweetest Days* by John Hough Jr (Gallery); *The Only Good Indians* by Stephen Graham Jones (Saga Press/Gallery); *The Bridge at La Fiere* by James Donovan (Dutton); *Night of the Mannequins* by Stephen Graham Jones (Tor.com); Pont Neuf by Max Byrd (Permuted Press); *Shoot for the Moon: The Perilous Voyage of Apollo 11,* by James Donovan (Little, Brown); *Mongrels*, by Stephen Graham Jones (William Morrow); *Blood Brothers: The Story of the Strange Friendship between Sitting Bull and Buffalo Bill*, by Deanne Stillman (Simon & Schuster); *Reliance, Illinois*, by Mary Volmer (Soho Press), *Mapping the Interior* by Stephen Graham Jones (Tor).

## ⊘ THE ROBBINS OFFICE, INC.

509 Madison Ave., New York NY 10022. (212)223-0720. **Fax:** (212)223-2535. **Website:** www.robbinsoffice.com. **Contact:** Kathy P. Robbins, owner.

**MEMBER AGENTS** Kathy P. Robbins; David Halpern.

**REPRESENTS** Novels.

☛ This agency specializes in selling serious nonfiction as well as commercial and literary fiction.

**HOW TO CONTACT** Accepts submissions by referral only. Do not cold query this market. Accepts simultaneous submissions.

**TERMS** Agent receives 15% commission on domestic, foreign, and film sales. Bills back specific expenses incurred in doing business for a client.

## RODEEN LITERARY MANAGEMENT

3501 N. Southport #497, Chicago IL 60657. **E-mail:** submissions@rodeenliterary.com. **Website:** www.rodeenliterary.com. **Contact:** Paul Rodeen. Estab. 2009. Member of AAR. Signatory of WGA.

○ Paul Rodeen established Rodeen Literary Management in 2009 after 7 years of experience with the literary agency Sterling Lord Literistic, Inc.

**REPRESENTS** Nonfiction, novels, juvenile books. illustrations, graphic novels. **Considers these fiction areas:** juvenile, middle grade, picture books, young adult, graphic novels, comics.

☞ Actively seeking "writers and illustrators of all genres of children's literature including picture books, early readers, middle-grade fiction and nonfiction, graphic novels and comic books, as well as young adult fiction and nonfiction." This is primarily an agency devoted to children's books.

**HOW TO CONTACT** Unsolicited submissions are accepted by e-mail only. Cover letters with synopsis and contact information should be included in the body of your e-mail. An initial submission of 50 pages from a novel or a longer work of nonfiction will suffice and should be pasted into the body of your e-mail. Accepts simultaneous submissions.

### ● ROGERS, COLERIDGE & WHITE

20 Powis Mews, London England W11 1JN United Kingdom. (44)(207)221-3717. **Fax:** (44)(207)229-9084. **E-mail:** info@rcwlitagency.com. **Website:** www.rcwlitagency.com. **Contact:** David Miller, agent. Estab. 1987.

○ Prior to opening the agency, Ms. Rogers was an agent with Peter Janson-Smith; Ms. Coleridge worked at Sidgwick & Jackson, Chatto & Windus, and Anthony Sheil Associates; Ms. White was an editor and rights director for Simon & Schuster; Mr. Straus worked at Hodder and Stoughton, Hamish Hamilton, and Macmillan; Mr. Miller worked as Ms. Rogers' assistant and was treasurer of the AAA; Ms. Waldie worked with Carole Smith.

**MEMBER AGENTS** Gill Coleridge; Georgia Garrett; Pat White (illustrated and children's books); Peter Straus; David Miller; Claire Wilson (children's and YA); Zoe Waldie (literary fiction and nonfiction); Emma Paterson; Laurence Laluyaux (foreign rights); Stephen Edwards (translation rights); Peter Robinson (fiction and nonfiction with particular interests in crime, thrillers and historical fiction, together with

history and popular science); Sam Copeland (literary and commercial fiction, all genre fiction, children's, and a smattering of nonfiction); Jenny Hewson (strong literary voices and compelling storytelling, both fiction and nonfiction); Jo Unwin (literary fiction, commercial women's fiction, Young Adult fiction and fiction for children aged 9+; comic writing; narrative nonfiction); Rebecca Jones (foreign rights); Cara Jones (fiction: particularly crime and thrillers; narrative nonfiction).

**REPRESENTS** Nonfiction, novels, juvenile books.

☞ This agency takes virtually all subjects and genres. Does not want to receive scripts for theatre, film or television.

**HOW TO CONTACT** "Submissions should include a covering letter telling us about yourself and the background of the book. In the case of fiction, they should consist of the first 3 chapters or approximately the first 50 pages of the work to a natural break, and a brief synopsis. Nonfiction submissions should take the form of a proposal up to 20 pages in length explaining what the work is about and why you are best placed to write it. Material should be printed out in 12-point font, in double-spacing and on one side only of A4 paper. YA and children's fiction should be submitted via email to clairewilson@rcwlitagency.com. We regret that this department cannot undertake to read submissions from the US due to the large volume received." Agents who are open to general e-mail submissions indicate so on their individual agent page on the website. Accepts simultaneous submissions. Tries to respond in 6-8 weeks to queries. Obtains most new clients through recommendations from others, solicitations, conferences.

**TERMS** Agent receives 15% commission on domestic sales. Agent receives 20% commission on foreign sales. Offers written contract.

### LINDA ROGHAAR LITERARY AGENCY, LLC

P.O. Box 3561, Amherst MA 01004. **E-mail:** contact@lindaroghaar.com. **Website:** www.lindaroghaar.com. **Contact:** Linda L. Roghaar. Estab. 1996. Member of AAR.

○ Prior to opening her agency, Ms. Roghaar worked in retail bookselling for 5 years and as a publishers' sales rep for 15 years.

**REPRESENTS** Nonfiction.

☞ The Linda Roghaar Literary Agency represents authors with substantial messages and specializes in nonfiction. We sell to major, independent, and university presses. Does not want fiction.

**HOW TO CONTACT** We prefer e-queries. Please mention "query" in the subject line, and do not include attachments. For queries by mail, please include an SASE. Accepts simultaneous submissions. Responds within 12 weeks if interested.

**TERMS** Agent receives 15% commission on domestic sales. Agent receives negotiable commission on foreign sales. Offers written contract.

## THE ROSENBERG GROUP

23 Lincoln Ave., Marblehead MA 01945. (781)990-1341. **Fax:** (781)990-1344. **Website:** www.rosenberg-group.com. **Contact:** Barbara Collins Rosenberg. Estab. 1998. Member of AAR. Recognized agent of the RWA. Represents 25 clients.

○ Prior to becoming an agent, Ms. Rosenberg was a senior editor for Harcourt.

**REPRESENTS** Nonfiction, novels, textbooks—college textbooks only. **Considers these nonfiction areas:** biography, current affairs, foods, music, popular culture, psychology, science, self-help, sports, women's issues, women's studies, women's health, wine/beverages. **Considers these fiction areas:** romance, women's, chick lit.

☛ Ms. Rosenberg is well-versed in the romance market (both category and single title). She is a frequent speaker at romance conferences. The Rosenberg Group is accepting new clients working in romance fiction (please see my Areas of Interest for specific romance subgenres); women's fiction and chick lit. Does not want to receive inspirational, time travel, futuristic or paranormal.

**HOW TO CONTACT** Query via QueryManager. Your query letter should not exceed one page in length. It should include the title of your work, the genre and/or subgenre; the manuscript's word count; and a brief description of the work. If you are writing category romance, please be certain to let her know the line for which your work is intended. Accepts simultaneous submissions. Obtains most new clients through recommendations from others, solicitations, conferences.

**TERMS** Agent receives 15% commission on domestic and foreign sales. Offers written contract; 1-month notice must be given to terminate contract. Charges maximum of $350/year for postage and photocopying.

**RECENT SALES** Sold 27 titles in the last year.

**WRITERS CONFERENCES** RWA National Conference; BookExpo America.

## RITA ROSENKRANZ LITERARY AGENCY

440 West End Ave., #15D, New York NY 10024. (212) 873-6333. **E-mail:** rrosenkranz@mindspring.com. **Website:** www.ritarosenkranzliteraryagency.com. **Contact:** Rita Rosenkranz. Member of AAR, Women's Media Group, Authors Guild. Represents 40 clients.

○ Prior to opening her agency, Ms. Rosenkranz worked as an editor at major New York publishing houses.

**REPRESENTS** Nonfiction. **Considers these nonfiction areas:** agriculture, Americana, animals, anthropology, archeology, architecture, art, autobiography, biography, business, child guidance, computers, cooking, crafts, creative nonfiction, cultural interests, current affairs, dance, decorating, diet/nutrition, design, economics, education, environment, ethnic, film, foods, gardening, gay/lesbian, government, health, history, hobbies, horticulture, how-to, humor, inspirational, interior design, investigative, language, law, literature, medicine, memoirs, military, money, multicultural, music, New Age, parenting, philosophy, photography, popular culture, politics, psychology, regional, religious, satire, science, self-help, sex, software, spirituality, sports, technology, theater, true crime, war, women's issues, women's studies.

☛ "This agency focuses on adult nonfiction, stresses strong editorial development and refinement before submitting to publishers, and brainstorms ideas with authors." Actively seeks authors who are well paired with their subject, either for professional or personal reasons.

**HOW TO CONTACT** Send query letter only (no proposal) via regular mail or e-mail. Submit proposal package with SASE only on request. No fax queries. Accepts simultaneous submissions. Responds in 2 weeks to queries. Obtains most new clients through directory listings, solicitations, conferences, word of mouth.

**TERMS** Agent receives 15% commission on domestic sales; 20% commission on foreign sales. Offers written contract, binding for 3 years; 3-month written notice must be given to terminate contract. Charges clients for photocopying. Makes referrals to editing services.

**RECENT SALES** *Pause. Breathe. Choose.: Become the CEO of Your Well-Being* by Naz Beheshti; *How to Communicate With Anyone, Anywhere: Your Passport to Connecting Globally* by Raul Sanchez and Dan Bullock; *Uncommon Sense Teaching* by Barbara Oakley, Beth Rogowsky, and Terrence Sejnowki; *Raising Critical Thinkers* by Julie Bogart.

**TIPS** "Identify the current competition for your project to make sure the project is valid. A strong cover letter is very important to help get to the next step."

## ANDY ROSS LITERARY AGENCY

767 Santa Ray Ave., Oakland CA 94610. (510)238-8965. **E-mail:** andyrossagency@hotmail.com. **Website:** www.andyrossagency.com. **Contact:** Andy Ross. Estab. 2008. Member of AAR. See website for client list.

○   I was the owner of Cody's Books in Berkeley, California for 30 years.

**REPRESENTS** Nonfiction, fiction, novels, juvenile books, scholarly books. **Considers these nonfiction areas:** anthropology, autobiography, biography, creative nonfiction, cultural interests, current affairs, economics, education, environment, ethnic, gay/lesbian, government, history, investigative, juvenile nonfiction, language, law, literature, memoirs, military, philosophy, popular culture, politics, psychology, science, sociology, technology, war, women's issues, women's studies, young adult. **Considers these fiction areas:** commercial, contemporary issues, historical, literary, middle grade, young adult.

☞   "This agency specializes in general nonfiction, politics and current events, history, biography, journalism and contemporary culture as well as literary, commercial, and YA fiction." Does not want to receive poetry.

**HOW TO CONTACT** Queries should be less than half page. Please put the word "query" in the title header of the e-mail. In the first sentence, state the category of the project. Give a short description of the book and your qualifications for writing. Accepts simultaneous submissions. Responds in 1 week to queries.

**TERMS** Agent receives 15% commission on domestic sales; 20% commission on foreign sales or other deals made through a subagent. Offers written contract.

**RECENT SALES** See my website.

## ROSS YOON AGENCY

1666 Connecticut Ave. NW, Suite 500, Washington, DC 20009. (202)328-3282. **E-mail:** submissions@rossyoon.com. **Website:** http://rossyoon.com. **Contact:** Jennifer Manguera. Member of AAR.

**MEMBER AGENTS** Gail Ross gail@rossyoon.com (represents important commercial nonfiction in a variety of areas; new projects must meet two criteria: it must make her daughters proud and offset their college educations); Howard Yoon howard@rossyoon.com (specializes in narrative nonfiction, memoir, current events, history, science, cookbooks, and popular culture ); Anna Sproul-Latimer anna@rossyoon.com (nonfiction of all kinds, particularly working with clients who are driven by curiosity: exploring new worlds, uncovering hidden communities, and creating new connections with enthusiasm so infectious that national audiences have already begun to pay attention).

**REPRESENTS** Nonfiction.

☞   "We are a Washington, D.C.-based literary agency specializing in serious nonfiction on a variety of topics: everything from memoir and history and biography to popular science, business, and psychology. Our clients include CEOs, Pulitzer Prize–winning journalists, academics, politicos, and radio and television personalities. We do not represent fiction, screenplays, poetry, YA, or children's titles."

**HOW TO CONTACT** E-query submissions@rossyoon.com with a query letter briefly explaining your idea, media platform, and qualifications for writing on this topic; or send a complete book proposal featuring an overview of your idea, author bio, media and marketing strategy, chapter outline, and 1-3 sample chapters. Please send these as attachments in .doc or .docx format. Accepts simultaneous submissions. Attempts to respond in 4-6 weeks to queries, but we cannot guarantee a reply. Obtains most new clients through referrals from current clients.

**TERMS** Agent receives 15% commission on domestic sales; 20% commission on foreign sales. Reserves the right to bill clients for office expenses.

## JANE ROTROSEN AGENCY LLC

318 E. 51st St., New York NY 10022. (212)593-4330. **Fax:** (212)935-6985. **E-mail:** info@janerotrosen.com. **Website:** www.janerotrosen.com. Estab. 1974. Mem-

ber of AAR, Authors Guild. Represents more than 100 clients.

**MEMBER AGENTS** Jane Rotrosen Berkey (not taking on clients); Andrea Cirillo, acirillo@janerotrosen.com (general fiction, suspense, and women's fiction); Annelise Robey, arobey@janerotrosen.com (women's fiction, suspense, mystery, literary fiction, and select nonfiction); Meg Ruley, mruley@janerotrosen.com (commercial fiction, including suspense, mysteries, romance, and general fiction); Christina Hogrebe, chogrebe@janerotrosen.com (young adult, new adult, book club fiction, romantic comedies, mystery, and suspense); Amy Tannenbaum, atannenbaum@janerotrosen.com (contemporary romance, psychological suspense, thrillers, and new adult, as well as women's fiction that falls into that sweet spot between literary and commercial, memoir, narrative and prescriptive nonfiction in the areas of health, business, pop culture, humor, and popular psychology); Rebecca Scherer, rscherer@janerotrosen.com (women's fiction, mystery, suspense, thriller, romance, upmarket/literary-leaning fiction); Jessica Errera (assistant to Christina and Rebecca); Kathy Scheider; Hannah Strouth; Logan Harper.

**REPRESENTS** Nonfiction, novels. **Considers these nonfiction areas:** business, health, humor, memoirs, popular culture, psychology, narrative nonfiction. **Considers these fiction areas:** commercial, literary, mainstream, mystery, new adult, romance, suspense, thriller, women's, young adult.

☛ Jane Rotrosen Agency is best known for representing writers of commercial fiction: thrillers, mystery, suspense, women's fiction, romance, historical novels, mainstream fiction, young adult, etc. We also work with authors of memoirs, narrative and prescriptive nonfiction.

**HOW TO CONTACT** Check website for guidelines. Accepts simultaneous submissions. Obtains most new clients through recommendations from others.

**TERMS** Agent receives 15% commission on domestic sales; 20% commission on foreign sales. Offers written contract, binding for 3 years; 2-month notice must be given to terminate contract. Charges clients for photocopying, express mail, overseas postage, book purchase.

## THE RUDY AGENCY

825 Wildlife Ln., Estes Park CO 80517. (970)577-8500. **E-mail:** mak@rudyagency.com. **Website:** www.rudy-agency.com. **Contact:** Maryann Karinch. Estab. 2004. Adheres to AAR canon of ethics; founder is a member of The Authors Guild. Represents 30 clients.

○ Prior to becoming an agent, Ms. Karinch was, and continues to be, an author of nonfiction books—primarily covering the subjects of health/medicine and human behavior. Prior to that, she was in public relations and marketing: areas of expertise she also applies in her practice as an agent.

**MEMBER AGENTS** Maryann Karinch.

**REPRESENTS** Nonfiction, fiction, novels, scholarly books. **Considers these nonfiction areas:** Americana, anthropology, archeology, architecture, autobiography, biography, business, computers, cooking, creative nonfiction, cultural interests, current affairs, diet/nutrition, economics, education, environment, gay/lesbian, government, health, history, how-to, investigative, law, literature, medicine, memoirs, military, money, multicultural, popular culture, politics, psychology, science, self-help, sex, sociology, sports, technology, theater, true crime, war, women's issues, women's studies. **Considers these fiction areas:** action, adventure, commercial, crime, erotica, historical, military, mystery, thriller.

☛ "We support authors from the proposal stage through promotion of the published work. We work in partnership with publishers to promote the published work and coach authors in their role in the marketing and public relations campaigns for the book." Actively seeking projects with social value, projects that open minds to new ideas and interesting lives, and projects that entertain through good storytelling. Does not want to receive poetry, screenplays, novellas, religion books, children's lit, and joke books.

**HOW TO CONTACT** "Query us via e-mail. If we like the query, we will invite a complete proposal (or complete ms if writing fiction). No phone queries, please. We won't hang up on you, but it makes it easier if you send us a note first." Accepts simultaneous submissions. Responds in under 3 weeks to nonfiction proposals and 12 weeks to invited manuscripts. Obtains most new clients through recommendations from others, solicitations.

**TERMS** Agent receives 15% commission on domestic sales. Offers written contract, binding for 1 year.

**RECENT SALES** *Cosmic Careers*, by Alastair Browne (HarperCollins Leadership); *Hospital Survival Guide*, by Dr. David Sherer (Humanix); *Operation Tidal Wave*, by Vincent dePaul Lupiano (Globe Pequot).

**TIPS** "Present yourself professionally. Know what we need to see in a query and what a proposal for a work of nonfiction must contain before you contact us."

## REGINA RYAN BOOKS

251 Central Park W., 7D, New York NY 10024. E-mail: queries@reginaryanbooks.com. **Website:** www.reginaryanbooks.com. **Contact:** Regina Ryan. Estab. 1976. Member of AAR.

○ Prior to becoming an agent, Ms. Ryan was an editor at Alfred A. Knopf, editor-in-chief of Macmillan Adult Trade, and a book producer.

**REPRESENTS** Nonfiction. **Considers these nonfiction areas:** Americana, animals, anthropology, archeology, architecture, autobiography, biography, business, child guidance, cooking, cultural interests, diet/nutrition, environment, foods, gardening, health, history, horticulture, medicine, parenting, popular culture, politics, psychology, recreation, science, self-help, sex, sports, travel, true crime, women's issues, women's studies, adult and juvenile nonfiction: narrative nonfiction; natural history (especially birds and birding); popular science, lifestyle, sustainability, mind-body-spirit.

☛ "We are always looking for new and exciting books in our areas of interest, including well-written narrative nonfiction, architecture, history, politics, natural history (especially birds), science (especially the brain), the environment, women's issues, parenting, cooking, psychology, health, wellness, diet, lifestyle, sustainability, popular reference, and leisure activities including sports, narrative travel, and gardening. We represent books that have something new and fresh to say, are well-written and that will, if possible, make the world a better place." Actively seeking narrative nonfiction, food related travel projects, brain science.

**HOW TO CONTACT** All queries must come through the following site https://app.authors.me/submit/regina-ryan-books. Accepts simultaneous submissions. "We try to respond in 4-6 weeks but only if we are interested in pursuing the project. If you don't hear from us in that time frame, it means that we are not interested." Obtains most new clients through internet submissions.

**TERMS** Agent receives 15% commission on domestic and foreign sales. Offers written contract. Charges clients for all out-of-pocket expenses (e.g., long-distance calls, messengers, freight, copying) if it's more than just a nominal amount.

**RECENT SALES** *The Friendly Orange Glow: The Untold Story of the PLATO Learning System and the Dawn of Cyberculture*, by Brian Dear; *What's Wrong With My Weed?*, by David Deardorff and Kathryn Wadsworth; *Itch! Everything You Didn't Want to Know about What Makes You Scratch*, by Anita Sanchez; *Craft Wines*, by Richard Bender; *Hair: A Human History*, by Kurt Stenn; *Wildlife Spectacles: Mass Migrations, Mating Rituals, and Other Fascinating Animal Behaviors*, by Vladimir Dinets; *Connecting in the Land of Dementia*, by Deborah Shouse; *The Backyard Birdsong Guide*, by Donald Kroodsma.

**TIPS** "It's important to include an analysis of comparable books that have had good sales, as well as an analysis of competitive books, that explains why your proposed book is different. Both are essential."

## THE SAGALYN AGENCY / ICM PARTNERS

Chevy Chase MD **E-mail:** info@sagalyn.com. **E-mail:** query@sagalyn.com. **Website:** www.sagalyn.com. Estab. 1980. Member of AAR.

**MEMBER AGENTS** Raphael Sagalyn.

**REPRESENTS** Nonfiction. **Considers these nonfiction areas:** biography, business, creative nonfiction, economics, popular culture, science, technology.

☛ "Our list includes upmarket nonfiction books in these areas: narrative history, biography, business, economics, popular culture, science, technology."

**HOW TO CONTACT** Please send e-mail queries only. Accepts simultaneous submissions.

**TIPS** "We receive 1,000-1,200 queries a year, which in turn lead to 2 or 3 new clients. See our website for sales information and recent projects."

## VICTORIA SANDERS & ASSOCIATES

440 Buck Rd., Stone Ridge NY 12484. (212)633-8811. **E-mail:** queriesvsa@gmail.com. **Website:** www.victoriasanders.com. **Contact:** Victoria Sanders. Estab. 1992. Member of AAR. Signatory of WGA. Represents 135 clients.

**MEMBER AGENTS** Victoria Sanders; Bernadette Baker-Baughman.

**REPRESENTS** Nonfiction, fiction, novels, short story collections, juvenile books. **Considers these nonfiction areas:** autobiography, biography, cooking, cultural interests, current affairs, ethnic, film, foods, gay/lesbian, government, history, humor, law, literature, memoirs, music, parenting, popular culture, politics, psychology, satire, theater, translation, women's issues, women's studies. **Considers these fiction areas:** action, adventure, cartoon, comic books, contemporary issues, crime, detective, ethnic, family saga, feminist, gay, historical, humor, inspirational, juvenile, lesbian, literary, mainstream, middle grade, multicultural, multimedia, mystery, new adult, picture books, suspense, thriller, women's, young adult.

**HOW TO CONTACT** Authors who wish to contact us regarding potential representation should send a query letter with the first 3 chapters (or about 25 pages) pasted into the body of the message to queriesvsa@gmail.com. We will only accept queries via e-mail. Query letters should describe the project and the author in the body of a single, 1-page e-mail that does not contain any attached files. Important note: Please paste the first 3 chapters of your manuscript (or about 25 pages, and feel free to round up to a chapter break) into the body of your e-mail. Accepts simultaneous submissions. Responds in 1-4 weeks, although occasionally it will take longer. "We will not respond to e-mails with attachments or attached files."

**TERMS** Agent receives 15% commission on domestic sales; 20% commission on foreign/film sales. Offers written contract.

**TIPS** "Limit query to letter (no calls) and give it your best shot. A good query is going to get a good response."

## WENDY SCHMALZ AGENCY

402 Union St., #831, Hudson NY 12534. (518)672-7697. **E-mail:** wendy@schmalzagency.com. **Website:** www.schmalzagency.com. **Contact:** Wendy Schmalz. Estab. 2002. Member of AAR.

**REPRESENTS** Juvenile books. **Considers these nonfiction areas:** young adult, many nonfiction subjects are of interest to this agency. **Considers these fiction areas:** middle grade, young adult.

☛    Not looking for picture books, science fiction or fantasy.

**HOW TO CONTACT** Accepts only e-mail queries. Paste synopsis into the e-mail. Do not attach the ms or sample chapters or synopsis. Replies to queries only if they want to read the ms. If you do not hear from this agency within 2 weeks, consider that a no. Accepts simultaneous submissions. Obtains clients through recommendations from others.

**TERMS** Agent receives 15% commission on domestic sales; 20% on foreign sales; 25% for Asia.

## SUSAN SCHULMAN LITERARY AGENCY LLC

454 W. 44th St., New York NY 10036. (212)713-1633. **E-mail:** susan@schulmanagency.com. **Website:** www.publishersmarketplace.com/members/Schulman/. **Contact:** Susan Schulman. Estab. 1980. Member of AAR. Signatory of WGA. Other memberships include Dramatists Guild, Writers Guild of America, East, New York Women in Film, Women's Media Group, Agents' Roundtable, League of New York Theater Women.

**REPRESENTS** Nonfiction, fiction, novels, juvenile books, feature film, TV scripts, theatrical stage play. **Considers these nonfiction areas:** anthropology, archeology, architecture, art, biography, business, child guidance, cooking, creative nonfiction, current affairs, economics, ethnic, government, health, history, juvenile nonfiction, law, money, popular culture, politics, psychology, religious, science, spirituality, women's issues, women's studies, young adult. **Considers these fiction areas:** commercial, contemporary issues, juvenile, literary, mainstream, new adult, religious, women's, young adult. **Considers these script areas:** theatrical stage play.

☛    "We specialize in books for, by and about women and women's issues including nonfiction self-help books, fiction, and theater projects. We also handle the film, television, and allied rights for several agencies as well as foreign rights for several publishing houses." Actively seeking new nonfiction. Considers plays. Does not want to receive poetry, television scripts or concepts for television.

**HOW TO CONTACT** "For fiction: query letter with outline and three sample chapters, résumé, and SASE. For nonfiction: query letter with complete description of subject, at least one chapter, résumé, and SASE. Queries may be sent via regular mail or e-mail. Please do not submit queries via UPS or Federal Express.

Please do not send attachments with e-mail queries Please incorporate the chapters into the body of the e-mail." Accepts simultaneous submissions. Responds in less than 1 week generally to a full query and 6 weeks to a full ms. Obtains most new clients through recommendations from others, solicitations, conferences.

**TERMS** Agent receives 15% commission on domestic sales; 20% commission on foreign sales. Offers written contract; 30-day notice must be given to terminate contract.

**RECENT SALES** Sold 70 titles in the last year; hundreds of subsidiary rights deals.

**WRITERS CONFERENCES** Geneva Writers' Conference (Switzerland); Columbus Writers' Conference; Skidmore Conference of the Independent Women's Writers Group. Attends Frankfurt Book Fair, London Book Fair, and BEA annually.

**TIPS** "Keep writing!" Schulman describes her agency as "professional boutique, long-standing, eclectic."

## THE SCIENCE FACTORY

Scheideweg 34C, 20253 Hamburg, Germany. **E-mail:** info@sciencefactory.co.uk. **Website:** www.sciencefactory.co.uk. **Contact:** Peter Tallack. Estab. 2008.

Prior to his current position, Mr. Tallack was a director of the UK agency Conville & Walsh, publishing director at Weidenfeld & Nicolson, and on the editorial staff of the science journal *Nature*. Ms. Takagi was an editor at Basic Books and Oxford University Press. Mr. Shreve worked as an editor at W. W. Norton.

**MEMBER AGENTS** Peter Tallack (mainly interested in popular science); Tisse Takagi (interested in a wide range of explanatory and narrative nonfiction, particularly science, biography, music, dance, food, and history); Jeff Shreve (drawn to astronomy, physics, genetics, neuroscience and biology and is also interested in business, technology, health and self-improvement; in short books that help readers grow, by giving them new knowledge, new perspectives and new tools to change their lives).

**REPRESENTS** Nonfiction.

"The Science Factory is a leading international literary agency specializing in stimulating nonfiction written by public intellectuals, academics and journalists. Experience of dealing directly in all markets, media and languages across the world." Represents "a diverse range of authors covering all areas of nonfiction." Founded in the UK and now headquartered in Germany, it currently has a particularly strong operation also in New York. Actively seeking serious popular upmarket nonfiction, including history, biography, memoir, politics, business, psychology, current affairs and travel as well as science, and particularly from public intellectuals, academics and journalists. Does not want poetry.

**HOW TO CONTACT** E-query to info@sciencefactory.co.uk. "In the subject line please include the word 'query' and the name of your project or your name. If you are attaching a file (sample chapter for fiction, or proposal for nonfiction), please name the file with your name (not ours). If we're interested, we often respond by email or by phone to let you know. We may then offer to represent you, or we may ask for additional information about you or your project. In any case, if you haven't had a 'no' within a few weeks, you can assume we're not interested." Accepts simultaneous submissions.

## SCOTT MEREDITH LITERARY AGENCY

1035 Park Avenue, 3A, New York NY 10028. (646)274-1970. **E-mail:** info@scottmeredith.com. **Website:** www.scottmeredith.com. **Contact:** Arthur Klebanoff, CEO. Adheres to the AAR canon of ethics. Represents 20 clients.

Prior to becoming an agent, Mr. Klebanoff was a lawyer.

**REPRESENTS** Nonfiction.

This agency's specialty lies in category nonfiction publishing programs. Actively seeking category leading nonfiction. Does not want to receive first fiction projects.

**HOW TO CONTACT** Query with SASE. Submit proposal package, author bio. Accepts simultaneous submissions. Responds in 2 weeks to queries; 4 weeks to mss. Obtains most new clients through recommendations from others.

**TERMS** Agent receives 15% commission on domestic sales. Offers written contract.

## SCRIBE AGENCY, LLC

5508 Joylynne Dr., Madison WI 53716. **E-mail:** whattheshizzle@scribeagency.com. **E-mail:** submissions@scribeagency.com. **Website:** www.scribeagency.com. **Contact:** Kristopher O'Higgins. Estab. 2004. Represents 8 clients.

"With more than 20 years experience in publishing, with time spent on both the agency and editorial sides, with marketing experience to boot, Scribe Agency is a full-service literary agency, working hands-on with its authors on their projects. Check the website (scribeagency.com) to make sure your work matches the Scribe aesthetic."

**MEMBER AGENTS** Kristopher O'Higgins.

**REPRESENTS** Fiction, novels, anthologies. **Considers these fiction areas:** fantasy, literary, paranormal, science fiction, urban fantasy.

"Scribe is currently closed to nonfiction and short fiction collections, and does not represent humor, cozy mysteries, faith-based fiction, screenplays, poetry, or works based on another's ideas."

**HOW TO CONTACT** E-queries only: submissions@scribeagency.com. See the website for submission info, as it may change. Accepts simultaneous submissions. Responds approximately 6 weeks to queries.

**TERMS** Agent receives 15% commission on domestic sales; 20% commission on foreign sales. Offers written contract.

**RECENT SALES** Juliette Wade's debut novel, and a sequel, sold to Sheila Gilbert at DAW Books.

**WRITERS CONFERENCES** BookExpo America; WisCon; Wisconsin Book Festival; World Fantasy Convention; WorldCon.

## ⊘ SELECTRIC ARTISTS

9 Union Square, #123, Southbury CT 06488. **E-mail:** christopher@selectricartists.com; query@selectricartists.com. **Website:** www.selectricartists.com. **Contact:** Christopher Schelling. Estab. 2011.

**REPRESENTS** Nonfiction, fiction, novels, short story collections, juvenile books. **Considers these nonfiction areas:** autobiography, biography, creative nonfiction, cultural interests, gay/lesbian, humor, juvenile nonfiction, literature, memoirs, multicultural, music, popular culture, young adult. **Considers these fiction areas:** commercial, fantasy, feminist, gay, historical, horror, humor, juvenile, lesbian, literary, mainstream, multicultural, science fiction, short story collections, suspense, thriller, young adult.

**HOW TO CONTACT** E-mail only. Consult agency website for status on open submissions. Accepts simultaneous submissions. Responds in 4-6 weeks.

## LYNN SELIGMAN, LITERARY AGENT

400 Highland Ave., Upper Montclair NJ 07043. (973)783-3631. **E-mail:** seliglit@aol.com. **Contact:** Lynn Seligman. Estab. 1986. Represents 35 clients.

Prior to opening her agency, Ms. Seligman worked in the subsidiary rights department of Doubleday and Simon & Schuster, and served as an agent with Julian Bach Literary Agency (which became IMG Literary Agency). Foreign rights are represented by Books Crossing Borders, Inc.

**REPRESENTS** Nonfiction, fiction, novels. **Considers these nonfiction areas:** animals, anthropology, art, biography, business, child guidance, cooking, creative nonfiction, cultural interests, current affairs, diet/nutrition, education, ethnic, film, foods, government, health, history, how-to, humor, language, medicine, memoirs, money, music, parenting, photography, popular culture, psychology, science, self-help, sociology, true crime, women's issues, young adult. **Considers these fiction areas:** commercial, ethnic, fantasy, feminist, historical, horror, humor, literary, mainstream, romance, satire, science fiction, women's, young adult.

"This agency specializes in general nonfiction and fiction. I also do illustrated and photography books and have represented several photographers for books."

**HOW TO CONTACT** Query with SASE or via e-mail with no attachments. Prefers to read materials exclusively but if not, please inform. Answers written and most email queries. Accepts simultaneous submissions. Responds in 2 weeks to queries; 2 months to mss. Obtains new clients through referrals from other writers and editors as well as unsolicited queries.

**TERMS** Agent receives 15% commission on domestic sales; 25% commission on foreign sales. Charges clients for photocopying, unusual postage, express mail, telephone expenses (checks with author first).

## SERENDIPITY LITERARY AGENCY, LLC

305 Gates Ave., Brooklyn NY 11216. **E-mail:** rbrooks@serendipitylit.com; info@serendipitylit.com. **Website:** www.serendipitylit.com; facebook.com/serendipitylit. **Contact:** Regina Brooks. Estab. 2000. Member of AAR. Signatory of WGA. Represents 150 clients.

Prior to becoming an agent, Ms. Brooks was an acquisitions editor for John Wiley & Sons, Inc. and McGraw-Hill Companies.

**MEMBER AGENTS** Regina Brooks; Christina Morgan (literary fiction, crime fiction, and narrative nonfiction in the categories of pop culture, sports, current events and memoir); Charles Kim; Kelly Thomas; Ameerah Holliday; Emma Loy-Santelli; Jitan Sharmayne Davidson.

**REPRESENTS** Nonfiction, fiction, novels, juvenile books. **Considers these nonfiction areas:** Americana, anthropology, architecture, art, autobiography, biography, business, cooking, creative nonfiction, cultural interests, current affairs, ethnic, foods, inspirational, interior design, juvenile nonfiction, memoirs, metaphysics, multicultural, music, parenting, popular culture, politics, psychology, religious, science, self-help, spirituality, sports, travel, true crime, women's issues, women's studies, young adult. **Considers these fiction areas:** commercial, gay, historical, lesbian, literary, middle grade, mystery, romance, thriller, women's, young adult, Christian.

**HOW TO CONTACT** Check the website, as there are online submission forms for fiction, nonfiction and juvenile. Website will also state if we're temporarily closed to submissions to any areas. Accepts simultaneous submissions. Obtains most new clients through conferences, referrals and social media.

**TERMS** Agent receives 15% commission on domestic sales; 20% commission on foreign sales. Offers written contract; 2-month notice must be given to terminate contract. Charges clients for office fees, which are taken from any advance.

**TIPS** "See the books *Writing Great Books For Young Adults* and *You Should Really Write A Book: How To Write, Sell, And Market Your Memoir*. We are looking for high concept ideas with big hooks. If you get writer's block try possibiliteas.co, it's a muse in a cup."

## ✪ SEVENTH AVENUE LITERARY AGENCY

2052-124th St., South Surrey BC Canada. (604)538-7252. **Fax:** (604)538-7252. **E-mail:** info@seventhavenuelit.com. **Website:** www.seventhavenuelit.com. **Contact:** Robert Mackwood, owner and principal agent. Estab. 1987. PACLA: Professional Association of Canadian Literary Agents. Represents 50 clients.

**REPRESENTS** Nonfiction. **Considers these nonfiction areas:** autobiography, biography, business, computers, cooking, creative nonfiction, economics, health, history, medicine, science, sports, technology, travel.

Seventh Avenue Literary Agency is both a literary agency and personal management agency, specializing in nonfiction. (The agency was originally Contemporary Management.) We also own and operate a self-publishing business imprint, Brilliant Idea Books, designed to help entrepreneurs and business owners develop their own "$20 business card" to further enhance their brand.

**HOW TO CONTACT** Query with SASE. Submit outline, synopsis, 1 sample chapter (nonfiction), publishing history, author bio, table of contents with proposal or query. Provide full contact information. Let us know the submission history. No fiction. Accepts simultaneous submissions. Obtains most new clients through recommendations from others, some solicitations. Does not add many new clients.

**WRITERS CONFERENCES** Willamette Writers Conference; Surrey Writers Conference; Okanagan Writers Conference.

**TIPS** "If you want your material returned, please include an SASE with adequate postage; otherwise, material will be recycled. (U.S. stamps are not adequate; they do not work in Canada.)"

## THE SEYMOUR AGENCY

475 Miner St., Canton NY 13617. (239)398-8209. **E-mail:** nicole@theseymouragency.com; julie@theseymouragency.com. **Website:** www.theseymouragency.com. Member of AAR. Signatory of WGA. Other memberships include RWA, Authors Guild, ACFW, HWA, MWA, SCBWI.

**MEMBER AGENTS** Nicole Rescinti, nicole@theseymouragency.com; Julie Gwinn, julie@theseymouragency.com; Tina Wainscott, tina@theseymouragency.com; Jennifer Wills, jennifer@theseymouragency.com; Lesley Sabga, lesley@theseymouragency.com; Elizabeth "Lizzie" Poteet; Elisa Houot; Michael L. Joy; Joyce Sweeney; Marisa Cleveland, marisa@theseymouragency.com; Lynette Novack.

**REPRESENTS** Nonfiction, fiction, novels, juvenile books. **Considers these nonfiction areas:** Americana, anthropology, business, child guidance, cooking, crafts, cultural interests, decorating, diet/nutrition, design, foods, gardening, gay/lesbian, health, history, hobbies, how-to, humor, inspirational, juvenile nonfiction, literature, memoirs, metaphysics, military, music, New Age, parenting, philosophy, photography, popular culture, politics, psychology, religious, self-help, sex, spirituality, sports, theater, travel, true crime, war, women's issues, women's studies, young adult, cookbooks; any well-written nonfiction that includes a proposal in standard format and 1 sample chapter. **Considers these fiction areas:** action, adventure, commercial, contemporary issues, crime, detective, erotica, ethnic, experimental, family saga, fantasy, feminist, frontier, gay, horror, humor, inspirational, lesbian, literary, mainstream, metaphysical, middle grade, military, multicultural, multimedia, mystery, new adult, New Age, occult, paranormal, picture books, police, religious, romance, science fiction, spiritual, sports, supernatural, suspense, thriller, translation, urban fantasy, war, westerns, women's, young adult.

**HOW TO CONTACT** Accepts e-mail queries or via QueryManager. Check online for guidelines. Accepts simultaneous submissions. Responds in 1 month to queries; 3 months to mss.

**TERMS** Agent receives 12-15% commission on domestic sales.

### DENISE SHANNON LITERARY AGENCY, INC.

121 W. 27th St., Suite 303, New York NY 10001. **E-mail:** info@deniseshannonagency.com; submissions@deniseshannonagency.com. **Website:** www.deniseshannonagency.com. **Contact:** Denise Shannon. Estab. 2002. Member of AAR.

○ Prior to opening her agency, Ms. Shannon worked for 16 years with Georges Borchardt and International Creative Management.

**REPRESENTS** Nonfiction, novels. **Considers these nonfiction areas:** biography, business, health, narrative nonfiction, politics, journalism, social history. **Considers these fiction areas:** literary.

☞ "We are a boutique agency with a distinguished list of fiction and nonfiction authors."

**HOW TO CONTACT** "Queries may be submitted by post, accompanied by a SASE, or by e-mail to submissions@deniseshannonagency.com. Please include a description of the available book project and a brief bio including details of any prior publications. We will reply and request more material if we are interested. We request that you inform us if you are submitting material simultaneously to other agencies." Accepts simultaneous submissions.

**RECENT SALES** *Mister Monkey*, by Francine Prose (Harper); *Hotel Solitaire*, by Gary Shteyngart (Random House); *White Flights*, by Jess Row (Graywolf Press); *The Underworld*, by Kevin Canty (Norton).

**TIPS** "Please do not send queries regarding fiction projects until a complete manuscript is available for review. We request that you inform us if you are submitting material simultaneously to other agencies."

### ⊘ KEN SHERMAN & ASSOCIATES

1275 N. Hayworth Ave., Suite 103, Los Angeles CA 90046. (310)273-8840. **E-mail:** kenshermanassociates@gmail.com. **E-mail:** ksasubmissions@gmail.com. **Website:** www.kenshermanassociates.com. **Contact:** Ken Sherman. Estab. 1989. BAFTA (British Academy of Film and Television Arts). Represents 35 clients.

○ Prior to opening his agency, Mr. Sherman was with The William Morris Agency, The Lantz Office, and Paul Kohner, Inc. He has taught The Business of Writing for Film and Television and the Book Worlds at UCLA and USC. He also lectures extensively at writer's conferences and film festivals around the U.S. He is currently a Commissioner of Arts and Cultural Affairs in the City of West Hollywood, and is on the International Advisory Board of the Christopher Isherwood Foundation.

**REPRESENTS** Nonfiction, fiction, novels, novellas, movie scripts, feature film, TV scripts, TV movie of the week, miniseries, theatrical stage play, stage plays, teleplays, life rights, film/TV rights to books and life rights. **Considers these nonfiction areas:** agriculture, Americana, animals, anthropology, art, biography, business, child guidance, computers, cooking, crafts, current affairs, education, ethnic, film, gardening, gay/lesbian, government, health, history, horticulture, how-to, humor, interior design, language, memoirs, military, money, multicultural, music, New Age, philosophy, photography, popular culture, psychology, recreation, regional, religious, science, self-help, sex, sociology, software, spirituality, sports, translation, travel, true crime, women's issues, young adult, creative nonfiction. **Considers these fiction areas:** action, adventure, commercial, crime, detective, family saga, gay, literary, mainstream, middle grade, mystery, police, romance, satire, science fiction, suspense, thriller, women's, young adult. **Considers these script areas:** action, adventure, autobiography, biography, comedy, detective, episodic drama, ethnic, family saga, fantasy, feature film, feminist, frontier, gay, historical, horror, inspirational, juvenile, lesbian, mainstream, miniseries, movie scripts, multimedia, mystery, police, regional, romantic comedy, romantic drama, science fiction, stage plays, supernatural, suspense, theatrical stage play, thriller, TV movie of the week. We represent book, film, TV writers and often sell film, TV, and stage rights to books.

**HOW TO CONTACT** Contact by referral only, please. Reports in approximately 1 month. Accepts simultaneous submissions. Obtains most new clients through recommendations from others.

**TERMS** Agent receives 15% commission on domestic and foreign sales; 10-15%, film and TV scripts, anything WGA, 10%. Offers written contract. Charges clients for reasonable office expenses (postage, photocopying, etc.).

**WRITERS CONFERENCES** Maui Writers' Conference; Squaw Valley Writers' Workshop; Santa Barbara Writers' Conference; Screenwriting Conference in Santa Fe; Aspen Summer Words Literary Festival including The Aspen Institute, the San Francisco Writer's Conference, Eugene International Film Festival, The Chautauqua Institute - Writer's Conference, La Jolla Writer's Conference, Central Coast Writer's Conference (California), etc.

### WENDY SHERMAN ASSOCIATES, INC.

138 W. 25th St., Suite 1018, New York NY 10001. (212)279-9027. **E-mail:** submissions@wsherman.com. **Website:** www.wsherman.com. **Contact:** Wendy Sherman. Estab. 1999. Member of AAR.

⬤    Prior to opening the agency, Ms. Sherman held positions as vice president, executive director, associate publisher, subsidiary rights director, and sales and marketing director for major publishers including Simon & Schuster and Henry Holt.

**MEMBER AGENTS** Wendy Sherman (women's fiction that hits that sweet spot between literary and mainstream, Southern voices, suspense with a well-developed protagonist, anything related to food, dogs, mothers and daughters). Cherise Fisher (upmarket commercial fiction, historical fiction, memoirs about the diversity of human experience, nonfiction on topics such as racial identity, personal development, health and sexuality, Christianity and spirituality, African American history, pop culture, and lifestyle books). Kelli Martin (Romance: romantic comedies, contemporary romance, romantic suspense; a wide variety of Women's Fiction and Commercial Fiction: love stories, suspense, family dramas, friendship dramas, beach reads, and women-coming-into-their-own stories). Nicki Richesin (literary and upmarket fiction with strong voices and unique perspectives, YA, big idea books, and select memoir). Callie Deitrick (upmarket and literary fiction, smart and entertaining, millennial, contemporary, unique hook, speculative, books about female friendships). Laura Mazer (adult nonfiction, feminism, intelligent pop culture, history/biography, celebrations of women and literary legacies, packaged gift or "concept" books).

**REPRESENTS** Nonfiction, fiction, novels, juvenile books. **Considers these nonfiction areas:** creative nonfiction, foods, humor, memoirs, parenting, popular culture, psychology, self-help, narrative nonfiction. **Considers these fiction areas:** mainstream fiction that hits the sweet spot between literary and commercial.

☛    "We specialize in developing new writers, as well as working with more established writers. My experience as a publisher has proven to be a great asset to my clients." Does not want genre fiction, picture books.

**HOW TO CONTACT** Query via e-mail only. "We ask that you include your last name, title, and the name of the agent you are submitting to in the subject line. For fiction, please include a query letter and your first 10 pages copied and pasted in the body of the e-mail. We will not open attachments unless they have been requested. For nonfiction, please include your query letter and author bio. Due to the large number of e-mail submissions that we receive, we only reply to e-mail queries in the affirmative. We respectfully ask that you do not send queries to our individual e-mail addresses." Accepts simultaneous submissions. Obtains most new clients through recommendations from other writers.

**TERMS** Agent receives standard 15% commission. Offers written contract.

**RECENT SALES** *Yellow Wife*, by Sadeqa Johnson; *Stationery Shop*, by Marjan Kamali; *A Good Neighborhood*, by Therese Anne Fowler; *Don't Look For Me*, by Wendy Walker; *Is Rape A Crime?*, by Michelle Bowdler; *Mercy House*, by Alena Dillon; *All Is Not Forgotten*, by Wendy Walker; *Z, A Novel of Zelda Fitzgerald*, by Therese Anne Fowler; *The Charm Bracelet*, by Viola Shipman; *The Silence of Bonaventure Arrow*, by

Rita Leganski; *Together Tea*, by Marjan Kamali; *A Long Long Time Ago and Essentially True*, by Brigid Pasulka; *Lunch in Paris*, by Elizabeth Bard; *The Rules of Inheritance*, by Claire Bidwell Smith; *Eight Flavors*, by Sarah Lohman; *How to Live a Good Life*, by Jonathan Fields; *The Essential Oil Hormone Solution*, by Dr. Mariza Snyder.

**TIPS** "The bottom line is: do your homework. Be as well prepared as possible. Read the books that will help you present yourself and your work with polish. You want your submission to stand out."

### BEVERLEY SLOPEN LITERARY AGENCY
131 Bloor St. W., Suite 711, Toronto ON M5S 1S3 Canada. (416)964-9598. **E-mail:** beverly@slopenagency.ca. **Website:** www.slopenagency.com. **Contact:** Beverley Slopen. Represents 100 clients.

Prior to opening her agency, Ms. Slopen worked in publishing and as a journalist.

**REPRESENTS** Nonfiction, novels. **Considers these nonfiction areas:** anthropology, autobiography, biography, creative nonfiction, history, investigative, psychology, sociology, true crime. **Considers these fiction areas:** commercial, literary, mystery, suspense.

"This agency has a strong bent toward Canadian writers." Actively seeking serious nonfiction that is accessible and appealing to the general reader. Does not want to receive fantasy, science fiction, or children's books.

**HOW TO CONTACT** Query by e-mail. Does not return materials. To submit a work for consideration, e-mail a short query letter and a few sample pages. Submit only one work at a time. "If we want to see more, we will contact the writer by phone or e-mail." Accepts simultaneous submissions. Responds in 1 month to queries only if interested.

**TERMS** Agent receives 15% commission on domestic sales; 10% commission on foreign sales. Offers written contract, binding for 2 years; 3-month notice must be given to terminate contract.

**TIPS** "Please, no unsolicited manuscripts."

### THE SLW AGENCY, LLC
360 West Erie St., Suite 9D, Chicago IL 60654. **E-mail:** shariwenk@swenkagency.com. **Contact:** Shari Wenk. **REPRESENTS** Nonfiction. **Considers these nonfiction areas:** sports.

"This agency specializes in representing books written by sports celebrities and sports journalists."

**HOW TO CONTACT** Query via e-mail, but note the agency's specific specialty. Accepts simultaneous submissions.

### ROBERT SMITH LITERARY AGENCY, LTD.
12 Bridge Wharf, 156 Caledonian Rd., London NI 9UU England. (44)(207)278-2444. **Fax:** (44)(207)833-5680. **E-mail:** robert@robertsmithliteraryagency.com. **Website:** www.robertsmithliteraryagency.com. **Contact:** Robert Smith. Member of AAA. Represents 40 clients.

Prior to becoming an agent, Mr. Smith was a book publisher (Ebury Press, Sidgwick & Jackson, Smith Gryphon).

**REPRESENTS** Nonfiction, syndicated material. **Considers these nonfiction areas:** autobiography, biography, business, cooking, cultural interests, current affairs, diet/nutrition, film, foods, health, history, inspirational, investigative, medicine, memoirs, military, music, popular culture, self-help, sports, theater, true crime, war, entertainment.

Actively seeking autobiographies.

**HOW TO CONTACT** Contact via e-mail or snail mail (with SASE), provide initially a synopsis of chapters, an overview of the whole book, a sample chapter (if one is available), a review of competitive books, your personal profile and details of any previous media coverage, which you or your book has received. Prefers to read materials exclusively; please specify exclusive or simultaneous submission. Responds to all submissions. Responds in 2 weeks to queries. Obtains most new clients through recommendations from others, direct approaches to prospective authors.

**TERMS** Agent receives 15% commission on domestic sales; 20% commission on foreign sales. Offers written contract, binding for 3 months; 3-month notice must be given to terminate contract. Charges clients for couriers, photocopying, overseas mailings of mss (subject to client authorization).

**RECENT SALES** *Shamed*, by Sarbjit Kaur Athwal; *Living with a Serial Killer*, by Delia Balmer; *The Ghosts of Happy Valley*, by Juliet Barnes.

## MICHAEL SNELL LITERARY AGENCY

H. Michael Snell, Inc., P.O. Box 1206, Truro MA 02666-1206. (508)214-0722. **E-mail:** query@michaelsnellagency.com. **Website:** michaelsnellagency.com. **Contact:** Patricia Snell, Michael Snell. 32 Bridge Road (for UPS, FedEx only) Estab. 1977. Represents 300 clients.

○ Prior to opening his agency in 1978, Mr. Snell served as a college textbook editor at Wadsworth and Addison-Wesley for 13 years.

**MEMBER AGENTS** Michael Snell (business, leadership, entrepreneurship, pets, sports); Patricia Snell, (business, business communications, parenting, relationships, health).

**REPRESENTS** Nonfiction. **Considers these nonfiction areas:** animals, business, creative nonfiction, health, how-to, parenting, psychology, science, self-help, women's issues, women's studies, fitness.

☞ This agency specializes in how-to, self-help, and all types of business, business leadership, entrepreneurship titles, as well as books for small-business owners. "We place a wide range of topics, from low-level how-to to professional and reference. We are especially interested in business leadership, management, communication, strategy, culture building, performance enhancement, marketing and sales, finance and investment, career development, executive skills, and organization development." Actively seeking strong book proposals in any area of business where a clear need exists for a new book. Does not want to receive memoirs, fiction, children's books, or complete mss (considers proposals only).

**HOW TO CONTACT** Query by e-mail. Visit the agency's website for proposal guidelines. "We only consider new clients on an exclusive basis." Responds in 1 week to queries; 2 weeks to mss. Obtains most new clients through unsolicited mss, word of mouth, *Literary Market Place*, *Guide to Literary Agents*.

**TERMS** Agent receives 15% commission on all sales, domestic and foreign.

**RECENT SALES** *Negotiating with a Bully*, by Greg Williams (Career Press); *The Oz Principle Next Generation*, by Craig Hickman; The Insider's Guide to *Culture*, by Siobhan McHale (HarperCollins); *Lead Right for Your Company Type*, by William Schneider (AMACOM); *Excuse Me: The Survival Guide to Modern Business Etiquette*, by Rosanne Thomas (AMACOM); *Finding Peace When Your Heart Is in Pieces*, by Paul Coleman (Adams Media); *Body Language Secrets to Win More Negotiations*, by Greg Williams (Career Press); *Career Courage*, by Katie Kelley (AMACOM); *The Disruption Revolution*, by Suman Sarkar (Berrett-Kohler).

**TIPS** "Visit the agency's website to view recent sales and publications and to review guidelines for writing a book proposal. Prospective authors can also download model book proposals at the website. The agency only considers new clients on an exclusive basis. Simultaneous queries are OK; multiple submissions are not."

## SPECTRUM LITERARY AGENCY

320 Central Park W., Suite 1-D, New York NY 10025. (212)362-4323. **Fax:** (212)362-4562. **Website:** www.spectrumliteraryagency.com. **Contact:** Eleanor Wood, president. Estab. 1976. Member of SFWA. Represents 90 clients.

**MEMBER AGENTS** Eleanor Wood (referrals only; commercial fiction: science fiction, fantasy, suspense, as well as select nonfiction); Justin Bell (science fiction, mysteries, and select nonfiction).

**REPRESENTS** Novels. **Considers these fiction areas:** commercial, fantasy, mystery, science fiction, suspense.

**HOW TO CONTACT** Unsolicited mss are not accepted. Send snail mail query with SASE. "The letter should describe your book briefly and include publishing credits and background information or qualifications relating to your work, and the first 10 pages of your work. Our response time is generally 2-3 months." Responds in 1-3 months to queries. Obtains most new clients through recommendations from authors.

**TERMS** Agent receives 15% commission on domestic sales. Deducts for photocopying and book orders.

**TIPS** "Spectrum's policy is to read only book-length manuscripts that we have specifically asked to see. Unsolicited manuscripts are not accepted. The letter should describe your book briefly and include publishing credits and background information or qualifications relating to your work, if any."

## SPEILBURG LITERARY AGENCY

**E-mail:** speilburgliterary@gmail.com. **Website:** speilburgliterary.com. **Contact:** Alice Speilburg. Estab. 2012. Member of SCBWI; MWA; RWA; Author's Guild.

**MEMBER AGENTS** Alice Speilburg worked for John Wiley & Sons and Howard Morhaim Literary Agency, before launching Speilburg Literary. She is a member of Romance Writers of America, Mystery Writers of America, and Society of Children's Book Writers and Illustrators, and she is a board member of Louisville Literary Arts. She represents commercial fiction and narrative nonfiction. Eva Scalzo has a B.A. in the Humanities from the University of Puerto Rico and a M.A. in Publishing and Writing from Emerson College. She has spent her career in scholarly publishing, working for Houghton Mifflin, Blackwell Publishing, John Wiley & Sons, and Cornell University in a variety of roles. Eva is looking to represent all subgenres of romance, with the exclusion of inspirational romance, as well as young adult fiction; Lindsey Smith.

**REPRESENTS** Nonfiction, fiction, novels. **Considers these nonfiction areas:** biography, cultural interests, health, history, investigative, music, popular culture, psychology, science, travel, women's issues, women's studies, young adult. **Considers these fiction areas:** adventure, commercial, detective, fantasy, feminist, historical, horror, mainstream, mystery, police, romance, science fiction, suspense, urban fantasy, westerns, women's, young adult.

☛ Does not want picture books; screenplays; poetry.

**HOW TO CONTACT** In the subject line of your query e-mail, please include "Query [AGENT's FIRST NAME]" followed by the title of your project. For fiction, please send the query letter and the first three chapters. For nonfiction, please send the query letter and a proposal, which should include a detailed TOC and a sample chapter. Accepts simultaneous submissions.

## SPENCERHILL ASSOCIATES

1767 Lakewood Ranch Blvd, #268, Bradenton FL 34211. (941)907-3700. **E-mail:** submission@spencerhillassociates.com. **Website:** www.spencerhillassociates.com. **Contact:** Karen Solem, Nalini Akolekar, Amanda Leuck, Sandy Harding, and Ali Herring. Estab. 2001. Member of AAR.

○ Prior to becoming an agent, Ms. Solem was editor-in-chief at HarperCollins and an associate publisher.

**MEMBER AGENTS** Karen Solem; Nalini Akolekar; Amanda Leuck; Sandy Harding; Ali Herring.

**REPRESENTS** Fiction, novels, juvenile books. **Considers these fiction areas:** commercial, contemporary issues, crime, detective, ethnic, family saga, fantasy, feminist, gay, historical, humor, inspirational, lesbian, literary, mainstream, middle grade, multicultural, mystery, new adult, paranormal, police, religious, romance, science fiction, supernatural, suspense, thriller, urban fantasy, women's, young adult.

☛ "We handle mostly commercial women's fiction, historical novels, romance (historical, contemporary, paranormal, urban fantasy), thrillers, and mysteries, in addition to middle grade and young adult novels. We also represent Christian fiction only—no nonfiction." No nonfiction, poetry, children's picture books, or scripts.

**HOW TO CONTACT** "We accept electronic submissions only. Please send us a query letter in the body of an e-mail, pitch us your project and tell us about yourself: Do you have prior publishing credits? Attach the first three chapters and synopsis preferably in .doc, rtf or txt format to your email. Send all queries to submission@spencerhillassociates.com. Or submit through the QueryManager link on our website. We do not have a preference for exclusive submissions, but do appreciate knowing if the submission is simultaneous. We receive thousands of submissions a year and each query receives our attention. Unfortunately, we are unable to respond to each query individually. If we are interested in your work, we will contact you within 12 weeks." Accepts simultaneous submissions. Responds in approximately 12 weeks.

**TERMS** Agent receives 15% commission on domestic sales; 20% commission on foreign sales. Offers written contract; 3-month notice must be given to terminate contract.

**RECENT SALES** A full list of sales and clients is available on the agency website.

## PHILIP G. SPITZER LITERARY AGENCY, INC

50 Talmage Farm Ln., East Hampton NY 11937. (631)329-3650. **E-mail:** lukas.ortiz@spitzeragency.com; annelise.spitzer@spitzeragency.com; kim.lombardini@spitzeragency.com. **Website:** www.spitzeragency.com. **Contact:** Lukas Ortiz. Estab. 1969. Member of AAR.

○ Prior to opening his agency, Mr. Spitzer served at New York University Press, McGraw-Hill, and the John Cushman Associates Literary Agency.

**MEMBER AGENTS** Philip G. Spitzer; Anne-Lise Spitzer; Lukas Ortiz.

**REPRESENTS** Nonfiction, fiction, novels. **Considers these nonfiction areas:** autobiography, biography, creative nonfiction, current affairs, ethnic, gay/lesbian, history, literature, memoirs, popular culture, politics, sociology, true crime. **Considers these fiction areas:** commercial, contemporary issues, crime, historical, horror, literary, mainstream, mystery, police, suspense, thriller.

☛ This agency specializes in mystery/suspense, literary fiction, sports, and general nonfiction (no how-to).

**HOW TO CONTACT** E-mail query containing synopsis of work, brief biography, and a sample chapter (pasted into the e-mail). Be aware that this agency openly says their client list is quite full. Obtains most new clients through recommendations from others.

**TERMS** Agent receives 15% commission on domestic sales; 20% commission on foreign sales.

**RECENT SALES** *New Iberia Blues*, by James Lee Burke (Simon & Schuster); *The Better Sister*, by Alafair Burke (HarperCollins); *Gone So Long*, by Andre Dubus III (Norton); *Two Kinds of Truth*, by Michael Connelly (Little, Brown & Co); *The Emerald Lie*, Ken Bruen (Mysterious Press/Grove-Atlantic); *Terror in the City of Champions*, by Tom Stanton (Lyons Press); *The Brain Defense*, by Kevin Davis (Penguin Press); *The Names of Dead Girls*, by Eric Rickstad (Harper-Collins); *Assume Nothing*, Gar Anthony Haywood (Severn House); *The Man on the Stair*, by Gary Inbinder (Norton); *Running in the Dark*, by Sam Reaves (Thomas & Mercer); *Green Sun*, by Kent Anderson (Mulholland Books).

**WRITERS CONFERENCES** London Book Fair, Frankfurt, BookExpo America, Bouchercon.

## NANCY STAUFFER ASSOCIATES

P.O. Box 1203, Darien CT 06820. (203)202-2500. **E-mail:** nancy@staufferliterary.com. **Website:** www.publishersmarketplace.com/members/nstauffer. **Contact:** Nancy Stauffer Cahoon. Member of Authors Guild.

○ "Over the course of my more than 20 year career, I've held positions in the editorial, marketing, business, and rights departments of *The New York Times*, McGraw-Hill, and Doubleday. Before founding Nancy Stauffer Associates, I was Director of Foreign and Performing Rights then Director, Subsidiary Rights, for Doubleday, where I was honored to have worked with a diverse range of internationally known and bestselling authors of all genres."

**REPRESENTS** **Considers these fiction areas:** literary.

☛ We do not represent mysteries, romance, action adventure, historical fiction, or thrillers.

**HOW TO CONTACT** Accepts simultaneous submissions. Obtains most new clients through referrals from existing clients.

**TERMS** Agent receives 15% commission on domestic sales.

**RECENT SALES** *You Don't Have To Say You Love Me*, by Sherman Alexie; *Our Souls At Night*, by Kent Haruf.

## STIMOLA LITERARY STUDIO, INC

308 Livingston Ct., Edgewater NJ 07020. **E-mail:** info@stimolaliterarystudio.com. **E-mail:** see submission page on website. **Website:** www.stimolaliterarystudio.com. **Contact:** Rosemary B. Stimola. Estab. 1997. Member of AAR, PEN, Authors Guild, ALA Represents 75 clients.

○ Prior to opening her agency, Rosemary Stimola was an independent children's bookseller. Erica Rand Silverman, Senior Agent, was a high school teacher and former senior agent at Sterling Lord Literistic. Allison Remcheck was an Assistant Editor at Feiwel & Friends/Macmillan, and then Editorial Assistant at the Stimola Literary Studio before acquiring for her own list. Adriana Stimola worked as Content Manager at Stone Barns, Food and Agricultural Institute. Peter Ryan continues to be the Director of Operations at the Stimola Literary Studio, and now represents graphic novels for all ages. Allison Hellegers was is a former Scout and Rights Manager at Rights People, and is now Foreign Rights Director at the Studio as well as acquiring for her own list.

**MEMBER AGENTS** Rosemary B. Stimola; Erica Rand Silverman; Allison Remcheck; Adriana Stimola, Peter Ryan.

**REPRESENTS** Nonfiction, fiction, juvenile books, poetry books. **Considers these nonfiction areas:** agriculture, cooking, foods, juvenile nonfiction, young adult. **Considers these fiction areas:** comic books, juvenile, middle grade, multicultural, mystery, picture books, suspense, thriller, young adult.

☛ Actively seeking remarkable middle grade, young adult fiction, and debut picture book author/illustrators. Also seeking fresh graphic novels for juvenile and adult readers. No institutional books.

**HOW TO CONTACT** Query via e-mail as per submission guidelines on website. Author/illustrators of picture books may attach text and sample art with query. A PDF dummy is preferred. Accepts simultaneous submissions. Responds in 3 weeks to queries "we wish to pursue further"; 2 months to requested mss. While unsolicited queries are welcome, most clients come through editor, agent, client referrals.

**TERMS** Agent receives 15% commission on domestic sales; 20% (if subagents are employed) commission on foreign sales. Offers written contract, binding for all children's projects. 60 days notice must be given to terminate contract.

**RECENT SALES** *Bear Island*, by Matthew Cordell; *The Bear and the Moon*, by Matthew Burgess and Catia Chen; *Blue Barry and Pancakes*, by Dan Abdo and Jason Patterson; *The Cat Man of Aleppo* by Irene Latham, Karim Shashi-Basha and Yuko Shimizu; *Lupe Wong Won't Dance*, by Donna Barba Higuera; *The Ballad of Songbirds and Snakes*, by Suzanne Collins; *Bear Mouth*, by Liz Hyder; *Bed Head Ted* by Scott San Giacomo; *The Cousins*, by Karen M. McManus; *Call Me Athena*, by Colby Cedar Smith; *Motherhood: Facing and Finding Yourself*, by Lisa Marchiano; *Mornings with Monet*, by Barb Rosenstock and Mary GrandPre; *I Am Courage*, by Susan Verde; *For the Table* by Anna Stockwell; *52 Weeks at Catbird Cottage* by Melina Hammer; *The People We Used to Be* by Kyle Scheele.

**TIPS** Agents are hands-on, no-nonsense. May request revisions. Does not line edit but may offer suggestions for improvement before submission. Well-respected by clients and editors. "Firm but reasonable deal negotiators."

## STONESONG

270 W. 39th St. #201, New York NY 10018. (212)929-4600. **E-mail:** editors@stonesong.com. **E-mail:** submissions@stonesong.com. **Website:** stonesong.com. Member of AAR. Signatory of WGA.

**MEMBER AGENTS** Alison Fargis; Ellen Scordato; Judy Linden; Emmanuelle Morgen; Leila Campoli (business, science, technology, and self improvement); Maria Ribas (cookbooks, self-help, health, diet, home, parenting, and humor, all from authors with demonstrable platforms; she's also interested in narrative nonfiction and select memoir); Melissa Edwards (children's fiction and adult commercial fiction, as well as select pop-culture nonfiction); Alyssa Jennette (children's and adult fiction and picture books, and has dabbled in humor and pop culture nonfiction); Madelyn Burt (adult and children's fiction, as well as select historical nonfiction); Adrienne Rosado; Kim Lindman.

**REPRESENTS** Nonfiction, fiction, novels, juvenile books. **Considers these nonfiction areas:** architecture, art, biography, business, cooking, crafts, creative nonfiction, cultural interests, current affairs, dance, decorating, diet/nutrition, design, economics, foods, gay/lesbian, health, history, hobbies, how-to, humor, interior design, investigative, literature, memoirs, money, music, New Age, parenting, photography, popular culture, politics, psychology, science, self-help, sociology, spirituality, sports, technology, women's issues, young adult. **Considers these fiction areas:** action, adventure, commercial, confession, contemporary issues, ethnic, experimental, family saga, fantasy, feminist, gay, historical, horror, humor, juvenile, lesbian, literary, mainstream, middle grade, military, multicultural, mystery, new adult, New Age, occult, paranormal, regional, romance, satire, science fiction, supernatural, suspense, thriller, urban fantasy, women's, young adult.

☛ Does not represent plays, screenplays, picture books, or poetry.

**HOW TO CONTACT** Accepts electronic queries for fiction and nonfiction. Submit query addressed to a specific agent. Include first chapter or first 10 pages of ms. Accepts simultaneous submissions.

**RECENT SALES** *Sweet Laurel*, by Laurel Gallucci and Claire Thomas; *Terrain: A Seasonal Guide to Nature at Home*, by Terrain; *The Prince's Bane*, by Alexandra Christo; *Deep Listening*, by Jillian Pransky; *Change Resilience*, by Lior Arussy; *A Thousand Words*, by Brigit Young.

## ⊘ STRACHAN LITERARY AGENCY

165 Green Street, Annapolis MD 21401. **E-mail:** query@strachanlit.com. **Website:** www.strachanlit.com. **Contact:** Laura Strachan. Estab. 1998.

**MEMBER AGENTS** Laura Strachan; Marisa Zeppieri-Caruana.

**REPRESENTS** Nonfiction, fiction, novels, short story collections, juvenile books. **Considers these nonfiction areas:** anthropology, art, creative nonfiction, cultural interests, current affairs, health, history, literature, memoirs, multicultural, spirituality, travel, women's issues, women's studies, narrative. **Considers these fiction areas:** contemporary issues, feminist, gay, lesbian, literary, multicultural, satire, short story collections, translation, young adult.

☞ "This agency specializes in literary fiction and narrative nonfiction."

**HOW TO CONTACT** Please query with description of project and short biographical statement. Do not paste or attach sample pages. Accepts simultaneous submissions.

## ROBIN STRAUS AGENCY, INC.

The Wallace Literary Agency, 229 E. 79th St., Suite 5A, New York NY 10075. (212)472-3282. **Fax:** (212)472-3833. **E-mail:** info@robinstrausagency.com. **Website:** www.robinstrausagency.com. **Contact:** Ms. Robin Straus. Estab. 1983. Member of AAR.

○ Prior to becoming an agent, Robin Straus served as a subsidiary rights manager at Random House and Doubleday. She began her career in the editorial department of Little, Brown.

**REPRESENTS Considers these nonfiction areas:** biography, cooking, creative nonfiction, current affairs, environment, foods, gay/lesbian, health, history, memoirs, multicultural, music, parenting, popular culture, politics, psychology, science, travel, women's issues, mainstream science. **Considers these fiction areas:** commercial, contemporary issues, fantasy, feminist, literary, mainstream, science fiction, translation, women's.

☞ Does not represent juvenile, young adult, horror, romance, Westerns, poetry, or screenplays.

**HOW TO CONTACT** E-query only. No physical mail accepted. See our website for full submission instructions. Email us a query letter with contact information, an autobiographical summary, a brief synopsis or description of your book project, submission history, and information on competition. If you wish, you may also include the opening chapter of your manuscript (pasted). While we do our best to reply to all queries, you can assume that if you haven't heard from us after six weeks, we are not interested. Accepts simultaneous submissions.

**TERMS** Agent receives 15% commission on domestic sales; 20% commission on foreign sales. Offers written contract.

## THE STRINGER LITERARY AGENCY LLC

P.O. Box 111255, Naples FL 34108. **E-mail:** mstringer@stringerlit.com. **E-mail:** via website. **Website:** www.stringerlit.com. **Contact:** Marlene Stringer. Estab. 2008. Member of AAR, RWA, MWA, ITW, SBCWI, The Writers Guild. Represents 50 +/- clients.

**MEMBER AGENTS** Marlene Stringer; Shari Maurer.

**REPRESENTS** Nonfiction, fiction, novels, juvenile books. **Considers these nonfiction areas:** biography, juvenile nonfiction, memoirs, multicultural, young adult. **Considers these fiction areas:** commercial, crime, detective, fantasy, historical, horror, juvenile, mainstream, middle grade, multicultural, mystery, new adult, paranormal, picture books, police, romance, science fiction, suspense, thriller, urban fantasy, women's, young adult, no space opera SF.

☞ This agency specializes in fiction, and select nonfiction. "We are an editorial agency, and work with clients to make their manuscripts the best they can be in preparation for submission. We focus on career planning, and help our clients reach their publishing goals. We advise clients on marketing and promotional strategies to help them reach their target readership. Because we are so hands-on, we limit the size of our list; however, we are always looking for exceptional voices and stories that demand we read to the end. You never know where the next great story is coming from." This agency is seeking thrillers, crime fiction, mystery, women's fiction, single title and category romance, fantasy (all subgenres), grounded science fiction (no aliens, etc.), YA/teen, MG, and picture books. Does not want to receive plays, short stories, scripts, or poetry. This is not the agency for inspirational romance or erotica. The agency is not seeking any nonfiction other than memoir, biography, or narrative nonfiction at this time.

**HOW TO CONTACT** Electronic submissions through website only. Please make sure your ms is as good as it can be before you submit. Agents are not first readers. For specific information on what we like to see in query letters, refer to the information at www.stringerlit.com. Accepts simultaneous submissions. "We strive to respond quickly, but current clients' work always comes first." Obtains new clients through referrals, submissions, conferences.

**TERMS** Standard commission. "We do not charge fees."

**RECENT SALES** *After She Was Mine* by Brian Charles; *The Dead Season* by Tessa Wegert; *Don't Believe It* by Charlie Donlea; *What's Left Unsaid*, by Emily Bleeker; Spellbreaker series, by Charlie N. Holmberg; *Belle Chasse*, by Suzanne Johnson; Wings of Fury series by Emily R. King; *Wilds of the Bayou*, by Susannah Sandlin; *Death in the Family*, by Tessa Wegert; *The Raven Sisters*, by Luanne Smith; The Swooning Virgins Society series, by Anna Bradley; *Fly by Night*, by Andrea Thalasinos; The Dragonsworn series, by Caitlyn McFarland; *The Devious Dr. Jekyll*, by Viola Carr; *The Dragon's Price*, by Bethany Wiggins; The Hundredth Queen series, by Emily R. King; film rights to *The Paper Magician*, by Charlie N. Holmberg.

**WRITERS CONFERENCES** Various conferences each year.

**TIPS** "Check our website for submission information and updates. If your ms falls between categories, or you are not sure of the category, query and we'll let you know if we'd like to take a look. We strive to respond as quickly as possible. If you have not received a response in the time period indicated on website, please re-query."

## THE STROTHMAN AGENCY, LLC

63 E. 9th St., 10X, New York NY 10003. **E-mail:** info@strothmanagency.com; strothmanagency@gmail.com. **Website:** www.strothmanagency.com. **Contact:** Wendy Strothman, Lauren MacLeod. Estab. 2003. Member of AAR. Represents 100+ clients.

○ Prior to becoming an agent, Ms. Strothman was head of Beacon Press (1983-1995) and executive vice president of Houghton Mifflin's Trade & Reference Division (1996-2002).

**MEMBER AGENTS** Wendy Strothman (history, narrative nonfiction, narrative journalism, science and nature, and current affairs); Lauren MacLeod (young adult fiction and nonfiction, middle grade novels, as well as adult narrative nonfiction, particularly food writing, science, pop culture and history).

**REPRESENTS** Nonfiction, juvenile books. **Considers these nonfiction areas:** anthropology, archeology, business, cooking, cultural interests, current affairs, economics, environment, foods, government, history, investigative, juvenile nonfiction, language, law, literature, popular culture, politics, science, sociology, true crime, war, women's issues, women's studies, young adult. **Considers these fiction areas:** middle grade, young adult.

➤ Specializes in history, science, biography, politics, narrative journalism, nature and the environment, current affairs, narrative nonfiction, business and economics, young adult fiction and nonfiction, and middle grade fiction and nonfiction. "The Strothman Agency seeks out scholars, journalists, and other acknowledged and emerging experts in their fields. We specialize in history, science, narrative journalism, nature and the environment, current affairs, narrative nonfiction, business and economics, young adult fiction and nonfiction, middle grade fiction and nonfiction. We are not signing up projects in romance, science fiction, picture books, or poetry."

**HOW TO CONTACT** Accepts queries only via e-mail. See submission guidelines online. Accepts simultaneous submissions. "All e-mails received will be responded to with an auto-reply. If we have not replied to your query within 6 weeks, we do not feel that it is right for us." Accepts simultaneous submissions. Obtains most new clients through recommendations from others.

**TERMS** Agent receives 15% commission on domestic sales; 20% commission on foreign sales. Offers written contract; 30-day notice must be given to terminate contract.

## THE STUART AGENCY

462 7th Ave., 6th Floor, New York NY 10018. (646)564-2983. **E-mail:** andrew@stuartagency.com. **Website:** stuartagency.com. **Contact:** Andrew Stuart. Estab. 2002.

○ Prior to his current position, Mr. Stuart was an agent with Literary Group International for five years. Prior to becoming an agent, he was an editor at Random House and Simon & Schuster.

**MEMBER AGENTS** Andrew Stuart (history, science, narrative nonfiction, business, current events, memoir, psychology, sports, literary fiction); Paul Starobin.

**REPRESENTS** Nonfiction, novels. **Considers these nonfiction areas:** art, business, creative nonfiction, current affairs, history, memoirs, popular culture, psychology, religious, science, sports. **Considers these fiction areas:** horror, literary, thriller.

**HOW TO CONTACT** Query via online submission form on the agency website. Accepts simultaneous submissions.

## EMMA SWEENEY AGENCY, LLC

245 E 80th St., Suite 7E, New York NY 10075. **E-mail:** info@emmasweeneyagency.com; queries@emmasweeneyagency.com. **Website:** www.emmasweeneyagency.com. Estab. 2006. Member of AAR, Women's Media Group. Represents 80 clients.

○ Prior to becoming an agent, Ms. Sweeney was director of subsidiary rights at Grove Press. Since 1990, she has been a literary agent. Ms. Sutherland Brown was an Associate Editor at St. Martin's Press/Thomas Dunne Books and a freelance editor. Ms. Watson attended Hunter College where she earned a BA in English (with a focus on Creative Writing) and a BA in Russian Language & Culture.

**MEMBER AGENTS** Emma Sweeney, president; Margaret Sutherland Brown (commercial and literary fiction, mysteries and thrillers, narrative nonfiction, lifestyle, and cookbook); Hannah Brattesani (poetry and literary fiction).

**REPRESENTS** Nonfiction, fiction, novels, poetry books. **Considers these nonfiction areas:** biography, cooking, creative nonfiction, cultural interests, decorating, diet/nutrition, design, environment, foods, gardening, history, how-to, interior design, literature, memoirs, popular culture, psychology, religious, science, self-help, sex, sociology. **Considers these fiction areas:** commercial, contemporary issues, crime, historical, horror, literary, mainstream, mystery, poetry, spiritual, suspense, thriller, women's.

☞ Does not want erotica.

**HOW TO CONTACT** "We accept only electronic queries, and ask that all queries be sent to queries@emmasweeneyagency.com rather than to any agent

directly. Please begin your query with a succinct (and hopefully catchy) description of your plot or proposal. Always include a brief cover letter telling us how you heard about ESA, your previous writing credits, and a few lines about yourself. We cannot open any attachments unless specifically requested, and ask that you paste the first 10 pages of your proposal or novel into the text of your e-mail." Accepts simultaneous submissions.

## STEPHANIE TADE AGENCY LLC

7A North Bank St., Easton PA 18042. (610)829-0035. **E-mail:** submissions@stephanietadeagency.com. **Website:** stephanietadeagency.com. **Contact:** Stephanie Tade.

○ Prior to becoming an agent, Ms. Tade was an executive editor at Rodale Press. She was also an agent with the Jane Rotrosen Agency.

**MEMBER AGENTS** Stephanie Tade, president and principal agent; Colleen Martell, editorial director and associate agent (cmartell@stadeagency.com).

**REPRESENTS** Nonfiction.

☞ Seeks prescriptive and narrative nonfiction, specializing in physical, emotional, psychological and spiritual wellness.

**HOW TO CONTACT** Query by e-mail. "When you write to the agency, please include information about your proposed book, your publishing history and any media or online platform you have developed." Accepts simultaneous submissions.

## TALCOTT NOTCH LITERARY SERVICES, LLC

31 Cherry St., Suite 100, Milford CT 06460. (203)876-4959. **Fax:** (203)876-9517. **E-mail:** editorial@talcottnotch.net. **Website:** www.talcottnotch.net. **Contact:** Gina Panettieri, founder. Estab. 2002. Member of SinC, MWA, SCBWI. Represents 150 clients.

○ Prior to becoming an agent, Ms. Panettieri was a freelance writer and editor. Ms. Munier was Director of Acquisitions for Adams Media Corporation and had previously worked for Disney. Ms. Sulaiman holds degrees from Wellesley and the University of Chicago and had completed an internship with Sourcebooks prior to joining Talcott Notch. Ms. Mele received her B.A. in English from the University of Connecticut and her Master's in Creative Writing from the University of Southern New Hampshire before completing an internship at

Talcott Notch and then joining the agency as an assistant.

**MEMBER AGENTS** Gina Panettieri, gpanettieri@talcottnotch.net (history, business, self-help, science, gardening, cookbooks, crafts, parenting, memoir, true crime and travel, YA, MG and women's fiction, paranormal, urban fantasy, horror, science fiction, historical, mystery, thrillers and suspense); Paula Munier, pmunier@talcottnotch.net (mystery/thriller, SF/fantasy, romance, YA, memoir, humor, pop culture, health & wellness, cooking, self-help, pop psych, New Age, inspirational, technology, science, and writing); Saba Sulaiman, ssulaiman@talcottnotch.net (upmarket literary and commercial fiction, romance [all subgenres except paranormal], character-driven psychological thrillers, cozy mysteries, memoir, young adult [except paranormal and sci-fi], middle grade, and nonfiction humor); Tia Mele, tmele@talcottnotch.net (YA and MG, fiction and nonfiction, limited adult projects); Amy Collins (nonfiction, gift, reference, history, fantasy, science fiction, historical fiction); Dennis Schleicher (biographies, Christian living, children's books, church life, devotional, inspirational, LGBTQ, theology, bible study, reference, health, finance, fiction, self-help, psychology, grief, suffering, marriage, family, women's, men's, philosophy, history, social issues, parenting, clean romance, LDS, and Mormonism).

**REPRESENTS** Nonfiction, fiction, novels, short story collections, novellas, juvenile books. **Considers these nonfiction areas:** autobiography, biography, business, cooking, crafts, creative nonfiction, cultural interests, current affairs, diet/nutrition, environment, ethnic, film, foods, gardening, gay/lesbian, government, health, history, how-to, humor, inspirational, investigative, juvenile nonfiction, language, law, literature, medicine, memoirs, military, money, multicultural, New Age, parenting, popular culture, politics, psychology, regional, religious, science, self-help, sex, sociology, spirituality, technology, travel, true crime, war, women's issues, women's studies, young adult. **Considers these fiction areas:** action, adventure, comic books, commercial, contemporary issues, crime, detective, erotica, ethnic, family saga, fantasy, feminist, gay, hi-lo, historical, horror, juvenile, lesbian, literary, mainstream, middle grade, military, multicultural, multimedia, mystery, new adult, New Age, paranormal, police, romance, science fiction, short story collections, sports, supernatural, suspense, thriller, urban fantasy, war, westerns, women's, young adult.

☞ "We are most actively seeking projects featuring diverse characters and stories which expand the reader's understanding of our society and the wider world we live in."

**HOW TO CONTACT** Query via e-mail (preferred) with first 10 pages of the ms pasted within the body of the e-mail, not as an attachment. Accepts simultaneous submissions. Responds in 2 weeks to queries; 6-10 weeks to mss. We find many of our new clients through conferences and online events that allow us to interact one-on-one with the authors, as well as through referrals by our clients.

**TERMS** Agent receives 15% commission on domestic sales; 20% commission on foreign sales. Offers written contract, binding for 1 year.

**RECENT SALES** Agency sold 65 titles in the last year, including *Lies She Told* by Cate Holahan (Crooked Lane Books); *American Operator*, by Brian Andrews and Jeffrey Wilson (Thomas & Mercer); *Reset*, by Brian Andrews (Thomas & Mercer); *A Lover's Pinch*, by Peter Tupper (Rowman & Littlefield); *Everlasting Nora*, by Marie Cruz (Tor); *A Borrowing of Bones*, by Paula Munier (St. Martin's); *Muslim Girls Rise*, by Saira Mir (Salaam Reads), *Belabored*, by Lyz Lenz (Nation Books); *Tarnished Are The Stars*, by Rosiee Thor (Scholastic): *The Complicated Math of Two Plus One*, by Cathleen Barnhart (Harper Children's); and many others.

**WRITERS CONFERENCES** Members of the agency usually appear at BEA, Thrillerfest, Bouchercon, Killer Nashville, New England Mystery Writers Crimebake, New York Pitch, The Monterey Writers Retreat and many other events. Please check each agent's page on our website for updated lists of their appearances.

**TIPS** "Know your market and how to reach them. A strong platform is essential in your book proposal. Can you effectively use social media/Are you a strong networker: Are you familiar with the book bloggers in your genre? Are you involved with the interest-specific groups that can help you? What can you do to break through the 'noise' and help present your book to your readers? Check our website for more tips and information on this topic."

**TESSLER LITERARY AGENCY, LLC**
27 W. 20th St., Suite 1003, New York NY 10011. (212)242-0466. **Website:** www.tessleragency.com.

**Contact:** Michelle Tessler. Estab. 2004. Member of AAR, Women's Media Group.

○ Prior to forming her own agency, Ms. Tessler worked at the prestigious literary agency Carlisle & Company (now Inkwell Management) and at the William Morris Agency.

**REPRESENTS** Nonfiction, fiction, novels. **Considers these nonfiction areas:** animals, autobiography, biography, business, cooking, creative nonfiction, cultural interests, current affairs, diet/nutrition, economics, education, environment, ethnic, foods, gardening, health, history, horticulture, how-to, humor, investigative, literature, medicine, memoirs, military, money, multicultural, parenting, philosophy, photography, popular culture, psychology, religious, science, self-help, spirituality, technology, travel, women's issues, women's studies. **Considers these fiction areas:** commercial, ethnic, family saga, historical, literary, multicultural, women's.

☛ "Tessler Literary Agency represents a select number of best-selling and emerging authors. Based in the Flatiron District in Manhattan, we are dedicated to writers of high quality fiction and nonfiction. Our clients include accomplished journalists, scientists, academics, experts in their field, as well as novelists and debut authors with unique voices and stories to tell. We value fresh, original writing that has a compelling point of view. Our list is diverse and far-reaching. In nonfiction, it includes narrative, popular science, memoir, history, psychology, business, biography, food, and travel. In many cases, we sign authors who are especially adept at writing books that cross many of these categories at once. In fiction, we represent literary, women's, and commercial. If your project is in keeping with the kind of books we take on, we want to hear from you." Does not want genre fiction or children's books or anthologies.

**HOW TO CONTACT** Submit query through online query form only. Accepts simultaneous submissions. New clients by queries/submissions through the website and recommendations from others.

**TERMS** Receives 15% commission on domestic sales; 20% on foreign sales. Offers written contract.

## THOMPSON LITERARY AGENCY

48 Great Jones St., #5F, New York NY 10012. (716)257-8153. **E-mail:** info@thompsonliterary.com. **Website:** thompsonliterary.com. **Contact:** Meg Thompson, founder. Estab. 2014. Member of AAR. Signatory of WGA.

○ Before her current position, Ms. Thompson was with LJK Literary and the Einstein Thompson Agency.

**MEMBER AGENTS** Kiele Raymond, senior agent; John Thorn, affiliate agent; Sandy Hodgman, director of foreign rights; Meg Thompson; Samantha Wekstein.

**REPRESENTS** Nonfiction, fiction, novels, juvenile books. **Considers these nonfiction areas:** autobiography, biography, business, cooking, crafts, creative nonfiction, current affairs, diet/nutrition, design, education, foods, health, history, how-to, humor, inspirational, interior design, juvenile nonfiction, memoirs, multicultural, popular culture, politics, science, self-help, sociology, sports, travel, women's issues, women's studies, young adult. **Considers these fiction areas:** commercial, contemporary issues, experimental, fantasy, feminist, historical, juvenile, literary, middle grade, multicultural, picture books, women's, young adult.

☛ The agency is always on the lookout for both commercial and literary fiction, as well as young adult and children's books. "Nonfiction, however, is our specialty, and our interests include biography, memoir, music, popular science, politics, blog-to-book projects, cookbooks, sports, health and wellness, fashion, art, and popular culture. Please note that we do not accept submissions for poetry collections or screenplays, and we only consider picture books by established illustrators."

**HOW TO CONTACT** "For fiction: Please send a query letter, including any salient biographical information or previous publications, and attach the first 25 pages of your manuscript. For nonfiction: Please send a query letter and a full proposal, including biographical information, previous publications, credentials that qualify you to write your book, marketing information, and sample material. You should address your query to whichever agent you think is best suited for your project." Use QueryManager. Accepts simultaneous submissions. Responds in 6 weeks if interested.

## THREE SEAS LITERARY AGENCY

P.O. Box 444, Sun Prairie WI 53590. (608)834-9317. **E-mail:** threeseaslit@aol.com. **E-mail:** See website for individual submission information. **Website:** three-seasagency.com. **Contact:** Michelle Grajkowski, Cori Deyoe, Stacey Graham. Estab. 2000. Member of AAR, RWA (Romance Writers of America), SCBWI. Represents 85 clients.

Since its inception, Three Seas has sold more than 900 titles worldwide. Ms. Grajkowski's authors have appeared on all the major lists including *The New York Times*, *USA Today* and *Publishers Weekly*. Prior to joining the agency in 2006, Ms. Deyoe was a multi-published author. She represents a wide range of authors and has sold many projects at auction.

**MEMBER AGENTS** Michelle Grajkowski (romance, women's fiction, young adult and middle grade fiction, select nonfiction projects); Cori Deyoe (all sub-genres of romance, women's fiction, young adult, middle grade, picture books, thrillers, mysteries and select nonfiction); Stacey Graham (women's fiction, thrillers, young adult, middle grade and romance).

**REPRESENTS** Nonfiction, fiction, novels, novellas, juvenile books, scholarly books. **Considers these nonfiction areas:** autobiography, biography, business, child guidance, cooking, crafts, cultural interests, economics, education, foods, gardening, government, health, history, hobbies, how-to, humor, inspirational, juvenile nonfiction, money, parenting, popular culture, politics, psychology, recreation, regional, religious, satire, science, self-help, sociology, spirituality, technology, travel, women's issues, women's studies, young adult. **Considers these fiction areas:** middle grade, mystery, picture books, romance, thriller, women's, young adult.

"We represent more than 85 authors who write romance, women's fiction, science fiction/fantasy, thrillers, young adult and middle grade fiction, as well as select nonfiction titles. Currently, we are looking for fantastic authors with a voice of their own." 3 Seas does not represent poetry or screenplays.

**HOW TO CONTACT** Please use the links below for the query submission form. Michelle: http://QueryManager.com/Michelle3Seas; Cori: https://QueryManager.com/Cori3Seas; Stacey: http://QueryManager.com/Stacey3Seas. Accepts simultaneous submissions. Each agent has their own submission process. Obtains most new clients through recommendations from others, conferences.

**TERMS** Agent receives 15% commission on domestic sales; 20% commission on foreign sales. Offers written contract.

**RECENT SALES** Bestselling authors include Abby Jimenez, former Governor Martin Schreiber, Liz Talley, Jennifer Brown, Katie MacAlister, Kerrelyn Sparks, and C. L. Wilson.

## TRANSATLANTIC LITERARY AGENCY

2 Bloor St. E., Suite 3500, Toronto ON M4W 1A8 Canada. (416)488-9214. **E-mail:** info@transatlanticagency.com. **Website:** transatlanticagency.com.

**MEMBER AGENTS** Amy Tompkins (adult: literary fiction, historical fiction, women's fiction including smart romance, narrative nonfiction, and quirky or original how-to books; children's: early readers, middle grade, young adult, and new adult); Samantha Haywood (literary fiction and upmarket commercial fiction, specifically literary thrillers and upmarket mystery, historical fiction, smart contemporary fiction, upmarket women's fiction and cross-over novels; narrative nonfiction, including investigative journalism, politics, women's issues, memoirs, environmental issues, historical narratives, sexuality, true crime; graphic novels (fiction/nonfiction): preferably full-length graphic novels, story collections considered, memoirs, biographies, travel narratives); Marie Campbell (middle grade fiction); Shaun Bradley (referrals only; adult literary fiction and narrative nonfiction, primarily science and investigative journalism); Sandra Bishop (fiction; nonfiction: biography, memoir, and positive or humorous how-to books on advice/relationships, mind/body/spirit, religion, healthy living, finances, life-hacks, traveling, living a better life); Fiona Kenshole (children's and young adult; only accepting submissions from referrals or conferences she attends as faculty); Elizabeth Bennett; Marilyn Biderman; Evan Brown; Cody Caetano; Laura Cameron; Andrea Cascardi; Brenna English-Loeb; Rob Firing; Carolyn Forde; Devon Halliday; Chelene Knight; Amanda Orozco; Timothy Travaglini; Leonicka Valcius.

**REPRESENTS** Nonfiction, novels, juvenile books.

"In both children's and adult literature, we market directly into the US, the United Kingdom and Canada." Represents adult and children's authors of all genres, including illustrators. Does not want to receive picture books, musicals, screenplays or stage plays.

**HOW TO CONTACT** Always refer to the website, as guidelines will change, and only various agents are open to new clients at any given time. Obtains most new clients through recommendations from others.

**TERMS** Agent receives 15% commission on domestic sales; 20% commission on foreign sales. Offers written contract; 45-day notice must be given to terminate contract. This agency charges for photocopying and postage when it exceeds $100.

**RECENT SALES** Sold 250 titles in the last year.

## ⊘ S©OTT TREIMEL NY

Scotty T., Inc., 434 Lafayette St., New York NY 10003. (212)505-8353. **E-mail:** general@scotttreimelny.com; submissions@scotttreimelny.com. **Website:** www. scotttreimelny.com. Estab. 1995. Member of AAR, The Authors Guild, SCBWI, PEN America.

 Mr. Treimel began his career as an assistant to Marilyn E. Marlow at Curtis Brown, a rights agent for Scholastic, a book packager and rights agent for United Feature Syndicate, a freelance editor, a rights consultant for HarperCollins Children's Books, and the founding director of Warner Bros. Worldwide Publishing.

**MEMBER AGENTS** Scott Treimel.

**REPRESENTS** Juvenile books. **Considers these nonfiction areas:** juvenile nonfiction, young adult. **Considers these fiction areas:** cartoon, hi-lo, juvenile, middle grade, new adult, picture books, young adult. All children's categories from board books through older YA, includes picture books, easy readers, chapter books, series, etc.

 This agency specializes in tightly focused segments of the trade and institutional markets, representing both authors and illustrators of books for children and teens, MG novels, YA.

**HOW TO CONTACT** No longer accepts unsolicited submissions. Wants—via e-mail only—queries from writers recommended by his clients and/or editor pals or that he has met at conferences. Accepts simultaneous submissions.

**TERMS** Agent receives 15% commission on domestic sales; 20% commission on foreign sales. Offers verbal or written contract, standard terms. Only charges fees for books needed to sell subsidiary rights—foreign, film, etc.

**RECENT SALES** *Misunderstood Shark*, by Ame Dyckman (Scholastic); *Tiny Barbarian*, by Ame Dyckman (HarperCollins); *The Purple Puffy Coat*, by Maribeth Boelts (Candlewick); *Other Word-ly*, by Yee-Lum Mak (Chronicle); *The Magician's Visit*, by Barbara Diamond Golden (Apples & Honey Press); *How Dinosaurs Went Extinct: A Safety Guide*, by Ame Dyckman (Little Brown); *The New Kid Has Fleas,* by Ame Dyckman (Roaring Brook Press); *Alaina*, by Eloise Greenfield (Alazar Press); *The Women Who Caught the Babies*, by Eloise Greenfield (Alazar Press).

**WRITERS CONFERENCES** Avalon Full Manuscript Writers Retreat; Pacific Coast Children's Writers Workshop; Pikes Peak Writers' Conference; Southwest Writers' Conference; SCBWI NY, NJ, PA, NC, SC, VA, Bologna; The New School.

**TIPS** "We look for dedicated authors and illustrators able to sustain longtime careers in our increasingly competitive field. I want fresh, not derivative story concepts with overly familiar characters. We look for gripping stories, characters, pacing, and themes. We read for an authentic (to the age) point-of-view, and look for original voices. We spend significant time hunting for the best new work and do launch debut talent each year. It is best not to send warm-up manuscripts or those already seen all over town."

## TRIADA US

P.O. Box 561, Sewickley PA 15143. (412)401-3376. **E-mail:** uwe@triadaus.com; brent@triadaus.com; laura@triadaus.com; lauren@triadaus.com; amelia@triadaus.com; elle@triadaus.com. **Website:** www.triadaus.com. **Contact:** Dr. Uwe Stender, President. Estab. 2004. Member of AAR.

**MEMBER AGENTS** Uwe Stender; Brent Taylor; Laura Crockett; Lauren Spieller; Amelia Appel; Elle Thompson.

**REPRESENTS** Nonfiction, fiction, novels, juvenile books. **Considers these nonfiction areas:** biography, business, cooking, crafts, creative nonfiction, cultural interests, current affairs, diet/nutrition, economics, education, environment, ethnic, foods, gardening, health, history, how-to, juvenile nonfiction, literature, memoirs, music, parenting, popular culture, politics, science, self-help, sports, true crime, women's issues, young adult. **Considers these fiction areas:** action, adventure, comic books, commercial, contemporary issues, crime, detective, ethnic, family saga, fantasy, feminist, gay, historical, horror, juvenile, lesbian, literary, mainstream, middle grade, multicultural, mystery, occult, picture books, police, suspense, thriller, urban fantasy, women's, young adult.

☛ Actively seeking fiction and nonfiction across a broad range of categories of all age levels.

**HOW TO CONTACT** E-mail queries preferred. Please paste your query letter and the first 10 pages of your ms into the body of a message e-mailed to the agent of your choice. Do not simultaneously query multiple Triada agents. Please query one and wait for their response before moving on to another agent within our agency. Triada US agents personally respond to all queries and requested material and pride themselves on having some of the fastest response times in the industry. Obtains most new clients through submission inbox (query letters and requested mss), client referrals, and conferences.

**TERMS** Triada US retains 15% commission on domestic sales and 20% commission on foreign and translation sales. Offers written contract; 30-day notice must be given prior to termination.

**RECENT SALES** *Always Young And Restless* by Melody Thomas Scott (Diversion Books), *Roman And Jewel* by Dana L. Davis (HarperCollins/Inkyard), *The Obsession* by Jesse Q. Sutanto (Sourcebooks), *Hani And Ishu's Guide To Fake Dating* by Adiba Jaigirdar (Page Street Kids), *Force of Fire* by Sayantani DasGupta (Scholastic), *Just Pretend* by Tori Sharp (Little, Brown), *Poultrygeist* by Eric Geron (Candlewick), *Red, White, and Whole* by Rajani LaRocca (Quill Tree), *Don't Date Rosa Santos* by Nina Moreno (Little Brown Young Readers), *These Violent Delights* by Chloe Gong (McElderry Books), *The Jasmine Throne* by Tasha Suri (Orbit), *Malice* by Heather Walter (Del Rey), *Within These Wicked Walls* by Lauren Blackwood (Wednesday Books), *Flower Crowns & Fearsome Things* by amanda lovelace (Andrews McMeel), *Barakah Beats* by Maleeha Siddiqui (Scholastic), *The Kill Club* by Wendy Heard (Mira), *The Devil Makes Three* by Tori Bovalino (Page Street Kids), *Throw Like a Girl, Cheer Like a Boy* by Robyn Ryle (Rowman & Littlefield Publishers), *The Unexpected Guest* by Michael Konik (Diversion Books).

## TRIDENT MEDIA GROUP

355 Lexington Ave., Floor 12, New York NY 10017. (212)333-1511. **E-mail:** info@tridentmediagroup.com.

**Website:** www.tridentmediagroup.com. **Contact:** Ellen Levine. Member of AAR.

**MEMBER AGENTS** Scott Miller, smiller@tridentmediagroup.com (commercial fiction, including thrillers, crime fiction, women's, book club fiction, middle grade, young adult; nonfiction, including military, celebrity and pop culture, narrative, sports, prescriptive, and current events); Don Fehr, dfehr@tridentmediagroup.com (literary and commercial fiction, young adult fiction, narrative nonfiction, memoirs, travel, science, and health); Erica Spellman-Silverman; Ellen Levine, levine.assistant@tridentmediagroup.com (popular commercial fiction and compelling nonfiction, including memoir, popular culture, narrative nonfiction, history, politics, biography, science, and the odd quirky book); Mark Gottlieb (fiction: science fiction, fantasy, young adult, graphic novels, historical, middle grade, mystery, romance, suspense, thrillers; nonfiction: business, finance, history, religious, health, cookbooks, sports, African-American, biography, memoir, travel, mind/body/spirit, narrative nonfiction, science, technology); Alexander Slater, aslater@tridentmdiagroup.com (children's, middle grade, and young adult fiction); Alexa Stark, astark@tridentmediagroup.com (literary fiction, upmarket commercial fiction, young adult, memoir, narrative nonfiction, popular science, cultural criticism and women's issues); Amanda Annis; Martha Wydysh; Tess Weitzner.

**REPRESENTS** Considers these nonfiction areas: biography, business, cooking, creative nonfiction, current affairs, economics, health, history, memoirs, military, popular culture, politics, religious, science, sports, technology, travel, women's issues, young adult, middle grade. **Considers these fiction areas:** commercial, crime, fantasy, historical, juvenile, literary, middle grade, mystery, new adult, paranormal, picture books, romance, science fiction, suspense, thriller, women's, young adult.

☛ Actively seeking new or established authors in a variety of fiction and nonfiction genres.

**HOW TO CONTACT** Submit through the agency's online submission form on the agency website. Query only one agent at a time. If you e-query, include no attachments. Accepts simultaneous submissions.

**TIPS** "If you have any questions, please check FAQ page before e-mailing us."

## UNION LITERARY

30 Vandam St., Suite 5A, New York NY 10013. (212)255-2112. **E-mail:** info@unionliterary.com; submissions@unionliterary.com. **Website:** http://unionliterary.com. Member of AAR. Signatory of WGA.

○ Prior to becoming an agent, Trena Keating was editor-in-chief of Dutton and associate publisher of Plume, both imprints of Penguin, senior editor at HarperCollins, and humanities assistant at Stanford University Press.

**MEMBER AGENTS** Trena Keating, tk@unionliterary.com (fiction and nonfiction, specifically a literary novel with an exotic setting, a YA/MG journey or transformation novel, a distinctly modern novel with a female protagonist, a creepy page-turner, a quest memoir that addresses larger issues, nonfiction based on primary research or a unique niche, a great essayist, and a voicy writer who is a great storyteller or makes her laugh); Sally Wofford-Girand, swg@unionliterary.com (history, memoir, women's issues, cultural studies, gripping literary fiction); Jenni Ferrari-Adler, jenni@unionliterary.com (fiction, cookbook/food, young adult and middle grade, narrative nonfiction); Christina Clifford, christina@unionliterary.com (literary fiction, international fiction, narrative nonfiction, specifically historical biography, memoir, business, and science).

➤ "Union Literary is a full-service boutique agency specializing in literary fiction, popular fiction, narrative nonfiction, memoir, social history, business and general big idea books, popular science, cookbooks and food writing." The agency does not represent romance, poetry, science fiction or illustrated books.

**HOW TO CONTACT** Nonfiction submissions: include a query letter, a proposal and a sample chapter. Fiction submissions: should include a query letter, synopsis, and either sample pages or full ms. "Due to the high volume of submissions we receive, we will only be in contact regarding projects that feel like a match for the respective agent." Accepts simultaneous submissions. Responds in 1 month.

**RECENT SALES** *White Ivy*, by Susie Yang; *Weather*, by Jenny Offill; *The Nightworkers*, by Brian Selfon; *You Know You Want This*, by Kristen Roupenian.

## UNITED TALENT AGENCY

888 7th Ave., 7th Floor, New York NY 10106. (212)659-2600. **Website:** unitedtalent.com. **Contact:** Marc Gerald.

○ Prior to becoming an agent, Mr. Gerald owned and ran an independent publishing and entertainment agency.

**MEMBER AGENTS** Marc Gerald (no queries); Juliet Mushens, UK Literary division, juliet.mushens@unitedtalent.com (high-concept novels, thrillers, YA, historical fiction, literary fiction, psychological suspense, reading group fiction, SF and fantasy); Sasha Raskin, sasah.raskin@unitedtalent.com (popular science, business books, historical narrative nonfiction, narrative and/or literary nonfiction, historical fiction, and genre fiction like sci-fi but when it fits the crossover space and isn't strictly confined to its genre); Sarah Manning, sarah.manning@unitedtalent.com (enjoys crime, thrillers, historical fiction, commercial women's fiction, accessible literary fiction, fantasy and YA); Diana Beaumont, UK Literary division, diana.beaumont@unitedtalent.com (accessible literary fiction with a strong hook, historical fiction, crime, thrillers, women's commercial fiction that isn't too marshmallowy, cookery, lifestyle, celebrity books and memoir with a distinctive voice).

**REPRESENTS** Nonfiction, novels. **Considers these nonfiction areas:** business, cooking, history, memoirs, popular science, narrative nonfiction, literary nonfiction, lifestyle, celebrity. **Considers these fiction areas:** commercial, crime, fantasy, historical, literary, science fiction, suspense, thriller, women's, young adult.

**HOW TO CONTACT** To query Juliet: Please send your cover letter, first 3 chapters and synopsis by e-mail. Juliet replies to all submissions, and aims to respond within 8-12 weeks of receipt of e-mail. To query Sasha: e-query. To query Sarah: Please send you cover letter in the body of your e-mail with synopsis and first 3 chapters by e-mail. She responds to all submissions within 8-12 weeks. Accepts simultaneous submissions.

## THE UNTER AGENCY

23 W. 73rd St., Suite 100, New York NY 10023. (212)401-4068. **E-mail:** jennifer@theunteragency.com. **Website:** www.theunteragency.com. **Contact:** Jennifer Unter. Estab. 2008. Member of AAR, Women Media Group.

Ms. Unter began her book publishing career in the editorial department at Henry Holt & Co. She later worked at the Karpfinger Agency while she attended law school. She then became an associate at the entertainment firm of Cowan, DeBaets, Abrahams & Sheppard LLP where she practiced primarily in the areas of publishing and copyright law.

**REPRESENTS** Nonfiction, fiction, novels, short story collections, juvenile books. **Considers these nonfiction areas:** animals, art, autobiography, biography, cooking, creative nonfiction, current affairs, diet/nutrition, environment, foods, health, history, how-to, humor, juvenile nonfiction, law, memoirs, popular culture, politics, spirituality, sports, travel, true crime, women's issues, young adult, nature subjects. **Considers these fiction areas:** action, adventure, cartoon, commercial, family saga, inspirational, juvenile, mainstream, middle grade, mystery, paranormal, picture books, thriller, women's, young adult.

This agency specializes in children's, nonfiction, and quality fiction.

**HOW TO CONTACT** Send an e-query. There is also an online submission form. If you do not hear back from this agency within 3 months, consider that a no. Accepts simultaneous submissions. Responds in 3 months.

**RECENT SALES** A full list of recent sales/titles is available on the agency website.

## UPSTART CROW LITERARY

594 Dean St., Office 47, Brooklyn NY 11238. **Website:** www.upstartcrowliterary.com. **Contact:** Danielle Chiotti, Alexandra Penfold. Estab. 2009. Member of AAR. Signatory of WGA.

**MEMBER AGENTS** Michael Stearns (not accepting submissions); Danielle Chiotti (all genres of young adult and middle grade fiction; adult upmarket commercial fiction [not considering romance, mystery/suspense/thriller, science fiction, horror, or erotica]; nonfiction in the areas of narrative/memoir, lifestyle, relationships, humor, current events, food, wine, and cooking); Ted Malawer (not accepting submissions); Alexandra Penfold (not accepting submissions); Susan Hawk (books for children and teens only); Kayla Cichello.

**REPRESENTS** **Considers these nonfiction areas:** cooking, current affairs, foods, humor, memoirs.

**Considers these fiction areas:** commercial, mainstream, middle grade, picture books, young adult.

**HOW TO CONTACT** Submit a query and 20 pages pasted into an e-mail. Accepts simultaneous submissions.

## VERITAS LITERARY AGENCY

601 Van Ness Ave., Opera Plaza, Suite E, San Francisco CA 94102. (415)647-7964. **Fax:** (415)647-6965. **E-mail:** submissions@veritasliterary.com. **Website:** www.veritasliterary.com. **Contact:** Katherine Boyle. Member of AAR, Author's Guild and SCBWI.

**MEMBER AGENTS** Katherine Boyle, katherine@veritasliterary.com (literary fiction, middle grade, young adult, narrative nonfiction/memoir, historical fiction, crime/suspense, history, pop culture, popular science, business/career); Michael Carr, michael@veritasliterary.com (historical fiction, women's fiction, science fiction and fantasy, nonfiction); Chiara Rosati, literary scout.

**REPRESENTS** Nonfiction, novels. **Considers these nonfiction areas:** business, history, memoirs, popular culture, women's issues. **Considers these fiction areas:** commercial, crime, fantasy, historical, literary, middle grade, new adult, science fiction, suspense, women's, young adult.

**HOW TO CONTACT** This agency accepts short queries or proposals via e-mail only. "Fiction: Please include a cover letter listing previously published work, a one-page summary and the first 5 pages in the body of the e-mail (not as an attachment). Nonfiction: If you are sending a proposal, please include an author biography, an overview, a chapter-by-chapter summary, and an analysis of competitive titles. We do our best to review all queries within 4-6 weeks; however, if you have not heard from us in 12 weeks, consider that a no." Accepts simultaneous submissions.

## WADE & CO. LITERARY AGENCY, LTD

33 Cormorant Lodge, Thomas More St., London E1W 1AU United Kingdom. (44)(207)488-4171. **E-mail:** rw@rwla.com. **Website:** www.rwla.com. **Contact:** Robin Wade. Estab. 2001.

Prior to opening his agency, Mr. Wade was an author.

**MEMBER AGENTS** Robin Wade.

**REPRESENTS** Nonfiction, fiction, novels.

"We are young and dynamic, and actively seek new writers across the literary spectrum."

Does not want to receive poetry, plays, screen-plays, young adult and children's books, film scripts, or short stories.

**HOW TO CONTACT** New proposals for full length adult books (excluding young adult, children's books or poetry, plays or film/tv scripts) are always welcome. We much prefer to receive queries and submissions by e-mail. There is no need to telephone in advance. Please provide a few details about yourself, a synopsis (i.e. a clear narrative summary of the complete story, of between say 1 and 6 pages in length) and the first 10,000 words or so (ideally as a Word doc or PDF attachments) over e-mail. Accepts simultaneous submissions. Responds in 1 week to queries; 1 month to mss.

**TERMS** Agent receives 10% commission on domestic sales; 20% commission on foreign sales. Offers written contract; 1-month notice must be given to terminate contract.

**TIPS** "We seek manuscripts that are well written, with strong characters and an original narrative voice. Our absolute priority is giving the best possible service to the authors we choose to represent, as well as maintaining routine friendly contact with them as we help develop their careers."

## WALES LITERARY AGENCY, INC.

1508 10th Ave. E. #401, Seattle WA 98102. (206)284-7114. **E-mail:** waleslit@waleslit.com. **Website:** www.waleslit.com. **Contact:** Elizabeth Wales; Neal Swain. Estab. 1990. Member of AAR. Other memberships include Authors Guild.

○  Prior to becoming an agent, Ms. Wales worked at Oxford University Press and Viking Penguin.

**MEMBER AGENTS** Elizabeth Wales; Neal Swain.

**REPRESENTS** Nonfiction, fiction, novels.

⚷  This agency specializes in quality mainstream fiction and narrative nonfiction. "We're looking for more narrative nonfiction writing about nature, science, and animals." Does not handle screenplays, children's picture books, genre fiction, or most category nonfiction (such as self-help or how-to books).

**HOW TO CONTACT** E-query with no attachments. Submission guidelines can be found at the agency website along with a list of current clients and titles. Accepts simultaneous submissions. Responds in 2 weeks to queries, 2 months to mss.

**TERMS** Agent receives 15% commission on domestic sales; 20% commission on foreign sales.

**RECENT SALES** *Wolf Odyssey* by Amaroq Weiss (Greystone); An untitled graphic novel by Josh Tuininga (Abrams); *Savage Love from A to Z* by Dan Savage (Sasquatch/Penguin Random House); *Rooted* by Lyanda Lynn Haupt (Little, Brown); *Half Broke*, by Ginger Gaffney (W.W. Norton).

**TIPS** "We are especially interested in work that espouses a progressive cultural or political view, projects a new voice, or simply shares an important, compelling story. We also encourage writers living in the Pacific Northwest, West Coast, Alaska, and Pacific Rim countries, and writers from historically underrepresented groups, such as gay and lesbian writers and writers of color, to submit work (but does not discourage writers outside these areas). Most importantly, whether in fiction or nonfiction, the agency is looking for talented storytellers."

## WATERSIDE PRODUCTIONS, INC.

2055 Oxford Ave., Cardiff CA 92007. (760)632-9190. **Fax:** (760)632-9295. **E-mail:** admin@waterside.com. **Website:** www.waterside.com. Estab. 1982.

**MEMBER AGENTS** Bill Gladstone (big nonfiction books); Margot Maley Hutchinson (computer, health, psychology, parenting, fitness, pop culture, and business); Carole Jelen, carole@jelenpub.com (innovation and thought leaders especially in business, technology, lifestyle and self-help); Jill Kramer, waterside-agentjk@aol.com (quality fiction with empowering themes for adults and YA (including crossovers); nonfiction, including mind-body-spirit, self-help, celebrity memoirs, relationships, sociology, finance, psychology, health and fitness, diet/nutrition, inspiration, business, family/parenting issues); Natasha Gladstone, (picture books, books with film tie-ins, books with established animated characters, and educational titles); Johanna Maaghul, johanna@waterside.com (nonfiction and select fiction); Kimberly Brabec, rights@waterside.com (Director of International Rights); Kristen Moeller (self-improvement/women); Michael Gosney.

**REPRESENTS Considers these nonfiction areas:** business, computers, diet/nutrition, health, inspirational, money, parenting, popular culture, psychology, self-help, sociology, technology, fitness. **Considers these fiction areas:** mainstream, picture books, young adult.

☞ Specializes in computer and technical titles, and also represents other nonfiction genres, including self-help, cooking, travel, and more. Note that most agents here are nonfiction only, so target your query to the appropriate agent.

**HOW TO CONTACT** "Please read each agent bio [on the website] to determine who you think would best represent your genre of work. When you have chosen your agent, please write his or her name in the subject line of your e-mail and send it to admin@waterside.com with your query letter in the body of the e-mail, and your proposal or sample material as an attached word document." Nonfiction submission guidelines are available on the website. Accepts simultaneous submissions. Obtains most new clients through referrals from established client and publisher list.

**TIPS** "For new writers, a quality proposal and a strong knowledge of the market you're writing for goes a long way toward helping us turn you into a published author. We like to see a strong author platform."

## ⊘ WATKINS LOOMIS AGENCY, INC.

P.O. Box 20925, New York NY 10025. (212)532-0080. **Fax:** (646)383-2449. **E-mail:** assistant@watkinsloomis.com. **Website:** www.watkinsloomis.com. Estab. 1980. Represents 50+ clients.

**MEMBER AGENTS** Gloria Loomis, president; Julia Masnik, junior agent.

**REPRESENTS** Nonfiction, novels. **Considers these nonfiction areas:** ethnic.

☞ This agency specializes in literary fiction, biography, memoir, and political journalism.

**HOW TO CONTACT** *No unsolicited mss.* This agency does not guarantee a response to queries.

**TERMS** Agent receives 15% commission on domestic sales; 20% commission on foreign sales.

**RECENT SALES** A list of sales is available on the agency website.

## WAXMAN LITERARY AGENCY, INC.

443 Park Ave. S, Suite 1004, New York NY 10016. **Fax:** (212)675-1381. **E-mail:** submit@waxmanagency.com. **Website:** www.waxmanagency.com.

**MEMBER AGENTS** Scott Waxman (nonfiction: history, biography, health and science, adventure, business, inspirational sports); Susan Canavan (narrative nonfiction, history, adventure, sports, memoir, journalism, health, science, pop culture, parenting,

nature, literary fiction, and historical fiction); Ashley Lopez (literary fiction, women's fiction (commercial and upmarket, memoir, narrative nonfiction, pop science/pop culture, cultural criticism).

**REPRESENTS** Nonfiction, fiction, novels, short story collections. **Considers these nonfiction areas:** biography, business, foods, health, history, humor, inspirational, memoirs, popular culture, science, sports, adventure. **Considers these fiction areas:** fantasy, historical, literary, mainstream, middle grade, mystery, paranormal, romance, science fiction, suspense, thriller, urban fantasy, women's, young adult.

**HOW TO CONTACT** To submit a project, please send a query letter only via e-mail to one of the addresses included on the website. Do not send attachments, though for fiction you may include 10 pages of your manuscript in the body of your e-mail. "Due to the high volume of submissions, agents will reach out to you directly if interested. The typical time range for consideration is 6-8 weeks. Please do not query more than 1 agent at our agency simultaneously." (To see the types of projects each agent is looking for, refer to the Agent Biographies page on website.) Accepts simultaneous submissions.

**TERMS** Agent receives 15% commission on domestic sales; 10% commission on foreign sales. Offers written contract; 2-month notice must be given to terminate contract.

## ⊘ CHERRY WEINER LITERARY AGENCY

925 Oak Bluff Ct., Dacula GA 30019-6660. (732)446-2096. **Fax:** (732)792-0506. **E-mail:** cherry8486@aol.com. **Contact:** Cherry Weiner. Estab. 1977. Represents 40 clients.

**REPRESENTS** Fiction, novels. **Considers these fiction areas:** action, adventure, commercial, contemporary issues, crime, detective, family saga, fantasy, frontier, gay, glitz, historical, horror, literary, mainstream, military, mystery, paranormal, police, psychic, romance, science fiction, supernatural, suspense, thriller, urban fantasy, westerns, women's.

☞ *This agency is currently not accepting new clients except by referral or by personal contact at writers' conferences.* Specializes in fantasy, science fiction, westerns, mysteries (both contemporary and historical), historical novels, Native American works, mainstream, and all genre romances. Children's, young adult, nonfiction or poetry.

**HOW TO CONTACT** Only wishes to receive submissions from referrals and from writers she has met at conferences/events. Responds in 1 week to queries; 2 months to requested mss.

**TERMS** Agent receives 15% commission on domestic sales; 15% commission on foreign sales. Offers written contract. Charges clients for extra copies of mss, first-class postage for author's copies, mailing of books first class, express mail for important documents/mss.

**RECENT SALES** This agency prefers not to share information on specific sales.

**TIPS** "Meet agents and publishers at conferences. Establish a relationship, then get in touch with them and remind them of the meeting and conference."

## THE WEINGEL-FIDEL AGENCY

310 E. 46th St., 21E, New York NY 10017. (212)599-2959. **Contact:** Loretta Weingel-Fidel.

○ Prior to opening her agency, Ms. Weingel-Fidel was a psychoeducational diagnostician.

**REPRESENTS** Nonfiction, fiction, novels. **Considers these nonfiction areas:** art, autobiography, biography, memoirs, investigative journalism. **Considers these fiction areas:** literary, mainstream.

☛ This agency specializes in commercial and literary fiction and nonfiction. Does not want to receive childrens books, self-help, science fiction, or fantasy.

**HOW TO CONTACT** Accepts writers by referral only. *No unsolicited mss.*

**TERMS** Agent receives 15% commission on domestic sales; 20% commission on foreign sales. Offers written contract, binding for 1 year with automatic renewal.

**TIPS** "A very small, selective list enables me to work very closely with my clients to develop and nurture talent. I only take on projects and writers about which I am extremely enthusiastic."

## WELLS ARMS LITERARY

In association with HSG Agency, New York NY. **Website:** www.wellsarms.com. Estab. 2013. Member of AAR, SCBWI, Society of Illustrators. Represents 25 clients.

○ Victoria's career began as an editor at Dial Books for Young Readers, then G. P. Putnam's Sons and then as the founding editorial director and Associate Publisher of Bloomsbury USA's Children's Division. She opened the agency in 2013.

**REPRESENTS** Nonfiction, fiction, novels, juvenile books, children's book illustrators. **Considers these nonfiction areas:** juvenile nonfiction, young adult. **Considers these fiction areas:** juvenile, middle grade, new adult, picture books, young adult.

☛ "We focus on books for young readers of all ages: board books, picture books, readers, chapter books, middle grade, and young adult fiction." Actively seeking middle grade, young adult, magical realism, contemporary, romance, fantasy. "We do not represent to the textbook, magazine, adult romance or fine art markets."

**HOW TO CONTACT** Wells Arms Literary is currently closed to queries or submissions "unless you've met me at a conference." Accepts simultaneous submissions. "We try to respond in a month's time." If no response, assume it's a no.

## WERNICK & PRATT AGENCY

**E-mail:** submissions@wernickpratt.com. **Website:** www.wernickpratt.com. **Contact:** Marcia Wernick; Linda Pratt; Emily Mitchell. Member of AAR. Signatory of WGA, SCBWI.

○ Prior to co-founding Wernick & Pratt Agency, Ms. Wernick worked at the Sheldon Fogelman Agency, in subsidiary rights, advancing to director of subsidiary rights; Ms. Pratt also worked at the Sheldon Fogelman Agency. Emily Mitchell began her publishing career at Sheldon Fogelman Agency and then spent eleven years as an editor at Charlesbridge Publishing.

**MEMBER AGENTS** Marcia Wernick, Linda Pratt, Emily Mitchell, Shannon Gallagher.

**REPRESENTS** Juvenile books. **Considers these fiction areas:** middle grade, young adult.

☛ "Wernick & Pratt Agency specializes in children's books of all genres, from picture books through young adult literature and everything in between. We represent both authors and illustrators. We do not represent authors of adult books." Wants people who both write and illustrate in the picture book genre; humorous young chapter books with strong voice, and which are unique and compelling; middle grade/YA novels, both literary and commercial. No picture book mss of more than 750 words, or mood pieces; work specifically targeted to the educational market; fiction about the American Revolution, Civil War, or World War II unless it is told from a very unique perspective.

**HOW TO CONTACT** Submit via e-mail only to submissions@wernickpratt.com. "Please indicate to which agent you are submitting." Detailed submission guidelines available on website. "Submissions will only be responded to further if we are interested in them. If you do not hear from us within 6 weeks of your submission, it should be considered declined." Accepts simultaneous submissions. Responds in 6 weeks.

## ☾ WESTWOOD CREATIVE ARTISTS, LTD.

386 Huron St., Toronto ON M5S 2G6 Canada. (416)964-3302. **E-mail:** submissions@wcaltd.com. **Website:** www.wcaltd.com. Represents 350+ clients.

**MEMBER AGENTS** Jackie Kaiser (President and COO); Michael A. Levine (Chairman); Hilary McMahon (Executive Vice President, fiction, nonfiction, children's); John Pearce (fiction and nonfiction); Bruce Westwood (Founder, Managing Director and CEO); Chris Casuccio; Emmy Nordstrom Higdon; Max Alexandre Tremblay; Meg Wheeler.

**REPRESENTS** Nonfiction, fiction, novels. **Considers these nonfiction areas:** biography, current affairs, history, parenting, science, journalism, practical nonfiction. **Considers these fiction areas:** commercial, juvenile, literary, thriller, women's, young adult.

☛ "We take on children's and young adult writers very selectively. The agents bring their diverse interests to their client lists, but are generally looking for authors with a mastery of language, a passionate, expert or original perspective on their subject, and a gift for storytelling. Please note that WCA does not represent screenwriters, and our agents are not currently seeking poetry or children's picture book submissions."

**HOW TO CONTACT** E-query only. Include credentials, synopsis, and no more than 10 pages. No attachments. Accepts simultaneous submissions.

**TIPS** "We will reject outright complete, unsolicited manuscripts, or projects that are presented poorly in the query letter. We prefer to receive exclusive submissions and request that you do not query more than one agent at the agency simultaneously. It's often best if you approach WCA after you have accumulated some publishing credits."

## WHIMSY LITERARY AGENCY, LLC

49 N. 8th St., 6G, Brooklyn NY 11249. (212)674-7162. **E-mail:** whimsynyc@aol.com. **Contact:** Jackie Meyer and Aria Gmitter, agents. Represents 35 clients.

○ Prior to becoming an agent, Ms. Meyer was a VP at Warner Books (now Grand Central/Hachette) for 20 years.

**MEMBER AGENTS** Jackie Meyer.

**REPRESENTS** Nonfiction. **Considers these nonfiction areas:** art, autobiography, biography, business, child guidance, cooking, current affairs, diet/nutrition, design, education, foods, gardening, health, history, how-to, humor, inspirational, interior design, literature, memoirs, money, multicultural, New Age, parenting, popular culture, politics, psychology, self-help, spirituality, technology, women's issues.

☛ "Whimsy looks for nonfiction projects that are concept- and platform-driven. We seek books that educate, inspire, and entertain." Actively seeking experts in their field with integrated and established platforms.

**HOW TO CONTACT** Send your proposal via e-mail to whimsynyc@aol.com (include your media platform, table of contents with full description of each chapter). First-time authors: "We appreciate proposals that are professional and complete. Please consult the many fine books available on writing book proposals. We are not considering poetry or screenplays. Please note: Due to the volume of queries and submissions, we are unable to respond unless they are of interest to us." Accepts simultaneous submissions. Responds "quickly, but only if interested" to queries. *Does not accept unsolicited mss.* Obtains most new clients through recommendations from others, solicitations.

**TERMS** Agent receives 15% commission on domestic sales; 20% commission on foreign sales. Offers written contract.

## PEREGRINE WHITTLESEY AGENCY

279 Central Park W., New York NY 10024. (212)787-1802. **Fax:** (212)787-4985. **E-mail:** pwwagy@aol.com. **Contact:** Peregrine Whittlesey. Estab. 1986. Signatory of WGA. Represents 30 clients.

○ Founder of the Manhattan Theatre Club, assistant to Elaine May, Literary Manager at the Goodman Theatre, Lit department of the Public Theatre, correspondent for "Plaisir du Theatre" for Antenne 2.

**REPRESENTS** Theatrical stage play, stage plays.

☞ This agency specializes in playwrights who also write for screen and TV.

**HOW TO CONTACT** Query with SASE. Prefers to read materials exclusively. Accepts simultaneous submissions. Responds in 1 week to queries; 1 month to mss. Obtains most new clients through recommendations from others and occasional over the transom submissions.

**TERMS** Agent receives 10% commission on domestic sales; 15% commission on foreign sales. Offers written contract, binding for 2 years.

**RECENT SALES** Portland Stage, Northern Stage, NJ Rep, 59E59, Colony Theatre, Stratford Shakespeare Festival, Canadian Stage, Huntington Theatre Company, Alliance Theatre, New York Theatre Workshop, Signature Theater Company, ACT San Francisco, Teatro Dallas, Actor's Shakespeare, Repertorio Español.

## WOLFSON LITERARY AGENCY

P.O. Box 266, New York NY 10276. **E-mail:** query@wolfsonliterary.com. **Website:** www.wolfsonliterary.com. **Contact:** Michelle Wolfson. Estab. 2007. Adheres to AAR canon of ethics.

○ Prior to forming her own agency in December 2007, Ms. Wolfson spent 2 years with Artists & Artisans, Inc. and 2 years with Ralph Vicinanza, Ltd.

**REPRESENTS** Nonfiction, fiction. **Considers these fiction areas:** commercial, ethnic, family saga, fantasy, gay, lesbian, mainstream, multicultural, new adult, paranormal, romance, sports, thriller, women's, young adult.

☞ Actively seeking commercial fiction: young adult, mainstream, women's fiction, romance. "I am not taking on new nonfiction clients at this time."

**HOW TO CONTACT** E-queries only. Accepts simultaneous submissions. Responds only if interested. Positive response is generally given within 2-4 weeks. Responds in 3 months to mss. Obtains most new clients through queries or recommendations from others.

**TERMS** Agent receives 15% commission on domestic sales; 25% commission on foreign sales. Offers written contract; 30-day notice must be given to terminate contract.

**TIPS** "Be persistent."

## WORDSERVE LITERARY GROUP

7500 E. Arapahoe Rd., Suite 285, Centennial CO 80112. **E-mail:** admin@wordserveliterary.com. **Website:** www.wordserveliterary.com. **Contact:** Greg Johnson. Estab. 2003. Represents 180 clients.

○ Prior to becoming an agent in 1994, Mr. Johnson was a magazine editor and freelance writer of more than 20 books and 200 articles.

**MEMBER AGENTS** Greg Johnson, Nick Harrison, Sarah Freese, and Keely Boeving.

**REPRESENTS** Nonfiction, fiction, novels. **Considers these nonfiction areas:** biography, business, cooking, creative nonfiction, current affairs, diet/nutrition, health, history, inspirational, literature, memoirs, military, money, parenting, religious, self-help, sports, war, women's issues. **Considers these fiction areas:** historical, inspirational, juvenile, literary, mainstream, military, religious, spiritual, suspense, thriller, war, women's, young adult.

☞ Materials with a faith-based angle, as well as the general market categories of business, health, history, military. No gift books, poetry, short stories, screenplays, graphic novels, children's picture books, science fiction or fantasy. Please do not send mss that are more than 120,000 words.

**HOW TO CONTACT** E-query admin@wordserveliterary.com. In the subject line, include the word "query." All queries should include the following three elements: a pitch for the book, information about you and your platform (for nonfiction) or writing background (for fiction), and the first 5 (or so) pages of the manuscript pasted into the e-mail. Please view our website for full guidelines: http://www.wordserveliterary.com/submission-guidlines/. Accepts simultaneous submissions. Response within 60 days. Obtains most new clients through recommendations from others.

**TERMS** Agent receives 15% commission on domestic sales; 10-15% commission on foreign sales. Offers written contract; up to 60-day notice must be given to terminate contract.

**TIPS** "We are looking for good proposals, great writing and authors willing to market their books. We specialize in projects with a faith element bent. See the website before submitting. Though we are not a member of AAR, we abide by all of the rules for agents."

## WRITERS HOUSE

21 W. 26th St., New York NY 10010. (212)685-2400. **Fax:** (212)685-1781. **Website:** www.writershouse.com. Estab. 1973. Member of AAR.

**MEMBER AGENTS** Amy Berkower; Stephen Barr; Susan Cohen; Dan Conaway; Lisa DiMona; Susan Ginsburg; Susan Golomb; Merrilee Heifetz; Brianne Johnson; Daniel Lazar; Simon Lipskar; Steven Malk; Jodi Reamer, Esq.; Robin Rue; Rebecca Sherman; Geri Thoma; Albert Zuckerman; Alec Shane; Stacy Testa; Victoria Doherty-Munro; Beth Miller; Andrea Morrison; Johanna V. Castillo; Lindsay Davis Auld; Alexandra Levick; Hannah Mann; Rebecca Eskildsen; Meredith Viguet.

**REPRESENTS** Nonfiction, novels. **Considers these nonfiction areas:** biography, business, cooking, economics, history, how-to, juvenile nonfiction, memoirs, parenting, psychology, science, self-help. **Considers these fiction areas:** commercial, fantasy, juvenile, literary, mainstream, middle grade, picture books, science fiction, women's, young adult.

☛ This agency specializes in all types of popular fiction and nonfiction, for both adult and juvenile books as well as illustrators. Does not want to receive scholarly, professional, poetry, plays, or screenplays.

**HOW TO CONTACT** Individual agent email addresses are available on the website. "Please e-mail us a query letter, which includes your credentials, an explanation of what makes your book unique and special, and a synopsis. Some agents within our agency have different requirements. Please consult their individual Publishers Marketplace (PM) profile for details. We respond to all queries, generally within six to eight weeks." If you prefer to submit by mail, address it to an individual agent, and please include SASE for our reply. (If submitting to Steven Malk: Writers House, 7660 Fay Ave., #338H, La Jolla, CA 92037.) Accepts simultaneous submissions. Obtains most new clients through recommendations from authors and editors.

**TERMS** Agent receives 15% commission on domestic sales. Agent receives 20% commission on foreign sales. Offers written contract, binding for 1 year. Agency charges fees for copying mss/proposals and overseas airmail of books.

**TIPS** "Do not send mss. Write a compelling letter. If you do, we'll ask to see your work. Follow submission guidelines and please do not simultaneously submit your work to more than one Writers House agent."

## WRITERS HOUSE

7660 Fay Ave., #338H, La Jolla CA 92037. **E-mail:** smalk@writershouse.com. **Website:** writershouse. com. **Contact:** Steve Malk. Member of AAR. Signatory of WGA.

**HOW TO CONTACT** Accepts simultaneous submissions.

## WRITERS' REPRESENTATIVES, LLC

116 W. 14th St., 11th Floor, New York NY 10011-7305. (212)620-0023. **E-mail:** transom@writersreps.com. **Website:** www.writersreps.com. **Contact:** Glen Hartley. Estab. 1985. Represents 120 clients.

◐ Prior to becoming an agent, Ms. Chu was a lawyer; Mr. Hartley worked at Simon & Schuster, Harper & Row and Cornell University Press.

**MEMBER AGENTS** Lynn Chu, Glen Hartley.

**REPRESENTS** Nonfiction, fiction.

☛ Serious nonfiction and quality fiction. No motion picture or television screenplays. "We generally will not consider science fiction or children's or young adult fiction unless it aspires to serious literature."

**HOW TO CONTACT** Query with SASE or by e-mail. Send ms, brief biography or CV, list of previously published works, and a table of contents. Advise on submission if the projects has been sent to other agents and if it was previously submitted to publishers. Accepts simultaneous submissions.

**TERMS** Agents receive 15% on domestic sales; 10% for screenwriting or other consulting services. No reading fee. "We may charge clients the costs of out-of-house photocopying or for buying books or galleys for manuscript or proposal submissions, messengers, long-distance telephone and long-distance courier services such as FedEx. Any other expenses must be approved by the author. We do our best to minimize all expenses."

## ⊘ THE WYLIE AGENCY

250 W. 57th St., Suite 2114, New York NY 10107. (212)246-0069. **Fax:** (212)586-8953. **E-mail:** mail@wylieagency.com. **Website:** www.wylieagency.com. Overseas address: 17 Bedford Square, London WC1B 3JA, United Kingdom; mail@wylieagency.co.uk.

**REPRESENTS** Novels.

This agency is not currently accepting unsolicited submissions; do not query unless you are asked.

**HOW TO CONTACT** This agency does not currently take unsolicited submissions. Accepts simultaneous submissions.

## JASON YARN LITERARY AGENCY

47 Fort Washington, Suite 67, New York NY 10032. **E-mail:** jason@jasonyarnliteraryagency.com. **Website:** www.jasonyarnliteraryagency.com. Member of AAR.
**REPRESENTS** Nonfiction, fiction. **Considers these nonfiction areas:** biography, business, cooking, creative nonfiction, current affairs, economics, foods, history, law, popular culture, politics, psychology, science, technology, young adult. **Considers these fiction areas:** adventure, comic books, commercial, contemporary issues, fantasy, horror, inspirational, juvenile, lesbian, literary, mainstream, middle grade, multicultural, paranormal, science fiction, supernatural, suspense, thriller, young adult, graphic novels, comics.

**HOW TO CONTACT** Please e-mail your query to jason@jasonyarnliteraryagency.com with the word "Query" in the subject line, and please paste the first 10 pages of your manuscript or proposal into the text of your e-mail. Do not send any attachments. "Visit the About page for information on what we are interested in, and please note that JYLA does not accept queries for film, TV, or stage scripts." Accepts simultaneous submissions.

## YATES & YATES

1551 N. Tustin Ave., Suite 710, Santa Ana CA 92705. (714)480-4000. **Website:** www.yates2.com. Represents 40 clients.
**REPRESENTS** **Considers these nonfiction areas:** religious.

## HELEN ZIMMERMANN LITERARY AGENCY

**E-mail:** submit@zimmagency.com. **Website:** www.zimmermannliterary.com. **Contact:** Helen Zimmermann. Estab. 2003.

Prior to opening her agency, Ms. Zimmermann was the director of advertising and promotion at Random House and the events coordinator at an independent bookstore.

**REPRESENTS** Nonfiction, fiction. **Considers these nonfiction areas:** diet/nutrition, health, interior design, memoirs, music, popular culture, sports, women's issues, relationships. **Considers these fiction areas:** family saga, literary, mainstream.

"I am currently concentrating my nonfiction efforts in health and wellness, relationships, popular culture, women's issues, lifestyle, sports, and music. I am also drawn to memoirs that speak to a larger social or historical circumstance, or introduce me to a new phenomenon. And I am always looking for a work of fiction that will keep me up at night!"

**HOW TO CONTACT** Accepts e-mail queries only. "For nonfiction queries, initial contact should just be a pitch letter. For fiction queries, I prefer a summary, your bio, and the first chapter as text in the email (not as an attachment). If I express interest I will need to see a full proposal for nonfiction and the remainder of the manuscript for fiction." Accepts simultaneous submissions. Responds in 2 weeks to queries, only if interested. Obtains most new clients through recommendations from others, solicitations.

**TERMS** Agent receives 15% commission on domestic sales. Offers written contract; 30-day notice must be given to terminate contract.

**WRITERS CONFERENCES** Washington Independent Review of Books Writers Conference; Yale Writers' Conference; American Society of Journalists and Authors Conference; Writer's Digest Conference; La-Jolla Writer's Conference; Gulf Coast Writers Conference; Kansas Writers Association Conference; New York Writers Workshop; Self-Publishing Book Expo; Burlington Writers' Conference; Southern Expressions Writers' Conference; Literary Writers' Conference, NYC.

# WRITERS CONFERENCES

Attending a writers conference that includes agents gives you the opportunity to learn more about what agents do and to show an agent your work. Ideally, a conference should include a panel or two with a number of agents to give writers a sense of the variety of personalities and tastes of different agents.

Not all agents are alike: Some are more personable, and sometimes you simply click better with one agent versus another. When only one agent attends a conference, there is a tendency for every writer at that conference to think, "Ah, this is the agent I've been looking for!" When the number of agents attending is larger, you have a wider group from which to choose, and you may have less competition for the agent's time.

Besides including panels of agents discussing what representation means and how to go about securing it, many of these gatherings also include time—either scheduled or impromptu—to meet briefly with an agent to discuss your work.

If they're impressed with what they see and hear about your work, they will invite you to submit a query, a proposal, a few sample chapters, or possibly your entire manuscript. Some conferences even arrange for agents to review manuscripts in advance and schedule one-on-one sessions during which you can receive specific feedback or advice regarding your work. Such meetings often cost a small fee, but the input you receive is usually worth the price.

Ask writers who attend conferences and they'll tell you that, at the very least, you'll walk away with new knowledge about the industry. At the very best, you'll receive an invitation to send an agent your material!

Many writers try to make it to at least one conference a year, but cost and location can count as much as subject matter when determining which one to attend. There are conferences in almost every state and province that can provide answers to your questions about writing and the publishing industry. Conferences also connect you with a community of other writers. Such connections help you learn about the pros and cons of different agents, and they can also give you a renewed sense of purpose and direction in your own writing.

## SUBHEADS

Each listing is divided into subheads to make locating specific information easier. In the first section, you'll find contact information for conference contacts. You'll also learn conference dates, specific focus, and the average number of attendees. Finally, names of agents who will be speaking or have spoken in the past are listed along with details about their availability during the conference. Contacting a conference director to verify the names of agents in attendance is always a good idea.

**COSTS:** Looking at the price of events, plus room and board, may help writers on a tight budget narrow their choices.

**ACCOMMODATIONS:** Here conferences list overnight accommodations and travel information. Often conferences held in hotels will reserve rooms at a discount rate and may provide a shuttle bus to and from the local airport.

**ADDITIONAL INFORMATION:** This section includes information on conference-sponsored contests, individual meetings, the availability of brochures, and more.

## AGENTS & EDITORS CONFERENCE

Writers' League of Texas, 611 S. Congress Ave., Suite 200 A-3, Austin TX 78704. (512)499-8914. **E-mail:** wlt@writersleague.org. **Website:** www.writersleague. org/38/conference. Estab. 1982. Annual conference held in summer. This standout conference gives each attendee the opportunity to become a publishing insider. Meet more than 25 top agents, editors, and industry professionals through one-on-one consultations and receptions. Get tips and strategies for revising and improving your manuscript from keynote speakers and presenters (including award-winning and best-selling writers).

**COSTS** Registration for the conference opens in the fall.

**ACCOMMODATIONS** Discounted rates are available at the conference hotel.

## ALASKA CONFERENCE FOR WRITERS & ILLUSTRATORS

Alaska Writers Guild, SCBWI Alaska, & RWA Alaska, P.O. Box 670014, Chugiak AK 99567. **E-mail:** alaskawritersguild.awg@gmail.com. **Website:** alaskawritersguild.com. Join the Alaska Writers Guild, SCBWI Alaska, and Alaska RWA for this annual 2-day conference event! Optional Friday workshops and round tables, 1:1 Manuscript Reviews and pitches, and an all-day event of keynotes, panels, and breakout sessions. Topics range from Writing 101 to advanced revisions, traditional to self-published, and Kidlit to steamy romance. Plus everything in between!

## ASJA ANNUAL WRITERS CONFERENCE

American Society of Journalists and Authors, 355 Lexington Ave., 15th Floor, New York NY 10017. (212)997-0947. **E-mail:** asjaoffice@asja.org. **Website:** www.asja.org. Estab. 1971. Annual conference held in New York each spring. Duration: 2 days. Average attendance: 600. Covers nonfiction. Site: New York. Speakers have included Kitty Kelley, Jennifer Finney Boylan, Daniel Jones, D.T. Max, and more.

**COSTS** Approximately $300/day, depending on when you sign up. Check website for details.

**ACCOMMODATIONS** Venue hotel has a block of rooms at discounted conference rate.

**ADDITIONAL INFORMATION** Conference program available online mid-January. Registration is online only. Sign up for e-mail updates online.

## ATLANTA WRITERS CONFERENCE

Atlanta Writers Club, Westin Atlanta Airport Hotel, 4736 Best Rd., Atlanta GA 30337. **E-mail:** awconference@gmail.com. **Website:** www.atlantawritersconference.com. **Contact:** George Weinstein. Estab. 2008. Annual conference held in spring and fall. Literary agents and editors are in attendance to take pitches and critique ms samples and query letters. Conference offers a writing craft workshop, instructional sessions with local authors, and separate question-and-answer panels with the agents and editors. Site: Westin Airport Atlanta Hotel.

**COSTS** Manuscript critiques are $170 each (2 spots/waitlists maximum). Pitches are $70 each (2 spots/waitlists maximum). There's no charge for waitlists unless a spot opens. Query letter critiques are $70 (1 spot maximum). Other workshops and panels may also cost extra; see website. The "all activities" option is $620 and includes 2 manuscript critiques, 2 pitches, and 1 of each remaining activity.

**ACCOMMODATIONS** A block of rooms is reserved at the conference hotel. Booking instructions will be sent in the registration confirmation e-mail.

**ADDITIONAL INFORMATION** A free shuttle runs between the airport and the hotel.

## BALTIMORE WRITERS' CONFERENCE

English Department, Liberal Arts Bldg., Towson University, 8000 York Rd., Towson MD 21252. (410)704-5452. **E-mail:** prwr@towson.edu. **Website:** baltimorewritersconference.org. Estab. 1994. Annual conference held in November at Towson University. Conference duration: 1 day. Average attendance: 150-200. Covers all areas of writing and getting published. Held at Towson University. Session topics include fiction, nonfiction, poetry, magazines and journals, and agents and publishers. Sign up the day of the conference for quick critiques to improve your stories, essays, and poems.

**ACCOMMODATIONS** Hotels are close by, if required.

**ADDITIONAL INFORMATION** Writers may register through the website. Send inquiries via e-mail.

## BAY TO OCEAN WRITERS CONFERENCE

P.O. Box 1773, Easton MD 21601. (410)482-6337. **E-mail:** easternshorewriters@gmail.com. **Website:** https://easternshorewriters.org. Estab. 1998. Annual conference held the second Saturday in March. Average attendance: 200. Approximately 30 speakers conduct workshops on publishing, agents, editing, marketing, craft, the internet, poetry, fiction, nonfiction, and freelance writing. Site: Chesapeake College, Rt. 213 and Rt. 50, Wye Mills, on Maryland's historic Eastern Shore. Accessible to individuals with disabilities.

**COSTS** Adults: $100-120. Students: $55. A paid ms review is also available; details on website. Includes continental breakfast and networking lunch.

**ADDITIONAL INFORMATION** Registration is on website. Pre-registration is required; no registration at door. Conference usually sells out 1 month in advance. Conference is for all levels of writers.

### BIG SUR WRITING WORKSHOP

P.O. Box 256, Quincy MA 02171. (617)479-5774. E-mail: lisa@bigsurchildrenswriters.com. **Website:** https://www.bigsurchildrenswriters.com/. Annual workshop focusing on children's writing (picture books, middle-grade, and young adult). Held every spring in Cape Cod, MA, and the first weekend in December at either the Big Sur Lodge in Pfeiffer State Park or the Hyatt. Cost for this workshop includes 4 mentoring sessions with agents, publishers and authors; panel discussions; meals and lodging. This event is helmed by the literary agents of the Andrea Brown Literary Agency. All attendees meet with at least 2 faculty members to have their work critiqued. Check website for conference dates. Due to the size of this workshop we want to be sure this is the right forum for you. Writers will need to submit material (1st three pages of MG or YA) or 1 PB, for consideration to attend the Workshop.

**COSTS** Please check the website.

**ACCOMMODATIONS** When we are at the Lodge, shared cabins are reserved with a few single cabins available. At the Hyatt and Sea Crest Beach Hotel, you will be paired with another writer. Unless you prefer a single room. Single rooms do come with an additional cost.

### BLUE RIDGE MOUNTAINS CHRISTIAN WRITERS CONFERENCE

**Website:** www.blueridgeconference.com. **Contact:** Edie Melson, director. Annual retreat held in May at Ridgecrest/LifeWay Conference Center near Asheville, North Carolina. Duration: Sunday through lunch on Thursday. Average attendance: 580. The conference is a training and networking event for both seasoned and aspiring writers that allows attendees to interact with editors, agents, professional writers, and readers. Workshops and continuing classes in a variety of creative categories are offered.

**COSTS** $325 for the conference; meal package is $145 per person (12 meals beginning with dinner Sunday and ending with lunch on Thursday). $350 conference fee for those not staying on campus. Room rates vary from $60-$70 per night.

**ADDITIONAL INFORMATION** For a PDF of the complete schedule (typically posted in April), visit the website.

### ERMA BOMBECK WRITERS' WORKSHOP

University of Dayton, 300 College Park, Dayton OH 45469-2940. **E-mail:** erma@udayton.edu. **Website:** go.udayton.edu/erma. **Contact:** Teri Rizvi. Estab. 2000. Biennial national conference held in even numbered years. This is a specialized writing conference for writers of humor and human interest (books, articles, essays, blogs, and film/television). "Through the workshop, the University of Dayton and the Bombeck family honor one of America's most celebrated storytellers and humorists. Over the years, the workshop has attracted such household names as Dave Barry, Art Buchwald, Phil Donahue, Roy Blount, Jr., Nancy Cartwright, Don Novello, Liza Donnelly, John Grogan, Gail Collins, Connie Schultz, Adriana Trigiani, Amy Ephron and Alan Zweibel. The workshop draws approximately 350 writers from around the country and typically sells out very quickly, so don't wait once registration opens."

**COSTS** $485, which includes meals.

**ACCOMMODATIONS** Marriott at the University of Dayton.

**ADDITIONAL INFORMATION** Special workshop rate available.

### BOOKS-IN-PROGRESS CONFERENCE

Carnegie Center for Literacy and Learning, 251 W. Second St., Lexington KY 40507. (859)254-4175. **E-mail:** info@carnegiecenterlex.org. **Website:** carnegiecenterlex.org. Estab. 2010. This is an annual writing conference at the Carnegie Center for Literacy and Learning in Lexington, Kentucky. It typically happens in June. "Each conference will offer writing and publishing workshops and includes a keynote presentation." Literary agents are flown in to meet with writers and hear pitches. Website is updated several months prior to each annual event.

**ACCOMMODATIONS** See website for list of area hotels.

### ❥ BREAD LOAF IN SICILY WRITERS' CONFERENCE

Middlebury College, 204 College St., Middlebury VT 05753. (802)443-5286. **Fax:** (802)443-2087. **E-mail:** blsicily@middlebury.edu. **Website:** www .middlebury.edu/bread-loaf-conferences/blsicily. Estab. 2011. Annual conference held in September in Erice, Sicily (western coast of the island). Duration: 7 days. Offers workshops for fiction, nonfiction, and poetry. Average attendance: 32.

**COSTS** $3,265/$3,010 (as a contributor with manuscript/as an auditor without manuscript). Includes the conference program, transfer to and from Palermo Airport, 6 nights of lodging, 3 meals daily (except for Wednesday), wine reception at the readings, and an excursion to the ancient ruins of Segesta. The charge for an additional person is $1,900. There is a $20 application fee and a deposit.

**ACCOMMODATIONS** Accommodations are single rooms with private bath. Breakfast and lunch are served at the hotel, and dinner is available at select Erice restaurants. A double room is possible for those who would like to be accompanied by a spouse or significant other.

**ADDITIONAL INFORMATION** Rolling admissions. Space is limited.

### BREAD LOAF ORION ENVIRONMENTAL WRITERS' CONFERENCE

Middlebury College, 204 College St., Middlebury VT 05753. (802)443-5286. **Fax:** (802)443-2087. **E-mail:** blorion@middlebury.edu. **Website:** www .middlebury.edu/bread-loaf-conferences/blorion. Estab. 2014. Annual specialized conference held in June. Duration: 7 days. Offers workshops for fiction, nonfiction, and poetry. Agents and editors will be in attendance. Average attendance: 70.

**COSTS** $2,205 for full participants and $1,875 for auditors. Both options include room and board.

**ACCOMMODATIONS** Mountain campus of Middlebury College in Vermont.

**ADDITIONAL INFORMATION** The event is designed to hone the skills of people interested in producing literary writing about the environment and the natural world. Rolling admissions. Space is limited.

### BREAD LOAF WRITERS' CONFERENCE

Middlebury College, 204 College St., Middlebury VT 05753. (802)443-5286. **Fax:** (802)443-2087. **E-mail:** blwc@middlebury.edu. **Website:** www .middlebury.edu/bread-loaf-conferences/bl_writers. Estab. 1926. Annual conference held in late August. Duration: 10 days. Average attendance: 230. Offers workshops for fiction, nonfiction, and poetry. Agents and editors attend.

**COSTS** $3,525 for general contributors and $3,380 for auditors. Both options include room and board.

**ACCOMMODATIONS** Bread Loaf campus of Middlebury College in Ripton, Vermont.

### CALIFORNIA CRIME WRITERS CONFERENCE

Sisters in Crime Los Angeles and Southern California Mystery Writers of America. **E-mail:** info@ccwconference.org. **Website:** www.ccwconference.org. **Contact:** Sisters in Crime Los Angeles and SoCal Mystery Writers of America. Estab. 1995. Biennial conference held in early June. Average attendance: 200. Two-day conference on mystery and crime writing. Offers craft, forensic, industry news, marketing, and career-building sessions; 2 keynote speakers; author, editor, and agent panels; ms critiques (additional fee); and pre-conference book giveaways. Keynote speakers have included Cara Black, Elizabeth Murray, and Jane Friedman.

**COSTS** $350 fee.

### CAPE COD WRITERS CENTER ANNUAL CONFERENCE

Cape Cod Writers Center, P.O. Box 408, Osterville MA 02655. (508)420-0200. **E-mail:** writers@capecodwriterscenter.org. **Website:** www.capecodwriterscenter.org. **Contact:** Nancy Rubin Stuart, executive director. Estab. 1963. Workshops in fiction, screenwriting, poetry, memoir, mystery, writing for children, writing for young adults, character, dialogue, setting and self-editing. Manuscript mentoring offered with editors and faculty.

**COSTS** Costs vary, depending on the number of courses and membership. Registration also includes annual membership to the Cape Cod Writers Center's year-round programs.

**ACCOMMODATIONS** Resort and Conference Center of Hyannis, Massachusetts.

## CHRISTOPHER NEWPORT UNIVERSITY WRITERS' CONFERENCE & WRITING CONTEST

(757)269-4368. **Website:** writers.cnu.edu. Estab. 1981. Annual conference held in spring. This is a working conference. Presentations made by editors, agents, fiction writers, poets, and more. Breakout sessions in fiction, nonfiction, poetry, juvenile fiction, and publishing. Previous panels have included publishing, proposal writing, and Internet research.

**ACCOMMODATIONS** Provides list of area hotels.

## CLARION WEST WRITERS WORKSHOP

P.O. Box 31264, Seattle WA 98103. (206)322-9083. **E-mail:** info@clarionwest.org. **Website:** www.clarionwest.org. **Contact:** Marnee Chua, executive director. Estab. 1984. Clarion West is a prestigious, intensive six-week workshop for writers preparing for professional careers in science fiction and fantasy, held annually in Seattle. Usually run from mid-June through the end of July. Average attendance: 18. Held near the University of Washington. Deadline for applications is March 1. Instructors are well-known writers and editors in the field.

**COSTS** $4,200 (for tuition, housing, most meals). Numerous scholarships are available. Students apply through our website and must submit 20-30 pages of ms with four-page biography and $60 fee ($35 if received by February 10).

**ACCOMMODATIONS** Students stay on-site in workshop housing near the University of Washington.

**ADDITIONAL INFORMATION** Information available in fall. For brochure/guidelines, send SASE, visit website, e-mail, or call.

## CLARKSVILLE WRITERS CONFERENCE

Clarksville Arts & Heritage Development Council, PO Box 555, Clarksville TN 37041-0555. (931)551-8870. **E-mail:** writers@artsandheritage.us. **Website:** www.artsandheritage.us/writers. **Contact:** Dr. Ellen Kanervo, Conference Chair. Estab. 2005. Valuable to writers and interesting to readers, our conference offers something for everyone. Sixteen writing workshops and presentations held in August on the campus of Austin Peay State University in Clarksville, Tennessee. Lunch and refreshments will be provided each day, and book signing will be available. Presenting authors have included Joshilyn Jackson, Kelly J. Beard, Dana Chamblee Carpenter, Kiezha Smith

Ferrell, Debra Coleman Jeter, Joy Jordan-Lake, Bobby Keel, Robert Mangeot, James Nihan, S.M. Williams and Renea Winchester.

**COSTS** We offer a complete package including all conference activities, as well as a la carte options. Discounted rates are available for early registration. Check website for more details.

**ADDITIONAL INFORMATION** Professional editing consultations are available. Appointments may be made on a first-come, first-served basis at the time of registration.

## COMMUNITY OF WRITERS AT SQUAW VALLEY

Community of Writers at Squaw Valley, P.O. Box 1416, Nevada City CA 95959. (530)470-8440 or (530)583-5200 (summer). **Website:** www.communityofwriters.org. **Contact:** Brett Hall Jones, Executive Director. P.O. Box 2352, Olympic Valley CA 96146 (summer). Estab. 1969.

**COSTS** Tuition is $1,350, which includes 6 dinners. Limited financial aid is available.

**ACCOMMODATIONS** The Community of Writers rents houses and condominiums in the Squaw Valley for participants to live in during the week of the conference. Single room (1 participant): $790/week. Double room (twin beds, room shared by conference participant of the same gender): $490/week. Multiple room (bunk beds, room shared with 2 or more participants of the same gender): $325/week. All rooms subject to availability; early requests are recommended. Can arrange airport shuttle pickups for a fee.

## FLORIDA CHRISTIAN WRITERS CONFERENCE

Word Weavers International, Inc., P O Box 520224, Longwood FL 32752. (407)414-8188. **E-mail:** floridacwc@aol.com. **Website:** word-weavers.com/floridaevents. **Contact:** Eva Marie Everson and Taryn Souders. Estab. 1988. Annual conference at Lake Yale Conference Center in Leesburg, Florida. Mid-Late October. Please check our website. FCWC workshops/classes geared toward all levels, from beginners to published authors. Open to students. Offers 6 keynote addresses, 10 continuing classes, and a number of 3-hour workshops, 1-hour workshops, and after-hours workshops. "FCWC brings in the finest the industry has to offer in editors, agents, freelancers, and marketing and media experts." Additionally, the conference offers a book proposal studio, a pitch studio, advanced critique services, a fun Meet-n-Greet Social on Wednesday evening and a "Just Deserts Desserts" awards ceremony on Saturday evening.

**COSTS** Ranges: $300 (daily rate—in advance, includes lunch and dinner; specify days) to $1,690 (Tuesday night, Wednesday intensive through conference for attendee and participating spouse/family member in same room). Scholarships offered. For more information or to register, go to the conference website.

**ACCOMMODATIONS** Offers private rooms and double occupancy as well as accommodations for participating and non-participating family members. Meals provided, including awards dessert banquet Saturday evening. For those flying into Orlando or Sanford airports, FCWC provides a shuttle to and from the conference center.

## GREEN MOUNTAIN WRITERS CONFERENCE

47 Hazel St., Rutland VT 05701. **E-mail:** yvonnedaley@me.com. **Website:** vermontwriters.com. **Contact:** Yvonne Daley, director. Estab. 1998. Annual conference held in the summer. Covers fiction, creative nonfiction, poetry, young adult fiction, journalism, nature writing, essay, memoir, personal narrative, and biography. Held at the Brandon Inn in the beautiful, walkable town of Brandon. Speakers have included T. Greenwood, Stephen Kiernan, Chard deNiord, Grace Paley, Ruth Stone, Howard Frank Mosher, Chris Bohjalian, Yvonne Daley, David Huddle, David Budbill, Jeffrey Lent, Verandah Porche, Tom Smith, and Chuck Clarino.

**COSTS** $600 (early); $650 (normal deadline). Partial scholarships are available.

**ACCOMMODATIONS** Dramatically reduced rates at the Brandon Inn for attendees. Close to other area hotels and bed-and-breakfasts.

**ADDITIONAL INFORMATION** Participants' mss can be read and commented on at a cost. Sponsors contests and publishes a literary magazine featuring work of participants. Brochures available on website or e-mail.

## HAMPTON ROADS WRITERS CONFERENCE

Hampton Roads Writers, P.O. Box 56228, Virginia Beach VA 23456. (757)639-6146. **E-mail:** info@hamptonroadswriters.org. **Website:** hamptonroadswriters.

org. Estab. 2008. Annual conference held in September. Workshops cover fiction, nonfiction, memoir, poetry, lyric writing, screenwriting, and the business of getting published. A bookshop, 3 free contests with cash prizes, free evening networking social, and many networking opportunities will be available. Multiple literary agents are in attendance each year to meet with writers and hear ten-minute pitches. Much more information available on the website.

**COSTS** Costs vary. There are discounts for members, for early bird registration, for students, and more.

## HOUSTON WRITERS GUILD CONFERENCE—READY, SET, PITCH!

Writefest Houston, Houston Writers Guild, P.O. Box 42255, Houston TX 77242. (281)736-7168. **E-mail:** info@houstonwritersguild.org. **Website:** houstonwritersguild.org. Estab. 1994. This annual conference, organized by the Houston Writers Guild, happens in the spring and has concurrent sessions and tracks on the craft and business of writing. Each year, multiple agents are in attendance taking pitches from writers. The festival, Writefest, is a weeklong event with various tracks of sessions during the weekday evenings as well as during the weekend of the festival. Literary journals as well as publishing companies and agents are featured.

**COSTS** Costs are different for members and nonmembers. Costs depend on how many days and events you sign up for.

**ADDITIONAL INFORMATION** Each year the conference takes place either the last weekend of April or the first weekend of May depending on venue availability.

The Guild also hosts a conference the last weekend of September called Indiepalooza. This conference focuses on marketing and branding for all authors and specific presentations and sessions for authors who are self-publishing.

## IDAHO WRITERS LEAGUE WRITERS' CONFERENCE

601 W. 75 St., Blackfoot ID 83221. (208)684-4200. **Website:** www.idahowritersleague.org. Estab. 1940. Annual floating conference, usually held in September. This conference has at least one agent in attendance every year, along with other writers and presenters.

**COSTS** Pricing varies. Check website for more information.

### IWWG ANNUAL SUMMER CONFERENCE

5 Penn Plaza, 19th Floor, PMB #19059, New York NY 10001. (617)792-7272. **E-mail:** iwwgquestions@iwwg.org. **Website:** https://iwwg.wildapricot.org/events. **Contact:** Michelle Miller, MEd, executive director. Estab. 1976. Held in July at Muhlenberg College in Allentown, Pennsylvania.

**COSTS** Varies. See website for details.

**ACCOMMODATIONS** Check website for updated pricing.

**ADDITIONAL INFORMATION** Choose from 30 workshops in poetry, fiction, memoir and personal narrative, social action/advocacy, and mind-body-spirit. Critique sessions; book fair; salons; open readings. No portfolio required.

### JACKSON HOLE WRITERS CONFERENCE

P.O. Box 1974, Jackson WY 83001. (307)413-3332. **E-mail:** info@jhwriters.org. **Website:** jacksonholewritersconference.com. Estab. 1991. Annual conference held in June. Conference duration: 3-4 days. Average attendance: 110. Covers fiction, creative nonfiction, poetry and KidsLit, and offers ms critiques from authors, agents, and editors. Agents in attendance will take pitches from writers. Paid ms critique programs are available.

**COSTS** $375; critiques additional.

**ACCOMMODATIONS** Accommodations not included.

**ADDITIONAL INFORMATION** Held at the Center for the Arts in Jackson, Wyoming, and online.

### JAMES RIVER WRITERS CONFERENCE

2319 E. Broad St., Richmond VA 23223. (804)433-3790. **E-mail:** info@jamesriverwriters.org. **Website:** www.jamesriverwriters.org. **Contact:** Katharine Herndon. Estab. 2003. Nonprofit supporting writers in the Richmond, VA, area and beyond. Annual conference held in October. The event has master classes, agent pitching, critiques, panels, and more. Previous attending speakers include Ellen Oh, Margot Lee Shetterly, David Baldacci, Jeannette Walls, Adriana Trigiani, Jacqueline Woodson, and more.

**COSTS** Check website for updated pricing.

### KACHEMAK BAY WRITERS' CONFERENCE

Kachemak Bay Campus—Kenai Peninsula College/University of Alaska Anchorage, 533 E. Pioneer Ave., Homer AK 99603. (907)235-7743. **E-mail:** KachemakBayWritersConf@alaska.edu. **Website:** http://writersconf.kpc.alaska.edu/. Annual conference held in May. This nationally recognized writing conference features workshops, readings, and panel presentations in fiction, poetry, nonfiction, and the business of writing. There are open mic sessions for conference registrants, evening readings open to the public, agent/editor consultations, and more.

**COSTS** See the website. Some scholarships available.

**ACCOMMODATIONS** Homer is 225 miles south of Anchorage, Alaska, on the southern tip of the Kenai Peninsula and the shores of Kachemak Bay. There are multiple hotels in the area.

### KENTUCKY WOMEN WRITERS CONFERENCE

University of Kentucky College of Arts & Sciences, 232 E. Maxwell St., Lexington KY 40506. (859)257-2874. **E-mail:** kentuckywomenwriters@gmail.com. **Website:** kentuckywomenwriters.org. **Contact:** Julie Wrinn, director. Estab. 1979. Conference held in second or third weekend of September. Duration: 2 days. Site: Carnegie Center for Literacy in Lexington, Kentucky. Average attendance: 150-200. Conference covers poetry, fiction, creative nonfiction, and playwriting. Includes writing workshops, panels, and readings featuring contemporary women writers.

**COSTS** $175-220 for workshops, agent meet up, general admission. Check website for variety of pricing options.

**ADDITIONAL INFORMATION** Sponsors prizes in poetry ($300), fiction ($300), nonfiction ($300), playwriting ($500), and spoken word ($500). Winners are also invited to read during the conference. Pre-registration opens May 1.

### KENTUCKY WRITERS CONFERENCE

Southern Kentucky Book Fest, WKU South Campus, 2355 Nashville Rd., Bowling Green KY 42101. (270)745-4502. **E-mail:** sara.volpi@wku.edu. **Website:** www.sokybookfest.org. **Contact:** Sara Volpi. This event is entirely free to the public. Duration: 2 days. Part of the 2-day Southern Kentucky Book Fest. Authors who will be participating in the Book Fest on Saturday will give attendees at the conference the benefit of their wisdom on Friday (16 sessions available). For the first time, additional workshops will be offered on Saturday! Free workshops on a variety of writing topics will be presented. Sessions run for 75 minutes, and the day begins at 9 a.m. and ends at 3:30 p.m. The conference is open to anyone who would like to attend, including high school students, college students, teachers, and the general public. Registration will open online in February.

## KILLER NASHVILLE

P.O. Box 680759, Franklin TN 37068. (615)599-4032. **Website:** www.killernashville.com. Estab. 2006. Annual conference held in late summer or fall. Duration: 4 days. Average attendance: more than 400. The event draws literary agents seeking thrillers as well as some of the industry's top thriller authors. Conference designed for writers and fans of mysteries and thrillers, including fiction and nonfiction authors, playwrights, and screenwriters. There are many opportunities for authors to sign books. Distinct session tracks may include general writing, genre-specific writing, publishing, publicity and promotion, forensics, and ms critiques (fiction, nonfiction, short stories, screenplays, and queries). The conference also offers a realistic mock crime scene for guests to solve and an opportunity for networking with best-selling authors, agents, editors, publishers, attorneys, publicists, and representatives from law and emergency services. Other activities include mystery games, an authors' bar, a wine tasting event, 2 cocktail receptions, a guest of honor dinner and awards program, giveaways, and more.

**COSTS** $419 for general registration. Includes networking lunches on Friday and Saturday and special sessions with best-selling authors and industry professionals.

**ADDITIONAL INFORMATION** Additional information about registration is provided online.

## LA JOLLA WRITERS CONFERENCE

P.O. Box 178122, San Diego CA 92177. **Website:** www.lajollawritersconference.com. Estab. 2001. Annual conference held in fall. Conference duration: 3 days. Attendance: 200 maximum. The La Jolla Writers Conference covers all genres in both fiction and nonfiction as well as the business of writing. "We take particular pride in educating our attendees on the business aspect of the book industry and have agents, editors, publishers, publicists, and distributors teach classes. There is unprecedented access to faculty. Our conference offers lecture sessions that run for 50 minutes and workshops that run for 110 minutes. Each block period is dedicated to either workshop or lecture-style classes with 6-8 classes on various topics available each block. For most workshop classes, you are

encouraged to bring written work for review. Literary agents from prestigious agencies such as the Andrea Brown Literary Agency, the Dijkstra Agency, the McBride Agency, Full Circle Literary Group, the Zimmermann Literary Agency, the Van Haitsma Literary Agency, the Farris Literary Agency, and more have participated in the past, teaching workshops in which they are familiarized with attendee work. Late night and early bird sessions are also available. The conference creates a strong sense of community, and it has seen many of its attendees successfully published."

**COSTS** $395 for full conference registration (doesn't include lodging or breakfast).

## LAS VEGAS WRITER'S CONFERENCE

Henderson Writers' Group, P.O. Box 92032, Henderson NV 89009. (702)953-5675. **E-mail:** confcoord@hendersonwritersgroup.com. **Website:** www.lasvegaswritersconference.com. Estab. 2001. Annual event held in spring. Conference duration: 3 days. Attendance: 175 maximum. "Join writing professionals, agents, industry experts, and your colleagues for 3 days in Las Vegas as they share their knowledge on all aspects of the writer's craft. While there are formal pitch sessions, panels, workshops, and seminars, the faculty is also available throughout the conference for informal discussions and advice. Workshops, seminars, and expert panels cover topics in both fiction and nonfiction, screenwriting, marketing, indie-publishing, and the craft of writing itself. There will be many question-and-answer panels for you to ask the experts all your questions." Site: Tuscany Suites and Casino (Las Vegas, Nevada).

**COSTS** Costs vary depending on the package. See the website. There are early bird rates through January 31.

**ADDITIONAL INFORMATION** Agents and editors participate in conference.

## MENDOCINO COAST WRITERS' CONFERENCE

P.O. Box 2087, Fort Bragg CA 95437. **E-mail:** info@mcwc.org. **Website:** www.mcwc.org. **Contact:** Lisa Locascio, Executive Director. Estab. 1989. Situated where summers are temperate and the seascape spectacular, this friendly conference emphasizes craft and community. Visiting faculty—top authors who are also outstanding teachers—will challenge you to find and express your own voice. Past faculty has included: Myriam Gurba, Ingrid Rojas Contreras, Shobha Rao, Mitali Perkins, Jeannie Vanasco, Scott Sigler,

Ismail Muhammad, Victoria Chang, and Charlotte Gullick with keynote speaker Sharon Olds. You will work closely with authors, editors, literary agents, and writers of many levels of experience, interests, ages, and backgrounds. Participants meet for three mornings with their intensive workshop group. Afternoons and evenings include craft seminars, pitch sessions, open-mics, literary readings, publishing panels, and social events. Optional manuscript consultations are available with the instructor, editor, or agent of your choice, on a limited first-come, first-served basis. All registrants may enter conference contests with cash prizes and possible publication in *Noyo River Review*.

**COSTS** $575 registration includes morning intensives, afternoon panels and seminars, social events, and most meals. Scholarships available. Opt-in for consultations and Publishing Boot Camp. Early application advised.

**ACCOMMODATIONS** Many lodging options in the scenic coastal area.

**ADDITIONAL INFORMATION** "Take your writing to the next level with encouragement, expertise, and inspiration in a literary community where authors are also fantastic teachers." General registration opens March 1.

## MIDWEST WRITERS WORKSHOP

Muncie IN 47306. (765)282-1055. **Website:** www.midwestwriters.org. **Contact:** Jama Kehoe Bigger, director. Writing conferences in east central Indiana, geared toward writers of all levels, including craft and business sessions. Topics include most genres. Faculty/speakers have included Angie Thomas, Becky Albertalli, Julie Murphy, Joyce Carol Oates, Marcus Sakey, William Kent Krueger, William Zinsser, John Gilstrap, Jane Friedman, and numerous best-selling mystery, literary fiction, young adult, and children's authors. Conferences with agent pitch sessions, ms evaluation, query letter critiques.

**COSTS** $155-425. Some meals included. Check website for details.

**ADDITIONAL INFORMATION** See website for more information. Keep in touch with the MWW at https://twitter.com/midwestwriters.

## MONTROSE CHRISTIAN WRITERS' CONFERENCE

Montrose Bible Conference, 218 Locust St., Montrose PA 18801. (570)278-1001 or (800)598-5030. **Fax:** (570)278-3061. **E-mail:** mbc@montrosebible.org.

**Website:** www.montrosebible.org. Estab. 1990. "Annual conference held in July. Offers workshops, editorial appointments, and professional critiques. We try to meet writing needs, for beginners and advanced, covering fiction, poetry, and writing for children. It is small enough to allow personal interaction between attendees and faculty. Speakers have included William Petersen, Mona Hodgson, Jim Watkins, and Bob Hostetler." Held in Montrose.

**COSTS** Tuition is around $200.

**ACCOMMODATIONS** Will meet planes in Binghamton, New York, and Scranton, Pennsylvania. Onsite accommodations: room and board $360-490/conference, including food. RV court available.

**ADDITIONAL INFORMATION** "Writers can send work ahead of time and have it critiqued for a small fee." The attendees are usually church related. The writing has a Christian emphasis. Conference information available in April. For brochure, visit website, e-mail, or call. Accepts inquiries by phone or e-mail.

## MOONLIGHT AND MAGNOLIAS WRITER'S CONFERENCE

Georgia Romance Writers, P.O. Box 1484, Buford GA 30515. **Website:** www.georgiaromancewriters.org/mm-conference. Director of Conference: Nicki Salcedo. Estab. 1982. Georgia Romance Writers Annual Conference. "Conference focuses on writing women's fiction with emphasis on romance. Includes agents and editors from major publishing houses. Previous workshops have included beginning writer sessions, research topics, writing basics, and professional issues for the published author, plus specialty sessions on writing young adult, multicultural, paranormal, and Regency." Keynote speakers, book fair, author signings, etc. complete this full conference.

**COSTS** $149-249. Visit website for exact amount.

## MUSE AND THE MARKETPLACE

Grub Street, P.O. Box 418, Boston MA 02476. (617)695-0075. **E-mail:** info@grubstreet.org. **Website:** museandthemarketplace.com. GrubStreet's national conference for writers. Held in the spring, such as in early April. Conference duration: 3 days. Average attendance: 550. Dozens of agents are in attendance to meet writers and give direct one-on-one feedback on manuscript samples. The conference has sessions on all aspects of writing.

**ACCOMMODATIONS** Boston Park Plaza Hotel.

## NAPA VALLEY WRITERS' CONFERENCE

Napa Valley College, Office 1753, 2277 Napa Valle-jo Highway, Napa CA 94558. (707)256-7417. **E-mail:** info@napawritersconference.og. **Website:** www.napawritersconference.org. **Contact:** Angela Pneuman, executive director. Estab. 1981. Annual week-long event in summer. Location: Upper Valley Campus in the historic town of St. Helena, 25 miles north of Napa in the heart of the valley's wine growing community. Average attendance: 48 in poetry and 48 in fiction. "Serious writers of all backgrounds and experience are welcome to apply." Offers poets and fiction writers workshops, lectures, faculty readings at Napa Valley wineries, and one-on-one faculty counseling. "Poetry session provides the opportunity to work both on generating new poems and on revising previously written ones."

**COSTS** The total participation fee for the program is $1,025, and includes daily breakfast and lunch, two dinners, wine tastings, and attendance at all conference events. $25 reading fee–Pay with your application. $1,025 participation fee–due on acceptance. Financial Assistance: A limited number of grants are available to cover all or part of the conference participation fee, with awards made on the basis of merit and need.

## NORTH CAROLINA WRITERS' NETWORK FALL CONFERENCE

P.O. Box 21591, Winston-Salem NC 27120. (336)293-8844. **E-mail:** mail@ncwriters.org. **Website:** www.nc-writers.org. Estab. 1985. Annual fall conference the first weekend of November rotates throughout the state each year. Average attendance: 225. This organization hosts 2 conferences: 1 in the spring and 1 in the fall. Each conference is a weekend full of workshops, panels, book signings, and readings (including open mic). There will be a keynote speaker, a variety of sessions on the craft and business of writing, and an opportunity to meet with agents and editors.

**COSTS** Approximately $260 (all days, with meals).

## NORTHERN COLORADO WRITERS CONFERENCE

2770 Arapahoe Rd., Suite 132-1110, Lafayette CO 80026. (575)430-7543. **E-mail:** info@northerncolora-dowriters.com. **Website:** www.northerncoloradowriters.com. Estab. 2006. Annual conference held in Fort Collins. Duration: 2-3 days. The conference features a variety of speakers, agents, and editors. There are workshops and presentations on fiction, nonfiction, screenwriting, children's books, marketing, magazine writing, staying inspired, and more. Previous agents who have attended and taken pitches from writers include Jessica Regel, Kristen Nelson, Jennifer March Soloway, Andrea Brown, Ken Sherman, Jessica Faust, Gordon Warnock, and Taylor Martindale. Each conference features more than 30 workshops from which to choose from. Previous keynotes include Chuck Wendig, Andrew McCarthy, and Stephen J. Cannell.

**COSTS** Prices vary depending on a number of factors. See website for details.

**ACCOMMODATIONS** Conference hotel offers rooms at a discounted rate.

## NORWESCON

100 Andover Park W. Suite 150-165, Tukwila WA 98188. (425)243-4692. **E-mail:** info@norwescon.org. **Website:** www.norwescon.org. Estab. 1978. Annual conference held on Easter weekend. Average attendance: 2,800-3,000. General convention (with multiple tracks) focusing on science fiction and fantasy literature with wide coverage of other media. Tracks cover science, sociocultural, literary, publishing, editing, writing, art, and other media of a science fiction/fantasy orientation. Literary agents will be speaking and available for meetings with attendees.

**ACCOMMODATIONS** Conference is held at the Doubletree Hotel Seattle Airport.

## ODYSSEY WRITING WORKSHOP

P.O. Box 75, Mont Vernon NH 03057. (603)673-6234. **E-mail:** jcavelos@odysseyworkshop.org. **Website:** www.odysseyworkshop.org. **Contact:** Jeanne Cavelos. Saint Anselm College, 100 Saint Anselm Dr., Manchester NH 03102. Estab. 1996. Annual workshop held in June (through July). Conference duration: 6 weeks. Average attendance: 15. A workshop for fantasy, science fiction, and horror writers that combines an intensive learning and writing experience with in-depth feedback on students' mss. Held on the campus of Saint Anselm College in Manchester, New Hampshire. Speakers have included George R.R. Martin, Elizabeth Hand, Jane Yolen, Catherynne M. Valente, Holly Black, and Dan Simmons.

**COSTS** $2,060 tuition, $195 textbook, $892 housing (double room), $1,784 housing (single room), $40 application fee, $600 food (approximate), $1,000 optional processing fee to receive college credit.

**ACCOMMODATIONS** Most students stay in Saint Anselm College apartments to get the full Odyssey experience. Each apartment has 2 bedrooms and can house a total of 2 to 3 people (with each bedroom holding 1 or 2 students). The apartments are equipped with kitchens, so you may buy and prepare your own food, which is a money-saving option, or you may eat at the college's Coffee Shop or Dining Hall. Wireless internet access and use of laundry facilities are provided at no cost. Students with cars will receive a campus parking permit.

**ADDITIONAL INFORMATION** Students must apply and include a writing sample. Application deadline: April 1. Students' works are critiqued throughout the 6 weeks. Workshop information available in October. For brochure/guidelines, send SASE, e-mail, visit website, or call.

### OKLAHOMA WRITERS' FEDERATION, INC. ANNUAL CONFERENCE

**Website:** www.owfi.org. Annual conference held first weekend in May, just outside Oklahoma City. Writer workshops geared toward all levels. "The goal of the conference is to create good stories with strong bones. We will be exploring cultural writing and cultural sensitivity in writing." Several literary agents are in attendance each year to meet with writers and hear pitches.

**COSTS** Costs vary depending on when registrants sign up. Cost includes awards banquet and famous author banquet. Three extra sessions are available for an extra fee. Visit the event website for more information and a complete faculty list.

### OREGON CHRISTIAN WRITERS SUMMER CONFERENCE

1075 Willow Lake Rd. N., Keizer OR 97303. **Website:** www.oregonchristianwriters.org. **Contact:** Christina Suzann Nelson, summer conference director. Estab. 1989. Annual conference held in August at the Red Lion Hotel on the River, a full-service hotel in Portland. Duration: 4 days. Average attendance: 280 (230 writers, 50 faculty). Top national editors, agents, and authors in the field of Christian publishing offer 10 intensive coaching classes and 24 workshops plus critique sessions. Published authors as well as emerging writers have opportunities to improve their craft, get feedback through ms reviews, meet one-on-one with editors and agents, and have half-hour mentoring appointments with published authors. Classes include fiction, nonfiction, memoir, suspense, screenwriting, young adult, poetry, magazine articles, devotional writing, children's books, websites, and marketing. Daily general sessions include worship and an inspirational keynote address. Each year contacts made during the OCW summer conference lead to publishing contracts.

**COSTS** $550 for OCW members, $595 for nonmembers. Registration fee includes all classes, workshops, and 2 lunches and 3 dinners. Lodging additional. Full-time registered attendees may also pre-submit 3 proposals for review by an editor (or agent) through the conference, plus sign up for a half-hour mentoring appointment with an author.

**ACCOMMODATIONS** Conference is held at the Red Lion on the River Hotel. Attendees wishing to stay at the hotel must make a reservation through the hotel. A block of rooms is reserved at a special rate and held until mid-July. The hotel reservation link is posted on the website in late spring. Shuttle bus transportation is provided from Portland Airport (PDX) to the hotel, which is 20 minutes away.

**ADDITIONAL INFORMATION** Conference details posted online beginning in January. All conferees are welcome to attend the Cascade Awards ceremony, which takes place Wednesday evening during the conference. For more information about the Cascade Writing Contest for published and unpublished writers—opens February 14. Please check the website for details.

### OZARK CREATIVE WRITERS, INC. CONFERENCE

207 W. Van Buren St., Eureka Springs AR 72632. (336)407-9098. **E-mail:** ozarkcreativewriters@ ozarkcreativewriters.com. **Website:** www.ozarkcreativewriters.com. The annual event is held in October at the Inn of the Ozarks, in the resort town of Eureka Springs, Arkansas. Approximately 200 writers attend each year; many also enter the creative writing competitions. Open to professional and amateur writers, workshops are geared toward all levels and all forms of the creative process and literary arts; sessions sometimes also include songwriting. Includes presentations by best-selling authors, editors, and agents. Offering writing competitions in all genres.

**COSTS** Full conference early bird registration: $185; regular: $248. Conference-only early bird registration: $140; regular: $150.

## PENNWRITERS CONFERENCE

P.O. Box 685, Dalton PA 18414. **E-mail:** info@pennwriters.org. **Website:** pennwriters.org/conference. Estab. 1987. The mission of Pennwriters, Inc. is to help writers of all levels, from the novice to the award-winning and multi-published, improve and succeed in their craft. The annual Pennwriters conference is held every year in May in Pennsylvania, switching between locations—Lancaster in even-numbered years and Pittsburgh in odd-numbered years. Literary agents are in attendance to meet with writers.

**ACCOMMODATIONS** Costs vary. Pennwriters members in good standing get a slightly reduced rate.

**ADDITIONAL INFORMATION** Sponsors contest. Published authors judge fiction in various categories. Agent/editor appointments are available on a first-come, first-served basis.

## PHILADELPHIA WRITERS' CONFERENCE

**Website:** pwcwriters.org. Estab. 1949. Annual conference held in June. Duration: 3 days. Average attendance: 160-200. Conference covers many forms of writing: novel, short story, genre fiction, nonfiction book, magazine writing, blogging, juvenile, poetry.

**ACCOMMODATIONS** See website for details. Hotel may offer discount for early registration.

**ADDITIONAL INFORMATION** Accepts inquiries by e-mail. Agents and editors attend the conference. Many questions are answered online.

## PIKES PEAK WRITERS CONFERENCE

Pikes Peak Writers, P.O. Box 64273, Colorado Springs CO 80962. (719)244-6220. **E-mail:** registrar@pikespeakwriters.com. **Website:** www.pikespeakwriters.com/ppwc. Estab. 1993. Annual conference held in April. Conference duration: 3 days. Average attendance: 300. Workshops, presentations, and panels focus on writing and publishing mainstream and genre fiction (romance, science fiction/fantasy, suspense/thrillers, action/adventure, mysteries, children's, young adult). Agents and editors are available for meetings with attendees on Saturday. Speakers have included Jeff Lindsay, Rachel Caine, and Kevin J. Anderson.

**COSTS** $405-465 (includes all 7 meals).

**ACCOMMODATIONS** Marriott Colorado Springs holds a block of rooms at a special rate for attendees until late March.

**ADDITIONAL INFORMATION** Readings with critiques are available on Friday afternoon. Registration forms are online; brochures are available in January. Send inquiries via e-mail.

## PNWA WRITERS CONFERENCE

Writers' Cottage, 317 NW Gilman Blvd. Suite 8, Issaquah WA 98027. (425)673-2665. **E-mail:** pnwa@pnwa.org. **Website:** www.pnwa.org. **Contact:** Pam Binder. Estab. 1955. Annual conference in September. Duration: 5 days. Average attendance: 400. Attendees have the chance to meet agents and editors, learn craft from authors, and uncover marketing secrets. Speakers have included J.A. Jance, Sheree Bykofsky, Kimberley Cameron, Jennie Dunham, Donald Maass, Jandy Nelson, Robert Dugoni, and Terry Brooks.

**COSTS** See website for costs.

## ROCKY MOUNTAIN FICTION WRITERS COLORADO GOLD CONFERENCE

Rocky Mountain Fiction Writers, P.O. Box 711, Monroe CO 81402. **Website:** www.rmfw.org. Estab. 1982. Annual conference held in September. Duration: 3 days. Average attendance: 400+. Themes include general fiction, genre fiction, contemporary romance, mystery, science fiction/fantasy, mainstream, young adult, screenwriting, short stories, and historical fiction, as well as marketing and career management. Past speakers have included Anne Hillerman, John Gilstrap, Marie Force, Kate Moretti, James Scott Bell, Christopher Paolini, Diana Gabaldon, Sherry Thomas, Lori Rader-Day, Ann Hood, Robert J. Sawyer, Jeffery Deaver, William Kent Krueger, Margaret George, Jodi Thomas, Bernard Cornwell, Terry Brooks, Dorothy Cannell, Patricia Gardner Evans, Diane Mott Davidson, Constance O'Day, and Connie Willis. Approximately 16 acquiring editors and agents attend annually.

**COSTS** Available on website.

**ACCOMMODATIONS** Special rates will be available at conference hotel.

**ADDITIONAL INFORMATION** Pitch appointments available at no charge. Add-on options include agent and editor critiques, master classes, pitch coaching, query letter coaching, special critiques, and more.

## ROMANCE WRITERS OF AMERICA NATIONAL CONFERENCE

5315-B Cypress Creek Parkway, #111, Houston TX 77069. (832)717-5200. **E-mail:** conference@rwa.org.

**Website:** www.rwa.org/conference. Estab. 1981. Annual conference held in July. The RWA Conference is the place where career-focused romance writers gather to make lasting connections and grow their careers—and so much more. When 2,000 romance writers and industry professionals assemble in one place, the sense of community is undeniable. At the conference, career-focused romance writers can anticipate: education and information, networking with fellow writers, interaction with editors, agents, publishers, vendors, retailers, and other romance publishing industry professionals.

**COSTS** $499-724 depending on your membership status as well as when you register.

**ADDITIONAL INFORMATION** Annual RTA awards are presented for romance authors. Annual Golden Heart awards are presented for unpublished writers.

### SAN FRANCISCO WRITERS CONFERENCE

Hyatt Regency San Francisco, San Francisco CA. (925)420-6223. **E-mail:** barbara@sfwriters.org. **Website:** sfwriters.org. **Contact:** Barbara Santos, marketing director. SFWC Main Office, P.O. Box 326, Oakley CA 94561 Estab. 2003. Annual conference held President's Day weekend in February. Average attendance: 700. "More than 100 top authors, respected literary agents, and major publishing houses are at the event so attendees can make face-to-face contact with all the right people. Writers of nonfiction, fiction, poetry, and specialty writing (children's books, lifestyle books, etc.) will all benefit from the event. There are important sessions on marketing, self-publishing, technology, and trends in the publishing industry. Plus, there's an optional session called Speed Dating with Agents AND individual meetings where attendees can meet with literary agents, editors and book marketing professionals. Past speakers have included Walter Mosley, Jane Smiley, Debbie Macomber, Clive Cussler, Guy Kawasaki, Jennifer Crusie, R.L. Stine, Lisa See, Steve Berry, and Jacquelyn Mitchard. Bestselling authors, agents and several editors from traditional publishing houses participate each year, and many will be available for meetings with attendees.

**COSTS** Full registration is $895 with a $795 early-bird registration rate.

**ACCOMMODATIONS** The Hyatt Regency San Francisco on the Embarcadero offers a discounted SFWC rate (based on availability). Use Code on the SFWC website or call directly: (415) 788-1234. Across from the Ferry Building in San Francisco, the hotel is located so that everyone arriving at the Oakland or San Francisco airports can take the BART to the Embarcadero exit, directly in front of the hotel.

**ADDITIONAL INFORMATION** "Present yourself in a professional manner, and the contacts you will make will be invaluable to your writing career. Fliers, details, and registration information are online."

### SAN FRANCISCO WRITING FOR CHANGE WORLDWIDE

San Francisco Writers Conference, P.O. Box 326, Oakley CA 94561. (925)420-6223. **E-mail:** barbara@sfwriters.org. **Website:** sfwritingforchange.org. **Contact:** Laurie McLean – Director. Estab. 2007. Annual conference in September. Writing to Make a Difference is the theme and it focuses on writing, publishing, and motivation from publishing professionals who specialize in the kind of writing that makes a difference with a wide-range of topics from diversity, spirituality, the environment, culture, memoir, and much more. The event is devoted to bringing together agents, editors, authors, and publishing professionals in order to enable writers to learn from the experts about writing, publishing, marketing, and technology. You'll come away knowing how to get your work published successfully, online and off. Includes one jam-packed day of workshops, panels, and keynote address. Attendees: 100.

**COSTS** $99. Please visit the website for details.

**ACCOMMODATIONS** Check website.

### SCBWI—AUSTIN CONFERENCE

**E-mail:** austin@scbwi.org. **Website:** austin.scbwi.org. **Contact:** Samantha Clark, regional advisor. Annual conference features a faculty of published authors and illustrators. Our conference has expanded this year. The schedule includes two keynotes; a publishing panel; 16 breakout sessions on writing, illustrating and professional development; intensives on picture books, novels and illustration; along with critiques, pitches, portfolio showcase, cookies and more. Editors and agents are in attendance to meet with writers. The schedule consists of keynotes and breakout sessions with tracks for writing (picture book and novel), illustrating, and professional development.

**COSTS** Costs vary for members, students, and non-members, and discounted early-bird pricing is available. Visit website for full pricing options.

## SCBWI—MID-ATLANTIC; ANNUAL FALL CONFERENCE

P.O. Box 3215, Reston VA 20195-1215. **E-mail:** midatlantic@scbwi.org. **Website:** midatlantic.scbwi.org/. **Contact:** Valerie Patterson and Erin Teagan, co-regional advisors. For updates and details, visit website. Registration limited to 250. Conference fills quickly. Includes continental breakfast and boxed lunch. Optional craft-focused workshops and individual consultations with conference faculty are available for additional fees.

## SCBWI WINTER CONFERENCE ON WRITING AND ILLUSTRATING FOR CHILDREN

4727 Wilshire Blvd #301, Los Angeles CA 90010. (323)782-1010. **E-mail:** info@scbwi.org. **Website:** www.scbwi.org. Estab. 2000. Average attendance: 1,000. Conference is to promote writing and illustrating for children (picture books, middle-grade, and young adult) and to give participants an opportunity to network with professionals. Covers financial planning for writers, marketing your book, art exhibitions, and more. The winter conference is held in Manhattan; the summer conference in Los Angeles.

**COSTS** See website for current cost and conference information; $525-675.

**ADDITIONAL INFORMATION** SCBWI also holds an annual summer conference in August in Los Angeles.

## SEWANEE WRITERS' CONFERENCE

735 University Ave., 119 Gailor Hall, Stamler Center, Sewanee TN 37383. (931)598-1654. **E-mail:** swc@sewanee.edu. **Website:** www.sewaneewriters.org. **Contact:** Adam Latham. Estab. 1990. Annual conference. Average attendance: 150. Accepting applications February 15-March 15. Thanks to the generosity of the Walter E. Dakin Memorial Fund, supported by the estate of the late Tennessee Williams, the Conference will gather a distinguished faculty to provide instruction and criticism through workshops and craft lectures in poetry, fiction, and playwriting. During a 12-day period, participants will read and critique workshop manuscripts under the leadership of faculty as well as attend craft lectures, master classes, and meet individually with editors and agents.

**COSTS** $1,100 for tuition, and $700 for room, board, and activity costs.

**ACCOMMODATIONS** Participants are housed in single rooms in university dormitories. Bathrooms are shared by small groups.

## SLEUTHFEST

Mystery Writers of America, Florida chapter. **Website:** sleuthfest.com. Annual conference held in February/March in Florida. Visit SleuthFest.com for dates and registration. Conference duration: 4 days. Hands-on workshops, 4 tracks of writing and business panels, forensics, and 2 keynote speakers for writers of mystery and crime fiction. We also offer agent and editor appointments and manuscript critiques. A full list of faculty, attending speakers, as well as agents and editors is at SleuthFest.com. This event is put on by the Florida chapter of the Mystery Writers of America.

## SOUTH CAROLINA WRITERS WORKSHOP

1219 Taylor St., Columbia SC 29201. **E-mail:** scwritersassociationpresident@gmail.com. **Website:** www.myscwa.org. Estab. 1991. Conference held in April in Columbia. Held almost every year. Conference duration: 3 days. Features critique sessions, open mic readings, and presentations from agents and editors. More than 50 different workshops for writers to choose from, dealing with all subjects of writing craft, writing business, getting an agent, and more. Agents will be in attendance.

## ◎ SURREY INTERNATIONAL WRITERS' CONFERENCE

SiWC, 151-10090 152 St., Suite 544, Surrey BC V3R 8X8 Canada. **E-mail:** kathychung@siwc.ca. **Website:** www.siwc.ca. **Contact:** Kathy Chung, proposals contact and conference coordinator. Annual professional development writing conference outside Vancouver, Canada, held every October. Writing workshops geared toward beginner, intermediate, and advanced levels. When in person, SiWC offers more than 80 workshops and panels, on all topics and genres, plus pre-conference master classes. Blue Pencil and agent/editor pitch sessions included. Different conference price packages available. Check the conference website for more information. This event has many literary agents in attendance taking pitches. Annual fiction writing contest open to all with $1,000 prize for first place. Conference registration opens in early June every year. Register very early to avoid disappointment as the conference is likely to sell out quickly.

### TAOS SUMMER WRITERS' CONFERENCE

P.O. Box 3225, Taos NM 87571. (575)758-0081. E-mail: somos@somostaos.org. **Website:** taosconf.unm.edu. **Contact:** Jan Smith, executive director. Estab. 1999. Annual conference held in July. Offers workshops and master classes in the novel, short story, poetry, creative nonfiction, memoir, prose style, screenwriting, humor writing, yoga and writing, literary translation, book proposal, the query letter, and revision. Participants may also schedule a consultation with a visiting agent/editor.

**COSTS** Week-long workshop registration: $700. Weekend workshop registration: $400. Master classes: $1,350-1,625. Publishing consultations: $175.

### THRILLERFEST

ITW, P.O. Box 1266, Eureka CA 95502. **E-mail:** kimberlyhowe@thrillerwriters.org; infocentral@thrillerwriters.org. **Website:** www.thrillerfest.com. **Contact:** Kimberley Howe, ITW Executive Director. Alternate Address: 811 7th Avenue, W 53rd St, New York, NY 10019. Estab. 2006. Annual workshop/conference/festival. Conference duration: 5 days. Average attendance: 1,000. "A great place to learn the craft of writing the thriller. Classes taught by best-selling authors." Speakers have included David Morrell, James Patterson, Sandra Brown, Ken Follett, Eric Van Lustbader, David Baldacci, Brad Meltzer, Steve Martini, R.L. Stine, Steve Berry, Kathleen Antrim, Douglas Preston, Gayle Lynds, Harlan Coben, Lee Child, Lisa Scottolini, Katherine Neville, Robin Cook, Andrew Gross, Kathy Reichs, Brad Thor, Clive Cussler, Donald Maass, M.J. Rose, and Al Zuckerman. 3 days of the conference are CraftFest, where the focus is on the craft of writing, and 2 days are ThrillerFest, which showcases the author-fan relationship. Also featured: PitchFest, a unique event where authors can pitch their work face-to-face to 50 top literary agents. Lastly, there is the International Thriller Awards and Banquet.

**COSTS** $160-1,260, depending on which events are selected. Various package deals are available, and early-bird pricing is offered beginning September of each year.

### UNICORN WRITERS CONFERENCE

P.O. Box 176, Redding CT 06876. (203)938-7405. E-mail: unicornwritersconference@gmail.com. **Website:** www.unicornwritersconference.com. **Contact:** Jan L. Kardys, chair. Estab. 2010. For all the information about our guest agents, editors, and speakers,

manuscript review sessions, and workshops please take a look through our site. This writers conference draws upon its close proximity to New York and pulls in over 40 literary agents and 15 major New York editors to pitch each year. There are manuscript review sessions (40 pages equals 30 minutes with an agent/editor), query/manuscript review sessions, and 6 different workshops every hour. Cost: $325, includes all workshops and 3 meals.

**ACCOMMODATIONS** Held at Reid Castle, Purchase, New York. Directions available on event website.

**ADDITIONAL INFORMATION** The first self-published authors will be featured on the website, and the bookstore will sell their books at the event.

### UNIVERSITY OF NORTH DAKOTA WRITERS CONFERENCE

Department of English, Merrifield Hall, Room 110, 276 Centennial Dr., Stop 7209, Grand Forks ND 58202. (701)777-2393. **Fax:** (701)777-2373. **E-mail:** crystal.alberts@und.edu. **Website:** und.edu/orgs/writers-conference. **Contact:** Crystal Alberts, director. Estab. 1970. Annual event. Duration: 3 days. Offers panels, readings, and films focused around a specific theme. Almost all events take place in the University of North Dakota Memorial Union, which has a variety of small rooms and a 600-seat main hall. Past speakers have included Art Spiegelman, Truman Capote, Colson Whitehead, Gwendolyn Brooks, Allen Ginsberg, Roxane Gay, Viet Thanh Nguyen, and Louise Erdrich.

**COSTS** All events are free and open to the public. Donations accepted.

**ACCOMMODATIONS** Information on overnight lodging & ADA accommodations available on website.

**ADDITIONAL INFORMATION** Schedule and other information available on website.

### WILLAMETTE WRITERS CONFERENCE

5331 SW Macadam Ave., Suite 258, PMB 215, Portland OR 97239. (971)200-5382. **E-mail:** conf.chair@willamettewriters.org. **Website:** willamettewriters.com/wwcon/. Estab. 1981. Over 700 attendees will gather for a weekend that's all about writers and writing. Meet industry professionals, learn from world-class faculty, and keynotes, and connect with a community of writers. Willamette Writers has hosted one of the largest and most-beloved writing conferences in North America. We have worked tirelessly to reach our golden anniversary, providing a wide array of opportunities for writers to build their craft, meet successful professionals, and become part of a dynamic group of writers from all walks of life.

**COSTS** Pricing schedule available online. Conference price includes breakfast, lunch, and an appetizer reception on Friday and Saturday. Workshops on Friday, Saturday, and Sunday are included — first come, first serve. No additional registration is required for workshops. You must sign up at an additional cost to participate in Master Classes and Sunday Intensives.

## WOMEN WRITING THE WEST

PO Box 1886, Durango, CO 81302. **E-mail:** wwwconference2021@gmail.com. **Website:** www.womenwritingthewest.org. **Contact:** Conference Chair: Kathy Sechrist. Women Writing the West is a nonprofit association of writers, editors, publishers, agents, booksellers, and other professionals writing and promoting the "Women's West." As such, they elevate literature that authentically portrays women and girls in the North American West. In addition, the organization provides support, encouragement, and inspiration to anyone writing about any facet of women's western experiences. Membership is open to all interested persons worldwide, including students. WWW membership also allows the choice of participation in our marketing marvel, the annual WWW Catalog of Author's Books. An annual conference is held every fall. The event covers research, writing techniques, multiple genres, marketing/promotion, and more. Agents and editors share ideas in a panel format as well as meeting one-on-one for pitch sessions with attendees. Conference location changes each year. The blog and social media outlets publish current WWW activities, features market research, and shares articles of interest pertaining to North American West literature and member news. WWW annually sponsors the WILLA Literary Awards, which is given in several categories for outstanding literature featuring women's or girls' stories set in the West. The winner of a WILLA Literary Award receives a cash award and a trophy at the annual conference. This competition is open to non-members. Visit www.womenwritingthewest.org. **COSTS** See website. Discounts available for members.

## WRITE ON THE SOUND

WOTS, City of Edmonds Arts Commission, Frances Anderson Center, 700 Main St., Edmonds WA 98020. (425)771-0228. **E-mail:** wots@edmondswa.gov. **Web-** site: www.writeonthesound.com. Estab. 1985. Small, affordable annual conference focused on the craft of writing. Held the first weekend in October. Conference duration: 3 days. Average attendance: 275. Features over 30 presenters, keynote, writing contest, ms critique appts, round table discussions, book signing reception, onsite bookstore, and opportunity to network with faculty and attendees. Edmonds is located just north of Seattle on the Puget Sound.

**COSTS** $90-300 (not including optional fees).

**ACCOMMODATIONS** Best Western Plus/Edmonds Harbor Inn is a conference partner.

**ADDITIONAL INFORMATION** Schedule posted on website late spring/early summer. Registration opens mid-July. Attendees are required to select the sessions when they register. Wait lists for conference and manuscript appointments are available.

## WRITERS CONFERENCE AT OCEAN PARK

P.O. Box 172, Assonet ME 02702. (401)598-1424. **E-mail:** opmewriter@gmail.com. **Website:** www.oceanpark.org/programs/education/writers/writers.html. Estab. 1941. Annual conference held in mid-August. Conference duration: 4 days. Average attendance: 50. "We try to present a balanced and eclectic conference. In addition to time and attention given to poetry, we also have children's literature, mystery writing, travel, fiction, nonfiction, journalism, and other issues of interest to writers. Our speakers are editors, writers, and other professionals. Our concentration is, by intention, a general view of writing to publish with supportive encouragement. We are located in Ocean Park, a small seashore village 14 miles south of Portland. Ours is a summer assembly center with many buildings from the Victorian age. The conference meets in Porter Hall, one of the assembly buildings which is listed in the National Register of Historic Places." Speakers have included Michael C. White (novelist/short story writer), Betsy Shool (poet), Suzanne Strempek Shea (novelist), John Perrault (poet), Anita Shreve (novelist), Dawn Potter (poet), Bruce Pratt (fiction writer), Amy McDonald (children's author), Sandell Morse (memoirist), Kate Chadbourne (singer/songwriter), Wesley McNair (poet and Maine faculty member), and others. "We usually have about 8 guest presenters each year." Writers/editors lead workshops and are available for meetings with attendees. Workshops start at 8:30 a.m. on Tuesday and continue through Friday until early afternoon. Opening event is Monday at 4 p.m.

**COSTS** $215. The fee does not include housing or meals, which must be arranged separately.

**ACCOMMODATIONS** "An accommodations list is available. We are in a summer resort area where motels, guest houses, and restaurants abound."

## WRITER'S DIGEST ANNUAL CONFERENCE

Active Interest Media, 4665 Malsbary Rd., Blue Ash OH 45242. **E-mail:** writersdigestconference@aimmedia.com; tsferra@aimmedia.com. **Website:** www.writersdigestconference.com. **Contact:** Taylor Sferra. Estab. 1995. The Writer's Digest conferences feature an amazing lineup of speakers to help writers with the craft and business of writing. Each calendar year typically features multiple conferences around the country. The most popular feature of the East Coast conference is the agent pitch slam in which potential authors are given the ability to pitch their books directly to agents. For more details, see the website.

**COSTS** Cost varies by location and year. There are typically different pricing options for those who wish attend the pitch slam and those who just want to attend the conference education.

**ACCOMMODATIONS** A block of rooms at the event hotel is reserved for guests. See the travel page on the website for more information.

**ADDITIONAL INFORMATION** Check https://novel.writersdigestconference.com for information on the annual Writer's Digest Novel Writing Conference in California.

## WRITERS IN PARADISE

Eckerd College, 4200 54th Ave. S., St. Petersburg FL 33711. (727)386-2264. **E-mail:** wip@eckerd.edu. **E-mail:** via Submittable only. **Website:** writersinparadise.com. Estab. 2005. Annual conference held in January. Conference duration: 8 days. Average attendance: 100 maximum. "Writers in Paradise offers workshop classes in fiction (novel and short story), poetry, and nonfiction. Working closely with our award-winning faculty, students will have stimulating opportunities to ask questions and learn valuable skills from fellow students and authors at the top of their form. Most importantly, the intimate size and secluded location of the Writers in Paradise experience allows you the time and opportunity to share your manuscripts, critique one another's work, and discuss the craft of writing with experts and peers

who can help guide you to the next level." Faculty have included Andre Dubus III (*House of Sand and Fog*), Laura Lippman (*Wilde Lake*), Dennis Lehane (*The Given Day*), Ann Hood (*The Book That Matters Most*), Lisa Gallagher (literary agent), Daniel Halpern (editor), and more.

**COSTS** See website for cost information.

**ADDITIONAL INFORMATION** Application materials including a writing submission are due November 1 and required for acceptance.

## WRITE-TO-PUBLISH CONFERENCE

WordPro Communication Services, 9118 W. Elmwood Dr., Suite 1G, Niles IL 60714. (847)296-3964. **E-mail:** lin@writetopublish.com. **Website:** www.writetopublish.com. **Contact:** Lin Johnson, director. Estab. 1971. Annual conference in June. Average attendance: 175. Conference is focused on the Christian market and includes classes for writers at all levels and appointments with editors and agents. Open to high school students. Site: Wheaton College, Wheaton, Illinois (Chicago area). [This is not a function of Wheaton College.]

**COSTS** See the website for current costs.

**ACCOMMODATIONS** Campus residence hall rooms available. See the website for current information and costs.

**ADDITIONAL INFORMATION** Conference information available in late January or early February. For details, visit website, or e-mail brochure@writetopublish.com. Accepts inquiries by e-mail, phone.

## WRITING AND ILLUSTRATING FOR YOUNG READERS CONFERENCE

WIFYR, 1480 E. 9400 S., Sandy UT 84093. **E-mail:** staff@wifyr.com. **Website:** www.wifyr.com. **Contact:** Carol Lynch Williams. Estab. 2000. Annual workshop held in June. Duration: 5 days. Average attendance: more than 100. Learn how to write, illustrate, and publish in the children's and young adult markets. Beginning and advanced writers and illustrators are tutored in a small-group workshop setting by published authors and artists and receive instruction from and network with editors, major publishing house representatives, and literary agents. Afternoon attendees get to hear practical writing and publishing tips from published authors, literary agents, and editors. Site: Waterford School in Sandy, UT. Speakers have included John Cusick, Stephen Fraser, Alyson Heller, David Farland, and Ruth Katcher.

**COSTS** Varies from $99-1,200.

**ACCOMMODATIONS** A block of rooms is available at the Best Western Cotton Tree Inn in Sandy, UT, at a discounted rate. This rate is good as long as there are available rooms.

**ADDITIONAL INFORMATION** There is an online form to contact this event.

## WYOMING WRITERS ANNUAL CONFERENCE

P. O. Box 454, Riverton WY 82501. **E-mail:** wyowriters@gmail.com. **Website:** wyowriters.org. **Contact:** J.G. Matheny, president. Estab. 1974. This is a three-day conference for writers of all genres, with attendees generally coming from Wyoming and neighboring states. Each year multiple published authors, editors, and literary agents come to meet with attendees, hold educational sessions, and take pitches. Open reading sessions, peer critique, and keynote speakers highlight the event. Each year the conference location moves to different Wyoming locales, so that attendees can experience the true flavor of this smaller western conference.

# GLOSSARY OF INDUSTRY TERMS

## Your Guide for Every Need-to-Know Term

**#10 ENVELOPE.** A standard, business-size envelope.

**ACKNOWLEDGMENTS PAGE.** The page of a book on which the author credits sources of assistance—both individuals and organizations.

**ACQUISITIONS EDITOR.** The person responsible for originating and/or acquiring new publishing projects.

**ADAPTATION.** The process of rewriting a composition (novel, story, film, article, play) into a form suitable for some other medium, such as television or the stage.

**ADVANCE.** Money a publisher pays a writer prior to book publication, usually paid in installments, such as one-half upon signing the contract and one-half upon delivery of the complete, satisfactory manuscript. An advance is paid against the royalty money to be earned by the book. Agents take their percentage off the top of the advance as well as from the royalties earned.

**ADVENTURE.** A genre of fiction in which action is the key element, overshadowing characters, theme, and setting.

**AUCTION.** Publishers sometimes bid for the acquisition of a book manuscript with excellent sales prospects. The bids are for the amount of the author's advance, guaranteed dollar amounts, advertising and promotional expenses, royalty percentage, etc. Auctions are conducted by agents.

**AUTHOR'S COPIES.** An author usually receives about ten free copies of his hardcover book from the publisher; more from a paperback firm. He can obtain additional copies at a reduced price by using his author's discount (usually 50 percent off the retail price).

**AUTOBIOGRAPHY.** A book-length account of a person's entire life written by the subject himself.

**BACKLIST.** A publisher's list of books that were not published during the current season, but that are still in print.

**BACKSTORY.** The history of what has happened before the action in your story takes place, affecting a character's current behavior.

**BIO.** A sentence or brief paragraph about the writer; includes work, any publishing history, and educational experience.

**BIOGRAPHY.** An account of a person's life (or the lives of a family or close-knit group) written by someone other than the subject(s). The work is set within the historical framework (i.e., the unique economic, social, and political conditions) existing during the subject's life.

**BLURB.** The copy on paperback book covers or hardcover book dust jackets, either promoting the book and the author or featuring testimonials from book reviewers or well-known people in the book's field. Also called flap copy or jacket copy.

**BOILERPLATE.** A standardized publishing contract. Most authors and agents make many changes to the boilerplate before accepting the contract.

**BOOK DOCTOR.** A freelance editor hired by a writer, agent, or book editor who analyzes problems that exist in a book manuscript or proposal, and offers solutions to those problems.

**BOOK PACKAGER.** Someone who draws elements of a book together—from initial concept to writing and marketing strategies—and then sells the book package to a book publisher and/or movie producer. Also known as book producer or book developer.

**BOUND GALLEYS.** A prepublication, often paperbound, edition of a book, usually prepared from photocopies of the final galley proofs. Designed for promotional purposes, bound galleys serve as the first set of review copies to be mailed out. Also called bound proofs.

**CATEGORY FICTION.** A term used to include all types of fiction. See *Genre*.

**CLIMAX.** The most intense point in the storyline of a fictional work.

**CLIPS.** Samples, usually from newspapers or magazines, of your published work. Also called tearsheets.

**COMMERCIAL FICTION.** Novels designed to appeal to a broad audience. These are often broken down into categories such as Western, mystery, and romance. See *Genre*.

**CONFESSION.** A first-person story in which the narrator is involved in an emotional situation that encourages sympathetic reader identification, concluding with the affirmation of a morally acceptable theme.

**CONFLICT.** A prime ingredient of fiction that usually represents some obstacle to the main character's (i.e., the protagonist's) goals.

**CONTRIBUTOR'S COPIES.** Copies of the book sent to the author. The exact number of contributor's copies is often negotiated in the publishing contract.

**CO-PUBLISHING.** Arrangement where author and publisher share publication costs and profits of a book. Also called cooperative publishing.

**COPYEDITING.** Editing of a manuscript for writing style, grammar, punctuation, and factual accuracy.

**COPYRIGHT.** A means to protect an author's work. A copyright is a proprietary right designed to give the creator of a work the power to control that work's reproduction, distribution, and public display or performance, as well as its adaptation to other forms.

**COVER LETTER.** A brief letter that accompanies the manuscript being sent to an agent or publisher.

**CREATIVE NONFICTION.** Type of writing where true stories are told by employing the techniques usually reserved for novelists and poets, such as scenes, character arc, a three-act structure, and detailed descriptions. This category is also called "narrative nonfiction" or "literary journalism."

**CRITIQUING SERVICE.** An editing service offered by some agents in which writers pay a fee for comments on the salability or other qualities of their manuscript. Sometimes the critique includes suggestions on how to improve the work. Fees vary, as does the quality of the critique.

**CURRICULUM VITAE (CV).** Short account of one's career or qualifications.

**DEADLINE.** A specified date and/or time that a project or draft must be turned into the editor. A deadline factors into a preproduction schedule, which involves copyediting, typesetting, and production.

**DEAL MEMO.** The memorandum of agreement between a publisher and author that precedes the actual contract and includes important issues such as royalty, advance, rights, distribution, and option clauses.

**DEUS EX MACHINA.** A term meaning "God from the machine" that refers to any unlikely, contrived, or trick resolution of a plot in any type of fiction.

**DIALOGUE.** An essential element of fiction. Dialogue consists of conversations between two or more people, and can be used heavily or sparsely.

**DIVISION.** An unincorporated branch of a publishing house/company.

**ELECTRONIC RIGHTS.** Secondary or subsidiary rights dealing with electronic/multimedia formats.

**EL-HI.** Elementary to high school. A term used to indicate reading or interest level.

**EROTICA.** A form of literature or film dealing with the sexual aspects of love. Erotic content ranges from subtle sexual innuendo to explicit descriptions of sexual acts.

**ETHNIC.** Stories and novels whose central characters are African American, Native American, Italian American, Jewish, Appalachian, or members of some other specific cultural group. Ethnic fiction usually deals with a protagonist caught between two conflicting ways of life: mainstream American culture and his ethnic heritage.

**EVALUATION FEES.** Fees an agent may charge to simply evaluate or consider material without further guarantee of representation. Paying up-front evaluation fees to agents is never recommended and strictly forbidden by the Association of Authors' Representations. An agent makes money through a standard commission—taking 15 percent of what you earn through advances, sales of subsidiary rights, and, if applicable, royalties.

**EXCLUSIVE.** Offering a manuscript, usually for a set period of time, such as one month, to just one agent and guaranteeing that agent is the only one looking at the manuscript.

**EXPERIMENTAL.** Type of fiction that focuses on style, structure, narrative technique, setting, and strong characterization rather than plot. This form depends on the revelation of a character's inner being, which elicits an emotional response from the reader.

**FAMILY SAGA.** A story that chronicles the lives of a family or a number of related or interconnected families over a period of time.

**FANTASY.** Stories set in fanciful, invented worlds or in a legendary, mythic past that rely on outright invention or magic for conflict and setting.

**FILM RIGHTS.** May be sold or optioned by the agent/author to a person in the film industry, enabling the book to be made into a movie.

**FLOOR BID.** If a publisher is very interested in a manuscript, he may offer to enter a floor bid when the book goes to auction. The publisher sits out of the auction, but agrees to take the book by topping the highest bid by an agreed-upon percentage (usually 10 percent).

**FOREIGN RIGHTS.** Translation or reprint rights to be sold abroad.

**FOREIGN RIGHTS AGENT.** An agent who handles selling the rights to a country other than that of the first book agent.

**GENRE.** Refers to either a general classification of writing, such as a novel, poem, or short story, or to the categories within those classifications, such as problem novels or sonnets.

**GENRE FICTION.** A term that covers various types of commercial novels, such as mystery, romance, Western, science fiction, fantasy, thriller, and horror.

**GHOSTWRITING.** A writer puts into literary form the words, ideas, or knowledge of another person under that person's name. Some agents offer this service; others pair ghostwriters with celebrities or experts.

**GOTHIC.** Novels characterized by historical settings and featuring young, beautiful women who win the favor of handsome, brooding heroes while simultaneously dealing with some life-threatening menace—either natural or supernatural.

**GRAPHIC NOVEL.** Contains comic-like drawings and captions, but deals more with everyday events and issues than with superheroes.

**HIGH CONCEPT.** A story idea easily expressed in a quick, one-line description.

**HI-LO.** A type of fiction that offers a high level of interest for readers at a low reading level.

**HISTORICAL.** A story set in a recognizable period of history. In addition to telling the stories of ordinary people's lives, historical fiction may involve political or social events of the time.

**HOOK.** Aspect of the work that sets it apart from others and draws in the reader/viewer.

**HORROR.** A story that aims to evoke some combination of fear, fascination, and revulsion in its readers—either through supernatural or psychological circumstances.

**HOW-TO.** A book that offers the reader a description of how something is accomplished. It includes both information and advice.

**IMPRINT.** The name applied to a publisher's specific line of books.

**IN MEDIAS RES.** A Latin term meaning "into the midst of things" that refers to the literary device of beginning a narrative at a dramatic point in a story well along in the sequence of events to immediately convey action and capture reader interest.

**IRC.** International Reply Coupon. Buy at a post office to enclose with material sent outside the country to cover the cost of return postage. The recipient turns them in for stamps in their own country.

**ISBN.** This acronym stands for International Standard Book Number. ISBN is a tool used for both ordering and cataloging purposes.

**JOINT CONTRACT.** A legal agreement between a publisher and two or more authors that establishes provisions for the division of royalties their co-written book generates.

**LIBEL.** A form of defamation, or injury to a person's name or reputation. Written or published defamation is called "libel," whereas spoken defamation is known as "slander."

**LITERARY.** A book where style and technique are often as important as subject matter. In literary fiction, character is typically more important than plot, and the writer's voice and skill with words are both essential. Also called "serious fiction."

**LOGLINE.** A one-sentence description of a plot.

**MAINSTREAM FICTION.** Fiction on subjects or trends that transcend popular novel categories like mystery or romance. Using conventional methods, this kind of fiction tells stories about people and their conflicts.

**MARKETING FEE.** Fee charged by some agents to cover marketing expenses. It may be used to cover postage, telephone calls, faxes, photocopying or any other legitimate expense incurred in marketing a manuscript. Recouping expenses associated with submissions and marketing is the one and only time agents should ask for out-of-pocket money from writers.

**MASS-MARKET PAPERBACKS.** Softcover books, usually 4×7 inches, on a popular subject directed at a general audience.

**MEMOIR.** An author's commentary on the personalities and events that have significantly influenced one phase of his life.

**MIDLIST.** Those titles on a publisher's list expected to have limited sales. Midlist books are mainstream, not literary, scholarly or genre, and are usually written by new or relatively unknown writers.

**MULTIPLE CONTRACT.** Book contract that includes an agreement for a future book(s).

**MYSTERY.** A form of narration in which one or more elements remain unknown or unexplained until the end of the story. Subgenres include amateur sleuth, caper, cozy, heist, malice domestic, police procedural, etc.

**NET RECEIPTS.** One method of royalty payment based on the amount of money a book publisher receives on the sale of the book after the booksellers' discounts, special sales discounts, and returned copies.

**NEW ADULT (NA).** Novels with characters in their late teens or early twenties who are exploring what it means to be an adult.

**NOVELIZATION.** A novel created from the script of a popular movie and published in paperback. Also called a movie tie-in.

**NOVELLA.** A short novel or long short story, usually 20,000–50,000 words. Also called a "novelette."

**OCCULT.** Supernatural phenomena, including ghosts, ESP, astrology, demonic possession, paranormal elements, and witchcraft.

**ONE-TIME RIGHTS.** This right allows a short story or portions of a fiction or nonfiction book to be published again without violating the contract.

**OPTION.** The act of a producer buying film rights to a book for a limited period of time (usually six months or one year) rather than purchasing said rights in full. A book can be optioned multiple times by different production companies.

**OPTION CLAUSE.** A contract clause giving a publisher the right to publish an author's next book.

**OUTLINE.** A summary of a book's content (up to fifteen double-spaced pages); often in the form of chapter headings with a descriptive sentence or two under each one to show the scope of the book.

**PICTURE BOOK.** A type of book aimed at ages two to nine that tells the story partially or entirely with artwork, with up to one thousand words. Agents interested in selling to publishers of these books often handle both artists and writers.

**PLATFORM.** A writer's speaking experience, interview skills, website, and other abilities that help form a following of potential buyers for his book.

**PROOFREADING.** Close reading and correction of a manuscript's typographical errors.

**PROPOSAL.** An offer to an editor or publisher to write a specific work, usually consists of an outline, sample chapters, a marketing plan, and more.

**PROSPECTUS.** A preliminary written description of a book, usually one page in length.

**PSYCHIC/SUPERNATURAL.** Fiction exploiting—or requiring as plot devices or themes—some contradictions of the commonplace natural world and materialist assumptions about it (including the traditional ghost story).

**QUERY.** A letter written to an agent or a potential market to elicit interest in a writer's work.

**READER.** A person employed by an agent to go through the slush pile of manuscripts and scripts, and select those worth considering.

**REGIONAL.** A book faithful to a particular geographic region and its people, including behavior, customs, speech, and history.

**RELEASE.** A statement that your idea is original, has never been sold to anyone else, and that you are selling negotiated rights to the idea upon payment. Some agents may ask that you sign a release before they request pages and review your work.

**REMAINDERS.** Leftover copies of an out-of-print or slow-selling book purchased from the publisher at a reduced rate. Depending on the contract, a reduced royalty or no royalty is paid to the author on remaindered books.

**REPRINT RIGHTS.** The right to republish a book after its initial printing.

**ROMANCE.** A type of category fiction in which the love relationship between a man and a woman pervades the plot. The story is told from the viewpoint of the heroine, who meets a man (the hero), falls in love with him, encounters a conflict that hinders their relationship, and then resolves the conflict with a happy ending.

**ROYALTIES.** A percentage of the retail price paid to the author for each copy of the book that is sold. Agents take their percentage from the royalties earned and from the advance.

**SASE.** Self-addressed, stamped envelope. It should be included with all postal mail correspondence and submissions.

**SCHOLARLY BOOKS.** Books written for an academic or research audience. These are usually heavily researched, technical, and often contain terms used only within a specific field.

**SCIENCE FICTION.** Literature involving elements of science and technology as a basis for conflict or as the setting for a story.

**SERIAL RIGHTS.** The right for a newspaper or magazine to publish sections of a manuscript.

**SIMULTANEOUS SUBMISSION.** Sending the same query or manuscript to several agents or publishers at the same time.

**SLICE OF LIFE.** A type of short story, novel, play, or film that takes a strong thematic approach, depending less on plot than on vivid detail in describing the setting and/or environment and the environment's effect on characters involved in it.

**SLUSH PILE.** A stack of unsolicited submissions in the office of an editor, agent, or publisher.

**STANDARD COMMISSION.** The commission an agent earns on the sales of a manuscript. The commission percentage (usually 15 percent) is taken from the advance and royalties paid to the writer.

**SUBAGENT.** An agent handling certain subsidiary rights, usually working in conjunction with the agent who handled the book rights. The percentage paid the book agent is increased to pay the subagent.

**SUBSIDIARY.** An incorporated branch of a company or conglomerate (for example, Crown Publishing Group is a subsidiary of Penguin Random House, Inc.).

**SUBSIDIARY RIGHTS.** All rights other than book publishing rights included in a book publishing contract, such as paperback rights, book club rights, and movie rights. Part of an agent's job is to negotiate those rights and advise the writer on which to sell and which to keep.

**SUSPENSE.** The element of both fiction and some nonfiction that makes the reader uncertain about the outcome. Suspense can be created through almost any element of a story, including the title, characters, plot, time restrictions, and word choice.

**SYNOPSIS.** A brief summary of a story, novel, or play. As a part of a book proposal, it is a comprehensive summary condensed in a page or page-and-a-half, single-spaced. Unlike a query letter or logline, a synopsis is a front-to-back explanation of the work—and will give away the story's ending.

**TERMS.** Financial provisions agreed upon in a contract, whether between writer and agent, or writer and editor.

**TEXTBOOK.** Book used in school classrooms at the elementary, high school, or college level.

**THEME.** The point a writer wishes to make. It poses a question—a human problem.

**THRILLER.** A story intended to arouse feelings of excitement or suspense. Works in this genre are highly sensational, usually focusing on illegal activities, international espionage, sex, and violence.

**TOC.** Table of Contents. A listing at the beginning of a book indicating chapter titles and their corresponding page numbers. It can also include chapter descriptions.

**TRADE BOOK.** Either a hardcover or softcover book sold mainly in bookstores. The subject matter frequently concerns a special interest for a more general audience.

**TRADE PAPERBACK.** A softbound volume, usually 5×8 inches, published and designed for the general public; available mainly in bookstores.

**TRANSLATION RIGHTS.** Sold to a foreign agent or foreign publisher.

**UNSOLICITED MANUSCRIPT.** An unrequested manuscript sent to an editor, agent, or publisher.

**VET.** A term used by editors when referring to the procedure of submitting a book manuscript to an outside expert (such as a lawyer) for review before publication. Memoirs are frequently vetted to confirm factual accuracy before the book is published.

**WESTERNS/FRONTIER.** Stories set in the American West, almost always in the nineteenth century, generally between the antebellum period and the turn of the century.

**YOUNG ADULT (YA).** The general classification of books written for ages twelve to sixteen. They run forty thousand to eighty thousand words and include category novels—adventure, sports, paranormal, science fiction, fantasy, multicultural, mysteries, romance, etc.

# LITERARY AGENT SPECIALTIES INDEX

**Mainstream**

## Metaphysical

## Middle Grade

## Military

## Thriller

## Business

## Popular Culture

# GENERAL INDEX